First Martyr of Liberty

First Martyr
of Liberty

*Crispus Attucks in
American Memory*

MITCH KACHUN

OXFORD
UNIVERSITY PRESS

OXFORD
UNIVERSITY PRESS

Oxford University Press is a department of the University of Oxford. It furthers
the University's objective of excellence in research, scholarship, and education
by publishing worldwide. Oxford is a registered trade mark of Oxford University
Press in the UK and certain other countries.

Published in the United States of America by Oxford University Press
198 Madison Avenue, New York, NY 10016, United States of America.

© Oxford University Press 2017

Library of Congress Cataloging-in-Publication Data
Names: Kachun, Mitchell A. (Mitchell Alan), author.
Title: First martyr of liberty : Crispus Attucks in American memory /
Mitch Kachun.
Description: New York, NY : Oxford University Press, 2017. |
Includes bibliographical references and index.
Identifiers: LCCN 2017003265 (print) | LCCN 2017017106 (ebook) |
ISBN 9780199875726 (Updf) | ISBN 9780199910861 (Epub) |
ISBN 9780199731619 (hardcover : alk. paper)
Subjects: LCSH: Attucks, Crispus, –1770—Influence. | African
Americans—Biography. | Revolutionaries—Massachusetts—Boston—Biography. |
Boston Massacre, 1770.
Classification: LCC E185.97.A86 (ebook) | LCC E185.97.A86 K33 2017 (print) |
DDC 973.3/113092 [B]—dc23
LC record available at https://lccn.loc.gov/2017003265

1 3 5 7 9 8 6 4 2
Printed by Sheridan Books, Inc., United States of America

For Michael Kammen,
a consummate historian whose work embraced the small details
and the big ideas

Contents

Acknowledgments

AS I OFTEN remind my students, the historian's craft requires many hours of solitary and often tedious work in archives, in microfilm rooms, in digital databases, and on the computer—researching, conceptualizing, categorizing, cross-referencing, outlining, writing, and rewriting. Then rewriting some more. Yet the core of historical scholarship involves collaboration and the exchange of ideas in the interest of advancing our understanding of the past. A book that has been over a decade in the making necessarily has benefited from my exchanging ideas with many colleagues, getting their feedback and critiques, and revising my thinking accordingly.

Portions of my research on Crispus Attucks have been presented at numerous academic gatherings, including meetings of the joint conference of the Society of Historians of the Early American Republic and British American Nineteenth Century Historians, the American Studies Association, the American Historical Association, the Southern Historical Association, and the Association for the Study of African American Life and History, as well as at invited talks for the Michigan State University History Department, the Robert Penn Warren Sawyer-Mellon Seminar at Vanderbilt University, the Africana Studies and Research Center at Cornell University, and the Indian Institute of Information Technology, Guwahati, Assam, India. Closer to home, I have shared my research at the Western Michigan University (WMU) Research and Creative Activities Day, the WMU History Department Ernst Breisach Faculty Research Colloquium, and the Kalamazoo Public Library. Parts of Chapters 2 and 3 were published in an earlier article (Mitch Kachun, "From Forgotten Founder to Indispensable Icon: Crispus Attucks, Black Citizenship, and Collective Memory," *Journal of the Early Republic* 29:2 [Summer 2009], 249–86), and I am grateful for being able to republish that material here, in revised form.

Many colleagues and friends have contributed to this project through casual conversations, Facebook exchanges, emails, discussions at public presentations, manuscript reviews, and formal comments on conference panels and seminars. I am grateful to all those named and to others whom I no doubt overlooked: J. L. Bell, David W. Blight, Richard Blackett, Clark Dougan, Roy E. Finkenbine, Teresa Goddu, Robert L. Harris Jr., Martha Hodes, James O. Horton, Stephen Kantrowitz, Catherine Kelly, Roderick MacDonald, Daniel Mandell, Maureen McAleer, Hilary J. Moss, Tavia Nyong'o, Sarah Purcell, John Saillant, John David Smith, Donald Yacovone, and Alfred F. Young. Several scholars gave generously of their time to read the entire manuscript, either at my request or at the behest of Oxford University Press. Pero Dagbovie, Kevin Kelley Gaines, Lois E. Horton, and Julie Winch each offered constructive critiques that in some cases prevented me from making embarrassing errors and more generally pushed me to engage issues that strengthened the manuscript. Of course, any errors, misattributions, or misinterpretations that remain are my own.

No historian can do without the support of librarians, archivists, and other information professionals who help us get our hands on the materials that make our interpretations possible. Special thanks are due the staff at the WMU Libraries Resource Sharing Office and Cecelia Moore at the WMU Libraries Digitization Center. Others who assisted me with the acquisition of materials include the staff at Columbia University Teachers College; the New York Public Library; the Schomburg Center for the Study of Black Culture; the Library Company of Philadelphia; the Massachusetts Historical Society; the American Antiquarian Society; and the Boston Public Library. Special thanks are due to Mr. Elliott Geisinger for graciously granting the rights to one of my favorite images of Crispus Attucks. Research funding for the project was provided by the Gilder Lehrman Institute of American History and the WMU Faculty Research and Creative Activities Fund. Grants from the WMU History Department Burnham Macmillan Fund and the WMU fund for the Publication of Papers and Exhibition of Creative Works supported the acquisition of the book's illustrations. A 2007–08 sabbatical leave from WMU allowed me to begin researching in earnest and an alternate academic year assignment in the spring of 2016 allowed time for thorough chapter revisions.

At Oxford University Press, Susan Ferber provided wholehearted support for the project from the outset. I still recall seeing her eyes light up when I responded to her casual conference query, "What are you working on now?" with, "a book on Crispus Attucks in American memory." Like me, she had been intrigued by Attucks for some time. As much as her enthusiasm, I appreciate Susan's keen editorial eye and her patience. I hope the wait has been worth it. Thanks are also due to the Oxford production staff for their careful work. In particular, production manager Julia Turner demonstrated remarkable patience, flexibility, and professionalism in guiding me through some unexpected challenges as we were getting down to the wire.

I am fortunate to have wonderful colleagues in the history department at WMU, for whose friendship, encouragement, and support I am extremely grateful. It is heartening to feel respected and appreciated within one's professional home. Over a decade's worth of graduate students, especially those in my History and Memory readings courses, have also contributed to my thinking, at times pointing out nuances and perspectives that had escaped me.

My family is once again owed the greatest debt for living with this project for a substantial chunk of their lives, even when they were no longer actually living in the same house as me. To my daughter Michelle Kachman, her partner Thom Monroe, and my son Silas Kachman—you give me hope that the emerging generation of Americans have their hearts and minds in the right place and will keep a watchful eye on the nation's leaders. And I am continually inspired by my wife, Karen Libman, whose own work on a different kind of stage challenges us all to envision a world of equity and justice. Karen, well, you're just everything.

First Martyr of Liberty

Introduction

Name in a footnote. Faceless name.
Moot hero shrouded in Betsy Ross
and Garvey flags—propped up
by bayonets, forever falling.

ROBERT HAYDEN (1975)

Dead men make such convenient heroes
For they cannot rise to challenge the images that we
might fashion from their lives

CARL WENDELL HINES (1969)

"THE ELECTION OF Barack Obama began on March Fifth 1770 at the Boston Massacre, with the death of Crispus Attucks."[1] This provocative opening line from the 2009 documentary, *We the People: From Crispus Attucks to Barack Obama*, is never fully explained. Viewers are left to wonder how the death of a mixed-race former slave during the first Revolutionary-era clash between American colonists and British soldiers led to the election of the nation's first African American president over two centuries later. While the connections between Obama and Attucks are tenuous and tangential at best, each man has occupied that intellectual and emotional juncture at which Americans attempt to understand how race has affected our understanding of what it means to be a patriot, a citizen, an American. These questions challenge us: first, to recognize the continuous black presence in American history and culture from the eighteenth century to the twenty-first; then to consider how Americans think about African Americans' place in the nation's story; and finally to ponder the process through which national heroes and myths are constructed. This book examines how Crispus Attucks has been remembered and forgotten, lionized and vilified, in the centuries-long debate over African American citizenship, patriotism, and inclusion.

As part of the struggle for full and equal citizenship rights in the United States, many African American leaders since the eighteenth century have consciously attempted to define black heroes, and by extension all black Americans, as integral parts of the American nation and its story. Perhaps no individual has filled this role better, and certainly none has done so for a longer time, than Crispus Attucks. These pages explore the meanings both black and white Americans have attached to Attucks's name, image, and story to shed light on some of the central questions of African American—and American—history and experience, particularly those relating to understandings of the nation's history and of who belongs in that history and who does not. The book investigates how Crispus Attucks came to serve as a symbolic embodiment of black patriotism who achieved mythic significance in African Americans' struggle to define their collective status as American citizens. It also considers the broader society's more uneven incorporation of Attucks, and blacks in general, into the mainstream of the American historical narrative. Central to this project is African Americans' use of Attucks in their efforts to incorporate their own story into the broader narrative the nation tells about itself.

There will likely never be a definitive biography of Crispus Attucks. Generations of scholars have probed the sources with only limited success in uncovering information about the man's actual life. While what can and cannot be known about Attucks is addressed here, the focus is on how he has been remembered, and why at times he has been forgotten, by different groups and individuals in different periods of American history. This approach to understanding the past, generally known as the study of "history and memory," considers not only how professional academic historians construct their interpretations of the past but also how broader societies arrive at shared understandings of historical events and individuals and how those understandings change over time. Examining these processes helps us come to terms with "history" in both senses of the word—the actual events of the past and the storylines that have developed to explain the meaning of those events. How have individuals and various socially constructed groups (defined by nation, ethnicity, special interests, region, religion, and so on) developed distinctively meaningful narratives about the past? What purposes (and whose interests) have those narratives served? Studying history and memory involves understanding how particular historical interpretations have been constructed, by whom, and to what end. While a few scholars have discussed select aspects of Attucks's historical significance in narrowly defined times or in particular places, this book is the first to examine the meanings both black and white Americans have attached to Attucks's name, image, and story over the course of two and a half centuries.[2]

But what do we really know about Crispus Attucks and his role in the Boston Massacre? There is little certainty about Attucks's life story. The most widely accepted interpretation suggests that he was born around 1723 near Natick, Massachusetts, a "praying town" of Christianized Indians about twenty miles west of Boston. He was likely of mixed African and Native American ancestry. He was a large man, over six feet, and was likely a slave owned by William Brown of Framingham until he liberated himself in 1750, after which he worked as a sailor and around the docks in Boston and elsewhere until his fateful role in the events of March 5, 1770.

Most modern historians of the American Revolution see the so-called Boston Massacre of March 5, 1770, as a noteworthy event in the colonists' growing disaffection with the British Empire. Available evidence confirms that Attucks was part of an unruly mob's confrontation with a small detachment of British soldiers outside the King Street Custom House, where he and four white colonists were killed after threatening the British guards with rocks, chunks of ice, and clubs. A few days later four of the victims—Crispus Attucks, Samuel Maverick, Samuel Gray, and James Caldwell—were buried in a single grave in Boston's Granary Burying Ground. A week or so later Patrick Carr, who lingered for several more days before dying, was placed in the grave with the others. Some months after that, the soldiers were tried in Boston for murder. All were acquitted of that charge, and only two were convicted of the lesser charge of manslaughter, lightly punished, and sent home to England.

Thousands of American colonists, and at least hundreds of Bostonians, were direct participants in mob actions between the early 1760s and the start of the Revolution in 1775. Crispus Attucks was one those colonists, and in the greater scheme of things he was no more important or significant than the rest. They all played a role in moving disgruntled colonists toward a bold and unprecedented struggle for independence. It is understandable that the first colonist to be killed by British soldiers might hold a memorable place in that Revolutionary saga, but the fact that the man was Crispus Attucks was largely happenstance. Had it been another person in the mob that day or in some other confrontation on another day, would that person be remembered at all? And why has Attucks's name been remembered in a way those of the men who died along with him have not? It makes sense to consider these questions because Attucks's incorporation into the story of the American Revolution was not a foregone conclusion. It was the result of a conscious campaign to construct an American hero—the First Martyr of Liberty. And that campaign was taken on only after Attucks had been almost completely ignored for decades by historians, Revolutionary veterans, and the general public.

Most twenty-first-century American schoolchildren learn about the Boston Massacre and Crispus Attucks fairly early in their introduction to the American Revolution and its heroes. Even as the other victims of the massacre have been largely ignored, Attucks's death on March 5, 1770, has led to his being singled out by many, especially African Americans, as the first to die in the cause of American independence. Attucks has come to signify African American patriotism, military service, sacrifice, and citizenship—he has become a black Founder. Since the 1850s both black and white Americans have commemorated Attucks in numerous ways, including Attucks Day celebrations, a monument on Boston Common, and institutions and organizations bearing his name. He has been the subject of juvenile biographies; a featured character in works of poetry, drama, and visual arts; and a presence in popular and academic histories and textbooks.

Attucks's place in American memory has waxed and waned since his death in 1770, and this book proceeds chronologically, following shifts in the extent and the nature of the attention Attucks received in different eras from different constituencies. Future United States president John Adams, in his role as defense attorney for the British soldiers on trial for murder, succeeded in portraying Attucks as an unsavory outsider, a threat to the social order who led the riotous mob that provoked the beleaguered troops into firing. Subsequently, American Revolutionaries in Boston used the memory of the massacre and its victims to serve their own political agendas during the Revolution by portraying the victims as respectable, innocent citizens struck down by a tyrannical military power.

Between 1771 and 1850 the Boston Massacre itself remained a part of the nation's collective memory of the American Revolution. Some characterized it as a key event in forging colonial unity while others preferred to distance the Revolution from what they considered a disorderly riot. In either case, Attucks's role and racial identity remained largely ignored, even among African Americans. A few scattered references to Attucks appeared during the first half of the nineteenth century, but he did not become a focal point for African American arguments for citizenship, inclusion, and equality until the 1850s.

Attucks's prominence among black and white abolitionists grew during the Civil War, as black men donned blue uniforms and risked their lives to preserve the Union and dismantle American slavery. As Jim Crow segregation came to define black Americans' place in the nation by the end of the nineteenth century, American memory also became largely segregated. African Americans continued to hold Attucks in high regard, but his name was invoked far less frequently in mainstream popular culture and historical scholarship. After World War I, African Americans intensified their attention to Attucks and other race heroes as they made more overt efforts to incorporate African American achievements into the national historical narrative. Interest in promoting Attucks as a national hero was redoubled as African Americans' heroic participation in World War II once again presented opportunities to sharpen activists' arguments for black inclusion and full citizenship rights.

As the integrationist civil rights movement took shape, Attucks became one of the most prominent black figures to enter elementary and secondary school curricula and textbooks. In most mainstream texts he became merely a token black presence, yet some white commentators took issue with even this superficial elevation to the status of Revolutionary Patriot, reviving the contention that Attucks was no more than a rabble rousing ruffian. Meanwhile, black writers characterized him as everything from a peaceful integrationist to an Afrocentric rebel to a sell-out Uncle Tom. The 1976 Bicentennial brought greater mainstream attention to Attucks and black participation in the Revolution, as well as increasing opportunities to disseminate interpretations of Attucks and other African American heroes in schools and in an ever-expanding mass media over the subsequent decades.

This general chronological narrative will explore how and why heroes and myths take shape in American history and collective memory and will interrogate the relationship between Attucks's *actual* biography, about which we know almost nothing, and the *mythic* biographies that have flourished over more than two centuries. The absence of clear facts about the man makes him a virtual blank slate upon which different groups and individuals have inscribed diverse meanings to suit a wide range of political and cultural agendas. These pages will address the extent to which this black hero has been accepted as an American hero within the broader society, while also examining the question of Attucks's legitimacy as a "Founding Father."

Popular fascination with the nation's founding generation has a long history, with the Founders' collective reputations shifting over time. The early twenty-first century has seen a particularly energetic revival of what one writer has labeled "Founders Chic," suggesting that "our reverence for the Fathers has gotten out of hand." Numerous admiring popular biographies tend to perpetuate the myth of a golden age in which a unique group of demigods

established God's best hope on earth. To be sure, historians have worked dil-
igently to complicate this simplistic understanding and to better appreciate
the struggles and conflicts of the founding generation. Even in popular culture, the 2015 Broadway musical sensation *Hamilton* has thrust a challenging,
if still highly laudatory, portrait of the Founders into the mainstream. Crispus
Attucks has largely been excluded from this popular attention, perhaps in part
because his life has been so scantly documented. But could it also be because
Founders tend to be recognized for having built things up, while Attucks and
the Boston mob may be more accurately described as tearing things down?[3]

Many other questions are germane to this study. Have representations and
commemorations of Attucks been directed more toward African Americans
in particular or toward the broader society? How have different media representing Attucks—monuments, art, literature, landscape, material culture, the
Internet—conveyed different meanings to different audiences? What meanings have been attached to Attucks in official governmental representations
like commemorative holidays, coins, and stamps, or in quasi-official sources
like school textbooks? How have non-black Americans—including Native
Americans, who have reason to claim him as one of their own—constructed,
or reacted to, Attucks's role in American history?

Following Crispus Attucks's career through both history and myth illu-
minates issues surrounding the incorporation of African Americans' actions,
experiences, and perspectives into the mainstream narrative Americans tell
themselves, each other, and the world about the nation's past. The creation of
a heroic Crispus Attucks, like the creation of all heroes, illustrates the power
of collective memory and the importance of pondering both what is remembered and what is forgotten, and why.

I

Who Was This Man?

Where shall we seek for a hero, and where shall we find
a story?

JOHN BOYLE O'REILLY (1888)

IN 1782, WHEN J. Hector St. John de Crèvecoeur asked the famous question in his *Letters from an American Farmer*—"What then is the American, this new man?"—he was not thinking about Crispus Attucks or other people of color. Crèvecoeur was trying to explain the nature of America and the emerging "American character" to a European audience intrigued by this land of distant colonials who were engaged in the modern world's first experiment in revolutionary nation-making. As far as Crèvecoeur was concerned, the "new man" he saw coming into being in the nascent United States was "either an European, or the descendant of an European." In other words, he was white.[1]

Yet during the era of the American Revolution, approximately 20 percent of Americans—one of every five people—was of African birth or descent. While fewer Native American people were as intimately connected with mainstream colonial American communities as were blacks, their presence on the fringes of those communities often played a significant role in shaping social, economic, and political realities. Diversity reigned even among the whites, with the various Protestant denominations and sects joined by Catholics and Jews, and the English and Welsh joined by people of Dutch, French, German, Irish, Scottish, and other ethnic or national origins. The English predominated most in New England, comprising about 70 percent of the total population there. But in the rest of colonial North America they made up less than half of the population; in fact, in the southern colonies Africans slightly outnumbered English, 39 percent to 37 percent.[2]

Multiethnic people like Crispus Attucks were very much a part of eighteenth-century America and, in ways Crèvecoeur failed to consider, they embodied much of what was new and distinctive in the revolutionary nation. In Attucks, the three primary ethnic and racial strains of American identity— African, European, and Native American—came together. While he may or may not have carried the blood of all three groups in his veins, Attucks almost certainly interacted closely with all three groups, and his life experience, as best as can be surmised, allowed him to see the best and worst of eighteenth-century America: the economic and social vitality of growing and prospering colonies, the oppression of racial slavery, the intermingling of diverse peoples and languages in bustling Atlantic seaports, the opportunities and dangers of life at sea, the fluidity of identity in America's formative era, and the language of liberty and natural rights that came to define the idealistic new nation's sense of itself.

Unfortunately, we have very little to go on in reconstructing Crispus Attucks's experiences and his own sense of self and place in this turbulent world. With almost no concrete evidence concerning Attucks's life, we must rely almost entirely on speculation in addressing the questions of who this particular American was and how he viewed his world. The most tangible information about Attucks comes from newspaper reports of the Boston Massacre and the court proceedings from the trial of the British soldiers. One of the most striking pieces of information in those accounts is that this man was identified in the first news reports of the massacre not as Crispus Attucks, but as "A Molatto man named, Johnson." The March 6 autopsy report referred to the deceased as "Michael Johnson." Not until the following week did newspapers print the correction that "The Name of the Molatto killed was Crispus Attucks, not Johnson."[3]

If Attucks did indeed use "Michael Johnson" as a pseudonym, it would lend credence to the idea that he had previously been a slave in eastern Massachusetts and avoided using his real name when his travels brought him back to that region. The records from 1770 do not suggest that Attucks had ever been a slave, nor do they provide more than superficial accounts of his appearance and biography. In terms of his physical characteristics, witnesses at the trials of Captain Thomas Preston and the accused soldiers consistently referred to him as "the Molatto" and described him as "a large stout man" who was "Dressed Sailor like." The term "stout" in eighteenth-century usage might have numerous meanings, but the most logical in this context is "strong in body" or "of powerful build."[4] Someone in Boston must have had some familiarity with Attucks, since he was identified in the press as having been "born in Framingham [Massachusetts], but lately belonging to New-Providence [The Bahamas], and was here [Boston] in order to go to North Carolina."[5] In his defense of the soldiers at the trial later that year, John Adams also empha-sized that he was "an *Attucks* from *Framingham*."[6]

These descriptions are consistent with the one apparent reference to Crispus Attucks that predates the Boston Massacre: an advertisement from 1750 that identified "a Molatto fellow, about 27 Years of Age, named *Crispas*," who "ran-away from his Master, *William Brown*, of *Framingham*," in late September of that year. The ad further described "Crispas" as being "6 Feet two Inches high, [with] short curl'd Hair, his Knees nearer together than common." A reward of £10 was offered, and "all Masters of Vessels and others" were duly "caution'd against concealing or carrying off said servant on Penalty of the Law."[7]

Of course, this man may not have been the same "Crispus" who died in Boston in 1770. But Crispus (or Crispas) was hardly a common name, and both men are described in contemporary accounts as being large mulatto men from Framingham. (In 1770, when only four of the three hundred soldiers in the British Twenty-Ninth regiment stationed in Boston exceeded six feet tall, a man of six foot two certainly qualified as "stout.") The 1750 advertisement's warning to ship captains might possibly mean that "Crispas" had some expe-rience with the sea, as did the 1770 "Crispus." The evidence is hardly ironclad, but the circumstantial connections suggest a strong likelihood that these two were indeed the same man.[8]

Regardless, we are left with the larger question of who this man was. Was he Crispus Attucks or Michael Johnson? A free man or a fugitive slave? African or Indian? Identity in the eighteenth-century Atlantic world could be fluid and variable.[9] Why, where, and how often might Attucks have identified him-self as Michael Johnson, or used other aliases? For all we know, Bostonians may have initially misidentified him as "Michael Johnson" because a different man by that name and resembling Attucks was living in Boston at the time. And any deeper attachments Attucks may have had to his African, Indian, or perhaps even European roots are far beyond what the existing sources reveal. The most widely accepted descriptions of the events leading up to the massacre suggest that he was not uncomfortable mixing with whites of his own social class in taverns, in workplaces, and even in a mob action. How comfortable was he among Africans or Indians? Did he speak other lan-guages? Could he read or write? Did he regularly adopt different identities that suited his particular circumstances at any given moment? If asked who he really was, how might Attucks have responded? In his own mind, would he agree with John Adams's disparaging characterization at the trial, that he was merely "an Attucks from Framingham"? Had Attucks's presumed (and largely undocumented) travels as a sailor along the Atlantic seaboard, into the Caribbean, and perhaps much farther overseas forged a more cosmopolitan man whose sense of self could not be so easily defined? Or, amid these diverse influences, did Attucks identify himself primarily as an American?

It is worth pondering these possibilities if we are to conjecture about why Crispus Attucks did what he did on the evening of March 5, 1770. While we can never presume to know his motives or mental state, we can imagine something about the man's worldview based on historical research into the lives of eighteenth-century Atlantic sailors. Sailors in this age of wooden sailing ships were an essential part of the era's booming international commerce and conflict as they crisscrossed the Atlantic. They sailed on merchantmen, slavers, military vessels, and pirate ships under the flags of many nations. As a sailor Attucks would have mixed with a wide variety of people, free and unfree, educated and illiterate, from various European and African ethnic groups, birthplaces, languages, and religions. Life on board sailing ships typically was filled with hard work, inadequate rations, brutal punishments, and the constant awareness of imminent danger. Shipmates recognized that their very lives were in the hands of their fellows. While stepping onto the deck did not eradicate racism among white sailors, sheer necessity forged bonds of respect and trust across the lines of race, ethnicity, and nationality that were all but unthinkable on the North American mainland.[10]

Contemporaries described these shipmates as a "motley crew," a term historians Peter Linebaugh and Marcus Rediker have used to emphasize not only sailors' ethnic diversity but also their centrality to "risings of the people" in eighteenth-century revolutionary movements. Sailors' resistance to oppressive authority was honed by the ever-present threat of impressment. During the virtually continuous eighteenth-century wars among the European powers, British Royal Navy vessels often lost crew to combat, disease, and desertion. In order to replenish their ranks, captains were authorized to board British merchant ships—including those hailing from the American colonies—and to conscript as many crew members as they needed. Sailors both black and white were vulnerable to "the press," and the period after the 1740s saw them respond with numerous shipboard mutinies and dry land riots. Boston experienced a major mob action, the Knowles Riot, in 1747 when some fifty sailors—including a number of New Englanders—deserted a Royal Navy vessel docked in the harbor. When the captain attempted to impress Bostonians on the wharves, a mob that may have numbered over a thousand controlled the streets of Boston for several days, taking the ship's officers hostage and forcing the colonial governor to seek refuge at Castle William in Boston

Harbor until the rioting subsided. The rioters were described by Boston's Town Meeting as "Foreign Seamen Servants Negroes and other Persons of Mean and Vile Condition."[11]

We have every reason to believe that Crispus Attucks was intimately familiar with the life and culture of the sea. During the 1740s, some 25 percent of the male slaves along the Massachusetts seaboard worked on ships, with a significant number of them engaged on vessels trading between North America, the West Indies, Africa, and Europe. Both free blacks and fugitive slaves attempting to sign on to a ship were often welcomed unquestioningly by captains desperate to assemble a full crew. Between 1750 and 1770, probably between 10 and 20 percent of north Atlantic deep-sea sailors were black. We know Attucks traveled widely, at least along the western Atlantic coast, since his reported home base in 1770 was New Providence in the Bahamas, a town reputed to have been the headquarters for the extensive pirating activity in that region between 1715 and 1725. Caribbean piracy had been largely contained by Attucks's time, but the buccaneers' vaunted radical egalitarianism still deeply affected sailors' worldview and contributed to their instigation of politicized mob actions.[12]

Sailors working out of American seaports, including Boston, became notably unruly during the late 1760s. Increasing numbers of British soldiers were stationed in Boston to quell the protests and mob actions—some well planned, but many spontaneous uprisings outside the control of patriot leader Samuel Adams and his Sons of Liberty. Having witnessed the Knowles Riot and other impressment riots by Boston sailors, Adams was well aware of mobs' effectiveness, but he and other patriot leaders generally exercised restraint in adapting those techniques to protest Britain's taxation of the colonies. The working classes in Boston were less cautious. They were hard hit in this period, especially those of the "lower sort" like laborers and sailors. Their situation was made even worse when off-duty British troops stationed in Boston competed with them for jobs, often accepting lower wages. Indeed, among the events precipitating the Boston Massacre in 1770 was a brawl between workers and British troops after an off-duty soldier looking for work was harassed by the regular hands at a ropewalk, where men engaged in the laborious task of twining strands of fiber into the long, heavy cables needed on sailing ships.[13]

Since the end of the French and Indian (or Seven Years) War in 1763, the British government attempted to exert greater control over its North American colonies and to expand its taxation of the colonies. One ill-fated attempt at taxation, the Stamp Act of 1765, prompted a vociferous colonial response in the form of both formal appeals and mob actions. The bill was promptly repealed, but colonial distrust remained. The immediate cause for the escalation of colonial outrage after 1767 was the Townshend Acts, which imposed duties on colonial imports of glass, lead, paints, paper, and tea; set up a Board of Customs Commissioners in Boston; and generally broadened customs officials' powers to enforce tax collection and curtail smuggling. Across the colonies, middling and upper-class leaders responded with coordinated agreements to boycott British goods. In Boston, lower-class mobs—often mixed-race groups of sailors, laborers, and young apprentices—took matters into their own hands, burning customs officials in effigy, seizing and destroying property, and threatening violence against both British authorities and colonial merchants who imported boycotted goods. The Crown's response was to send four regiments—probably around twelve hundred men—to maintain order in a city of approximately 16,000. Bostonians of all social levels objected to the very visible military presence, which involved public drilling, patrolling, and the posting of sentries throughout the city. Sentries regularly exercised their right to challenge and question any passerby, a practice that in turn helped provoke harassment, theft, and all manner of "ill treatment" at the hands of the locals. Ultimately, the troops sent to preserve order only served to escalate conflicts between soldiers and the citizenry through 1768.[14]

After a winter and spring with no major incidents, the British removed most of the military force in June 1769, leaving only the Fourteenth and Twenty-Ninth regiments in the Boston garrison. The calm proved misleading, and conflicts grew more frequent and severe during the fall and winter of 1769–1770. The isolated regiments, probably numbering around six hundred men, justifiably believed themselves to be in physical danger, yet even Boston's courts consistently ruled against soldiers in cases that pitted them against civilians. Mobs targeting troops, importers, and Tory informers became ever bolder as their violent acts against both property and people consistently went unpunished. Some victims barely escaped with their lives. Then in February 1770 came the inevitable tragedy. A large mob was harassing the home of an importing merchant, when his neighbor, a notorious Tory informer named Ebenezer Richardson, confronted them. He was bombarded with rocks and sticks, took refuge in his home, and shouted threats at the crowd. His home then became the target of a major barrage of projectiles. Eventually Richardson fired his musket through an upstairs window, wounding one youth and killing an eleven-year-old boy named Christopher Seider. The lad's funeral on February 26 was at the time said to be "the largest perhaps ever known in America."[15]

With Seider's death the crescendo of conflict approached its climax. Bostonians' intensified outrage against the occupation was countered by increasing frustration and anger among the troops themselves. A mere four days after Seider's funeral, on March 2, a British soldier looking for work at John Gray's ropewalk was told by one of the ropemakers that if he wanted a job, he could "go and clean my shithouse." After a brief scuffle, the soldier retreated but soon returned with reinforcements from the nearby barracks of the Twenty-Ninth regiment. A major melee among dozens of soldiers and civilians ended with the troops being driven back to their barracks. The next two days witnessed numerous small-scale clashes that resulted in various injuries, and a growing sense on both sides that a culminating confrontation was imminent.[16]

The foot of snow on the ground did little to cool the simmering rage that permeated Boston on Monday, March 5, a day on which both citizens and soldiers were said to be hot for a fight. During the day, knots of soldiers and gangs of club-wielding civilians were seen "driving about the streets" as if they "had something more than ordinary in mind." When a sentry rifle-butted a young wigmaker's apprentice after the boy insulted an officer of the Fourteenth regiment, townsmen rallied. Ringing church bells—normally an alarm for fire—brought scores more people into the streets. By around 9:00 in the evening, a group of about twenty to thirty teenage boys and young men gathered around the offending sentry, Hugh White, and began pelting him with insults, snowballs, and chunks of ice. White loaded his rifle, retreated to the door of the King Street Custom House, and called for the main guard (see Fig. 1.1). Meanwhile, a few blocks away, dozens of townsmen, many carrying sticks and clubs, chastised the officers of Murray's Barracks for not keeping their soldiers indoors. Rumors of British violence circulated as church bells continued to pull people into the streets.

Hugh White's call for assistance brought Captain Thomas Preston and seven soldiers from the Twenty-Ninth regiment to his side, with bayonets fixed and muskets loaded with powder and ball. Several of these men, including White, had been involved in the March 2 brawl at the ropewalk. Groups of twenty or thirty citizens formed spontaneously in Dock Square, the North End, and other sections. With "huzzas" and shouts of "kill them," "to the main guard," and general calls for an assault on "the bloody-back rascals," both individuals and crowds, many armed with clubs or even broadswords, poured into King Street from every direction. Eventually upward of two hundred had assembled before the Custom House. Many of these were sailors, laborers, and young apprentices, though a number of merchants and higher-status patriot

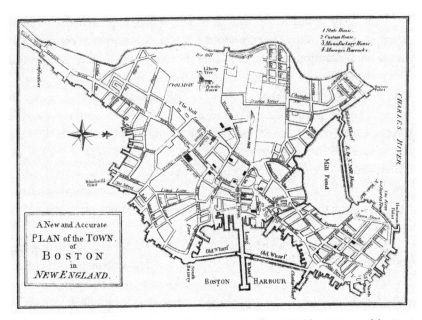

FIG. 1.1 A 1770 map of Boston, reproduced from Frederick Kidder, *History of the Boston Massacre* (1870). Photo: Western Michigan University Libraries Digitization Center.

activists were among them as well. Confusion reigned. The swelling crowd continued hurling sticks and snowballs, daring the soldiers to fire. Some witnesses described several among the mob striking the soldiers and their weapons with sticks. At last Private Edward (or Hugh) Montgomery was knocked to the ground. Amid continued cries from the mob of "Fire! Fire!" and "They dare not fire!" Montgomery discharged his rifle, with several more soldiers soon following his lead. Attucks and three others—Samuel Gray, James Caldwell, and Samuel Maverick—were killed instantly and at least seven others were wounded. One of these, Patrick Carr, died several days later. The identities of the victims suggest the range of people in the crowd. Caldwell and Attucks were both sailors; Maverick, the youngest at seventeen, was apprenticed to an ivory turner; Carr, an immigrant from Ireland, was apprenticed to a leather-breeches maker; Gray worked on a ropewalk. The wounded included a wheelwright's apprentice, a shipwright's apprentice, a merchant, a tailor, and a sailor. Two of the wounded, like Maverick, were just seventeen years old.[17]

Captain Preston and the soldiers were eventually tried for murder, resulting in two privates being convicted only of the lesser charge of manslaughter. Each was branded on the hand and dismissed from service. Several witnesses at the trials offered testimony regarding Crispus Attucks's actions leading up to the shooting. Thomas Symmonds reported that Attucks had dined at his victualing house near Murray's Barracks that evening. A newspaper report shortly after the soldiers' trial confirmed that Attucks was "at supper" when the ringing of bells brought him into the streets. He then witnessed "the affray at Murray's Barracks" and was prompted to join another man who threatened to drive all the soldiers back indoors. Around nine o'clock, Patrick Keaton saw "the tall mulatto fellow, the same that was killed" with a large group "coming from the north end, with sticks and clubs in their hands." Attucks carried two cordwood sticks, one of which he gave to Keaton. Then Attucks continued on, "cursing and swearing at the soldiers." Sailor James Bailey claimed to have been standing very near the Custom House when he also saw "the mulatto fellow" about seven or eight minutes before the firing, at the head of twenty or thirty sailors heading up Cornhill toward the town pump, "huzzaing, whistling and carrying their sticks upright over their heads" and generally "making a noise." While only about "seven or eight" of the group had sticks, Bailey was certain that "the mulatto fellow had a large cord-wood stick." John Danbrooke later saw Attucks about twelve feet in front of the soldiers, "leaning over a long stick he had, resting his breast upon it."[18]

In his testimony, Bailey also claimed that Private Montgomery, the first to have fired, was felled when he was struck with a club wielded by "a stout man" whom Bailey could not identify. That "stout man" apparently was seen more clearly by Andrew, a black slave of merchant and patriot activist Oliver Wendell. Andrew testified to have gotten "as close to the officer [Preston] as I could." From that vantage point, he saw "a number" of men approach the Custom House

from Jackson's corner, huzzaing and crying, damn them, they dare not fire, we are not afraid of them. One of these people, a stout man with a long cord wood stick, threw himself in, and made a blow at the officer; I saw the officer try to ward off the stroke; whether he struck him or not I do not know; the stout man then turned round, and struck the grenadier's gun at the captain's right hand, and immediately fell in with his club, and knocked his gun away, and struck him over the head; the blow came either on the soldier's cheek or hat. This stout man held the bayonet with his left hand, and twitched it, and cried, kill the dogs, knock them over.

When asked who the stout man was, Andrew replied, "I thought, and still think, it was the mulatto who was shot."[19]

A member of the crowd, John Hickling, saw both Attucks and Gray fall. After discovering "a hole as big as my hand" in Gray's head, Hickling "then went to Attucks and found him gasping, pulled his head out of the gutter and left him." Another bystander, Robert Goddard, then "went and helped the mulatto man, who was shot, into Mr. Stone's house. After we got him in there, I saw him give one gasp. I then opened his breast, and saw two holes, one in each breast, where the balls had entered." Attucks succumbed soon after.[20]

Samuel Adams's cousin John Adams, one of the soldiers' defense attorneys, summed up Attucks's role in his closing arguments. Attucks, he claimed,

> appears to have undertaken to be the hero of the night; and to lead this army with banners, to form them in the first place in Dock square, and march them up to King-street with their clubs; they passed through the main street up to the main-guard, in order to make the attack. . . . Attucks with his mirmidons comes round Jackson's corner, and down to the party by the sentry-box; when the soldiers pushed the people off, this man with his party cried, do not be afraid of them, they dare not fire, kill them! kill them! knock them over!—and he tried to knock their brains out. . . . [N]ow to have this reinforcement coming down under the command of a stout mulatto fellow, whose very looks was enough to terrify any person, what had not the soldiers then to fear? He had hardiness enough to fall in upon them, and with one hand took hold of a bayonet, and with the other knocked the man down: this was the behaviour of Attucks: to whose mad behaviour, in all probability, the dreadful carnage of that night is chiefly to be ascribed.[21]

Adams, as the soldiers' defense attorney, had an obvious motive for casting Attucks in as negative a light as possible, and we can easily imagine him exaggerating Attucks's aggressiveness. Following his summary of Attucks's alleged "mad behaviour," Adams did his best to characterize the entire mob as a rabble that did not reflect the demeanor, or represent the interests, of the good people of Boston. "And it is in this manner," he lamented, "this town has been often treated. A Carr from Ireland, and an Attucks from Framingham, happening to be here, shall sally out upon their thoughtless enterprises, at the head of such a rabble of negroes &c., as they can collect together, and then there are not wanting persons to ascribe all their doings to the good people of the town." The reference to "an Attucks from Framingham," a town known for its proximity to the Native American community in Natick, immediately cast Attucks in the eyes of Bostonians as a racially mixed and disreputable outsider. In other words, it was these foreigners—an Irish immigrant and a mixed-race thug—who roused a pack of sailors and lower-class ruffians to outnumber, corner, and assault beleaguered British troops. They were not Bostonians, they were not patriots, and the troops had every right to fire in order to protect themselves from the "motley rabble of saucy boys, negroes and mulattoes; Irish teagues and outlandish jack tars." To even call them a mob, Adams claimed, "is too respectable for them."[22]

Even accounting for Adams's exaggeration, however, the collective testimony of several witnesses—and especially that of Andrew—does suggest that Attucks was at the forefront of the mob and one of the most aggressive among those accosting the troops. He was heard cursing the soldiers, huzzaing and waving a club, handing a club to at least one other person, and positioning himself a few short paces from the besieged soldiers. Andrew is the only witness to describe Attucks physically assaulting the guards, but that deed cannot be ruled out, given his other actions that were corroborated by more than one observer.

Still, John Adams's characterization represents merely one of many possible reconstructions of the events of March 5. The local newspapers presented a very different point of view. Massachusetts's contemporary patriot press, pamphleteers, and engravers mourned the martyrdom of upright citizens—victims of a standing army's capricious abuse of arbitrary power. Though some of the earliest press reports made brief mention of Attucks (or Michael Johnson) being a mulatto, and denied him the title "mister" that was applied to the other victims, many subsequent accounts ignored the racial and class identities of the victims, referring to all the fallen men with the title "mister," which would have suggested to readers that all of them—including Attucks—were both respectable and white. Contemporary Bostonians would likely have known the truth of Attucks's identity, but those from other colonies who picked up the press accounts, and especially those who had seen the well-dressed, and apparently white, victims in Paul Revere's popular, propagandistic engraving of the event—provocatively titled "The BLOODY MASSACRE"—would have had no reason to suspect anything but an arbitrary attack on respectable white citizens by an abusive standing army (see Fig. 1.2). This reinterpretation of the massacre was specifically geared toward provoking outrage against British tyranny across the colonies.[23]

Boston's reaction to the events of March 5 was unequivocal. Three days after the "bloody massacre" a funeral for the fallen men dwarfed that of Christopher Seider, which was still fresh in everyone's memory. Ten to twelve thousand people—perhaps three quarters of Boston's total population—participated in

FIG. 1.2 Paul Revere, engraver. *The Bloody Massacre Perpetrated in King Street Boston on March 5th 1770 by a Party of the 29th Regt.* Boston: Engraved, Printed & Sold by Paul Revere, 1770. Library of Congress.

the massive commemoration. The body of Samuel Maverick was brought out from the house of "his distressed mother" and Samuel Gray's from that of his brother. Since the two sailors, Attucks and James Caldwell, were "strangers," they were conveyed from Faneuil Hall. The hearses came together on King Street and, followed by "an immense concourse of People" from all social ranks, formed a procession that traveled up the main streets, around the Liberty Tree, and ended at the Granary Burying Ground, where the four martyrs were laid to rest in a common grave (see Fig. 1.3). A history of the event written a generation later emphasized the solemnity of the ceremony, which

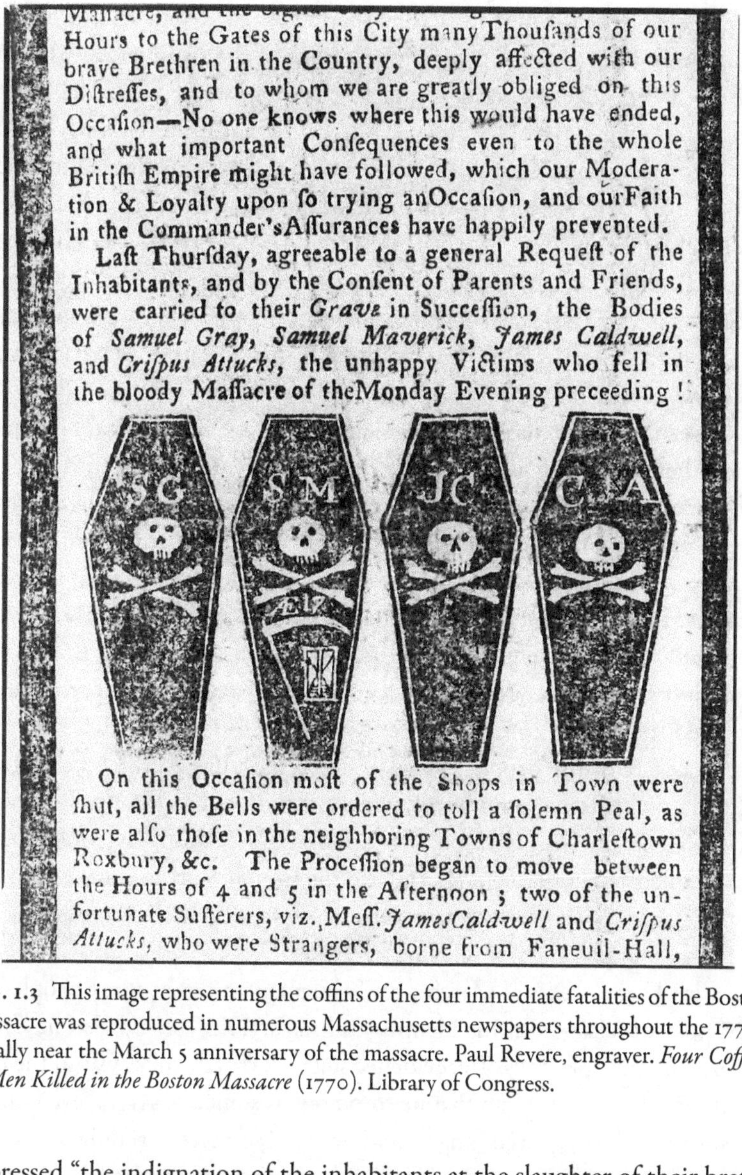

Hours to the Gates of this City many Thousands of our brave Brethren in the Country, deeply affected with our Distresses, and to whom we are greatly obliged on this Occasion—No one knows where this would have ended, and what important Consequences even to the whole British Empire might have followed, which our Moderation & Loyalty upon so trying an Occasion, and our Faith in the Commander's Assurances have happily prevented.

Last Thursday, agreeable to a general Request of the Inhabitants, and by the Consent of Parents and Friends, were carried to their *Grave* in Succession, the Bodies of *Samuel Gray, Samuel Maverick, James Caldwell,* and *Crispus Attucks,* the unhappy Victims who fell in the bloody Massacre of the Monday Evening preceeding!

On this Occasion most of the Shops in Town were shut, all the Bells were ordered to toll a solemn Peal, as were also those in the neighboring Towns of Charlestown Roxbury, &c. The Procession began to move between the Hours of 4 and 5 in the Afternoon ; two of the unfortunate Sufferers, viz. Mess. *James Caldwell* and *Crispus Attucks,* who were Strangers, borne from Faneuil-Hall,

FIG. 1.3 This image representing the coffins of the four immediate fatalities of the Boston Massacre was reproduced in numerous Massachusetts newspapers throughout the 1770s, usually near the March 5 anniversary of the massacre. Paul Revere, engraver. *Four Coffins of Men Killed in the Boston Massacre* (1770). Library of Congress.

expressed "the indignation of the inhabitants at the slaughter of their brethren, by soldiers quartered among them, in violation of their civil liberties."[24]

The orators at Boston Massacre commemorations similarly constructed the event in public consciousness as an emblem of a virtuous people's resistance to tyranny. Annual March 5 commemorations were held in Boston from 1771 until 1783, when the observances were replaced with annual celebrations of American independence on July 4. In the orations delivered at the March 5 ceremonies, the victims were discussed collectively, with few

references to specific individuals and sparing use of specific names. Most orators used telling phrases to stir the emotions of their audiences: "the horrid
bloody scene" (James Lovell, 1771, 1); "streets . . . stained with the BLOOD
OF OUR BRETHREN" (Joseph Warren, 1772, 6); our "murdered *fellow-
citizens*" (Benjamin Church, 1773, 12); "the blood of slaughtered innocents"
(John Hancock, 1774, 15). Only three orators mentioned any of the victims
by name, and only John Hancock (1774) mentioned Attucks, and then merely
while listing all of the victims. In none of the addresses was any mention
made of the victims' racial or ethnic identities; rather, they were consistently
referred to collectively as "our brethren," "our countrymen," "citizens," or
"fellow-citizens."[25]

Not surprisingly Massachusetts Lieutenant Governor Thomas Hutchinson
and other British officials refused to acknowledge the events of March 5 as a
massacre and exercised a large degree of tact in their characterizations of the
event in official correspondence. While making clear that the British troops
were provoked by an unruly mob, Hutchinson used neutral language. He
referred to it as "a most unfortunate affair." Lieutenant General Thomas Gage
called it "an unhappy quarrel" that excited "a general rising" of Boston's citizens. John Pownall, undersecretary of state of the American department, recognized the patriot construction only by mentioning it as "(what is called)
the massacre of the people." Pownall was responding to the official Report
of the Boston Town Committee, which was printed in the April 1770 issue
of *Gentleman's Magazine*, a popular London publication. The *Magazine* also
maintained a neutral tone, referring to "the late Tumult" in Boston, and publishing Captain Thomas Preston's version of events in the same issue. For others, it was simply "the riot on King street."[26]

Clearly, the events of March 5 could be many things to many people. And
Crispus Attucks—both his identity and his actions—could also be characterized in multiple ways. The evidence suggests that Attucks was in the thick
of things that evening and that he stood out as someone several eyewitnesses
characterized as agitated, angry, and active. He most certainly was *not* an
innocent bystander who happened to be at the wrong place at the wrong
time. As a sailor and a man who likely sought work around the docks when
he was in port, Attucks conceivably bore some resentment against the British
troops in Boston. Perhaps his bitterness toward the Crown was also fed by
previous experiences with impressment, harsh service on British naval vessels,
or prior altercations with British soldiers. But we cannot know for sure, and
we certainly have no evidence of his prior participation in anti-British actions
or his attitudes regarding American independence and the revolutionary

movement. No surviving sources connect him with Boston's Sons of Liberty or any other individuals or groups affiliated with the patriot cause. He seems to have been an outsider with whom Bostonians were largely unfamiliar. Trial witnesses never used his name, almost always describing him merely as "the molatto," and he was specifically identified as a "stranger" in descriptions of the funeral.

Yet Attucks has since been ascribed personal attributes, political loyalties, and a public persona far beyond what the meager evidence supports. Some of the most widespread assumptions about Attucks relate to his background and family history. Over the years interested parties have hypothesized that Attucks may have been fully Native American or African, or various combinations of European, African, and Indian. Most people, however, believe that Attucks was of African and Native American ancestry, which is most likely the case. While the transcript of the 1770 Boston Massacre trial contains one reference to Attucks as an "Indian," it was the term "mulatto" (or "molatto") which was most consistently applied to Attucks both during the trial and in the 1750 runaway advertisement. This term was commonly used in the eighteenth century to describe a person of mixed race and sometimes specifically "those who are begotten by a Negro Man on an Indian Woman; or an Indian Man on a Negro Woman." William Brown's description of "Crispas" in his 1750 runaway ad also noted the fugitive's "short curl'd hair," a trait that would be more likely in a person with some African, rather than purely Native American, ancestry.[27]

The case for Attucks's Indian ancestors is circumstantial but strong. Hailing from Framingham placed him very near Natick, a "praying town" of Christianized Indians from various Algonquian-speaking groups. The surname "Peterattucks"—which one early historian said "savors of Indian origin"—was known in that area, and the word "attuck" (or "ahtuk") is said to be a Natick area word meaning "young deer." Also, a Native American man from the region named John Auttuck (or "Uktuck") was executed in 1676 for his alleged participation in King Philip's War. Some believe Crispus Attucks to be a descendant of this man, but the only evidence is the similarity of their last names (and perhaps the proclivity toward confrontation with colonial authorities). There has also been considerable speculation about whether Attucks's Native and African blood came from the maternal or paternal sides. Most accounts posit that his mother was Indian and his father African, but there is no firm evidence supporting either position. Similarly, we have no idea whether Attucks had any siblings or extended family around Framingham; nor do we know whether he ever married or had children.[28]

While he was almost certainly a sailor, we cannot know how long he had
been plying that trade or under what circumstances. One persistent story
holds that Attucks had sailed on a Nantucket whaler captained by a man
named Folger, but that story comes solely from the secondhand recollections of an elderly Boston man some six decades after the fact. A later mid-
nineteenth century source repeats the Nantucket whaler story and also claims
that Attucks was employed in a North End ropewalk at the time of the massacre. While possible, contemporary evidence placing Attucks at a ropewalk
is conspicuously absent.[29]

Likewise, it is difficult to place much confidence in the stories involving
the Brown family of Framingham, from which Attucks presumably fled
in 1750. Josiah H. Temple's 1887 *History of Framingham* claimed, with no
attribution, that Attucks had come to the Brown family "as early as 1747."
Temple quoted a Brown descendant that "Crispus was well informed, . . .
was a good judge of cattle, and was allowed to buy and sell upon his own
judgment of their value." In 1858, at the first commemoration of Attucks
organized by black abolitionists in Boston, a grandson of Deacon William
Brown reportedly "narrated to several persons the traditions extant in
the family relating to Crispus Attucks—of his goblet, powder-horn, &c."
The latter items were said to be on display at the 1858 Faneuil Hall observance. In the early twenty-first century, the Society for the Preservation of
New England Antiquities (SPNEA) sponsored a traveling museum exhibit
titled "Cherished Possessions," which included a teapot purportedly
belonging to Attucks and also said to have been displayed at nineteenth-
century Attucks Day observances. The curator of the exhibit, however,
questioned the likelihood of the teapot actually having been Attucks's personal property. Indeed, it strains credibility to think that the family would
connect a slave who had escaped in 1750 with the massacre martyr twenty
years later, and it seems even more incredible that a slave's ostensible possessions would be preserved over several generations as honored relics.[30]

These nineteenth-century tales have had an indirect impact on twenty-
first-century thinking. Popular contemporary beliefs about Attucks are probably best measured by the information readily available through "Crispus
Attucks" Internet searches. While some of these sources are more careful and
accurate than others, many accept and propagate very similar—and often
unreliable—stories. Numerous myths about Attucks have emerged since his
first appearance in the historical record, but much of the information that is
widely accepted today can be traced to a single source: a 1965 juvenile biography titled *Crispus Attucks: Boy of Valor*, written by Dharathula H. Millender,

an African American librarian and columnist from Gary, Indiana. *Boy of Valor* seems to be the first black-authored work to appear in publisher Bobbs-Merrill's popular "Childhood of Famous Americans" series. When the Crispus Attucks volume appeared in 1965 he joined Booker T. Washington and George Washington Carver as the only African Americans in the series. Begun in the early 1930s and still active, this series presents "fictionalized biographies" of dozens of Americans, with a particular emphasis on their experiences as children. The series editors claimed in 2003 that their stories are "fleshed out with fictionalized details . . . but every reasonable effort has been made to make the stories consistent with the events, ethics, and character of their subjects." However, when Millender's Attucks biography appeared, books in the series were *not* clearly identified as "fictionalized," and readers had little reason to distrust their biographical details.[31]

Crispus Attucks presented a formidable task for Millender, since so little is known about the actual events of his life. Nonetheless, the author produced nearly two hundred pages of large-font text. We learn about young "Cris" and his parents, Nancy and Prince, and his big sister Phebe. Prince was born the son of an African king, and Nancy was one of the "praying Indians" residing near Natick before she chose to live as a slave in order to marry the man she loved. The family was owned by Colonel Buckminster of Framingham, and Prince was the Colonel's "favorite slave." The colonel was always "very nice to the Attucks family," and they had a comfortable "cottage" some distance from the other slaves' cabins. Early in the story Cris is baptized in the Buckminsters' church.[32]

Millender reiterated some of the speculation that had long existed regarding Attucks's mixed-race parentage. She has Nancy explain to young Cris his Indian heritage, claiming "John Uktuck" as her great-grandfather, while Prince tells Cris about his own African homeland. Millender provides some elementary, but generally sound, historical context about the process of Africans being captured in ethnic conflict before being sold to Europeans; the fairly common intermixture of Indians and Africans in New England; the history of King Philip's War and the Native community in Natick; and the distinctions between black slaves and white indentured servants.

While in some cases Millender engages in reasonable speculation, she throws caution to the wind in inventing many "events" of Attucks's life. Despite the family's relatively comfortable existence and his parents' admonitions to enjoy his privileges, since "We hardly know that we're slaves here" (95), Cris couldn't help but "want to be free rather than a slave" (97). But he minded his parents and remained on the farm until he was unexpectedly "sold without his being consulted. He just couldn't believe it!" (117). Over the next ten years as a slave of "Deacon Brown," Cris earned his master's trust and was allowed to travel on his own, trading in cattle and buying sperm oil from whalers for the deacon's chandlery. Cris grew to become "a huge man, powerful and brave" (123), and finally escaped to pursue his long-held dream of becoming a sailor. He became a highly skilled and respected harpooner on Captain Folger's whaler. While staying for a time in Boston, Cris witnessed atrocities committed by British soldiers and listened to speeches by American leaders like James Otis and John Adams. When tensions increased one evening in March 1770, Cris "mounted a platform that had been erected for speakers" and "spoke briefly to the crowd in the square . . . as if he had been speaking in public for years" (171). He spoke of taxation and slavery, of unfair trade restrictions and the courage to stand up to the British. A confrontation almost broke out, but Attucks was able to calm the crowd and send them all home (172–74). A few days later the British killed Attucks in the Boston Massacre, when he led a crowd of sailors coming to the aid of a small group of citizens who were being threatened by the guard. During the funeral exercises a few days later, "speeches made special mention of Crispus Attucks," a man "filled with a passion for freedom . . . intolerant of intolerance . . . [and] endowed . . . with native daring. . . . His sacrifice serves as a rallying cry for freedom" (182–84).

Millender's portrayal of Attucks has permeated much of the popular understanding of the man. The impact of this 1965 text expanded when it was reissued verbatim in 1986 under Simon and Schuster's Aladdin imprint as *Crispus Attucks, Black Leader of Colonial Patriots*. It is still in print and over one thousand American libraries hold either *Boy of Valor* or *Black Leader*.[33] A google search using the combined terms "crispus," "attucks," "nancy," and "prince" (not in quotes) yields over 27,000 websites that include the parents' names among the biographical details about Attucks, many presenting details of Millender's fictional account as fact. Millender's heroic and freedom-loving Cris thus continues to influence popular knowledge of Attucks.[34]

Although Millender's construction of Attucks's life clearly should not be accepted as ironclad truth, some of her speculations are based on historically verifiable evidence. Beginning with what can be most easily dismissed as fabrication, Millender's depiction of Attucks's participation in the Boston Massacre bears little resemblance to the historical record. While it is quite possible that Attucks had been in Boston prior to March 1770, we have no clear evidence of that, let alone that he was inspired by, or even heard, the speeches of patriot leaders. The idea that he "mounted a platform" and displayed his oratorical skills with a discourse on taxation, slavery, and other matters is complete invention, as is the idea that he calmed a crowd and avoided a confrontation just prior to March 5. Millender's claim that Attucks led a group on March 5 to protect citizens threatened by British troops clearly distorts the reality of that encounter, and we have no evidence that Attucks was singled out for praise during the funeral or at any time after the massacre. The only singular public notice he received was from John Adams during the trial, and that notice was hardly favorable.

Millender's account of Attucks's experiences between his 1750 escape from William Brown and his appearance in Boston, while unverifiable, indicates that the author used nineteenth-century sources, especially Temple's 1887 *History of Framingham*, to piece together a plausible life for the fugitive slave. Millender occasionally uses Temple's exact language, as when she refers to "Cris" as "a huge man, powerful and brave, almost to recklessness." Temple had described Attucks as being "of huge bodily proportions, and brave almost to recklessness." Millender repeats the Brown descendant's assertion of Attucks's skill in judging cattle and his relative freedom to travel on his master's business. She also accepts Temple's speculation that Attucks "was fond of a seafaring life and, probably with consent of his master, was accustomed to taking coasting voyages," as well the elderly Bostonian's uncorroborated recollection from the 1830s that Attucks served on Captain Folger's whaler out of Nantucket. She provides an extensive fictitious narrative of Cris's experiences on the whaler, during which he earned his mates' and his captain's respect by working hard to "become a trusted and daring harpooner."[35]

In her treatment of Attucks's life as a slave of Framingham's Brown and Buckminster families, Millender once again relies on Temple's *History*, and perhaps an earlier nineteenth-century town history by William Barry that was used extensively by Temple, as a basis for her tale. Indeed, the Browns and Buckminsters were well-known Framingham families during the eighteenth century, and the superficial descriptions Millender provides accurately reflect their status in that community. Colonel Joseph Buckminster was a prominent landowner there from 1693 until his death in 1747 at the age of eighty-one. During that time he served as a selectman for seventeen years, a representative for twelve, and attained his rank of colonel as commander of a company of Royal Grenadiers and as the head of a colonial militia unit.[36]

More pertinent to Millender's tale of the Attucks family, the colonel owned an African-born slave named Prince Yongey (sometimes noted as Young, Yonger, or Jonar), who was said to have been "a person of consideration in his native land." Acquired by Buckminster in the early 1720s when he was around the age of twenty-five, Yongey lived a remarkably long life in Framingham and came to be "the most noted individual" among the blacks living in that region. According to William Barry's 1847 *History of Framingham*, Prince "was a faithful servant, and by his general honesty, temperance and prudence, so gained the confidence of his first master, Col. Buckminster, that for about a quarter of a century, he was left with the management of a large farm, during his master's absence at the General Court." A literate and religious man, in his later years "Old Prince" was well known for his "simplicity, intelligence, and humor." He died in 1797 at the age of ninety-nine, still a slave of Colonel Buckminster's son, Deacon Thomas Buckminster, even though slavery had been abolished in Massachusetts by 1783. Apparently, Prince had been offered his liberty, but "had the sagacity to decline; pithily saying, 'massa eat the meat; he now pick the bone.'" Millender even depicts this scene, without the colorful language, in her fictionalized biography (152–54).[37]

Adding to the interest of the existence of this African-born slave named Prince is his 1737 marriage to a local woman named Nanny Peterattucks, "by whom he had several children, among them a son, who died young, and a daughter Phebe, who never married." Both Nanny and Jacob Peterattucks— identified by Temple in his "Genealogical Register" as "Prob. descts. [probable descendants] of John Attuck, the Indian"—worked for Joseph Buckminster. Jacob may not have been a slave, but he was said to have been "at work" for Buckminster in 1730. Nanny, however, was apparently the colonel's slave at least at the time of his death in 1747, when "a negro woman, Nanny" appeared in his estate inventory, valued at £80.[38]

Nanny's identification as a probable descendant of the Indian John Attucks and her later designation as "a negro woman" raises some question about her actual racial heritage. Perhaps there had been racial mixing among the Peterattucks clan prior to Nanny's marriage to Prince, or perhaps her marriage and her status as a slave made her "negro" by association in the eyes of those compiling the 1747 estate inventory. In any event, if we change "Nanny" to "Nancy," we have Millender's married slave couple, their daughter Phebe, and perhaps another living child, all part of Buckminster's extended household during the period Crispus Attucks likely was growing up in the Framingham area. William Barry's description of Prince certainly fits with Millender's presentation of him as the colonel's "favorite" slave. In fact, Barry informs us that Prince lived in his own "cabin near the Turnpike, and cultivated, for his own use, a piece of meadow." This would seem a special privilege for a favored bondsman. Prince's arrival in the early 1720s corresponds almost exactly with the generally accepted time of Crispus Attucks's birth, but it is not clear whether Nanny lived with Buckminster prior to 1730. Neither do we have the birth date of Phebe or the couple's other children. It is certainly possible that Prince and Nanny had been cohabiting and having children for some time prior to their wedding. If that were the case, they very well could have had a son named Crispus in 1723.[39]

So it seems that the further back Millender's construction of "Cris's" life is traced, the more plausible it becomes. To be sure, her evidence is completely circumstantial and the story she constructs about Cris's life experiences is utterly fictional. Yet the family in which she places Cris did exist. The timing of Prince's arrival and the surname of his wife are highly suggestive. But one also must wonder why there is no eighteenth-century record in Framingham or elsewhere connecting the famous "Old Prince" with the much publicized exploits of his son in Boston in 1770. Prince was in his early seventies at the time and by all accounts still had his wits about him. Along with the Browns and Buckminsters, Prince remained well known in the community, and the press reports from nearby Boston clearly identified Crispus Attucks as both a Framingham native and a central figure in the massacre. If Prince or the Browns or the Buckminsters had any connection with the massacre martyr, there surely would have been some mention in local sources. None have yet been found. While Millender's story of Crispus Attucks's family and child-hood connects with verifiable elements of local history, the reality of the man's early life remains a shadow in the mist of time.

Even in 1847, William Barry's *History of Framingham*, on which J. H. Temple relied heavily in preparing his own 1887 treatise, fails to mention Crispus Attucks at all, despite the details he provides on John Uktuck, Prince Yongey and Nanny Peterattucks, and the Browns and Buckminsters. Yet Temple's 1887 history does make those connections, going so far as to locate Attucks's birthplace as an "old cellar-hole" located "near the Framingham town line, a short distance to the eastward of the State Arsenal." Frederic Kidder's 1870 *History of the Boston Massacre* also identifies an "old cellar hole" located "near the Chochituate lake and not far from the line of Natick." Neither author cites a source for this information, but they may have relied on William Barry's description of Prince Yongey's "cabin near the Turnpike" where he cultivated land that was subsequently known as "Prince's meadow." Crossed by multiple highways, Lake Chochituate is located near the current Natick Mall. Perhaps the location of Prince's Meadow was still known in the nineteenth century, and Kidder and Temple were able thereby to locate Attucks's supposed birthplace.[40]

Yet the question remains: Why did Kidder in 1870 and Temple in 1887 have so much to say about Crispus Attucks and his connections in Framingham while he is completely absent from Barry's otherwise very thorough 1847 volume? Attucks's differing treatment in those histories is actually part of a larger story of forgetting and remembering, and of his disappearance and reemergence in America's collective memory between the 1770s and the 1850s.

2

The Dustbin of History

CRISPUS ATTUCKS AND AMERICAN AMNESIA,
1770S–1840S

Here, on the long-remembered night of the 5th of ——,
1770, Attucks, a colored man, Caldwell, a stranger,
Maverick, a widow's son, seventeen years of age, with Gray
and Carr, were shot by soldiers of the 29th British regi-
ment, under the command of Captain Preston. This day
was celebrated for many years, but the event has somewhat
faded from the minds of men.

NEW YORK SPECTATOR (June 14, 1845)

I have been unable to find out much of the History of
Attucks.

WILLIAM C. NELL (1841)

IN HIS DEFENSE of the British soldiers at their 1770 trial, John Adams had
emphasized the "outlandish" nature of the March 5 mob and its composition
of people of the lower sort. They were anything but patriots, Adams argued;
they were a rabble whose actions threatened not merely the British guard
but the very social order of the colony. Eastern Massachusetts's contemporary Revolutionaries, on the other hand, mourned the martyrdom of upright
citizens—victims of a standing army's reckless abuse of power. When Adams
was no longer constrained by his role as defense attorney, however, he suggested that his view of Attucks and the other massacre victims may have been
more in line with his patriot contemporaries. In July 1773, with the colonies'
relations with Britain continuing to deteriorate, he copied into his diary the
text of a letter—apparently never sent or published—to Governor Thomas
Hutchinson, condemning the governor's "premeditated malice" in inciting
the "Murder" of Americans at the Boston Massacre and threatening that "You

will hear further from Us hereafter." While it was written in the collective voice of the massacre martyrs, Adams signed the letter "Chrispus Attucks."[1]

This reference almost two years after the soldiers' trial is unusual because it offers one of the few indications that anyone in Boston or elsewhere retained any memory of Crispus Attucks. To be sure, between 1770 and the Revolution's formal conclusion in 1783, the Boston Massacre and its victims continued to serve the political agenda of the patriot cause. Orators at March 5 commemorations in Boston provided annual reminders of the supposed atrocities perpetrated by the British against peaceful and virtuous citizens, but they rarely mentioned the victims by name. Attucks was named in passing only once. So why did John Adams's diary entry have "Crispus Attucks" sign the letter to Hutchinson? Was it because Adams recognized Attucks as the first to die in freedom's cause? Did he in fact see Attucks as a patriot leader, the man he described (albeit pejoratively) at the trial as having "undertaken to be the hero of the night"? Or was Adams tapping into the terror Attucks presumably inspired—this "stout mulatto fellow," as Adams had also said at the trial, "whose very looks was enough to terrify any person." The diary entry is all the more interesting because, after the 1770s, Crispus Attucks disappeared almost completely from American memory for more than half a century.[2]

Even the March 5 commemorations ended in 1783 in favor of the celebration of July 4. With the Revolution completed and American independence achieved, the massacre was no longer needed to rally patriotic outrage against British injustice. Independence Day seemed a far more relevant commemoration. The massacre, however, continued to be widely acknowledged as a key event—some argued *the* key event—leading to the colonies' demand for independence. In private correspondence in 1786, John Adams, this time with no reference to Attucks, asserted that on the "5th of March, 1770 . . . the foundation of American independence was laid."[3]

Many histories and reminiscences of the Revolution published between the 1790s and 1850s paid some attention to the Boston Massacre, though many did not. One of the earliest histories of the Revolution contains one of the most thorough accounts of the events surrounding the massacre, including Crispus Attucks's role. William Gordon's *The History of the Rise, Progress, and Establishment of the Independence of the United States of America . . .* (1789) devoted about ten pages to the events, starting with the March 2 confrontation at the Boston ropewalk that precipitated the fatal clash of March 5 and continuing through the March 8 group burial of the patriotic martyrs. Gordon's present tense reenactment portrayed Attucks as the instigator. The mob accosting the British guard, he reported, "appears to be headed by the mulatto Attucks," who "aims a blow at Captain Preston, strikes down one of the guns, seizes the bayonet with his left hand, and shows a hardy disposition answering to the threats which have been uttered." Attucks's subsequent "assault" on another soldier, Hugh Montgomery, provoked the soldier to shoot and kill his "mulatto" assailant.[4]

While David Ramsay's *The History of the American Revolution* (1795) did not mention Attucks, it emphasized the significance of ceremonies surrounding the interment of the martyrs, who "were buried in one vault, and in a most respectful manner to express the indignation of the inhabitants at the slaughter of their brethren, by soldiers quartered among them, in violation of their civil liberties." Ramsay also accurately characterized the spirit of the subsequent anniversary observances, which were "observed with great solemnity." Orators "preserve[d] the remembrance of [the massacre]" in the minds of the people and "administered fuel to the fire of liberty, and kept it burning, with an incessant flame."[5]

Beyond published histories, the nation's collective memory of the Revolution was preserved in the public sphere of the early republic in various ways. Popular biographies of George Washington, John Paul Jones, Patrick Henry, Francis Marion, and others established an early heroic pantheon. Visual representations of individuals and battles were created by engravers like Paul Revere and painters like John Trumbull, culminating with the installation of Trumbull's four scenes of the Revolution in the Capitol's rotunda, completed between 1818 and 1824. As the 1826 semicentennial of independence approached, Americans memorialized key Revolutionary events with projects like Trumbull's paintings; the Bunker Hill Monument in Boston, which was begun in 1825; celebrations of George Washington's birthday; and the continuing commemoration of July Fourth. The Boston Massacre entered into this conversation primarily in text, with 1807 and 1824 republications of the transcript of the soldiers' trial, which had originally appeared in 1770.[6]

Nonetheless, public attention to the Boston Massacre waned after 1783, and it disappeared from the commemorative calendar even in Boston. Meanwhile, the event drew only sporadic attention in early American newspapers, perhaps in part because it virtually coincided with the "Republican Jubilee" that Jefferson's supporters began celebrating every March 4, to honor the Sage of Monticello's inauguration as president in 1801. March 4 had been inauguration day since George Washington's second inauguration in 1793, but it took on new meaning for Democratic-Republicans after Jefferson's "Revolution of 1800" removed Federalists from the presidency. March 4, 1802, was celebrated by "Republican Citizens" across Massachusetts as the first anniversary of "the Era of Renovation of Republicanism in the United States, in the advancement of the Sage, the Philosopher, Patriot, and genuine Republican, Thomas Jefferson, to the Presidential Chair of the Union." Subsequent years continued this new partisan tradition, perhaps limiting the possibility that anyone would think about reviving the celebration of another anniversary a day later.[7]

The proximity of March 4 and March 5 was rarely commented on in early republic newspapers, though in 1807 Boston's *Independent Chronicle* explicitly juxtaposed the two dates: "The contrast between this day (*the Fifth of March*) in the American annals, and that of the *Fourth*, must be striking to every Republican; for while the *former* brings to our remembrance the MASSACRE IN STATE-STREET, the *latter* leads us to the reflection of the inauguration of our beloved PRESIDENT." Pundits did occasionally try to restore the Boston Massacre to national consciousness. In 1784, for example, a Vermont newspaper reprinted the exact text from the March 12, 1770, *Boston Gazette* account that described the event in detail (referring to Attucks as a "mulatto man"), and a similar account appeared in a New Jersey periodical in 1787. But these appear to be the last occasions for several decades on which Attucks would be identified racially in the public media.[8]

The massacre occasionally did work its way back into public discourse, as in 1795 when several newspapers paid homage to the victims on the massacre's twenty-fifth anniversary and in 1799 when a journalist used the massacre to illustrate the dangers inherent in standing armies. During Jefferson's second term, escalating tensions between the United States and Great Britain—over impressment, trade restrictions, and other issues—presented a politically opportune moment for Republican editors to recall Britain's past atrocities. Boston's *Independent Chronicle* complemented its column-length coverage of the March 4, 1806, "republican celebration" with an editorial urging city residents to remember "the thirty-sixth anniversary of the BOSTON MASSACRE! ... [when] the blood of our fellow-citizens was spilt in a wanton manner, by British troops. . . . The Old Whigs of Boston remember that night, and it is their duty to instill an abhorrence of such barbarity into the minds of their children." Later that year, a twenty-three-year-old Daniel Webster used the massacre to kindle patriotic outrage in a July Fourth audience of "federal gentlemen" at Concord, New Hampshire. Webster identified the massacre as the seminal event leading to revolution and compared it with a recent incident in which a British naval captain "wantonly and inhumanly" fired on an American vessel in New York's harbor, killing a crew member.

Webster chastised authorities for their tepid proclamation of protest, asserting that "national honor" called for a more "heated" response. He reminded his audience that in 1770, when British troops "fired among our citizens, kill[ing] some and wound[ing] others . . . the continent rose to arms! The cry of blood was abroad in the land, and from that moment we may date the severance of the British Empire."[9]

On the massacre's fortieth anniversary in 1810, one Republican editor recalled "the cruel outrages of a British soldiery" and asked his readers, "Can cordiality ever be renewed between those who thus wantonly shed the blood of our townsmen?" In 1812, just a few months before Congress's declaration of war against Great Britain, Boston's Republican press intensified its rhetoric, calling attention to British abuses with articles entitled "OUR RIGHTS— Shall We Defend Them" and "AMERICANS IN SLAVERY." In the midst of these pieces was another, boldly headlined "5th of March—or, BOSTON MASSACRE!" which characterized the massacre as a "catastrophe which never ought to be obliterated from the memory of patriotic citizens . . . [and which had] evinced the temper and designs of the British government at that early period of our controversy." The massacre showed "nothing short of a determination to subjugate America to the despotism of England." The article argued that "the debates of that day . . . and those of the present time [were] on the same subject." The patriotic response of leaders like "Adams and Hancock, Warren and Quincy" did not flatter present day Bostonians, who, according to the paper's editor, were reluctant to act because they "paid court to a British faction." Two years later the *Salem Gazette* reprinted an excerpt from a July 4, 1807, oration by Samuel Dana, which recalled the "injured shades of Maverick, Gray, Caldwell, Carr and Attucks, slain by the soldiers of a mercenary army on the 5th of March, 1770." The names of the massacre martyrs may have been preserved, but few, if any, Americans knew or cared who these men were.[10]

During this same period a rather cryptic reference to Crispus Attucks appeared in a short-lived Boston newspaper devoted to political lampooning. *The Scourge* only produced a few issues in 1811 before its editor, Merrill Butler (publishing under the pseudonym "Tim Touchstone"), was sentenced to six months' imprisonment for libel in December of that year. In an October issue, Butler included the following blurb: "The extract from the Journal of an OLD MAN, on our first page, will 'cause gnashing of teeth' among the friends and adherents 'of Crispus Attux and Holder Slocum.'" The clearly fictitious "Journal" offers a vaguely scatological insult to an unnamed and deceased "late worthy patriot of the revolution," harking back to that person's residence in the Netherlands in the early 1780s. But the journal entry does not seem germane in any way to Crispus Attucks, the massacre, or other related issues. It is not clear why any "gnashing of teeth" would beset Attucks's ostensible "friends and adherents."[11]

Yet the passage's mention of Holder Slocum is intriguing. Slocum (1747–1827) was from a prominent family that owned land in Dartmouth, Massachusetts, and on Cuttyhunk Island off the coast. Holder served as a Massachusetts state legislator from about 1805 to 1826, and perhaps drew the attention of the *Scourge*'s editor because of some political dispute. More pertinent to a possible Attucks connection, during the eighteenth century Holder's older relatives, Ebenezer Slocum and later John Slocum, had owned an African-born slave named Kofi Slocum, who John, following his Quaker principles, freed during the 1740s. Kofi married a Wampanoag woman and for many years continued to live in the same region as the white Slocums, either in Dartmouth, on nearby Cuttyhunk Island, or farther offshore in the Indian community of Chilmark on Martha's Vineyard. Kofi is of particular interest because one of his sons, Paul, later adopted his father's African name as a surname and became known as Paul Cuffe. Born in 1759, Paul Cuffe became an accomplished sailor and wealthy shipping entrepreneur who used his shipping business during the 1810s to actively pursue establishing a black American colony on the west coast of Africa.[12]

Between the 1740s and 1770s, Kofi and his family lived along Buzzard's Bay, the very active waterway between Martha's Vineyard and what would soon become the prolific whaling port of New Bedford, Massachusetts. Kofi and his children crisscrossed the waters between the coast, Martha's Vineyard, and the Elizabeth Islands on a regular basis. Kofi Slocum would have been just a few years older than Crispus Attucks, who probably began working on ships in this general region after his escape from slavery in 1750. During the 1760s, the former slave Kofi Slocum prospered. He learned to read and write, and he achieved considerable success as a carpenter, merchant, and farmer. Kofi made a good living ferrying and trading supplies between Martha's Vineyard and the mainland. Thus he and his family would have had considerable contact with sailors plying their trade in those waters. In 1766, Kofi purchased 116 acres of farmland in the mainland community of Dartmouth, where he lived until his death in 1772.[13]

Is it possible that the Afro-Indian sailor Crispus Attucks had some contact with this Afro-Indian family? Can we imagine an eleven-year-old Paul mourning the death of this seafaring family friend in 1770? Would the thirteen-year-old Holder Slocum have been a playmate of Paul's? Might he too have had some contact with Crispus Attucks? Could the plausible connections among these men explain a malicious Boston journalist's 1811 reference to "the friends and adherents of Holder Slocum and Crispus Attux"? Like so much of Attucks's life and legacy, we may never know.

These periodic references to Attucks and the massacre notwithstanding, Americans made no concerted effort to commemorate the Boston Massacre after 1783, and the names of Crispus Attucks and the other victims faded from Americans' memories and most written historical accounts of the Revolutionary era. This is not terribly surprising, since early nineteenth-century historians, and the era's collective memory of the Revolution in general, tended to ignore the deeds of the common folk. Generals, political leaders, great battles, and momentous events took center stage, and the disorderly mob of March 5, 1770, to the extent that it was discussed at all, was depersonalized and made into a respectable gathering of upstanding citizens in most histories published prior to 1820. Attucks's racial identity made him even less likely a candidate for individual attention than the other massacre martyrs, though none of them was ever singled out.[14]

Still, Attucks did not disappear entirely. Three authors published in the United States in the half-century after Gordon's 1789 *History* specifically discussed Crispus Attucks's role in the massacre and identified him racially: Revolutionary veteran and memoirist George Robert Twelves Hewes; Italian historian Carlo (Charles) Botta; and Samuel G. Goodrich, the prolific author of numerous popular histories for young readers.

The semicentennial of the Declaration of Independence in 1826 stimulated popular attention to remembering and commemorating the Revolution while also drawing attention to the dwindling number of the war's veterans. By the 1830s the appropriation of republican ideology by the working classes helped generate a good deal of interest in the memoirs of a working-class hero like Hewes, a shoemaker who had witnessed and participated in many of the key events in Revolutionary Boston. In his reminiscences in James Hawkes's *A Retrospect of the Boston Tea Party* (1834), Hewes gave no details about Attucks's role in the massacre but did include him in the list of those who fell: "Gray, a rope maker, Marverick, a young man, Colwell, who was the mate of Captain Colton; Attuck, a mulatto, and Carr, who was an Irishman." Hewes made similar references to Attucks a year later in another edited memoir, *Traits of the Tea Party*. That text also quoted an elderly Boston barber named William Pierce, who claimed to have witnessed the massacre, and who "remember[ed] Attucks distinctly," particularly a "frightful war-whoop which he yelled." Pierce had never seen Attucks before, but his fading memory provided the uncorroborated recollection that he was "a Nantucket Indian, belonging on board a whale-ship of Mr. Folger's." If Attucks indeed had some connection with Nantucket, that island's proximity to Martha's Vineyard and New Bedford would strengthen a possible connection between Attucks and Paul Cuffe.[15]

The historian Botta gave a more thorough and well-documented account of the incidents of March 5 in his *History of the War of the Independence of the United States of America* (1820). He was critical of the mob, describing "a band of the populace, led by a mulatto named Attucks, who brandished their clubs, and pelted [the soldiers] with snowballs." As the confrontation escalated, "the mulatto and twelve of his companions" taunted the soldiers, and incited the crowd to "kill them . . . crush them at once." Then, Botta wrote, "the mulatto lifted his arm against captain Preston, and having turned one of the muskets, he seized the bayonet in his left hand, as if to execute his threat," and when the soldiers finally fired, "Attucks is slain." Botta's account is significant because of its popularity in the United States. It went through numerous American editions in the 1830s, and when historian Jared Sparks lectured on the Revolution at Harvard College in 1839, he used Botta (probably the 1838 edition) as the assigned text "because I can procure no other; all the other histories of the same period being out of print."[16]

Samuel Goodrich's books would not have been suitable for Sparks's Harvard audience, but they were very much in print and reached a much broader readership than either Botta or Hewes. Goodrich had an enormous impact on young Americans' historical education through nationally popular common school textbooks published under both his own name and his "Peter Parley" pseudonym. Echoing Botta, the 1831 edition of Goodrich's *The First Book of History for Children and Youth* provided a detailed account of the Boston Massacre which not only identified Attucks but vilified both him and the Boston mob. A "noisy" crowd, he recounted, "rushed furiously" upon the British soldiers:

Led on by a giant of a negro, named Attucks; they brandished their clubs, and pelted [the soldiers] with snow-balls, abused them with all manner of harsh words, shouted in their faces, surrounded them, and challenged them to fire. . . . At last, Attucks, with twelve of his men, began to strike upon their muskets with clubs. . . . Attucks lifted his arm against Captain Preston, and seized upon a bayonet. . . . At this instant, the firing began. The negro dropped dead upon the ground.

After describing the immediate aftermath and the victims' funeral, Goodrich accorded "much . . . honor to the jury" that acquitted the soldiers and to John Adams and Josiah Quincy, who defended them. Had the troops not fired, Goodrich informed his young readers, "the irritated and unreasonable populace would have torn the soldiers to pieces." A small illustration in the text shows an unruly mob led by a dark-skinned man wielding a club and advancing into the British line. The caption reads, "People attacking the Soldiers" (see Fig. 2.1). Goodrich's *First Book of History* was one of the most widely used antebellum texts, and editions in 1834, 1838, 1847, 1851, and 1859 contained the same description and illustration.[17]

Goodrich's tone seems to confirm journalist and popular historian Frances FitzGerald's observation that "nineteenth-century text writers had decided opinions on things" and vigorously imparted "moral instruction" to their young readers.[18] Casting "a giant of a negro" as the primary instigator surely helped Goodrich create an impression of the mob as not merely "unreasonable" but downright frightful. This characterization was not solely due to the presence of Attucks. During the eighteenth century, crowd or mob

FIG. 2.1 "People Attacking the Soldiers," from Samuel Goodrich, *The First Book of History for Children and Youth* (1851). The Library Company of Philadelphia.

actions were more or less accepted forms of political expression, but by the mid-nineteenth century, an era during which all white men were granted voting rights, cultural leaders tended to characterize mobs as illegitimate and unacceptable threats to the social order.[19] Yet one historian of schoolbooks, Ruth Miller Elson, argues that nineteenth-century texts generally character- ized "American rebellions before the Revolution [as] part of the Revolution." "The Revolution," these texts suggested, was not "carried out in the spirit of a riot. . . . The men who participated in the American Revolution were not reb- els, but men of law and order." For example, Elson points out that the destruc- tion of private property during 1773 Boston Tea Party was justified in one 1874 schoolbook because "the British sea chests symbolized oppression and the loss of liberty. No way was open for freedom but to strike at oppression through them."[20]

Elson's interpretation is corroborated by historian Alfred F. Young, who has demonstrated that, like the Boston Massacre, the so-called Boston Tea Party "was virtually lost in the sixty years after the Revolution as the elites who established their cultural domination chose to erase the radical or 'popular' side of the Revolution." To be sure, this event too was generally acknowledged in published histories as an important step toward revolution and indepen- dence, but as it was popularized through the notoriety of the working-class hero George R. T. Hewes during the 1830s, this act of radicalism was stripped of its belligerence. In fact, the event had been commonly known merely as "the destruction of the tea," and Young suggests that it only took on the "Tea Party" label in the 1830s to render an aggressive assault on imperial policy and private property less threatening. Hewes himself was transformed from a radical young workingman into a "kindly old codger" who hardly seemed a threat to the social order.[21]

The fact that the massacre, unlike the Tea Party, threatened personal vio- lence against British troops and resulted in bloodshed made it more difficult to sanitize. A few early school histories did clearly side with the massacre mob, as when J. E. Worcester concluded in 1836 that "To a free and high-spirited people, the presence of an insolent soldiery, sent with design to intimidate them, could not but be extremely odious and provoking." In fact, Worcester lifted much of that passage from Noah Webster's 1833 *History of the United States*. Other early texts were noncommittal. Even Samuel Goodrich, in *Peter Parley's Common School History* (1839), described the Boston Massacre as merely "a quarrel" during which "British red-coats . . . fired upon a crowd of unarmed people." None of these texts mentioned Attucks.[22]

If American schoolchildren of the 1830s received a biased account of Attucks and the massacre from Goodrich, the adult population remained almost completely uninformed. Other than the accounts by Hewes, Botta, and Goodrich, two passing mentions of Attucks appeared in 1830s newspapers, and only one of those identifies him racially, referring to him simply and without elaboration as "a mulatto man."[23]

African American intellectuals and activists through the late 1830s seem to have been just as oblivious to Crispus Attucks and his racial identity as their white American contemporaries. Between 1770 and 1839, both African Americans and white abolitionists ignored Attucks completely, even when they referred to the massacre. In "A Sermon on the Evacuation of Charlestown," published in 1783, a writer signing as "An AEthiopian" insisted that the most appropriate homage to the military heroes who had risked all to win national freedom would be to abolish slavery in the newly independent United States. Attucks is mentioned only in passing, in conjunction with the other victims of the Boston Massacre, and he is not identified explicitly by race: "The fair fields of Boston stand as eternal monuments to [the British soldiers'] savage proceedings;—the blood of an Attucks and a Maverick can tell!" This self-identified African then calls for white Americans to "say with the Psalmist, *Unto thee, O God, do we give thanks, for delivering us. . . .* May we be thankful, and make our states independent states indeed, by gradually abolishing slavery, and making the Aethiopian race comfortable amongst us."[24]

The important white abolitionist William Lloyd Garrison provides a compelling piece of negative evidence for Attucks's absence from the intellectual landscape of early antebellum America. After surviving a brutal assault by an anti-abolitionist Boston mob in 1835—around the time Hewes and his memoirs were the most popular—Garrison marveled that he had been violently dragged "over the very ground that was stained with the blood of the first martyrs in the cause of LIBERTY and INDEPENDENCE, by the memorable massacre of 1770." It is interesting here that Garrison acknowledges the massacre victims as the Revolution's "first martyrs." Had he been aware of Attucks's racial identity, Garrison almost certainly would have singled him out. Similarly, the abolitionist Lydia Maria Child published a book in 1850 entitled *The Rebels; or, Boston before the Revolution*, which culminates in a description of the Boston Massacre with no mention of Attucks or any people of color. White activists were not alone in their omissions. In 1849, black activist Abner H. Francis failed to mention Attucks in his address at an August First commemoration of British West Indian emancipation, even though he quoted from Joseph Warren's speech at the 1772 Boston Massacre commemoration.[25]

While Attucks was not part of the nation's, or the race's, collective memory during the early nineteenth century, a number of African American orators and writers from that period did call attention to blacks' military service in the Revolution and the War of 1812 in their arguments for black citizenship. As early as 1782 a sermon by a writer identifying himself as a "Black Whig" addressed fellow South Carolinians "with all the affection of a fellow-citizen, though a descendant of Africa," and demanded that the blood blacks had spilled in the Revolution be repaid with freedom. While Boston still commemorated the massacre, this black writer explicitly condemned the British for "the murderous bayonet . . . shewn to the virtuous sons of Boston" but without any mention of Crispus Attucks. In an 1816 oration commemorating the 1808 abolition of the Atlantic slave trade, black Philadelphia minister Russell Parrott claimed that American blacks had earned their citizenship rights through national service in the Revolution and the more recent war against Britain. The black citizen-soldier had fought "with noble daring, mingling his blood, with the ungrateful soil, that refused him everything but a grave" and had demonstrated the race's possession of "all the rich materials for the formation of the good, the useful citizen." In 1837, the black abolitionist Hosea Easton discussed African Americans' Revolutionary service at Dorchester, Lexington, and Bunker Hill as well as Andrew Jackson's praise for the black "Sons of Freedom" who had fought under him in Louisiana during the War of 1812. The following year Robert Purvis, in his futile plea against black disfranchisement in Pennsylvania, also recalled Jackson's comments, and Henry Scott of Worcester, Massachusetts, wrote to the *Liberator* that "my forefathers at the old South fought heroically in the Revolution, for independence."[26]

In September 1846, the black sailor and activist William P. Powell complained that "very little, if anything, is recorded in history as to the active part our people took in the great struggle for national rights." A month later he condemned the treatment of black sailors going ashore in New Orleans, where, during the War of 1812, "coloured men POURED out their life's blood, to defend their wives, their children, and their homes, from British bayonets, rapine and murder!" Surely the black sailor Crispus Attucks would have entered into this appeal had Powell been aware of him. In July 1847, the white abolitionist and poet John Greenleaf Whittier contributed a piece to the abolitionist weekly, the *National Era*, arguing that the nation should heed "certain historical facts, which, for the last half century, have been quietly elbowed aside," relating to black Americans' patriotic sacrifices in both the Revolution and the War of 1812. He also lamented that the "colored soldiers of the Revolution . . . have had no historian. With here and there an exception, they have all passed away, and only some faint tradition of their campaigns under Washington, and Greene, and Lafayette, and of their cruisings under Decatur and Barry, linger among their descendants." Again, however, no reference to Attucks.[27]

The earliest surviving reference to Crispus Attucks by a black American appeared in 1839 in a brief description of an August First commemoration of British West Indian emancipation, held in Boston and initially reported in a letter to Garrison's *Liberator*. The Reverend Jehiel C. Beman, who was active regionally in temperance and abolitionist organizations throughout the antebellum era, informed a sizable mixed-race audience at the Belknap Street meeting house "that the first blood spilt for independence in this country was by a colored man by the name of Airtiks." The report does not indicate whether Beman elaborated on the subject in his oration, but despite the inaccurate transcription of the name, there is little doubt whom he was talking about. Beman's father, Caesar Beman, was a veteran of the Revolution, and the younger Beman's speeches and letters often used black military service to argue for black citizenship rights. Whether Beman's knowledge of Attucks was derived from oral traditions through his father or from the recently published works by Goodrich, Botta, and Hewes is unclear. Another possibility is that he learned about Attucks from a contemporary resident of Boston, the abolitionist and early black historian William C. Nell.[28]

An 1841 letter from Nell to the white abolitionist Wendell Phillips provides the next reference to Attucks by an African American. Nell, who regularly received both books and intellectual guidance from Phillips, wrote him that "I am not at all as familiar with History as I ought to be," and confided that

I have been unable to find out much of the History of Attucks. Botta contains an allusion to him as the first who fell in libertys cause and a work entitled, Memoirs of Hewes with traits of the Tea Party, mentions him in one place as a colored man, and in another as a Nantucket Indian and adds that he was buried from Faneuil Hall as one of the strangers who fell in the struggle. Mr. William Pierce a Barbar and an old Tea Party Veteran could if alive probably give me any information concerning him, but I shall continue to make inquiries that I believe will furnish me with some *interesting* facts in the Biography of Attucks.

The tone of Nell's letter suggests that he and Phillips had previously discussed Attucks, although how Nell first learned about him is unclear. Nell might possibly have heard of him from Jehiel C. Beman, since he attended the 1839 August First celebration at which Beman spoke of the "colored man" named "Airtiks."[29]

Regardless of their origins, the observations of Beman and Nell signal the beginning of a profound shift that moved Attucks from virtual invisibility before the late 1830s and placed him at the center of African American arguments for citizenship rights after 1850. Historians Roy Finkenbine and Richard Newman have concluded that Attucks—along with African Methodist Episcopal Church founder Richard Allen and Revolutionary veteran, entrepreneur, and activist James Forten—was one of "the most popular early figures identified by antebellum black reformers." This was a truly meteoric rise in popularity and status, given the absence of any abolitionist references to him prior to 1839.[30]

After 1850 Attucks's name was invoked readily and regularly in the struggle for black citizenship. As Tavia Nyong'o has observed, antebellum black activists carefully reconstructed an image of Attucks and the massacre to serve their political purposes. For the patriot press and Boston Massacre orators of the 1770s and 1780s, the massacre victims were noble martyrs—respectable American citizens and patriots who gave their lives while opposing tyranny and injustice. Those eighteenth-century propagandists projected a generic group identity on the crowd of March 5 that implied both whiteness and a respectably "middling" social status. Once antebellum abolitionists learned about Attucks, they similarly constructed the massacre as a courageous stand against arbitrary power that provided "the impetus to the American Revolution." Unlike their eighteenth-century predecessors, however, these nineteenth-century activists focused specifically on Crispus Attucks, whom they unequivocally defined as both a black man and the leader of the patriots. Attucks thereby became, in essence, a black Founder, and as such he embodied a compelling argument for African American liberty, patriotism, and citizenship.[31]

The post-1840s revitalization of Attucks makes the absolute silence about him prior to 1839 all the more intriguing and raises questions about why Attucks was not used as a symbol of black citizenship during the years of the early republic. Between the 1790s and 1830s, white American intellectuals and political leaders constructed meaningful symbols and traditions surrounding the Revolution and the American past in general. The absence of Crispus Attucks from these traditions is consistent with that era's broader tendency to exclude the exploits of "ordinary" citizens from the public memory of the Revolution and, more pointedly, to ignore or dismiss black claims to American citizenship.[32]

Historian David Waldstreicher has argued that, for black intellectuals and activists between the 1790s and 1820s, "the struggles of the post-Revolutionary generation might not have led them to articulate or stress their Americanness." This may help explain their inattention to Attucks, as they placed their emphasis on forging coherent communities and networks, opposing slavery, and even pondering the potential benefits of emigration. But the memory of blacks' military service in the Revolution and the War of 1812 had been politicized and used in black arguments for citizenship throughout this period, so why not Attucks? It seems quite possible that he was completely unknown among African Americans before the late 1830s.[33]

Still, it is conceivable that some knowledge of Attucks continued through this period. The puzzling 1811 reference to the "friends and adherents of Holder Slocum and Crispus Attux" suggests that some people in the early republic may indeed have retained a memory of Attucks and his exploits. But the conjecture that Holder Slocum or Paul Cuffe had known Attucks or at least attached some significance to his place in the history of the Revolution requires a leap of faith from a shaky and circumstantial evidentiary base. If an oral tradition existed, African American leaders' concerns with demonstrating their respectability and presenting positive images to the white public may have influenced how they responded to Attucks's controversial role in the massacre. In some quarters, the Boston Massacre mob was still seen as a bunch of ruffians rather than part of a legitimate Revolutionary heritage. African American activists in the early nineteenth century may well have thought it advantageous to distance themselves from Attucks and the Boston Massacre mob to avoid being associated in the public mind with lawlessness and disorder.[34]

If there had been a suppressed oral tradition, perhaps among black seamen, Revolutionary veterans, or Bostonians, it seems reasonable that William C. Nell, born and raised in the seaport of Boston, well-educated and well-connected with his elders, would have been aware of it. The evidence from his writings indicates that he was not. By 1839, however, both Nell and Jehiel Beman knew about Attucks and his racial identity, suggesting that the published works of Botta and Hewes, and possibly Goodrich, generated this awareness rather than any underground oral tradition.

Alfred Young has emphasized how the social and political climate of the 1830s brought greater attention to the Revolutionary exploits of common folk and provided a context for a contentious public discourse surrounding mob actions among the working classes. The convergence of publications by Goodrich, Hewes, and Botta called attention to Attucks within a context in which "forgotten Founders" from the middling and lower orders of society began to receive their due and where the radical republicanism of actions like the Boston Tea Party and the Boston Massacre became a matter of public discussion. The decade also witnessed the emergence of an organized abolitionist movement that stridently called for the immediate end to slavery. As common people in the 1830s attached the legacy of the Revolution to their own causes, abolitionists' identification of Attucks as an American hero and a symbol of black citizenship fit neatly with the intellectual and activist climate of the period, even as they suffered violent attacks from anti-abolitionist mobs.[35]

The absence of black attention to Attucks before the 1840s and his subsequent rise to iconic status raises broad questions about black heroes and historical mythology and about their function in the struggle for black citizenship. As historian Joanne Pope Melish has shown, race occupied a particular intellectual and ideological place in the discourse surrounding citizenship in the antebellum North. She suggests that "New England whites 'racialized' themselves and people of color in response to concerns about citizenship and autonomy posed by emancipation and post-Revolutionary dislocation in their own region." This discourse affected how whites and free blacks throughout the North went about constructing their respective notions of who might claim what racial identity and who had the right to claim American citizenship. And citizenship was the point. Focusing on Massachusetts, historian Margot Minardi argues that antebellum black Bay Staters' central goal was the broader society's recognition of their full rights as American citizens, a goal that required them not merely to be free but also to demonstrate "their autonomy as historical actors." African Americans' citizenship hinged on their full "incorporation into the community, including the community of memory."[36]

African Americans staked their claim to citizenship in part by shaping a collective memory to confront the dominant racialist ideology and demonstrate their agency and belonging. They engaged the past and their present plight by constructing traditions and drawing upon symbolic resources that addressed the question of whether racial identity might exclude one group from national citizenship. Blacks generally were excluded (often forcibly) from participating in national rituals or claiming a legitimate role in the national story. But African Americans' development of distinctive historical and commemorative traditions did not merely respond to this exclusion. Their written histories and their public observances of the 1808 abolition of the Atlantic slave trade, the 1827 abolition of slavery in New York, and West Indian Emancipation in the 1830s illustrate African Americans' efforts to establish a program of commemoration and a politicized engagement with the past that highlighted their own experiences and achievements and that advanced their own cultural and political agendas.

In the mid-nineteenth century, black intellectuals and activists consciously went about constructing a proud African American history and heritage whose heroes were to be celebrated and emulated. As early as 1827, the Reverend Nathaniel Paul had observed that all great nations "have been careful to select the most important events, peculiar to themselves, and have them recorded for the good of the people that should succeed them," and in 1839 Amos G. Beman, the son of Jehiel Beman, emphasized how vital it was for a people's orators to "recount the glory of their ancestors." Twenty years later, Jacob C. White pointed out that black Americans "should remember *who* they are, and *why* they are."[37] By the 1840s a handful of black activists became aware of Crispus Attucks, his racial identity, and his actions in 1770. As they went about constructing a story asserting blacks' rightful place in the nation, African American activists recognized the central role Attucks might play and began the process of reinscribing him into the history of the American Revolution and the pantheon of American patriot heroes.

3

First Martyr of Liberty

CRISPUS ATTUCKS AND THE STRUGGLE FOR
CITIZENSHIP IN THE CIVIL WAR ERA

When British laws oppressed the land
The people rose on every hand,
He must fight who would be free—
"Rouse, Patriots! Strike for Liberty!"
Foremost Crispus Attucks stands,
With club uplifted in his hands.
"Beat back the tyrants!" Attucks said—
A moment more and he fell dead.

'Twas not in vain that Attucks fell
History's pages often tell,
And Freedom's Patriots freely own
That Attucks was a stepping stone.
The valor of the martyred sire
Doth the courage of his race inspire;
Through North and South on every hand,
Our honor's bright all o'er the land!

GEORGE W. POTTER, "Our Honor's Bright All o'er the Land" (1870)

WILLIAM COOPER NELL was a man deeply committed to the pursuit of equality and racial justice. His father, William Guion Nell, was a veteran of the War of 1812 and a prominent member of Boston's African American community. The Nells lived on Beacon Hill near many other black activists, including David Walker, arguably the most erudite and powerful black abolitionist and writer of the 1820s. The younger Nell, born in 1816, was a stellar student at the segregated colored school that met at the African Meeting House on Belknap Street, and he was understandably appalled and insulted when the city refused to award him and other black scholars the academic medals white scholars of their caliber received, solely on account of their race. Nell was almost certainly the young black apprentice who assisted William Lloyd Garrison in publishing the *Liberator* in its earliest years, and he maintained close ties with Garrison, Wendell Phillips, and other abolitionist leaders. From his teenage years on, William C. Nell seems to have participated in virtually every abolitionist meeting that took place wherever he was living.[1]

It was Nell, more than anyone, who was responsible for resuscitating the nation's memory of Crispus Attucks and thrusting him into antebellum public debate surrounding black citizenship. Nell's two major publications, a brief pamphlet titled *Services of Colored Americans in the Wars of 1776 and 1812* (1851) and the full-length book *The Colored Patriots of the Revolution* (1855), were pathbreaking works of African American history as well as important abolitionist tracts that publicized the military role blacks had played in the nation's founding and early defense. His 1841 correspondence with Wendell Phillips indicates that he had been researching the history of black military service for at least a decade before his work was published.[2]

In May 1848, Nell first introduced Crispus Attucks to a broad abolitionist readership in an essay demanding black citizenship, published in Frederick Douglass's *North Star*:

Colored Americans have ever been ready to worship at Freedom's shrine; in every struggle for their country's cause, have they zealously engaged. They have contributed to the support of government as loyal citizens—services, alas! Which have been liquidated only by insult and persecution. The page of impartial history bears testimony to the fact, that the first martyr in the American Revolution was a colored man by the name of Attacks [*sic*], who fell in King street, Boston. The seven years' conflict, and also the war of 1812, were both dotted by instances of the loyalty of colored soldiers—a fact which is of at least significance enough to claim for their descendants treatment equal to those of a paler hue.[3]

A few months later, Henry W. Johnson, a black activist from Canandaigua, New York, followed Douglass on the speakers' platform at a Rochester, New York, West Indian emancipation celebration. He made a similarly impassioned appeal for the protection of black citizenship rights, based on their long-standing patriotic services that began with the Boston Massacre.

Johnson despaired that "this soil, once watered with the life-blood of the martyrs of freedom, is now saturated with the tears and stained with the blood of
the slave!" In this "free republic," he claimed,

> there is not one spot upon which a colored man can rest his feet, and
> declare that he is free. . . . He may go to . . . proud and glorious New
> England—a land . . . watered by the first blood that was shed in the
> great struggle of the revolution . . . he may go to Faneuil Hall, that
> old cradle of liberty, . . . that sacred spot from within whose walls
> was borne away the mangled form of that brave black man, Benjamin
> Attucks, from whose veins flowed the first drop of blood that mingled
> with American soil, in defence of American liberty—even there he
> finds no protection.

Nell, who was present at the celebration and served as one of the event's secre-
taries, would no doubt have corrected Johnson regarding Attucks's first name.[4]

Attucks featured prominently in Nell's *Services of Colored Americans*
(1851), which he also used to publicize a petition that Boston blacks presented,
without success, to the state legislature "asking an appropriation of $1,500 for
erecting a monument to the memory of Crispus Attucks, the first martyr in
the Boston Massacre." Nell resurrected Attucks as "the first martyr" sacrificed on the altar of American freedom and demanded not merely his rein-
sertion into the historical record but also his redemption. Nell cited "Botta's
History, and Hewes's Reminiscences (the tea party survivor), [to] establish
that fact that the colored man, ATTUCKS, was *of* and *with* the people, and
was never regarded otherwise." Responding to opponents of the monument
petition who claimed that Attucks was merely a "firebrand of disorder," leader
of a disruptive rabble, and deserving not praise but disparagement, Nell cited
both the published texts of the Boston Massacre orations and Ramsay's 1795
History to establish the solemnity and importance of the anniversary observances and the patriotic credentials of the Boston mob. Nell's bitter response
was that the "rejection of the petition was to be expected" since "the colored
man never gets justice done him in the United States."[5]

After the publication of *Services of Colored Americans* and the unsuccess-
ful monument campaign, Attucks quickly became more of a household name
among both black and white abolitionists. Black activist Martin Delany, who
had worked with Douglass and Nell on the *North Star*, helped publicize
Attucks's place in American history in his 1852 book *The Condition, Elevation,
and Destiny of the Colored People of the United States*. This remarkable work

surveyed European, African, and American history, including colonialism and the Atlantic slave trade, leading to an assessment of blacks' history and status in the United States. One chapter was titled "Claims of Colored Men as Citizens of the United States" and was followed by another, "Colored American Warriors," in which Delany used black military service and sacrifice to bolster the argument for citizenship. Attucks figured prominently. Delany noted that "the hero and the warrior, have long been estimated, the favorite sons of a favored people" and sought in part on those grounds to "establish our right of equal claims of citizenship with other American people." He argued "that colored men, not only took part in the great scene of the first act for independence, but that they were the actors—a colored man was really the hero in the great drama, and actually the first victim in the revolutionary tragedy." Citing Nell's 1851 pamphlet, he called attention to the Boston Massacre, during which the storm of colonial discontent "broke out in terrible blasts, drenching the virgin soil of America, with the blood of her own native sons— Crispus Attuck [*sic*], a colored man, was the first who headed, the first who commanded, the first who charged, who struck the first blow, and the first whose blood was spilt, and baptized the colony, as a peace-offering on the altar of American liberty." Attucks's sacrifice, he argued, constituted "a monument of fame to the history of our deeds, more lasting than that pile that stands on Bunker Hill."[6]

Attucks's renown was also boosted by the Fugitive Slave Act of 1850, which gave southern slaveholders unprecedented power to intrude into northern communities in pursuit of escaped slaves. This latest assault on black freedom provided a proximate cause for magnifying Attucks's symbolic embodiment of black citizenship. The effect was immediate and enduring. In the 1850 "Declaration of Sentiments of the Colored Citizens of Boston on the Fugitive Slave Bill," Nell, Garrison, Lewis Hayden, John T. Hilton, and several other black and white abolitionists emphasized blacks' Revolutionary services, in part, by asserting "that the first martyr in the attack on residents was a colored man, Crispus Attucks by name, who fell in State street on the 5th of March, 1770."[7]

As southern slave catchers moved into northern communities and abducted fugitives for return to slavery, many blacks and whites responded with outrage at the affront to personal liberty the new law represented. Abductions in Boston, in particular, angered abolitionists who decried the travesty of this new American injustice occurring on the very ground where Attucks's blood was spilled. The notorious case of Anthony Burns in 1854, in particular, provoked considerable civil conflict and public expense, and required a military force to return Burns to slavery. White abolitionist Thomas Wentworth Higginson, recalling the attempt to liberate Burns from his captors, praised a black man who was first to shoulder his way into the jail as a "modern Crispus Attucks." After Burns's return to slavery, white abolitionist Theodore Parker invoked the spirit of Attucks in a sermon describing Burns's departure and condemning the incident in terms that echoed the Revolutionary generation's fears of arbitrary power imposed by force of arms:

> The scene last Friday you will never forget. . . . all the citizen soldiery under arms; ball cartridges were made of the city Government on Thursday afternoon in Dock Square, to be fired into your bosoms and mine; United States soldiers loaded their pieces in Court square, to be discharged into the crowd of Boston citizens whenever a drunken officer should give command; a nine-pound cannon, furnished with forty round of canister shot, planted in Court Square, manned by United States soldiers. . . . And at high [charge?], over the spot where on the 5th of March, 1770, fell the first victim in the Boston Massacre—where the Negro blood of Christopher [*sic*] Attucks stained the ground,— over that spot Boston authorities carried a citizen of Massachusetts to Alexandria as a slave.

Frederick Douglass also chided the US military forces which "occupied the streets of Boston,—insulted the citizens[,] pricked little boys with their bayonets[,] cut down peaceful citizens with their sabers[,] and when Anthony Burns was led forth to slavery, by the valor of their arms, over the hallowed spot where Attucks fell, they nobly greeted him with the generous, chivalrous strain of 'Carry me back to Ole Virginny.'"[8]

The same kind of rhetorical reference to Attucks was applied to the 1851 case of the captured fugitive, Thomas Sims. "Boston was a garrisoned town while the poor boy was in custody," the abolitionist newspaper the *National Era* recalled several years after the event. As Boston's mayor led the procession taking Sims to the ship that would bear him into bondage, the paper reported that "they trod over the spot where the black martyr, Attucks, fell, in the gray dawn . . . on the 5th of March, 1770." Nell's publication of *Colored Patriots of the Revolution* in 1855 provided him yet another opportunity to express outrage that Sims and Burns had been "dragged back to slavery,—both marching over the very ground that ATTUCKS trod." The white Boston abolitionist Samuel Bowditch used the same imagery of the spot "where Attucks fell" when he and others took to the streets to protest the Sims and Burns incidents.[9]

In Boston and across the North, African Americans invoked Attucks's memory in their arguments for citizenship rights and racial justice. In 1854, the correspondent "W." bemoaned his expulsion from the main seating area of a church "in Boston, not far from the spot on which Crispus Attucks, the nobel [*sic*] colored man fell in defense of his country."[10] In 1851, James McCune Smith ridiculed claims by whites that colonization to Africa was a responsibility that African Americans would be cowardly not to accept. McCune interjected his own mocking parenthetical commentary in a passage by an unidentified white writer in the *New York Tribune*, who argued that whites' "fathers were treated very unjustly by George III and his ministry, but that injustice was the means of their entire emancipation from foreign control. If the blacks will confront their disabilities in the same spirit (spirit of Attucks, listen!) they may yet achieve for their race a glorious destiny, for themselves an enduring fame."[11]

A committee of Philadelphia blacks in 1855 used Attucks in their call for the reinstatement of African American voting rights in Pennsylvania. After demonstrating that they were "a useful and productive class of citizens" by citing real estate and taxation figures, the committee asserted that

> we, of all other men, have the highest claims to the privilege of citizenship, since the first blood shed upon the altar of American Republicanism, and consecrated its soil to liberty and independence, was that of Crispus Attucks, a "colored man." In that trying hour . . . when no reward seemed to await the heroes' struggles, when adversity, like rigid sentinel, challenged the bold, the daring, and the brave; he, tinged with a complexion now scorned and despised, led on that little band of patriots.

Similarly, a meeting of black activists in Ithaca, New York, claimed suffrage as "our rightful heritage, in view of the heroic efforts made by our forefathers to secure the independence of this country, and free her people from the galling yoke of British tyranny—as shown in the person of Crispus Attucks, the first patriot martyr of the Revolution."[12]

Along with these numerous written references, during the 1850s new images of Attucks and the Boston Massacre emerged which reflected Attucks's new status as an African American hero and patriot. The frontispiece of Nell's 1855 *Colored Patriots* displayed an image of the massacre that bore some resemblance to the 1770 Revere/Pelham print, in that it depicted respectably dressed, unarmed citizens being fired on by a phalanx of British

Crispus Attucks, the First Martyr of the American Revolution, King (now State) Street, Boston, March 5th, 1770. Page 16.

FIG. 3.1 "Crispus Attucks, the First Martyr of the American Revolution." Frontispiece from William Cooper Nell, *Colored Patriots of the Revolution* (1855). Library of Congress.

soldiers, with several fallen figures being tended to by their comrades (see Fig. 3.1). While the image shows the Old State House in the background, no other buildings are represented; the focus is entirely on the troops and the citizens. The citizens are completely unintimidating. One man carries a slender walking stick and is extending his hand toward the soldiers in a "Hold your fire" gesture. Another walking stick—notably less threatening than the cordwood club Attucks had been seen carrying—lies in the street next to a fallen dark-skinned figure in the foreground. This victim is identified in the caption as "Crispus Attucks, the First Martyr of the American Revolution." The Attucks in this image is indeed a blameless martyr, felled by an unprovoked fusillade. The slain Attucks, in fact, is a Christlike *pietà*, posed in much the same position as the slain body of another revolutionary martyr, General Joseph Warren, in John Trumbull's well-known painting, *The Death of General Warren at the Battle of Bunker's Hill, April 17, 1775* (see Fig. 3.2). As Nell described him, this Attucks is clearly "of and with the people" and is as worthy a martyr as the much admired Warren.[13]

A second image from the mid-1850s, a chromolithograph by John Bufford, based on a print by William Champney, projects a distinctly different impression (see Fig. 3.3). The image's background more closely resembles that in the

FIG. 3.2 Archer & Boilly, John Trumbull, and Samuel Walker. *The Battle at Bunker's Hill Near Boston. June 17, 1775.* Boston: Printed and published by Samuel Walker, 1834. Library of Congress.

FIG. 3.3 Boston Massacre, March 5th, 1770. Champney, W. L. Boston: Published by Henry Q. Smith: [Printed by] J. H. Bufford's Lith., 1856. Boston Athenæum.

Revere/Pelham print, with buildings on either side of the street receding to the State House tower at the rear center. Like the Nell image, the foreground depicts an unmistakably black man at the center of the fray. Unlike Nell's, however, this scene shows the black man aggressively engaging the troops in the manner described in several eyewitness and historical accounts. Attucks's left hand is seizing the bayonet of a soldier's rifle and his right is wielding a heavy club. Another soldier lies on the ground at his feet, apparently victim of a blow from the black assailant. Attucks's chest is stained with blood, his head is thrown back, and his body is leaning away from the standing soldier, as if in the very act of being shot. Another white citizen is raising a club against the troops, and others are already on the ground. Rather than the passive victim of Nell's image, this Crispus Attucks is bold, defiant, and belligerent—taking the fight to the British foes. In some respects this image of an aggressive Attucks resembles that in Samuel Goodrich's *First Book of History*, except that Goodrich shows an unharmed Attucks about to clobber a soldier; Goodrich suggests a lawless assault, while Bufford/Champney evokes heroic resistance.[14]

Historian Margot Minardi argues that, "for Nell and other black civil rights leaders of the 1850s, claiming a history of military heroism was critical to reclaiming black men's image" from the feminized notions of black manhood that were prevalent at the time. This emphasis on black "agency and manliness" also bolstered the argument that black men had earned "the privileges and obligations of citizenship." If Nell's visual depiction of a rather passive Attucks seems to work against this argument, his assertion that Attucks "was *of* and *with* the people" and deserving to be included among the "gallant Americans" who fought for independence was consistent with Minardi's point. Bufford's depiction of Attucks as an aggressive champion of resistance made the case even more compelling.[15]

Yet another image of Attucks was purely imaginary. Black Brooklyn activist William J. Wilson, writing under the pen name "Ethiop," took his readers on a tour of a nonexistent "Afric-American Picture Gallery" containing selected scenes from the annals of black history from the slave trade through the underground railroad. Wilson's third image was a likeness of Attucks, "the first martyr of the American Revolution." Hanging "at the north east end of the [imaginary] Gallery," the "fine likeness" was that "of a bold, vigorous man,—just such, as would be likely to head a revolution to throw off oppression."[16]

Wilson's bold Revolutionary and the Bufford/Champney image are accurate reflections of the assertive stance taken by many African Americans during this period. As blacks in northern communities formed vigilance committees and armed militias to protect themselves against slave catchers and kidnappers, "sixty-five colored petitioners" in Massachusetts sought state sanction "for a charter to form an Independent Military Company." In his 1853 address to a legislative committee, William J. Watkins drew extensively on Carlo Botta's account of the Boston Massacre, along with Nell's *Services of Colored Americans*, to demonstrate "the fact of our Fathers' having fought to achieve this country's Independence." Black Ohioan Charles H. Langston made a similar argument for African Americans' right to serve in militias in an 1855 address: "But why have we been denied enrollment on the militia? Have we proved ourselves enemies to our country? Have not our fathers stood side by side with your fathers in the battles of the revolution and the war of 1812? Was not the first blood shed in the revolution that of Crispus Attucks a colored man?"[17]

With or without governmental approval, between 1848 and 1865 African Americans formed over two dozen military companies in Massachusetts, Connecticut, New York, Rhode Island, New Jersey, Pennsylvania, Ohio, Michigan, and Canada West. Some communities, like New York City, Staten Island, and New Bedford, Massachusetts, had more than one. By now, Attucks had achieved such renown that more military companies were named for him than for any other individual. These included Cincinnati's Attucks Blues, New Bedford's Attucks Frontiers, New York's Attucks Guards, and possibly Brooklyn's Independent Attee Guard and Long Island's Attic Guards. In his praise for the Attucks Blues, William Nell reveled in "the fact that a colored soldiery, named in honor of Crispus Attucks, (a colored man, be it remembered, and the first martyr in the Revolution,) can now, in 1856, peaceably parade the streets of Cincinnati, within a stone's throw of the slavery-cursed soil of Kentucky." Historian Jeffrey Kerr-Ritchie argues that these black militias were not merely for show but were part of a "trajectory toward militarization from vigilance committees to independent companies to enrollment in Union armies." The use of Attucks's name paid homage to his martial valor and sacrifice, and linked his legacy to contemporary issues surrounding the rights of citizenship and community self-defense.[18]

In 1860, another African American organization calling itself the Attucks Guards was formed as a "Wide Awakes" political association in Boston's Sixth Ward. Wide Awakes were Republican marching companies, made up mainly of young white men, which performed at pro-Lincoln rallies across the North during the 1860 presidential election campaign. As an all–African American company, the Attucks Guards was an unusual Wide Awake unit, but the company made it clear that "it recognizes the equality of all men, and will cheerfully admit into its ranks any white Republican who may desire to give this practical proof of devotion to the principles of his party." Some historians characterize the Wide Awakes as little more than social clubs, but while their functions were largely non-military, they were uniformed, often well drilled, and organized according to quasi-military divisions, with head-quarters, captains, lieutenants, and grand marshals who issued general orders. The Republican press characterized them as "thorough military men" with the appearance of "an orderly, disciplined, and effective force." After Lincoln's inauguration, the Wide Awakes disbanded, but at one Chicago meeting in April 1861, the motion to disband was followed by a resolution to open a mus-ter roll at which former members were "invited to enroll themselves as a band of brothers in defence of the Union and Constitution of their country."[19]

Information on the Attucks Guards does not indicate whether any of its members answered Lincoln's 1861 call for volunteers to put down the rebel-lion in the South or eventually served in one of the United States Colored Troops regiments formed later in the war, but they and their fellow black Bostonians were uniquely positioned to be both well informed about Crispus Attucks and highly politicized in the struggle for black rights. If local radical-ism in opposition to the Fugitive Slave Act were not enough, blacks in Boston and across the nation were all affected by the Dred Scott decision of 1857 that denied African Americans' claims to United States citizenship. William C. Nell seized on this "annihilation of the citizenship of Colored Americans" as yet another opportunity to invoke the spirit of Attucks.[20]

The Supreme Court announced its decision in the case on March 6, 1857, a day after the Boston Massacre anniversary. Nell took advantage of this coin-cidence with a massive commemorative festival to mark Crispus Attucks Day on March 5, 1858. The festival—held at Faneuil Hall, where Attucks's body lay before being conveyed to the martyrs' grave—accentuated the bitter irony that characterized many black invocations of Attucks during this era. As his-torian Elizabeth Rauh Bethel has observed, "Crispus Attucks had sacrificed his life for the liberty of a nation that had denied Dred Scott his personal lib-erty." Bethel argues that Nell's festival was "designed specifically to revise and expand the myth of the nation's beginnings to include African Americans" and to construct "an historical validation for contemporary protests against injustice and demands for full and unconditional rights as American citizens." Who better to personify this message than the first martyr of the Revolution? The public invitation in Garrison's *Liberator* called on all "friends of freedom" to "rally and commemorate the massacre of 1770, when Attucks fell, and bled for Liberty!" The Attucks Glee Club performed the anthem "Freedom's Battle," written for the occasion by the African American essayist and poet Frances Ellen Watkins, and the platform was graced by Garrison, Charles L. Remond, Wendell Phillips, Theodore Parker, John S. Rock, and other black and white antislavery luminaries. The event fulfilled Nell's desire to "Rock the Cradle of Freedom," and Attucks Day celebrations continued at least into the 1870s.[21]

This explosion of interest in Attucks during the 1850s also resulted in some new historical evidence. In a July 1859 letter to Garrison's *Liberator*, Nell informed the abolitionist readership that his friend "Charles H. Morse, Esq., whose zeal as a collector of autographs and relics of the olden time is well known hereabouts," had alerted him to the existence of the 1750 runaway advertisement for the "mulatto fellow . . . named Crispus." What is odd about this apparently new discovery is that it came a year *after* Nell's first Attucks Day celebration, at which Samuel H. Brown, a descendant of Attucks's former owner, "narrated to several persons the traditions extant in the family relating to Crispus Attucks,—of his goblet, powder-horn, &c." These last named objects were displayed at the 1858 celebration. Brown's participation in that event, a year prior to Nell's knowledge of the runaway ad, raises the question of how Brown became involved with Nell and Attucks Day. It also lends some credence to the idea that the Brown family, indeed, had retained its memory of the escaped slave Crispus.[22]

Regardless of the possible connections with Framingham's Brown family, Attucks's prominence among antislavery activists perhaps made it unavoidable that they would link him to a very different Brown after the white abolitionist John Brown's 1859 raid on the federal arsenal at Harpers Ferry, Virginia. Meeting at Pittsburgh's Wylie Street African Methodist Episcopal Church, Lewis Woodson, Benjamin Tanner, Jonathan Peck, George B. Vashon, and other black leaders "acknowledge[d] in the person of John Brown a hero, patriot, and Christian," and they resolved that "we see in the Harpers Ferry affair what Daniel Webster saw when speaking of Crispus Attucks, the black Revolutionary martyr who fell in Boston—viz. the severance of two antagonistic principles." While Webster's 1806 statement about the Boston Massacre—"From that moment we may date the severance of the British empire"—actually made reference only to the massacre itself and did not mention Attucks, that distinction was lost on Attucks's later admirers.[23]

As for Attucks's connection with John Brown's raid, Osborne Anderson, a black man who participated in the raid and escaped to tell the tale, drew his own comparison. "As in the war of the American Revolution," Anderson wrote, "the first blood shed was a black man's, Crispus Attuck's, so at Harpers Ferry, the first blood shed by our party, after the arrival of the United States troops, was that of a slave." Speaking at Boston's 1860 Attucks Day obser-vance, black minister J. Sella Martin offered "a beautiful tribute to Crispus and John Brown." John S. Rock, speaking at the same celebration, drew a more nuanced comparison. "Crispus Attucks," he granted, "was a brave man, and he fought with our fathers in a good cause; but they were not victorious. They fought for liberty, but they got slavery." Rock added that he was

> not yet ready to idolize the actions of Crispus Attucks, who was a leader among those who resorted to forcible measures to create a new government which has used every means in its power to outrage his race and posterity, in order to oppress them more easily, and to render their condition more hopeless in the country. . . . The only events in the history of this country which I think deserve to be commemorated, are the organization of the Anti-Slavery Society and the insurrections of Nat Turner and John Brown.

Still, Rock recognized Attucks's leadership and claimed to "believe in insur-rections." Perhaps Attucks's willingness to use force in a noble cause allowed Rock to suggest that "the John Brown of the second Revolution, is but the Crispus Attucks of the first."[24]

The Civil War, Rock's "second Revolution," provided the first of many moments in which African Americans connected the memory of Attucks with contemporary questions concerning black patriotism and military ser-vice. As Lincoln moved toward supporting black enlistment in the United States military, debate raged over whether African Americans should be mus-tered and whether they would be effective soldiers. Crispus Attucks bolstered affirmative responses to both questions. Fugitive slave and militant aboli-tionist Jermain W. Loguen used history to affirm African Americans' eager-ness to fight the Confederacy. "Colored men have not been backward, when treated as men, in standing up for the liberties of our country," he asserted in September 1861. "It is not denied that in the Revolutionary war, the black man made as good a soldier as the white.—The *first* martyr in the Boston Massacre of 1770, was a colored man, *Crispus Attucks*, who was a brave man, and fought as did the bravest whites."[25]

One anonymous writer, echoing John Rock's misgivings about the fruits of Attucks's sacrifice, was reluctant to risk black lives without guarantees that they would "have all the rights and privileges of other citizens in every state of the Union." But on the question of African Americans' courage and military prowess, the same author cited "the many instances which occurred in those days which 'tried men's souls,'" noting with pride that "Attucks, one of the heroes of the Revolution, spilt the first blood that was offered up on the altar of American independence." After black units served admirably in 1863 and 1864, a black Philadelphian wrote with satisfaction that "Port Hudson, Fort Wagner, Milliken's Bend, Olustee, and numerous other engagements have proved what the colored soldiers are," and he recalled that "in the first blow struck for American Independence, the crowd were led on to the attack by a negro man, of gigantic size, named Attucks, who was killed in that engagement; thus proving, that the negro man was identified with the interests of the American people from the very first struggle for national existence." Many blacks in the Civil War era hoped, along with the poet George W. Potter, that "'twas not in vain that Attucks fell." They worked to promote his heroism, connect his patriotism with that of black Civil War soldiers, and use both in their arguments for citizenship.[26]

By the time of the Civil War, even the opponents of black citizenship were more aware of Crispus Attucks. In an 1861 letter to the *Weekly Anglo-African*, a writer signing as "Ivanhoe" claimed, "Every schoolboy knows of 'the giant of a negro Crispus Attucks.'" Yet even as abolitionists presented Attucks as a heroic American patriot, most of the school textbooks published during the Civil War era still ignored him in their discussions of the Boston Massacre. Regarding the massacre itself, textbooks offered a range of opinion. Some were mildly critical of the British. Benson J. Lossing's *A Primary History of the United States for Schools and Families* (1860) noted that the "insolent" behavior of the troops led to a "quarrel" and later a "riot" in which three were killed. Another Civil War–era text contended that the troops' presence "exasperated the people; and affrays ensued, in one of which, called the Boston Massacre, the soldiers fired upon the populace, killing three men, and wounding others." In 1866, John Bonner defended the mob, describing "bands of soldiers . . . beating every man they met, and seeking a quarrel" before the confrontation. British bullets came in response to mere "jeering and name calling" and "the people of Boston never acted rashly or hastily," even after the shooting. Attucks was absent from all these accounts.[27]

Other school textbooks from this period unequivocally condemned the Americans' actions on March 5, 1770. Not surprisingly, Samuel Goodrich provides a good example. His 1868 *A Pictorial History of the United States* featured a detailed and didactic account of the mob provoking the British troops, arguing that "mobs are seldom just or reasonable" and that "there is no doubt that in most of these transactions the mob were in the wrong."[28] Many other textbooks echoed Goodrich's discomfort with the 1770 crowd action, usually without ever calling attention to its racial composition, even though by the 1860s they certainly would have been aware of Attucks's presence. John G. Shea's 1858 *A School History of the United States* noted that the troops were goaded into firing after they "had been constantly insulted by the rabble." A. B. Berard's 1863 *School History of the United States* did not identify Attucks by name but did mention the death of the "negro who excited the disturbance." Like Goodrich, he concluded that "the people" were "much at fault" for the confrontation.[29]

If mainstream textbooks of the period tended to ignore Attucks, the opposite was true of black writers. The Civil War and the promise of emancipation stimulated the emergence of a new wave of African American historical writing, building on the work of William Nell and others. The most important black historical writer of the 1860s was William Wells Brown, a former slave who liberated himself in the 1830s and became a prominent orator, memoirist, novelist, travel writer, and historian. Brown wrote several important historical works, the first of which was published shortly after the Emancipation Proclamation went into effect. *The Black Man* (1863) launched postbellum black writers' production of numerous biographical compilations outlining the lives and accomplishments of notable men (and occasionally women) of African descent.[30]

Brown wrote *The Black Man* explicitly to counter the widespread assumption among white Americans that African peoples were intellectually inferior and had produced no great thinkers, leaders, or contributions to civilization. Just a few months before issuing the Emancipation Proclamation, Brown pointed out, even President Lincoln had told "a committee of the colored citizens of the District of Columbia . . . that the whites and the blacks could not live together in peace, on account of one race being superior intellectually to the other." Brown set out to "vindicate[e] the Negro's character, and show that he is endowed with those intellectual and amiable qualities which adorn and dignify human nature." He argued that the preceding several centuries of racial slavery were to blame for blacks' appearing to lag behind Europeans, pointing not only to the great accomplishments of ancient Ethiopia and Egypt, but also to the backward state of the ancient Britons, whose early history was "not very flattering to the President's ancestors." When encountered by their Roman conquerors, Brown claimed, "Britons were "a rude and barbarous people, divided into numerous tribes, dressed in the skins of wild beasts." Brown quoted Cicero advising an associate "not to buy slaves from England, 'because . . . they cannot be taught to read, and are the ugliest and most stupid race I ever saw.' I am sorry," Brown went on, "that Mr. Lincoln came from such a low origin; but he is not to blame. I only find fault with him for making mouths at me."[31]

Brown used brief biographical sketches of fifty-three notable African-descended men and women to "refut[e] . . . the charge of the natural inferiority of the negro" and demonstrate the valuable contributions African Americans could make to the nation as free and equal citizens. In his four-page treatment of Crispus Attucks, Brown provided a little background on the colonies' conflict with Britain before inserting Attucks into the fray. Grossly distorting the historical record and inventing events out of whole cloth, Brown described a "crowded and enthusiastic meeting, held in Boston in the latter part of the year 1769." Speeches were made "by the ablest talent that the progressive element could produce. Standing in the back part of the hall, eagerly listening to the speakers, was a dark mulatto man, very tall, rather good looking, and apparently about fifty years of age. This was Crispus Attucks." Of course, no evidence, then or now, places Attucks in Boston prior to March 5, 1770. Nor was there ever any indication that Attucks's "heroism was imitated by both whites and blacks," that "his name was a rallying cry for the brave colored men who fought at the battle of Bunker's Hill," or that his skin color was particularly "dark," let alone that he was "good looking." Brown maintained the now ubiquitous language identifying Attucks as "the first martyr to American liberty, and the inaugurator of the revolution"; he also wrote of the injustice that

> no monument has yet been erected to him. An effort was made in the legislature of Massachusetts a few years since, but without success. Five generations of accumulated prejudice against the negro had excluded from the American mind all inclination to do justice to one of her bravest sons. When negro slavery shall be abolished in our land, then we may hope to see a monument raised to commemorate the heroism of Crispus Attucks.[32]

It would take another generation before Brown's hopes for a monument would be fulfilled.

Brown's invention of details regarding Attucks's exploits went much further than that of earlier writers who had speculated about the life of this enigmatic hero. But such exaggerations and pure fabrications would become common practice in the decades to follow. Given the scarcity of reliable information, writers across subsequent generations would often rely primarily on their imaginations as they inscribed upon Attucks whatever details suited their purposes.

Historian Frederic Kidder's *The Boston Massacre* (1870) offered a refreshingly thorough and largely dispassionate coverage of events to mark the massacre's centennial. Rather than crafting an interpretive history, Kidder was more a compiler. Beyond a brief introduction, the volume contained the published trial transcripts and witness depositions; the 1770 account produced by the Town of Boston; and previously unpublished notes taken at the time of trial by John Adams, the authenticity of which Kidder claimed was "verified by his grandson, and biographer, the Hon. Charles Francis Adams." Kidder acknowledged the mixed public opinion regarding the massacre among his contemporaries but claimed he would not be "undertaking to decide this question." Nonetheless, he did offer quotations from John Adams and Daniel Webster asserting the massacre's foundational role in the movement toward independence. As for Attucks, Kidder added little to the references included in his various sources, though he did add one lengthy footnote explaining that

Crispus Attucks is described as a mulatto; he was born in Framingham near the Chochituate lake and not far from the line of Natick. Here an old cellar hole remains where the Attucks family formerly lived. Attuck is an Indian word meaning a deer, and was often given to children; his ancestors were probably of the Natick tribe, who had intermarried with negroes who were slaves, and as their descendants were held as such; he inherited their condition, although it is likely the blood of three races coursed through his veins.

Kidder may have relied on William Barry's 1847 *History of Framingham* and possibly visits to the Natick area in formulating his conjectures about the Attucks family's home. He also added the text of William Brown's 1750 runaway advertisement for the fugitive mulatto, Crispus.[33]

The Boston Massacre's centennial anniversary and the appearance of Kidder's volume may help explain a small flurry of attention to Attucks in the pages of a popular history periodical during the early 1870s. Edited by the prolific historical writer Benson J. Lossing, the *American Historical Record*, published monthly from 1872 through 1874, offered a range of letters and essays "concerning the history and antiquities of America and biography of Americans." Its third issue, in March 1872, contained a reminder of the massacre's one hundred second anniversary, accompanied by the account published in a 1770 issue of the *Boston Gazette* after the victims' funeral. Lossing noted the massacre as "the first collision between British troops and the people," and mentioned that the "leader of the mob was a powerful mulatto, named Crispus Attucks," who along with the other victims was "buried with great Parade." Perhaps not coincidentally, another essay in the same issue mentioned "a *Negro Regiment* employed in the Revolutionary war" and commented favorably on the "colored, mulattoes, and full blacks" who served with distinction under Commodore Stephen Decatur during the War of 1812.[34]

Later that year, a Philadelphian named J. B. Fisher apparently was spurred by recent attention to Attucks to do a bit of historical investigation. Writing to the *Record* with his ruminations on the question, "Who was Crispus Attucks?" Fisher tried to make a case that "evidence does not in the least prove him to be of African origin," and "that Crispus Attucks was a Natick Indian from Framingham." At the time Fisher was writing, both black and white abolitionists had created the image of an unequivocally black Attucks, completely ignoring his Indian parentage. Fisher used the trial transcript, William Barry's 1847 discussion of Nanny Peterattucks (which he conveniently revised to "Nancy Peter Attucks"), the etymology of the term "attuk" (meaning young deer), and the seventeenth-century case of John Uktuck to make the case for Crispus's Indian identity. Implicitly challenging the dominant story black writers had crafted, he completely discounted any possible African ancestry based on shaky premises and shoddy logic. First, he argued that "the terms Mulatto and Indian were synonymously used" during the eighteenth century, and very few "negroes" were listed in eighteenth-century Framingham records. Second, he reasoned that, since "the negro occupied the most servile position" in that time and place, it would have been extremely unlikely that "if Attucks was a negro . . . he should have been the leader of a mob of sailors." On the other hand, Fisher falsely asserted, "the Indian occupied [a position] of almost social equality with the white population."[35]

It is difficult to assess Fisher's motives and interest in the question. His statements about terminology and social relations simply don't hold water. Was he so intent upon denying Attucks's African ancestry that he purposely misled his readers, or was he simply an unreliable investigator? Over the subsequent weeks, Fisher's essay "attracted much attention" from readers of the *Record*. One writer, "in order to render the subject more complete," called Fisher's attention to the 1750 runaway advertisement that seemed to identify Attucks as a slave of the Brown family. The writer, Grace Greenwood, did not overtly challenge Fisher's interpretation, but Fisher evidently recognized that Attucks being a slave would add credibility to claims of his African heritage. Fisher first contended that the ad may well have been written in regard to another mulatto named Crispus and then disputed as "simply ridiculous" the Brown family's claims to have his drinking cup and powder horn. He seemed to imply that the Browns' claim to Attucks was a self-serving attempt to prove that theirs was "the first blood shed in the revolution" since "if they owned Crispus Attucks . . . his blood was theirs as well as his body." Fisher held rather defensively to his original position, emphasizing that "I have not written these articles as an argument, but to demonstrate a fact, and unveil an error."[36]

So by the Reconstruction era several different kinds of efforts were being made to complicate the image of the patriotic black martyr that was being shouted from the rooftops by African American activists. Writers like Fisher and Kidder called attention to Attucks's likely Indian roots, which had the potential to weaken blacks' claims to Attucks and his usefulness as an icon of their Americanness and belonging. Taking a different tack, authors of many school histories either vilified Attucks and the entire massacre mob, or they excluded the putative black hero from their accounts altogether. Whether these competing narratives were developed consciously to undermine African Americans' claims to citizenship or were the result of less malicious editorial decisions is difficult to discern. Regardless, blacks' commitment and connection to their hero of the Revolution only grew stronger.

During the decades preceding the Civil War, black Americans struggled both to end slavery and to establish their status as United States citizens. Their military service during the sectional conflict lent considerable weight to their arguments for citizenship, and the Thirteenth, Fourteenth, and Fifteenth Amendments formally accomplished those goals by 1870. White Americans, however, proved intransigent when it came to fully accepting blacks as part of the American national family. African Americans worked through official judicial and legislative processes to secure and maintain their rights, but they also recognized the need to wage a broader cultural campaign in the American public sphere. Public presentations of both historical discussions and symbolic cultural resources were spread through books, speeches, newspapers, naming patterns, and public commemorations and were significant in constructing an empowering race history that demonstrated African Americans' rightful status as American citizens. In that campaign, Crispus Attucks emerged as a powerful and enduring symbol—not merely as a "race hero" but as a legitimately "American hero" who lent weight to black claims for inclusion. By the time of the Civil War, Attucks had become virtually a household name among those sympathetic to the cause of racial justice.

Crispus Attucks quite literally became a household name during the 1870s, as both black parents and organizational leaders chose to honor the first martyr of liberty by passing on his name. In September 1873, the Attucks Guard of Richmond, Virginia, opened an account in the Freedmen's Bank, which had been established by the federal government in 1865 to promote the economic security of African Americans. In 1871, Captain William J. Brodie and his fellow officers established a similar account for the Attucks Light Infantry in Charleston, South Carolina. Despite the return to power of a white supremacist government in the state, the "colored . . . military organization" was still in existence in 1879. In that same year, an African American family in Norfolk, Virginia, named their new baby boy Crispus Attucks Palmer.[37]

Crispus Attucks burst onto the American scene during the 1850s and 1860s as the seminal exemplar of black patriotism and virtuous citizenship. In the emerging mythology, Attucks was unequivocally identified as a black man who was the first to sacrifice his life on the altar of American freedom. His identification with the nation's founding and his construction as the "first martyr of liberty" in retrospect seems a logical and obvious tactic to employ in the argument for African American citizenship. But in fact this was a careful historical reconstruction that emphasized evidence that was useful while ignoring anything that tarnished the hero's image or complicated his ancestry. The heroic martyr also emerged within a particular historical context. In the aftermath of the fiftieth anniversary of American independence in 1826, the common people turned to the past and appropriated the Revolution's republican legacy to bolster their own causes. The reclamation of the Tea Party was one example of the Revolution's working-class heroes that attracted attention during the 1830s. That decade also saw the rise of an abolitionist movement calling for the immediate end to American slavery. As that movement became more radicalized in reaction against the 1850 Fugitive Slave Act, the rediscovery of Crispus Attucks allowed abolitionists to craft an American hero to play an important symbolic role in their crusade for racial justice.

But this memory of a heroic Attucks was contested by other Americans who saw abolitionism and radicalism in general as a threat to the social order. These voices—whether from writers of school textbooks or Boston councilmen rejecting a petition for the Attucks monument—highlighted Attucks's roughness and violence and the chaos and violence the massacre mob had instigated. Textbooks in particular likely had a lasting effect on the malleable minds of young readers. But those who would vilify Attucks during the 1850s and 1860s had to compete against a groundswell of public acclaim. Attucks proponents used virtually every form of media available in the

mid-nineteenth century to sing the martyred hero's praises. Through political orations, newspaper editorials, historical and biographical essays, poems,
monument campaigns, Attucks Day celebrations, and named institutions like
militia companies and glee clubs, the American public rapidly became saturated with the heroic version of Attucks's story.

The mid-nineteenth century was a heady period for the construction of
heroes. Writing in 1841, Thomas Carlyle famously conceived of heroes as history's "Great Men," who were "leaders of men . . . modellers . . . of whatso-
ever the general mass of men contrived to do or to attain." Historian William
L. Van Deburg argues that African American heroes serve as "the personi-
fication of predominating ideals, the embodiment of a people's ineffable
desires." According to Van Deburg, "in order to define, sustain, and promote
the concept of a viable African American heroic," nineteenth-century writers like Nell, William Wells Brown, and others pioneered efforts "to conduct
research in black history"; such was the case with Nell's construction of a
heroic Crispus Attucks.[38]

Nineteenth-century African Americans sought a usable past that incorporated both their distinctive history and heritage as black people and their
uncompromising claim to the full fruits of American citizenship. By 1850,
Crispus Attucks began playing a significant role in African Americans' affirm-
ation of their essential Americanness. But the Crispus Attucks who emerged
late in the antebellum period was a shrewd construction. His mixed racial background was muted in favor of a fully African American one, and his possible
reasons for being part of the Boston mob were left unscrutinized as he assumed
the mantle of an American patriot committed to independent nationhood.
Like Carlyle's "Great Men," he was courageous, daring, and loyal, devoted to
the cause of liberty, and willing to sacrifice his life while protecting the nation
from an external threat. Reflecting the needs of the time, Attucks emerged as
a black patriot and Founder, a hero who, in Van Deburg's terms, personified
a people's "predominating ideals" and embodied their "ineffable desires." As
the nation slowly and haltingly distanced itself from an era of civil war, sectional reconciliation relied heavily on a tacit agreement that the white South
would be left alone to manage its racial affairs and that the national interest
did not include racial justice for black Americans. In the coming generations
of Jim Crow segregation, African Americans would be left largely to their own
devices to empower themselves politically, socially, and economically. In their
efforts to reap the rewards of the full citizenship they had been promised they
forged doggedly ahead in an increasingly more segregated America.

4

Crispus Attucks Meets Jim Crow

THE SEGREGATION OF AMERICAN MEMORY,
1870S–1910S

And honor to Crispus Attucks, who was leader and voice that day;
The first to defy, and the first to die, with Maverick, Carr, and Gray.
JOHN BOYLE O'REILLY (1888)

Crispus Attucks—that half Indian, half negro and altogether
rowdy . . . should have been strangled the day he was born.
JAMES R. GILMORE (1897)

ON A CHILL January day in 1879, William H. Palmer, an African American revenue inspector at the Norfolk, Virginia, county Alms House, awaited the birth of his fourth child. We cannot know the conversations he, his wife Annie, and their family had about naming that child. But when the baby boy came into the world he became known as Crispus Attucks Palmer. At the age of twenty-one, Crispus Palmer still lived in Norfolk county with his mother, by then a widow, and all six of his siblings, all with less illustrious names, who ranged in age from thirteen to thirty-one. Ten years later Crispus was married and on his own, and he and his wife Mary had three young daughters. When their only son was born in 1912, he was named Crispus Attucks Palmer Jr.[1]

A few years later, thirty-eight-year-old Crispus senior registered for the World War I draft, though he did not serve. By 1920 he was a widower and had moved with his four children to Norfolk City, where he owned his home free and clear and worked as a clerk at the post office. Later that year Crispus remarried. He and his second wife, Rose, provided well for their family. Their home was worth $3,500, they purchased a radio to keep up with the rapidly changing times, and they placed a high priority on education. Crispus still held his post office position, and both Rose and his eldest daughter, Marian, were schoolteachers.

Seventeen-year-old Crispus junior was soon off on his own adventures. He completed four years of college—an impressive achievement for a black man in early twentieth-century America—and was working as a film editor in the motion picture industry until May 1942, when he enlisted in the US army to help defend a country at war. He earned the rank of technician fifth grade (the equivalent of corporal) and gave his life serving his country in Epinal, France, where he was buried. Young Crispus Palmer Jr. never married or had children, so we can only speculate as to whether he would have carried on his family's tribute to the first martyr of the Revolution.[2]

The Palmer family personifies important aspects of the culture of "racial uplift" among middle-class African Americans during the late nineteenth and early twentieth centuries. They placed a high value on family, education, and economic advancement. William Palmer was very likely a slave prior to 1865. In 1870, he was listed as a domestic servant, and while he could read and write, his wife Annie could not. By 1880, Annie was literate and William had risen to the position of county revenue inspector. Successive generations of Palmers illustrate the emergence of a postbellum southern black middle class with jobs increasingly removed from the subservience of slavery and with stable two-parent households in which the children's education was a priority. They became homeowners and had the expectation that the next generation would exceed their own accomplishments. In naming a male child after a black patriot and hero, two generations of Palmers also claimed their place as American citizens while illustrating an attention to history and race pride that signifies the solidification of Crispus Attucks's indelible status in black communities across the nation.[3]

Despite the upward mobility of families like the Palmers, black Americans generally saw their stock decline during the years after the Civil War. African Americans' hopes for equality, opportunity, and acceptance in American society expanded briefly after constitutional amendments between 1865 and 1870 abolished slavery and guaranteed blacks' full and equal citizenship rights, but those hopes steadily eroded after the 1870s. By 1879, when Crispus Attucks Palmer was born, nearly two thousand black men had held political offices in the southern states, sixteen of them in the US Congress; at the birth of his namesake in 1912 there were no African Americans in Congress and very few held elected office at any level. Even the right to vote, let alone hold office, was undermined by convoluted voting rules, racially restrictive laws, intimidation, and violence. While black literacy rates climbed from barely 10 percent to over 70 percent in that period, blacks' hopes to pursue a fulfilling education were slim. The passage of Jim Crow laws across the South restricted African Americans' access to schools, jobs, libraries, and other public facilities. After the withdrawal of federal troops from the South in 1877 and the return to power of white supremacist former slaveholders, even basic constitutional legal protections for black Americans disappeared. In 1882, forty-nine lynchings of African Americans were recorded, a number that climbed steadily over the next several decades, with the total reaching well over three thousand by 1920. Countless others no doubt went unreported.[4]

In times like these, when white America had all but abandoned its concern for the basic welfare and rights of black citizens, a black hero like Crispus Attucks had little chance to enter the heroic pantheon of the nation. White Americans and mainstream popular culture virtually erased Attucks from the story of the American Revolution, just as black service in the Civil War disappeared from popular conceptions of that conflict. As white northerners and southerners gradually left behind the hatred spawned by civil war and reconciled their differences over the half-century after 1865, blacks were left to preserve their own contributions in segregated spheres of public and personal memory. As both legal and de facto segregation kept the races separate in public spaces and services, the realm of collective memory also developed along racially exclusive parallel paths. With few exceptions, African Americans had to rely on their own written histories, public commemorations, and private acts of memory like the naming of children to define and preserve a meaningful history of the race's role in shaping American society.[5]

One sign of the nation's disregard for African Americans' participation in the nation's history was blacks' almost complete exclusion from mainstream schoolbooks and written histories of any kind. Frances FitzGerald, in her study of American history schoolbooks, argues that by the 1890s, textbook authors were exercising greater "restraint" in articulating their moral judgments, striving for "a tone of objectivity and authoritativeness." Yet in discussions of the Boston Massacre one can discern distinct anti-mob sentiments in turn-of-the-century textbooks, even as they excised Crispus Attucks from their accounts. John Bach McMaster described British troops "intended for the defense of the colony" being "annoyed" by impatient Bostonians. He called the subsequent conflict "the Boston Riot." Susan Pendleton Lee took a firmer stance, asserting that the British soldiers were "quartered there to enforce the law" and that they "only fired into the mob to preserve their own lives, and were not very much to blame." Albert Bushnell Hart similarly noted

that the British troops only fired "under great provocation" in this "unfortunate affair." Attucks was invisible.[6]

And he remained invisible. Samuel G. Goodrich's 1881 *The American
Child's Pictorial History of the United States* had described the Boston
Massacre as had his earlier schoolbooks, with the British firing after extreme
provocation when "a negro named Attucks began to strike their muskets with
his club." But Goodrich seems to have been the last writer for many years to
include Attucks in that story. The period after the turn of the century brought
an explosion of textbook writing, with numerous texts being produced to
fill an expanding school market. But I have not been able to find a single
mainstream American history schoolbook prior to the 1960s that mentions
Crispus Attucks.[7]

Black authors during the late nineteenth and early twentieth centuries
made a concerted effort to redress the omissions of white authors and tell
African Americans' story. Historian Laurie F. Maffly-Kipp has observed
that late nineteenth-century black historical writers, more explicitly than
earlier authors, incorporated black heroes and "the account of the African
American journey to freedom" into a new historical narrative which "stressed
the dawning of a distinctive era, one in which blacks would take their rightful place as equals among the nations of the world." She also sees in this new
genre of the black-authored "race history" a general assumption of race progress as well as a distinctly spiritual rendering of the past that held moral lessons for the present generation. Not surprisingly, Crispus Attucks featured
prominently in the many histories, textbooks, and biographical collections
published during this period.[8]

Two important historical works from the 1880s illustrate Maffly-Kipp's
points. George Washington Williams's *History of the Negro Race in America,
1619–1880* (1883), subtitled "Negroes as Slaves, as Soldiers, and as Citizens,"
left no doubt as to the primary objective of the author's enterprise. In perhaps the earliest attempt at a comprehensive and scholarly history of African
Americans, Williams emphasized the "progress of the race": from early African
cultures, through the dark days of slavery, and into an ever brighter future in
which black accomplishments and contributions would lead to full equality
in American society. William Simmons's *Men of Mark: Eminent, Progressive,
and Rising* (1887) is not a race history like Williams's but rather a biographical catalog. In accounts sprawling over one thousand pages, Simmons offered
brief biographies of 177 African American men (and no women), most of
whom were still living when the book was published. Like Williams, Simmons
was intent on demonstrating black accomplishment, with an emphasis on

inspiring black youth and convincing white America of the race's potential for helping to shape a positive future for the American nation.[9]

These two black historical writers presented Crispus Attucks as a redemptive figure whose actions simultaneously defined what it meant to be an American, while embodying the centrality of African American people to the nation's founding. Williams preceded his coverage of the Boston Massacre with a discussion of the incongruity of white Americans demanding liberty while they enslaved hundreds of thousands of Africans. The failure to pass measures outlawing slavery, Williams claimed, "led [blacks] to regard the colonists as their enemies." In this "critical" situation, "a bold, clear-headed, loyal-hearted man was needed." He then presented William Brown's 1750 runaway ad to illustrate that, with Attucks's "soul and body . . . beyond the cruel touch of master," he was then free to become, twenty years later, "the Negro patriot, soldier, and martyr to the ripening cause of the American Revolution." Williams boldly contrasted the "obsequious humility" of many American colonists with the "sterner stuff" of the "manly-looking" and "commanding figure" of "the intrepid Attucks," who "[gave] his life as an offering upon the altar of *American liberty*."[10]

In highlighting Attucks's leadership and martyrdom, Williams built on the work of William Nell and William Wells Brown while also extending the practice of embellishing the details of Attucks's life. Admitting that Attucks's whereabouts between 1750 and 1770 were unknown, Williams nevertheless had no qualms about asserting that he was "doubtless in Boston, where he heard the fiery eloquence of Otis, the convincing arguments of Sewall, and the tender pleadings of Belknap." Attucks "was not a madcap, as some would have the world believe. He was not ignorant of the issues. . . . His patriotism was not a mere spasm produced by sudden and exciting circumstances. It was an education; and knowledge comes from experience; and the experience of this black hero was not of a single day." To prove the latter point, Williams reproduced the letter to Thomas Hutchinson from John Adams's diary and claimed that it was in fact written by Attucks himself, "some time before the memorable 5th of March." Williams, an ordained Baptist minister, made a biblical comparison. Eighteen centuries before Attucks's sacrifice, another "Negro [Simon the Cyrenian] bore the cross of Christ to Calvary for him. And when the colonists were staggering wearily under their cross of woe, a Negro came to the front, and bore that cross to the victory of a glorious martyrdom."[11]

William Simmons was no less effusive, and in fact he drew heavily from Williams, "the historian of the race," as a source for portions of his biographical profile of Attucks, including another full reproduction of the Hutchinson letter. While Williams had clearly implied that Attucks was literate by accepting his authorship of the letter, Simmons explicitly stated that Attucks "learned to read at odd times, and he used this accomplishment in understanding the fundamental principles that underlie all regulated forms of government." Attucks had escaped from slavery "determined to be a free American citizen," and a "fiery patriotism burned in his breast." Attucks's need "to avenge oppression in every form" caused him to take the lead in 1770. He was "the first to resist and the first slain. His patriotism was the declaration of war. It was liberty to the oppressed; it opened the way to modern civilization and independence." Like Williams, Simmons could not resist employing a spiritual tone in praising Attucks's sacrifice. "It has blessed and will continue to bless generations yet unborn. He is rightly claimed as the savior of his country."[12]

Williams and Simmons mark a high point of exaggerated claims about Crispus Attucks and his seemingly single-handed and messianic role, leading the colonists in that initial fatal confrontation with British troops. The Attucks they present is undoubtedly black, brave, and saintly—indeed, almost Christ-like in his sacrifice. He was not only literate but he was also familiar with the Boston patriots' oratory and well informed about the nature of the people's rights and government's responsibilities. His burning desire for freedom, to the point of martyrdom, was an inspiration to his contemporaries and to subsequent generations of Americans, black and white.

One of the earliest and most well-known African American histories designed for use in schools, Edward A. Johnson's *School History of the Negro Race in America* (1891), presented Attucks in a similar vein, though with a somewhat tempered tone. Within a ten-page section on "Negro Heroes of the Revolution," Johnson identified Attucks in a subheading as "The Leader Who Fell in the Famous Boston Massacre," and he incorporated earlier writers' unfounded and idealized assertions. For example, he repeated the claim that "Attucks had no doubt been listening to the fiery eloquence of the patriots of those burning times. The words of the eloquent Otis had kindled his soul, and though a runaway slave, his patriotism was so deep that he it was who sacrificed his life *first* on the altar of American Liberty." Johnson also repeated the false claim that "many orators spoke in the highest terms of Crispus Attucks."[13] Similarly, in their 1902 history of black progress in America, J. W. Gibson and W. H. Crogman labeled Attucks in a bold subheading as the "Hero and Martyr" of the Boston Massacre and the man who "cut the cord and knot that held us to Britain." Attucks's courageous leadership "touched the people of the colonies as they had never been touched before. Orators poured out upon this former slave, now a hero and martyr, their unstinted praise." These authors' presentations were only slightly less exaggerated than the fabrications of Williams and Simmons.[14]

Historical texts by black authors in the first decades of the twentieth century were generally a bit more measured in their treatment of the first martyr of liberty. Perhaps later writers began to heed the advice given by African American educator and diplomat John Stephens Durham in his 1897 book, *To Teach the Negro History*. Durham had taught black students in decrepit and backward classrooms in the United States, with virtually no materials, and also during his foreign appointments in Haiti and Santo Domingo. Durham observed that "in our own country, the negro has greater opportunities for advancement, and gives indications of more rapid, more essential, progress than in any other country in which I know members of the race to reside in relatively large numbers." He concluded that "an unbiased and philosophic method of teaching the growing generation is necessary to making the best of this opportunity." Durham counseled those teaching black students to avoid racial chauvinism and to teach them, not as black students, but as students who were "member[s] of the universal human family." "On the one hand," Durham recognized,

> the negro has been ignorantly denounced by historians and ethnologists. . . . On the other hand, colored historians, in a spirit of resentment quite natural, all things considered, have written books to excite what they call race pride. Teach your boy that nature did not make one special creation and color it white, and another special creation and paint it black.

In his brief section discussing African Americans' participation in the American Revolution, Durham made no mention of Crispus Attucks.[15]

Few subsequent black-authored texts completely excluded Attucks, but many treated him with greater detachment than had nineteenth-century authors. John W. Cromwell's *The Negro in American History* (1914) perhaps exercised the most care with both historical fact and objective tone, stating merely that "Crispus Attucks, the mulatto, was one of the first to fall March 5, 1770, in the Boston Massacre, in which the first blood of the Revolution was shed." Still, the frontispiece of Cromwell's book depicts "The Boston Massacre," with an engraving loosely based on the Revere print, but showing a man front and center grabbing a bayonet and holding a club, as in the 1856 Champney image (see Fig. 4.1). The white writer John Daniels's study

FIG 4.1 "The Boston Massacre." Frontispiece for John W. Cromwell, *The Negro in American History* (1914). The Library Company of Philadelphia.

of blacks in Boston, *In Freedom's Birthplace* (1914), was rare among texts on black history in acknowledging Attucks's probable Indian ancestry in his discussion of the massacre: "The central hero of that incident was a Negro, or a Negro-Indian half-breed, Crispus Attucks." Daniels also included the quotations about the Boston Massacre by John Adams and Daniel Webster that were by then well known to many Bostonians thanks to their presence on the most prominent biracial commemoration of Crispus Attucks to appear in the nineteenth century.[16]

In fact, the most public gesture honoring Crispus Attucks that was undertaken with significant biracial support between 1770 and the 1920s was perhaps the grandest gesture of all and one that made the most lasting mark on the public landscape. William C. Nell had died in 1874, but his dream of a statue commemorating Crispus Attucks, first put forward in 1851, was taken up in the mid-1880s by both black activists and white political leaders in Boston. In 1888, the City of Boston finally unveiled an impressive monument on Boston Common that was formally and popularly known as the "Memorial to Crispus Attucks" or simply "the Attucks monument" (see Fig. 4.2).

This monument met with considerable opposition and criticism, both prior to its approval and erection and for several years afterward. Given the general disregard for African American participation in the national story

FIG. 4.2 Boston Massacre Monument. Detroit Publishing Co., Publisher. Between 1890 and 1906. Library of Congress.

and the growing fear of mob violence during the 1880s, it is somewhat surprising that the monument was approved at all. The revival of Nell's monument movement came to fruition in 1887, just a year after an explosion during a labor protest in Chicago's Haymarket Square resulted in the death of seven police officers and four civilians, along with numerous casualties. Eight anarchists were hastily tried and convicted on flimsy evidence, and the nation entered a period of profound fear and suspicion of working-class organizations and public demonstrations of any kind. It hardly seemed an ideal moment to honor a rowdy Revolutionary mob. Nonetheless, when a coalition of black activists and white political leaders submitted their 1887 petition "that a suitable monument may be erected to the memory of these early patriots of the Revolution," they seemed to have little difficulty getting the approval of the state legislature and Governor Oliver Ames.[17]

In his thoughtful study of the meanings surrounding the Attucks monument, Stephen H. Browne argues that the monument was a device through which Boston addressed the "social transformations" brought by increasing numbers of immigrants who needed to be Americanized in order to maintain the city's "civic character." The Attucks monument served this agenda by fixing in the community's public memory a tribute to the inclusiveness of "an essentially American quality of heart, mind, and spirit." The sacrifices Attucks and his fellow martyrs made in the name of American liberty, according to Browne, were meant "to exemplify all Americans." The monument would bring Boston's "New Americans, Americans without memory," into the national fold by drawing them into the collective memory of the nation. As commentator George Nelson put it in 1888, "the Nation [had begun] to experience difficulty in assimilating [its] foreign born population," and commemorations like the Attucks monument were "occasions on which the people at large were to be educated in the history of the Nation and instructed in the principles on which the nation was founded."[18]

The monument featured a twenty-five-foot-high "Concord granite" obelisk, upon a pedestal bearing a bronze bas relief depicting the massacre, showing Attucks lying in the foreground. The upper corners of the plaque displayed the quotations by Webster (the "Moment [from which] we may date the Severance of the British Empire") and Adams ("On that Night the Foundation of American Independence was laid"). Above the bas relief, and in front of the obelisk, stood Robert Kraus's seven-foot-high bronze statue of a female figure, "Free America," which was described glowingly in the official account of the unveiling:

> With her left hand she clasps a flag about to be unfurled, while she holds aloft in her right hand the broken chain of oppression, and crushes beneath her right foot the royal crown, which, twisted and torn, is falling off the plinth. At her left side, clinging to the edge of the plinth, is an eagle. Its wings are raised, its beak is open, and it has apparently just lit. Its pose is in unison with the fiery spirit of its mistress, shown in the serious, determined, and heroic gaze of her upturned face.

The obelisk bears the names of the five victims, with Attucks listed first, and the base is inscribed with the date, March 5, 1770.[19]

Supporters articulated the significance of the monument at the November 14, 1888, dedication ceremony, which included venerable black abolitionist Lewis Hayden, prominent North Carolina black educator J. C. Price, former Louisiana lieutenant governor P. B. S. Pinchback, Massachusetts congressman George F. Hoar, Governor Ames, Boston mayor Hugh O'Brien, and other black and white dignitaries. A large procession included public figures, marching bands, militia units, and black organizations, including forty members of the [Robert Gould] Shaw Guard Veterans Association and thirty from the Crispus Attucks Lodge of the Knights of Pythias. The throng wended its way past the state house, city hall, and other prominent spots, before ending at the monument site on the Common near Tremont Street, where the organizers and their honored guests mounted a platform. The Germania band played "America" and the Reverend Eli Smith of Springfield offered a prayer that praised Massachusetts for recognizing the "manhood" of the Negro and for being "the first to do honor to him in rearing a monument to commemorate his valor and patriotism in a great conflict."[20]

Black Bostonian William H. DuPree, chairman of the Citizens Committee, followed Smith with a clear statement of what Attucks and the monument signified for American freedom. "On the 5th," he proclaimed, "by the death of Attucks and his comrades, submission to English law gave place to active opposition," which forced the removal of British troops from the town of Boston. Their assertive actions demonstrated to the Crown that "the people were masters. The real authority had been wrested from the king, and assumed by his subjects. The death of these men made the republic secure." Attucks's sacrifice "forever affirmed the right of rebellion against tyranny." After the unveiling, the procession marched to Faneuil Hall, where Attucks's body had lain before the 1770 group funeral. There Governor Ames praised the "memory of a noble race and noble men" as well as the contemporary "representatives of a race whose brother, Attucks, was the first one to fall" and who "did much toward freeing our nation from British rule." Mayor O'Brien acknowledged the naysayers who directed "adverse criticism" toward "Attucks and his martyr associates," saying that they were merely "rioters, who deserved their fate." O'Brien expressed "no doubt" that the massacre martyrs played a major role "in uniting the colonists as one man" and "made possible the war of the Revolution and the Declaration of Independence, that immortal document which pronounced all men free and equal without regard to color, creed, or nationality."[21]

In his featured oration, historian John Fiske set out explicitly to explain "the real significance of the Boston Massacre and its place in American history." After a lengthy review of the events of the late 1760s that led up to the massacre, Fiske essentially reiterated the case laid out by William Dupree, that the citizens' revolt on March 5 forced the "removal of the instruments of tyranny"—the British troops—from Boston. The actions of Attucks and his fellow citizens "effected in a moment what seventeen months of petition and discussion had failed to accomplish. . . . It is, therefore, historically correct to regard them as the first martyrs to the cause of American independence." Like Mayor O'Brien, Fiske was disturbed by the "present generation of historical students" who "seem to have swung around into the Tory view of the events which ushered in the Revolution" and who had said things "about the Boston Massacre which one would think fit to make glorious old Samuel Adams turn in his grave." Fiske admitted that the men who fell that day "did not belong to our 'first families,'" and—showing more respect for historical evidence than contemporary black writers—that little could be said with certainty "about their motives and purposes." Yet Fiske had no doubt that those first families who turned out to escort the martyrs "to their grave in the Old Granary Burying-ground, unquestionably regarded them as victims who had suffered in the common cause." Fiske praised both Attucks (who "likely . . . had both Indian and African blood in his veins") and all the "brave men of his race" (presumably blacks) who had "nobly acquit[ted] themselves" in many Revolutionary era engagements.[22]

John Boyle O'Reilly's poem, "Crispus Attucks," written especially for the occasion, suggested that whether one called the massacre "riot or revolution" and its victims "mob or crowd" depended on one's point of view: "They were lawless hinds to the lackeys [of the British Crown]—but martyrs to Paul Revere;/And Otis and Hancock and Warren read spirit and meaning clear." A modern patriot surely had to side with the latter. O'Reilly began his poem with a question: "Where shall we seek for a hero, and where shall we find a story?" Like Fiske, he acknowledged the humble social status of Attucks, "this negro slave with unfamiliar name," and "his poor companions, nameless too, till their lives leaped forth in flame." O'Reilly emphasized the motley diversity represented by the massacre martyrs—"Indian and Negro, Saxon and Celt, Teuton and Latin and Gaul." Through the flowing blood of the five victims "the streams of several races in the well of a nation meet." O'Reilly questioned whether all Americans might see, as "our Crispus Attucks knew—/When right is stricken the white and black are counted one, not two?"

And so must we come to the learning of Boston's lesson today;
The moral that Crispus Attucks taught in the old heroic way;

God made mankind to be one in blood, as one in spirit and thought;
And so great a boon, by a brave man's death, is never dearly bought.[23]

The monument's critics, however, imposed a different significance on both the Boston Massacre and the monument and raised unsettling questions about just what sort of lessons the behavior of Attucks and the monument were likely to instill. Some cynically saw Governor Ames's support for the monument as politically driven. The *New York Sun* claimed that "it is said" that Ames had been asked to veto the legislature's $10,000 appropriation for the monument, but that he refused, fearing that he would "lose the colored vote of the state." The venerable patricians at the Massachusetts Historical Society (MHS) mounted a vehement opposition, "declar[ing] that the proposed monument was a waste of the public's money" and that "these men were rioters, not patriots." Attucks in particular was "not a fit candidate for monumental honors" since "the famous mulatto was a rowdyish person, killed while engaged in a defiance of law." Bostonian Nora Perry noted the "storm of criticism and questioning concerning" the monument and agreed that "the Crispus Attucks monument, as it is called," was based on "prejudiced and sensational interpretations." "It was," she agreed, "the spark that brought on the crisis. Yet, all the same, the instigators were not heroic, and were not so considered at the time. They were rioters—nothing more nor less." A writer for the *Boston Globe* sarcastically observed that Attucks was "not the only American who has made history without meaning to" and suggested that perhaps Chicago's Mrs. O'Leary and her cow might be equally worthy of public commemoration.[24]

To counter these objections to the monument in the mainstream media, African Americans mobilized through their own public print outlets. After the Civil War, African Americans established newspapers and periodicals across the North, South, and West, and black journalists remained among the most vocal champions of black history and advocates for black citizenship rights. The black press was instrumental in informing the public about books, celebrations, monuments, and other tools of memory that affirmed African Americans' historical accomplishments and contributions and their identity as Americans. Crispus Attucks had become an important part of this campaign, and during the 1880s the celebration of a black hero and patriot from the Revolution resonated with contemporary efforts to honor other black heroes like those who had served in the Civil War. Like black Civil War veterans, Attucks was presented not merely as a "race hero" but as a legitimately "American hero" who lent weight to black claims for inclusion.

New York City editor T. Thomas Fortune was exceptional in his attention to black veterans, black history, and the need to construct an empowering collective memory for the race. During the 1880s, his succession of newspapers regularly provided information about Decoration Day services and meetings of black Civil War veterans' organizations as well as information about black history and its commemoration. In 1886, the *Freeman* reported on Decoration Day celebrations in Boston that included "a procession . . . to the grave of Crispus Attucks," where attendees heard a "forcible oration" and "impressive prayer" before placing flowers on the martyr's grave and heading to their next stop—the grave of abolitionist William Lloyd Garrison.[25] In early 1887, without any mention of the monument petition, Fortune gave space to numerous pieces related to Attucks. One printed just after the March 5 anniversary of Attucks's death responded to a white editor's denial of black troops' importance in the Civil War, in part by asserting that "the colored man has been the Alpha and Omega of this country's struggle for liberty. The first blood shed in the Revolution, the first martyr to the cause of freedom was Crispus Attucks, a Negro. . . . Crispus Attucks—Appomattox. How they rhyme!"[26]

In a June 1887 essay supporting the formation of a new civil rights organization, the Afro-American League, Fortune called on blacks to demonstrate their courage and manhood and to confront white violence and "the reign of lynch and mob law," in part by recalling past black martial heroes:

Attucks, the black patriot—he was no coward! Toussaint L'Ouverture —he was no coward! Nat Turner—he was no coward! And the two hundred thousand black soldiers of the last war—they were no cowards! If we have work to do, let us do it. And if there is violence, let those who oppose our just cause "throw the first stone!"[27]

So it is not surprising that Fortune also lent considerable publicity and support for the Attucks monument on Boston Common. At least two issues of his *New York Age* featured drawings of the monument, and at least half-a-dozen issues contained extensive discussions of Attucks's heroism, calls for race pride, and rejoinders to the monument's many critics.[28]

One Boston civic leader who had signed the petition supporting the monument later changed his view. Abner Goodell Jr., writing in 1893, expressed concern that the tribute to the massacre mob would give sanction to modern ruffians in an era that had seen mob violence in the Haymarket incident, the 1892 Homestead steelworkers strike, and other aggressive actions by the working classes. "I think there is little consistency in our rebuking the mob violence with which we are threatened today," he argued, when "we . . . single out the prowess of Crispus Attucks, in his cowardly, unprovoked attack upon men who . . . could not strike back without express authority from the civil magistrate." Goodell questioned "what possible connection has the brutal conduct of this man, partly intoxicated, and with no grievance, and no motive but a frenzied impulse . . . with the subsequent achievement of political independence by the Anglo-Saxon sons of New England?"[29]

Goodell's was hardly a lone voice. Newspaper correspondent Arlo Bates found it absurd that "the colored brethren of Boston . . . have made of Crispus Attucks the most popular martyr on the list of popular martyrs." Despite the MHS position "that Crispus Attucks was a drunken and disreputable half-caste who in a scandalous riot was shot by the British soldiers . . . it is still the popular feeling in Boston, as it likely is elsewhere, that Crispus Attucks was one of the heroes of the Revolution." He further mocked the idea of "the colored gentlemen of Boston" forming "a Crispus Attucks club for the annual celebration of the death of the martyr." Echoing Goodell's fear of mob violence, Bates pondered how Bostonians might feel if, "in an age of imitation . . . another should get his head full of beer and impudence and do what Crispus Attucks did."[30]

Writing in 1893, a year after the violent conflict at Homestead, John Douglas Lindsay, a New York City assistant district attorney and member of the Sons of the Revolution, captured the nation's apprehensive mood regarding mob violence in his detailed account of the massacre. While he made no mention of the monument or recent public unrest, Lindsay's judgment on the events of 1770 left little doubt about where he stood on those issues. He acknowledged the legitimacy of Bostonians' distaste for the troops stationed among them and the steady deterioration of relations, and he claimed that it was "not the purpose of this writer to say one word in defense of the soldiers, except for their action in this single instance." Yet Lindsay's narration made explicit his judgment of the crowd's and especially Attucks's culpability in that "instance," in the process feeding a growing cultural trope that defined black men in particular as dangerous and savage brutes.[31] "Large numbers of people were in the streets" on March 5, "many bent on mischief." Stirred by "exaggerated and garbled accounts of the behavior of the soldiers," groups of "impetuous, heedless men . . . act[ed] upon impulse rather than reason . . . [and] rush[ed] recklessly" toward the troops, "in their frenzy wholly unmindful of the consequences." Still it seemed that a fatal confrontation might be avoided. "There was a lull and the people were apparently about to turn

[back], when suddenly there appeared upon the scene a burly mulatto giant named Attucks, to whose mad behavior in all probability the dreadful slaughter that shortly after followed was due." This "half breed Indian negro" led his "myrmidons of bloodthirsty sailors" into the fray. Attucks wildly attacked Captain Preston and Private Montgomery, and the latter was "so frightfully provoked by the bloodthirsty Attucks" that he fired and killed his assailant. Lindsay went on to expose the "engraving by Paul Revere . . . of the so-called 'massacre'" as a misrepresentation of the event; in reality, the unruly mob, and Attucks in particular, was "wholly responsible, legally and morally," for having "murderously assaulted the soldiers."[32]

Another highly unflattering characterization of Attucks, first appearing in print in 1897, is even more damning of the ostensible hero: "I stood with Parson Byles on the corner of what are now School and Washington Streets, in March, 1770, and watched the funeral of Crispus Attucks—that half Indian, half negro and altogether rowdy, who should have been strangled the day he was born."[33] This statement was related by author and journalist James R. Gilmore, who claimed to have been recalling a conversation he had over a half-century earlier, in 1840, with the then ninety-five-year-old Calvinist minister Nathanael Emmons. Noting the passage of so much time, Gilmore warned his readers that "it will not be expected that I shall repeat his conversation verbatim; but I remember its substance distinctly." Gilmore's essay was a fond remembrance of Emmons, who had a marked influence on the writer's early years. As Gilmore told it, he had, as a youth of eighteen, approached Emmons after being assigned "to defend the old Tory," Parson Mather Byles, in his debating club, as he knew that Emmons had been "the bosom friend of Parson Byles from 1770 until 1788."[34] Crispus Attucks was in no way a part of Gilmore's debating assignment, and he was incidental to Emmons's attempt to illustrate Byles's well-known wit. Watching the funeral of Attucks and the other martyrs was merely the context for Byles's alleged statement: "'They call me a brainless Tory; but tell me, my young friend, which is better—to be ruled by one tyrant three thousand miles away, or by three thousand tyrants not one mile away?'"[35]

This "three thousand tyrants" quip, or some variation of it, has been widely repeated since its first appearance in 1897, perhaps most famously in the 2000 feature film, The Patriot, in which Mel Gibson's South Carolina farmer used it to express his reluctance to go to war with England. But it is unclear whether Byles really said it or whether Nathanael Emmons was even present in Boston to have heard it that day. Even if we discount pure fabrication on the part of Gilmore or Emmons, we are dealing with a seventy-five-year-old's memory of a fifty-seven-year-old conversation with a ninety-five-year-old man, recalling events from seventy years earlier. That left plenty of room for a lapse of memory, as Gilmore himself acknowledged.[36]

But it was Emmons, not Byles, whom Gilmore recalled making the comments about Attucks. The historian of Revolutionary Boston J. L. Bell questions whether Emmons was even in Boston on the day of the funeral, since biographies of Emmons placed him in Connecticut, New York, and New Hampshire—not Massachusetts—between 1769 and 1772.[37] Even if he did happen to have attended the funeral, since Emmons was not a resident of Boston, or even Massachusetts, in 1770, it is hard to imagine him knowing enough about Attucks at that time to have wished him strangled at birth. It is not even clear that Attucks was well known among people actually living in Boston, let alone a visitor from outside the colony. Emmons may possibly have held the massacre mob in contempt in 1840, since a negative view of mobs was not uncommon at the time and the event had just reentered public discussion through the publications of Botta, Goodrich, and Hewes. But unless he had some undocumented familiarity with Attucks or had uncannily strong memories of John Adams's disparaging comments about Attucks at the soldiers' trial—both of which seem unlikely—then it seems odd that he would express such a violent hatred of the man.

James R. Gilmore appears to have made no other public comments about Attucks. Yet he was a longtime Bostonian who surely had extensive knowledge of the debates surrounding Attucks, from the Attucks Day celebrations of the Civil War era through the flurry of pro- and anti-Attucks rhetoric surrounding the 1888 Boston Common monument. Boston in particular saw an unprecedented level of Attucks vilification in the years immediately before Gilmore wrote his reminiscence, so it seems that he, rather than Emmons, would have been far more familiar with arguments that Attucks was a disreputable troublemaker. Therefore I strongly suspect that the 1897 reference to the "altogether rowdy" Attucks who "should have been strangled the day he was born" emanated from Gilmore rather than Emmons.[38]

Among these turn-of-the-century critics of Attucks and his compatriots, there remained many Bostonians, white and black, who revered the martyrs' memory enough to seek further commemoration by addressing an often overlooked component of the 1887 monument petition. In addition to calling for a public monument, the petition also noted that, while the names of "the first Martyrs in the cause of American Liberty" had been recorded in history, "no stone marks their burial place." The Commonwealth of Massachusetts responded by resolving not only that "a suitable memorial or monument" be erected to the martyrs, but also that "suitable headstones" be placed "at the graves of said persons, where their locations can be ascertained."[39]

Numerous writers over the years have suggested that there was an original gravestone placed over the massacre martyrs' grave, but no contemporaneous evidence indicates that such a stone was ever erected. The earliest assertion I have found suggesting a gravestone's existence comes in an 1860 piece in William Lloyd Garrison's *Liberator*. "A stone was erected, and on it carved this inscription:—

> *Long as in Freedom's cause the wise contend,*
> *Dear to your country, shall your fame extend;*
> *While to the world the lettered stone shall tell*
> *How Caldwell, Attucks, Gray and Maverick fell.*

"No remains of the stone are now visible," the *Liberator* item continued, "as it was probably destroyed by British regulars."[40] The same verse and a similar assertion about an original grave marker were repeated a few years later by George Livermore in an address to the Massachusetts Historical Society.[41]

The source cited for these assertions, including the lines of verse, was the 1852 volume, *The Hundred Boston Orators*, which reprinted all the Boston Massacre orations between 1771 and 1783, as well as the annual Boston Independence Day orations from 1783 to 1851. However, the 1852 source does not support these assertions; the relevant passage in the editor's introductory essay is significantly misconstrued by the 1860s writers. The *Orators* editor, James Spear Loring, did reproduce twelve lines of verse that included the four lines above, but he indicated merely that it had been published in a contemporary Boston newspaper—not that it had been inscribed on the martyrs' gravestone. In fact, Loring did not even confirm that a gravestone was ever erected. His statement was that "no stone [in 1852] appears on the spot where they were buried. Indeed, *if* any stone were ever erected over their remains, it *may* have been destroyed by British regulars, or removed in making repairs on the ground." Frederic Kidder, in his 1870 book, *The Boston Massacre*, confirmed that no headstone existed in the mid-nineteenth century and indicated that, to his knowledge, none had ever been placed. "It is singular," Kidder wrote, "that no stone has *ever* marked their place of interment, and it is not certain as the locality can now be found."[42]

It was well documented that Attucks and the others had been buried in Boston's Granary Burying Ground, but Kidder speculated that, in 1870 at least, many of his readers might be "unable to call to mind the locality of this cemetery." While the location of the Burying Ground was in fact well known, historian J. L. Bell has questioned whether the bodies of the massacre victims could be located within its boundaries, since many bodies were removed from the cemetery during the nineteenth century. But workers installing a fence around the Burying Ground in 1840 stumbled upon a collection of human bones, including a skull with evidence of a gunshot wound. These were assumed by many to be the four immediate massacre victims—Attucks, James Caldwell, Samuel Maverick, and Samuel Gray—along with Patrick Carr, who died about a week after the first four, and young Christopher Seider, who had been killed on February 22. The *Boston Evening-Post* reported on March 19, 1770, that on March 17 Carr's body had been "buried in the same grave with the other four persons" killed on March 5. As for Seider, however, the *Boston Gazette*'s account of his funeral stated that he was not buried in the Granary Burying Ground at all, but rather "the little Corpse was let down under the Tree of Liberty," which was located several blocks away. No contemporaneous accounts suggest that Seider's remains were ever moved to join the massacre martyrs.[43] Regardless of whose bones actually inhabit the present Granary gravesite, in 1906 Boston's chapter of the Sons of the American Revolution, a fraternal order open to those whose ancestors had participated in the Revolutionary struggle, finally fulfilled the goals of the 1887 petitioners by placing a headstone to memorialize all six martyrs' sacrifice (see Fig. 4.3). Oddly, in light of the controversy inspired by the monument, the placing of the gravestone attracted minimal attention.[44]

Boston's use of the monument and gravestone to publicly memorialize Attucks as an American patriot and hero was somewhat out of step with the norm during the emerging Jim Crow era. The vilification of Attucks that came in the wake of the monument controversy was part of a larger assault in mainstream American culture on black claims to citizenship and inclusion. By the turn of the twentieth century, it was clear to many African Americans that they were fighting a losing battle to secure and maintain their rights through official judicial and legislative processes. They were fighting a similar uphill battle in the realm of popular culture, and they rose to the challenge of waging a broad cultural campaign in the American public sphere. Black authors were consistent in including positive presentations of African Americans in histories, biographies, and school texts during this period in order to offset their complete erasure from mainstream histories. But these texts had a limited audience. To augment those efforts, black Americans turned to newspapers, literary and activist organizations, and commemorative activities both

FIG. 4.3 "The Boston Massacre Monument in Boston [*sic*]." Undated photograph.
Watertown (Massachusetts) Free Public Library.

to solidify their communities and to present their case for racial justice to a
broader black and white audience. Attucks's name and spirit infused these
efforts.

As one monument critic noted, Boston's African American community
established a Crispus Attucks club that held annual March 5 commemorations to maintain the memory of the fallen hero. Commenting on their 1894
annual dinner observance at the Quincy House hotel, one newspaper identified the club as "the leading colored organization of the state." Attucks clubs
were not limited to Boston or the East Coast. During the 1890s, Kansas City
had an Attucks Reading Club to promote the discussion of literary and social
topics, and the city also was one of the earliest to have a colored Attucks
School. Hopkinsville, Kentucky, also had an Attucks High School. The Los
Angeles Young Men's Afro-American League formed the Crispus Attucks
Light Guard, a marching club of "over one hundred members" that would
"take an active part in the coming [1904] Republican campaign." A number of other Attucks Clubs were involved with Republican Party politics. In
1908, the black Cleveland journalist and activist Harry C. Smith responded
with outrage to a report that his city's Attucks Club was endorsing William
Taft for the Republican nomination. "When Afro-Americans support Taft,"

Smith bristled, "they indorse [*sic*] disfranchisement and 'Jim Crow' cars in the South. . . . We are not foolish or crazy enough to do that." Smith suggested that the Attucks Club, along with "99 percent" of Ohio's 40,000 black voters, would back the state's own Senator Joseph B. Foraker, who was well known for his support of African American causes.[45]

Washington, DC's Crispus Attucks Relief Association was founded in 1903 "for the purpose of relieving the wants of each other in times of sickness, and to assist in the burial of our members when they die." The officers and members were said to include "the best element of colored citizens," and a ladies auxiliary was formed to expand upon the work of the men. Its first public social event was a "smoker" featuring food, drink, "good cigars," music, speeches, and toasts. The five hundred members in attendance showed it already to be "one of the strongest organizations in the city" only a month after its founding. Shortly afterward, Massachusetts congressman Samuel L. Powers presented the association with what was said to be "the first oil painting of Crispus Attucks, hero of the Boston massacre, reproduced from a photogravure" (see Fig. 4.4). The organization continued to do humanitarian work at least through the next decade, distributing "more than $1,200 in . . . sick and death benefits" in 1913, while maintaining a balance of $2,500 in reserve. After World War I the association expanded its mission to provide support for "officers and overseas men" who had returned from Europe.[46]

Community service, activist, social, and fraternal organizations, as well as businesses and schools, began adopting Attucks's name with greater frequency during the early twentieth century. In addition to its Attucks political club, Cleveland also fielded the Attucks Colts baseball team. New York's Gotham-Attucks Music Publishing Company placed its imprint on sheet music distributed to meet the huge demand for "coon songs," rags, and other racially themed musical forms, including compositions by Will Marion Cook and Bert Williams's biggest hit, "Nobody." Syracuse, New York, boasted the Crispus Attucks Lodge of the Grand United Order of Odd Fellows. The Springfield, Massachusetts, Crispus Attucks Lodge of the Knights of Pythias that had attended the Attucks monument unveiling in 1888 was still active, and Memphis, Tennessee's Pythians had an Attucks Lodge at least as early as 1916. In 1915, Ida B. Wells Barnett addressed the Joliet, Illinois, Crispus Attucks Club regarding an Arkansas racial violence case she had investigated recently. In St. Paul, Minnesota, local African Americans opened the Crispus Attucks Old Folks Home and Orphanage in 1906 and in 1913 were caring for twenty-two children and eight elderly adults. In 1917, six "elevator apartment buildings in upper Harlem" acquired for rental to over three hundred African

FIG. 4.4 This likeness of Crispus Attucks seems to be the foundation for the most commonly reproduced depictions of Attucks in the twentieth and twenty-first centuries. There is no clear evidence suggesting that this image might be the portrait presented to Washington, DC's Crispus Attucks Relief Association in 1904, though it seems to originate from the same time period. This exact image was reproduced in Baltimore's *Afro-American Ledger* newspaper on March 2, 1912, which is the earliest confirmed appearance the author has found. The date in the lower left of the image is not clearly legible but seems to resemble either 1908 or 1903. If 1903, it could have been the same image presented to the Relief Association. The image may also have been the model for various portraits of Attucks that were occasionally advertised for sale in early twentieth-century black newspapers. New York Public Library, Schomburg Center for Research in Black Culture, Photographs and Prints Division.

American families would each bear the names of historical "negroes of prominence," from Phillis Wheatley to Booker T. Washington; the first would "commemorate the memory of Crispus Attucks." And in 1919, Norfolk's black community could attend movies and performances at the brand new Attucks Theatre, whose curtain depicted the scene of the Boston Massacre (see Fig. 4.5).[47]

Other forms of commemoration also began to appear around this time. The Abyssinia Club of Greater Boston commissioned a "life sized marble

FIG. 4.5 Exterior of Attucks Theatre, Norfolk, Virginia. From *Norfolk's Thirty-Six Percent* (1927). Sargeant Memorial Collection, Norfolk Public Library.

bust of Crispus Attucks" which they planned to display and then "present . . . to the city with the request that it be placed in some suitable place." In 1915, Chicago's Douglas Specialties Company advertised a series of 11x14-inch, framed "Negro pictures of the highest quality" depicting race heroes, including Booker T. Washington, W. E. B. Du Bois, Frederick Douglass, Sojourner Truth, Crispus Attucks, and many others. Both Washington and Du Bois recognized Attucks's martyrdom in their respective books from this period, with Du Bois speculating that his possible presence among the "roistering band of rope walk hands whose rashness precipitated the Boston Massacre" linked Attucks—and hence "Negro workingmen" generally—with the roots of American organized labor.[48]

African American activists from Virginia appealed to Boston officials in 1907 to allow the Attucks monument to be shipped to Jamestown for the Negro exhibit at the tercentenary celebration of the establishment of the colony of Virginia. This raised questions about Attucks's racial identity in some quarters, with one prominent white Maryland educator insisting that "the colored people were wrong in erecting a monument to Attucks at the Jamestown Exposition for the reason that he was not a negro, but an Indian." Members of the black Odd Fellows lodge in Frostburg, Maryland, undertook an investigation of the question and turned up various sources supporting a range of positions, including one supporting the white professor's claim and another suggesting that Attucks was descended from "Natick Indians who had intermarried with negro slaves." Nonetheless, the Odd Fellows "still contend upon the authority of our own book that Attucks was a genuine Simon-pure negro." The book they consulted identifying Attucks as "a negro" was "Goodrich's History."[49]

America's involvement in military conflicts provided additional opportunities for Attucks to exemplify black patriotism and martial valor. In 1899, a "large reception" was given for members of the black Eighth Illinois Volunteers "in token of their services in Cuba." The white colonel addressing the troops extended the thanks of the nation and suggested that it was fitting that "the first man to die for liberty on the Western hemisphere was Crispus Attucks, a negro, and the last to die for it was John Coombs, a negro member of the Eighth, who died at Santiago."[50] When President William McKinley was shot at the 1901 Buffalo Pan-American Exposition, James "Big Jim" Parker, a black Exposition employee, wrestled the assassin to the ground. Cyrus Field Adams saw Parker's "heroic act" of bravery and patriotism, like that of Crispus Attucks, as proof that "the Afro-American . . . can be depended upon whenever the nation is in peril." The *Chicago Defender* conjured up the martial aspects of Attucks's memory in a somewhat different way, praising the black citizens of Jackson, Tennessee, after they "armed themselves with Winchesters and revolvers" to defend the home of a black man against a lynch mob, after the man had struck a white co-worker. These "members of the race were ready to sacrifice their lives, to do or die like the brave Crispus Attucks in the Revolution."[51]

Yet African Americans' long record of service to the nation had not led to their enjoyment of equal citizenship rights. The Baltimore *Afro-American Ledger* complained in 1912 about "the prejudice that has long existed against colored soldiers in the United States army." Conditions in the navy were "even worse." Fearful that an upcoming military conference would recommend "the elimination of the negro from the army," the reporter recalled "the valuable service [black troops] had rendered in the Civil and Spanish American Wars," as well as the War of 1812 and the Mexican war, and that "the first man to die in the Revolutionary War was Crispus Attucks, a colored soldier."[52]

Once the nation entered World War I, short pieces in the *Chicago Defender* publicized blacks' contributions to the war effort and illustrated the wide association of Attucks's name with such causes. Omaha, Nebraska's "Crispus Attucks auxiliary prepared one hundred Christmas boxes" for black troops at Camps Dix, Funston, and Dodge. The Crispus Attucks chapter of the Daughters of the American Flag was formed in Chicago to support one company of the African American Eighth Illinois Infantry Regiment. Philadelphia's "Crispus Attucks circle" sponsored a "great patriotic demonstration" in a local theater to raise funds for a military base hospital. And after the war, Washington, DC's "Crispus Attucks Relief Association and its women's auxiliary" offered support and comfort for returning troops.[53]

The participation of black troops during the war also raised the familiar debate over whether blacks should fight for a nation that denied them basic rights. Poet, statesman, novelist, activist, and journalist James Weldon Johnson used his "Views and Reviews" column in the *New York Age* to respond affirmatively to the rhetorical query, "Shall the Negro Fight?" Holding that "the Negro must continue to claim every right of American citizenship as his own, and always be ready to perform the corresponding duties," Johnson noted that "the first blood shed for America's Independence was by Crispus Attucks, a black man." A later column likened Attucks's sacrifice to that of black troops in the recent US incursion into Mexico by maintaining that "the Negro should not do anything to mar his splendid record from the Boston Massacre to the slaughter of Carrizal," a Mexican engagement in which black soldiers lost their lives.[54]

The debate surrounding black enlistment also reanimated many white Americans' presumptions that blacks were somehow lacking in courage, loyalty, or both. White journalist Herbert Kaufman, writing for the *New York American*, conveniently erased African Americans' Civil War service as he called for blacks to "do your duty" in the present conflict in payment to "the half a million white men . . . that died for your salvation" between 1861 and 1865. Black journalist Ralph W. Tyler was quick to supply Kaufman with a history lesson regarding the "one hundred and seventy thousand Negroes [who] donned the blue of the Union Army and offered their lives" as well as those "valiant hosts of blacks, who fought from Lexington down to Carrizal." Another writer noted that "the Negro has shown his loyalty and bravery from the time that Crispus Attucks fell a martyr on the Commons of Boston." "It shall never be said," Tyler asserted, "that any Americans rendered a better account of themselves and served the Stars and Stripes, whose folds do not protect us below where sweeps the Ohio, with a greater loyalty than the American Negro. We ARE doing our duty." It is worth noting that the same issue of the *New York Age* covered the NAACP's silent protest parade held in New York after deadly white attacks on the black community in East St. Louis, Illinois. One banner in the parade, held aloft by members of the women's section, read, "The First Blood for American Independence Was Shed by a Negro—Crispus Attucks" (see Fig. 4.6).[55]

As was the case after the Civil War, African Americans used Decoration or Memorial Day commemorations after World War I to "give honor to the fallen" black soldiers for their "valor and deeds" on the fields of Europe, often connecting the recent patriots with those from the past, including Attucks. In 1919, a piece in the *Chicago Defender* exalted "the memory of Attucks," along with other white and black notables, military or otherwise, who "contributed mightily to our advancement." Frederick Douglass, Nat Turner, Blanche

FIG. 4.6 Silent protest parade in New York City against the East St. Louis riots, 1917. Library of Congress.

K. Bruce, Booker Washington, Paul Lawrence Dunbar, and even whites like Garrison, Wendell Phillips, and Owen Lovejoy joined the martial ranks of the heroes of Fort Wagner and Carrizal, and the "boys of '98."[56]

As this list of black (and white) race heroes suggests, Crispus Attucks was not the only African American to be raised to a patriotic pantheon in the black press. Far from it. Black newspapers featured essays and promoted commemorations honoring Nat Turner, Frederick Douglass, Henry Highland Garnet, Toussaint Louverture, Harriet Tubman, and many others. As early as the 1880s, as blacks in Boston pushed for the Attucks monument, the African Methodist Episcopal (AME) Church, through its weekly newspaper the *Christian Recorder*, had mounted a sustained campaign to exalt the life and example of the denomination's founder and first bishop Richard Allen. The church published biographical essays on Allen, including a serialization of his memoir. It promoted the observance of February 14 as "Allen Day," a date for reflecting on their founder's life and his importance for the church and the race. In fact, Allen was held up not merely as an AME or race hero; like Attucks, he was constructed as a legitimate national hero, a black Founder of the Revolutionary generation.[57]

Crispus Attucks, however, played a special role, not merely because he was the first black hero but because he was the first to sacrifice his life for the American nation. Yet most white Americans either remained ignorant of Attucks's existence or rejected his legitimacy as an American hero and patriot. After showing some mild curiosity about Attucks in the 1870s, perhaps connected with the centennial anniversary of the massacre, Attucks faded from white memory and was excised from mainstream textbooks. During the mid-1880s, Boston's Attucks monument revived popular attention, but not all of that attention was positive. While the monument itself honored Attucks and surely expanded his name recognition and stature for some, it also opened the door to frank and unbridled criticism and even vilification. While the era's anxiety over mobs was a factor, Attucks's race unquestionably played a significant role in his denigration, as evidenced by the disparaging references to him as a disreputable half-breed. Fears of race mixing, black male violence, and the deluge of pseudoscientific and Social Darwinist treatises on the fixity of racial characteristics and race hierarchies raised serious concerns about Attucks's potential for heroic action and his status as an American hero.

The comparison to Mrs. O'Leary's cow suggests the ways in which many whites trivialized and even dehumanized his actions, implying that his role in the Boston Massacre was as conscious and intentional as that of a cow kicking a lantern. He was a drunken brute in the wrong place at the wrong time,

they felt. Even a relatively thoughtful and sympathetic assessment of the massacre mob published in 1900 by Samuel A. Green, in the *Proceedings of the
American Antiquarian Society*, rendered Attucks an unthinking participant.
He was "not a very useful member of society" and "but a bird of passage in the
town, who chanced to take part in the affray and was shot down in the street."
This "transient visitor" was "reckless in his conduct" and "itching for a fight."
His actions were not well considered but merely "the most natural thing in
the world" for a man "in his position" to do.[58] Even if the Boston Massacre
could be construed as an important and patriotic rallying point for colonial
resistance and independence, Attucks was at best an inadvertent hero. By the
early twentieth century, with few exceptions, whites tended largely to ignore
him altogether.

But African Americans would have none of that. The period from the 1880s
through World War I saw a steady acceleration of black attention to Attucks.
The 1888 monument was surely a high point, but it did not fundamentally
alter the overall trajectory of African Americans' commitment to honoring
a race hero and promoting his rightful place in the nation's pantheon. Race
histories, biographical essays, and school books were important and increasing in number, and the black press played a growing role in spreading the
word as newspapers in the early twentieth century became more widespread
and established, with a rapidly expanding readership. This was true across the
nation, but particularly in northern cities like Chicago and New York that
were magnets for the tremendous numbers of black southerners seeking new
freedoms and opportunities through the era's Great Migration.

The commemorative act of naming was perhaps the most notable development in popularizing Attucks during the early twentieth century. School
texts and historical works were crucial in bringing Attucks and black history
more generally into the understanding of black children and adults alike. But
the new flood of references in popular culture was at least as significant in
placing Attucks's name before the American public. With his name associated
with everything from apartment buildings, schools, mutual aid societies, and
political clubs to coon songs, theaters, and sports teams—not to mention the
grand public monument in Boston—Crispus Attucks became a household
name for unprecedented numbers of black Americans.

And as the naming of two generations of Crispus Attucks Palmers suggests, that name indeed became quite literally a member of more and more
households across the nation. Between the 1880s and 1920s, census, military,
and other vital records list Chrispus Attucks Jackson (born in Pennsylvania in
1887), Crispus Attucks Henderson (Louisiana 1889), Crispus Attucks Walker

(Georgia 1892), Ernest Attucks White (West Virginia 1894), Lowell Attucks Woods (Illinois 1892), Charles Attucks Aerie (New Jersey 1885), Roscoe Attucks Bowser (Massachusetts 1888), Crispus Attucks Wright (California 1914), and Attucks Agobert (Illinois 1915), among others.[59]

Several of these men served during World War I. As they and other black veterans returned from war after 1918, they entered an America whose racial environment had not improved since they shipped out. Their service to their country, like Attucks's a century and a half earlier, did little to affect their prospects in a world ruled by Jim Crow. But with a rush of migration to the cities of the North, an invigorated sense of race pride, and a growing unwillingness to acquiesce to the status quo, black America was changing. As W. E. B. Du Bois famously put it after African American soldiers returned from heroic service in the Great War, "We return from fighting. We return fighting. Make way for Democracy! We saved it in France, and by the Great Jehovah, we will save it in the United States of America, or know the reason why." Perhaps the poet Claude McKay had both the returning troops and Crispus Attucks in the back of his mind when he penned his unflinching 1919 poem, "If We Must Die":

> *If we must die—oh, let us nobly die,*
> *So that our precious blood may not be shed*
> *In vain; then even the monsters we defy*
> *Shall be constrained to honor us though dead!*
>
> *Oh, Kinsmen! We must meet the common foe;*
> *Though far outnumbered, let us still be brave,*
> *And for their thousand blows deal one death-blow!*
> *What though before us lies the open grave?*
> *Like men we'll face the murderous, cowardly pack,*
> *Pressed to the wall, dying, but—fighting back!*[60]

As the era of Jim Crow intersected with the era of the New Negro, McKay's words and Attucks's example helped provide an impetus for a newly empowered sense of race pride and race history.

5

Crispus Attucks Meets the New Negro

BLACK HISTORY AND BLACK HEROES BETWEEN
THE WORLD WARS

The tendency today is to ignore the Negro or else to belittle his part in the making of the nation.... Americans, white and black, should be proud of the Negroes who rendered valiant service in defense of the country from Crispus Attucks through the Great War, yet ... the name of Attucks has been submerged and few are the white children who know that this hero of the Revolution was a Negro.

NEW YORK AMSTERDAM NEWS (1923)

The New Negro
Breaks the icons of his detractors,
Wipes out the conspiracy of silence,
Speaks to his America.

MELVIN B. TOLSON (1939)

IN 1913, AS Crispus Attucks Palmer Jr. celebrated his first birthday, the Afro-Caribbean historian and bibliophile Arthur A. Schomburg issued an intellectual call to arms to include "Negro history" in American school and college curricula. "The white institutions have their chair of history," he observed, "and whenever the Negro is mentioned in the text-books it dwindles down to a footnote. The white scholar's mind and heart are fired because in the temple of learning he is told how on March 5, 1770, the Americans were able to beat the English; but to find Crispus Attucks it is necessary to go deep into special books." While Schomburg mildly distorted both the outcome of the Boston Massacre and its treatment in contemporary textbooks, his larger point was that the time was overdue "to teach the people our own history" in order to help African Americans "feel prouder of the achievements of our sires" and "give us the background for our futures."[1]

Schomburg's manifesto reflected the surge of race pride that typified the era of the New Negro, which accelerated further in the years after World War I. The Great Migration out of the rural South into cities swelled the black population of northern centers like Chicago and New York. In these northern cities especially, black educators, writers, visual artists, journalists, entrepreneurs, scholars, and political activists used multiple modes of expression and organization to advance their varied agendas. While New York's Harlem district was undoubtedly the most visible and vibrant center of activity, the New Negro Renaissance found ways of expressing itself all over the country. This was no organized movement but rather a diffuse set of ideas and leaders promoting racial consciousness, self-respect, and self-reliance through cultural expression and political activism among urban African American communities all over the country.

African Americans' concerns with promoting race pride and collective identity were also consistent with broader patterns that emerged more forcefully in the 1920s, which saw a cultural clash between white American nativists and traditionalists, and the increasingly visible and vocal ethnic minorities seeking to incorporate themselves into the American story. Millions of recent immigrants and their American-born children struggled with the process of "Americanization" as they strived to claim full acceptance as citizens in the face of considerable hostility. At the same time, the nearly two million African Americans migrating into northern cities embraced somewhat greater opportunity to pursue educational, economic, and political advancement. Leaders of both groups saw education as critical, and they wanted their groups' contributions infused into the curriculum. As one historian has observed, American history textbooks became key battlegrounds as minority representatives sought "to insert new heroes such as Crispus Attucks and Thaddeus Kosciusko" into America's master narrative.[2]

The decades after 1920 saw an expansion of both textual and nontextual attention to black history as well as increasing complaints from black commentators about the exclusion of that history from school curricula and public life. While mainstream textbooks failed to incorporate Attucks or African Americans in general, black authors attempting to replace or supplement the white narrative apparently were frustrated by how little was actually known about their purported first martyr of liberty.

For Crispus Attucks, the 1920s brought both increased attention and the continued fabrication of missing details of his life in books primarily targeted at school-aged readers. Even while acknowledging the scant documentation of Attucks's life, Elizabeth Ross Haynes, in *Unsung Heroes* (1921), repeated George Washington Williams and William Simmons's revelation that he "had been around Boston for some years and had listened to the fiery speeches of some of the orators of the day." She even included an illustration of Attucks on a raised platform giving a speech to a crowd of white Bostonians.[3] Bessie Landrum's *Stories of Black Folk for Little Folk* (1923) set out to "provide the youth with some facts of Negro history," but she offered speculation as well, at times borrowing language from Simmons and Williams. Attucks was "as bold as a knight," and after achieving his freedom, he "became a big-hearted, loyal American" and "the first Black martyr of the Revolution."[4] A few years later Arthur Huff Fauset admitted that "not much [was] known" about Attucks's early life, yet he attributed Attucks with being "too intelligent and too strong to be kept in slavery." Moreover, "he had that daring, courageous, almost reckless spirit that makes men die rather than not be free." Fauset's seven-page account speculated that after his 1750 escape, Attucks "very likely . . . followed the wide, rolling seas," though he also offered the bizarre speculation that Attucks may have "lived off somewhere in a cave and planned how some day he should help the world attain a larger portion of freedom." By early 1770, however, Fauset placed Attucks in Boston, "eager to offer his aid in the cause of Liberty." In fact, "people were attracted to him" as he delivered "fiery speeches" for freedom and exchanged ideas with "the people who thronged around him." Like Haynes, Fauset accompanied his text with the unlikely image of Attucks holding forth to a white audience (see Fig. 5.1).[5]

The pattern of accepting and repeating fabricated stories about Attucks—like those originating with Williams and Simmons in the 1880s—would continue to confound historical understanding into the twenty-first century. Notwithstanding the 1920s expansion of the unsubstantiated tales, the decade also saw a parallel expansion of legitimate scholarly research on the history of African Americans. Arthur A. Schomburg captured the new interest African Americans displayed for recovering and disseminating their history in his contribution to Alain Locke's collection, *The New Negro* (1925). In "The Negro Digs Up His Past," Schomburg echoed some of the themes he introduced in his 1913 essay. "The American Negro," he insisted, "must remake his past in order to make his future." It was a "prime social necessity" for the race to build a "group tradition" and "pride of race," and to think "more collectively, more retrospectively than the rest" of American society. Having said that, Schomburg also explicitly criticized biographical writings that provided "vindicating evidences of individual achievement" that he considered

FIG. 5.1 "Along Came Crispus Attucks," illustration from Arthur Huff Fauset, *For Freedom: A Biographical Story of the Negro* (1927). Photo: Western Michigan University Libraries Digitization Center.

"pathetically overcorrective, [and] ridiculously over-laudatory." While he did not mention any specific examples, some of the recent biographical sketches of Attucks clearly fit his criteria. Yet Schomburg understood the motivations of such writers, who, he said, recognized "the definite desire and determination to have a history, well documented, widely known at least within race circles, and administered as a stimulating and inspiring tradition for the coming generations." Schomburg called for the development of a "true historical sense" that was not based on "the petty braggadocio with which the effort for race history first started." He took heart in the recent emergence of a new cadre of trained academic professionals and serious amateurs who approached the race's past with a "truly scientific attitude" and who were investigating race history "not merely that we may not wrongfully be deprived of the spiritual nourishment of our cultural past, but also that the full story of human collaboration and interdependence may be told and realized."[6]

One of the most important contributors to the era's new vision of black historical study was Carter G. Woodson, who had earned a PhD in history from Harvard in 1912. Woodson founded the Association for the Study of Negro Life and History (ASNLH) in 1915 and, thanks to substantial funding from the Carnegie Foundation in 1920, the organization entered "a period of great growth and expansion" in its efforts to present the American public with "information to show what the Negro has thought and felt and done" throughout history. One of Woodson's most important scholarly contributions was his editing of the *Journal of Negro History*, a publication established in 1916 to present authoritative historical scholarship challenging the biased histories of the mainstream historical profession, which persisted in either ignoring or denigrating the role of African Americans in the nation's past. While the *Journal* did not feature any articles specifically investigating Attucks during its early decades, his name did appear in passing with some regularity.[7]

In 1926, Woodson used the ASNLH to spearhead one of the most enduring of the Association's public outreach programs—Negro History Week. For one week in February, selected to honor the birthdays of Abraham Lincoln (February 12) and Frederick Douglass (February 14), scholars, educators, ministers, and community leaders highlighted black historical accomplishments in speeches, pageants, parades, school programs, and community events. The idea became popular very quickly, and Woodson early on considered it "one of the most fortunate steps ever taken by the Association." He explained the dire need for Negro History Week to counter "the race hate of this age" and belie the widespread notion that "the Negro has never contributed anything to the progress of mankind." This "doctrine" of racial incompetence, Woodson claimed, "has been thoroughly drilled into the whites and the Negroes have learned well the lesson themselves; for many of them look upon other races as superior and accept the status of recognized inferiority." Woodson intended Negro History Week to underscore for both black and white Americans "the achievements of the Negro" in order to demonstrate that the race had been "a factor in early human progress and a maker of modern civilization." Several contemporary black leaders saw Negro History Week as "Woodson's most impressive achievement."[8]

Negro History Week remained a cornerstone of Association activities, eventually expanding during the 1970s to become Black History Month. From the outset, Crispus Attucks was frequently at the center of Negro History Week activities. This was especially true after the early 1930s. A 1929 questionnaire filled out by 497 black Virginia students ("two-thirds of whom are in the eighth and ninth grades") indicated that Attucks had a fairly high name recognition compared with other black historical figures, with 182 of the respondents claiming to "have a knowledge of [his] life and work." This placed Attucks among the top eleven of the twenty-three names listed, and fifth among those who had not lived during the twentieth century. Topping the list was contemporary singer Roland Hayes, followed closely by Booker T. Washington and Paul Lawrence Dunbar; among pre-twentieth-century figures, Attucks was preceded only by Frederick Douglass, Phillis Wheatley, Nat Turner, and Reconstruction-era South Carolina congressman Robert Brown Elliott. Attucks was better known than Sojourner Truth, Harriet Tubman, Denmark Vesey, Gabriel Prosser, Toussaint Louverture, and Richard Allen, as well as Matthew Henson, George Washington Carver, and several other twentieth-century figures. Within a few years, Attucks's name would reach an even broader audience, thanks to attention from both national and local commemorative activities.[9]

In 1932, Carter Woodson applauded both "the increasing interest in the study of the Negro" and the success and growth of Negro History Week. He also noted that the six-year-old February event had recently "received new stimulus from the protest of Negroes against the elimination of their achievements from ... the celebration of the George Washington Bicentennial." Washington's two hundredth birthday in 1932 prompted a host of local and national commemorative activities that exemplified the nation's recent revival of interest in celebrating its colonial and Revolutionary heritage. The period between the world wars was notable for Americans' accelerating interest in all sorts of nostalgic and commemorative attention to Americana, as evidenced by a colonial architectural revival, a surge in antique collecting, a boom in "see America" tourism, the creation of monuments like Mount Rushmore and the Lincoln Memorial as well as historical sites like Colonial Williamsburg and Henry Ford's Greenfield Village, and more. But the Washington Bicentennial stood out. Arrangements began with a congressional planning committee established in 1925 and, according to historian Michael Kammen, by the early 1930s the bicentennial generated "as much [popular appeal] as any celebration of its kind in U.S. history." In conjunction with the bicentennial, New York congressman and Bicentennial Commission chairman Sol Bloom saw to it that Gilbert Stuart's iconic portrait of Washington was placed in some 750,000 school classrooms.[10]

As the nation gloried in celebrating the "Father of His Country," Woodson wanted to ensure that African American Revolutionary patriots had their proper place in the festivities. But thanks to the "biased and unhistoric attitude of the politicians who directed the celebration," Woodson complained, Sol Bloom and the federally funded Bicentennial Commission "undertook to restrict the Negroes' participation to that of slaves." Woodson expressed his disappointment that some "thoughtless Negroes, not learned in history, were inclined to support this role without much protest." The ASNLH was not about to take this denigration lying down. Woodson approached commission chairman Bloom, "offer[ing] to cooperate with his commission . . . to emphasize the more commendable things about the Negroes of that day" and suggesting that both the ASNLH and the commission each contribute $5,000 for that purpose. "The Commission," Woodson reported, "manifested no interest, and nothing was done."[11]

Acknowledging that the commission had some historical rationale for its treatment of blacks, since "most Negroes of Washington's day were slaves," Woodson went on to point out that "most American white men of George Washington's day were serfs" who had little freedom and no political rights. He wondered sardonically whether "Sol Bloom's commission will try to dramatize this part played by a large element of whites at that time." In the name of fair play, Woodson called for some attention to "certain neglected characters" among the eighteenth-century black population—poet Phillis Wheatley, scientist Benjamin Banneker, religious leader Richard Allen, and others—who had not only "become free" but who "during Washington's time impressed their worth upon the public." But Woodson "invited attention especially to the martyrdom of Crispus Attucks, who in the Boston Massacre on March 5, 1770, shed the first blood in behalf of American independence." Woodson also mentioned Peter Salem, Salem Poor, and the thousands of other "Negroes [who] displayed unusual valor" during the Revolution. "To ignore those heroes who thus sacrificed their lives and dramatize the Negro as merely a servant or slave leading Washington's horse," Woodson fumed, "is a distortion of history and a reflection on the intelligence of our citizenry." Woodson commended black scholars like Benjamin Brawley and Charles Harris Wesley who spread this message through speeches and appearances during Negro History Week, and called attention to his personal mission, which took him in February 1932 on a nine-city tour from Buffalo, New York, to Lincoln, Nebraska, to Charleston, South Carolina, during which he spoke at public schools, community meetings, churches, and universities.[12]

Some black citizens, however, did not view Attucks quite as positively as Woodson. "One of these highly educated fellows" commented to Woodson that Attucks was "the first national fool produced in the United States" for having "sacrifice[d] his life for a country which held his people as slaves." Woodson took the opportunity to publicly defend Attucks and "to inform biased instructors of history and prejudiced directors of the George Washington Bicentennial that the record of Crispus Attucks is just as honorable as that of any man who has ever lived in America." After reviewing Attucks's credentials and justifying his patriotic sacrifice, Woodson noted with contempt that even when whites "feel that they cannot get rid of Crispus Attucks altogether and that he must be given some consideration in the history of this country," they tried to distort his racial identity. Woodson railed against what he called the "Bureau of Misinformation" supplied by a white syndicated journalist who had recently dug out the old objection that Attucks "was a white man of Indian blood. In other words," Woodson explained, "if this unusual character must be kept in history [whites must] Caucasianize him in some way or make him the hero of some other race, for it will never do to let it be said that he was a man of Negro blood." To underscore the point that Attucks was "distinctively a Negro," Woodson observed that "if living in this country today, he would be subjected to all the inconveniences and insults that people of this race now encounter."[13]

Woodson's energetic defense of Attucks is interesting, since in one of his earliest books, *The Negro in Our History* (1922), he identified Attucks merely as "one of the first four to shed blood in behalf of American liberty," without any further elaboration or detail. During the 1930s, however, Woodson found it necessary to promote Attucks as a distinguished American hero. One critic in 1937 mocked the race's pride in Attucks, saying "this hero was nothing but a roustabout." Woodson pointed out that many of the soldiers who proudly served with George Washington "came from the lowest ranks" of society. He even resorted to his own historical slurs by referring to Thomas Jefferson as "a poor uplander," Patrick Henry as "all but a ragamuffin failure," and Alexander Hamilton as "an illegitimate immigrant from the West Indies." Woodson was particularly miffed by black spokespersons who continued to question Attucks's credentials, blaming whites for their manipulations of history and blacks for their credulousness:

> The unfortunate and discouraging aspect of this effort to have the Negro forget his contributions to world progress is that it is accepted by a number of Negroes who are highly trained in what the traducers of the race would have them memorize but have not learned to think and do for themselves. They see the Negro as a misfit and a failure just as the enemies of the race would have them see the race.

Woodson urged blacks to give "all honor to Crispus Attucks. Venerate his memory. Dramatize the story to teach the youth patriotism. . . . To forget him would brand us with the sin of ingratitude. Crispus Attucks has his place among the great. No traducer can deprive him of his high rank among the immortals."[14]

Despite inspiring published accounts of Attucks's heroism and unprecedented interest in the black past through both scholarly publications and popular vehicles like Negro History Week, other black spokespersons joined Woodson in bemoaning the lack of interest African Americans had in their own history. The Pan-Africanist teacher and author Drusilla Dunjee Houston, in touting her own book on ancient Africa in the *Atlanta Daily World* in 1934, wondered why "the Negro will not accept Negro history." Houston did not understand why, with the growth of information about Negro history, so many were "apathetic." But she recognized that a "vast number of Negro teachers FEAR to teach Negro history—the fear of losing their jobs." Therefore it was up to black community institutions and especially parents to use these books, along with other resources, to disseminate information about black heroes.[15]

Three years later, Josephine T. Washington, a retired schoolteacher from Cleveland, expressed her "astonishment" at the "ignorance as to racial matters" she found among fellow blacks. Both adults and children "know little about their own race," including the names of Frederick Douglass, Benjamin Banneker, Crispus Attucks, and other heroes. "A course in negro history," she advised, "is a corrective greatly needed." She called for ministers, lecturers, teachers, and parents to use whatever materials they could, "despite the absence of what children call 'a history book,'" to impart, to the children especially, the "worthwhile facts in their racial history." But there were growing numbers of history books in print, and some African Americans praised segregated "colored" schools for providing the youth with a solid introduction to the race's history and heroes. In a debate over segregated schools in 1934, John H. Young III, president of Morehouse College, argued that "a Negro youth who has completed all of his education in a white (mixed) institution, is worthless along lines of race intelligence and leadership. . . . Ask this student . . . about Vesey, Banneker, Wheatley, Nat Turner, Attucks, and he will think you are speaking a foreign language."[16]

Many black commentators agreed that mainstream institutions systematically failed their black students in this regard. Addressing African American children in a 1935 editorial, the *New York Amsterdam News* recognized that "colored boys and girls" aspiring to heroism were denied role models of their own race. "What we are trying to say, children, is that most heroes you have read and heard about have been white men and women. . . . Those are the ones they tell you about in school, do they not?" Even if occasionally blacks were known for some accomplishment, school curricula as a whole ingrained the idea "that the standard heroes, the real ones, are white." In this environment, "it is easy for you to conclude that you belong to a second-rate race, and secretly regret that God did not make you white so that you, too, might be of the stuff from which real heroes are made." The editor expressed the hope that the race's children could recognize and move beyond such mental restrictions more easily than members of their parents' generation, who had been "deceived about the greatness of their own people when they were children and have never been able to see the greatness in colored men and women until the white man told them about it." The writer skillfully contrasted the white hero Patrick Henry's demand for liberty or death, with Attucks. "Does it not seem strange that these books [on the "heroes of the Revolution"] never mention Crispus Attucks, a colored man, who was the first to give his life in the Revolutionary War?" While Henry offered only rhetorical heroism, Attucks considered the choice between liberty and death and "chose to die for freedom." It was children's "duty" to exercise their critical thinking: to realize that "the white man" tends to idealize his own "as inspiration for future generations of whites." Since blacks had far fewer resources to do the same for their own race, black children had a responsibility to keep an eye open for black heroes and to "grow up to be proud of yourself and your race."[17] Several years later, African American

poet Melvin B. Tolson made a similar, if more lyrical, comparison between
Attucks and Henry:

> *Black Crispus Attucks taught*
> *Us how to die*
> *Before white Patrick Henry's bugle breath*
> *Uttered the vertical*
> *Transmitting cry:*
> *"Yea, give me liberty or give me death."*[18]

If the mainstream schools and textbooks gave insufficient attention to
Attucks and other race heroes, and black schools were limited in resources,
African American children and adults were educated about his heroism in
numerous less formal ways, including Negro History Week events, the efforts
of concerned parents, the black press, and black spokespersons. Even Marcus
Garvey—better known for his internationalist Pan-African agenda—lauded
"a black man by the name of Crispus Attucks, who on Boston Common shed
the first drop of blood for American independence," calling him "equally as
great" as George Washington. Columnist George S. Schuyler recalled that
during his early years around the turn of the century, his parents had introduced him to black history. He had "learned about Crispus Attucks, Toussaint
L'Ouverture, Hannibal, [and others], . . . and some of the part Negroes played
in the development of American civilization before I entered the first grade."
Surely many parents in the 1930s were doing the same. And by that time they
had additional resources, including the powerful voice of the black press.[19]

Black newspapers continued to expand their role in presenting the views
and aspirations of the race to the American public, including a strong advocacy for black history, through editorials, coverage of Negro History Week
activities, and individual stories on historical topics. One resource fueling
the black press's role as history educator was popular historian J. A. Rogers
and the history lessons he provided through his syndicated columns and car-
toons. The latter provided one-panel illustrations of black (or purportedly
black) heroes of history with a brief summary of their accomplishments (see
Fig. 5.2). Rogers's essays were thoughtful and well documented, and served as
a much needed corrective that was widely available to a broad black reading
audience. While Rogers was arguably the most popular and prolific historical essayist of the period, many others contributed historical pieces to the
black press. In May 1935, the *Chicago Defender* published a full-page essay
telling the story of Crispus Attucks and his heroism at the Boston Massacre.

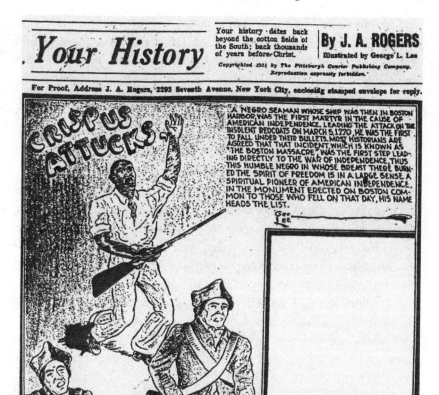

FIG. 5.2 J. A. Rogers, "Your History," illustration by George L. Lee, *Pittsburgh Courier*, May 16, 1936. Photo: Western Michigan University Libraries Digitization Center.

Arthur A. Schomburg authored a similar lengthy piece on Attucks a few months later for the *New York Amsterdam News*.[20]

African Americans themselves were the most ardent advocates for the study of black history and the promotion of heroes like Crispus Attucks. But during the interwar years their efforts occasionally had an impact on the broader society. During the same year Negro History Week was established during the mid-1920s, Crispus Attucks's reputation got a big boost in Boston, thanks largely to the efforts of black activist and journalist William Monroe Trotter. Trotter was a longtime Boston activist whose father had served in the 55th Massachusetts Volunteer Infantry during the Civil War and whose uncle, William H. DuPree, had chaired the Citizens Committee that organized the 1888 dedication ceremony for the city's Attucks monument. Trotter himself earned both bachelor's and master's degrees from Harvard during the 1890s and was the first African American inducted into that university's Phi Beta Kappa chapter. He devoted his life to racial causes and became notorious for butting heads with Booker T. Washington and several US presidents in his demand for the protection of African Americans' rights and opportunities. Through public demonstrations and his newspaper, the *Boston Guardian*, Trotter had established himself as one of the most radical of the era's black rights activists.[21]

In 1926, after several years of lobbying, Trotter and other Boston members of the National Equal Rights League (NERL) succeeded in their efforts to have the state of Massachusetts officially honor Crispus Attucks, some four decades after the dedication of the Attucks monument on Boston Common. In the year marking the sesquicentennial of the Declaration of Independence, Massachusetts governor Alvin T. Fuller "issued an official proclamation for Boston Massacre Day, [and] eulogizing Crispus Attucks." At the Faneuil Hall ceremony, the Reverend D. Leroy Ferguson delivered "a masterly Attucks oration in which he urged that March 5 be made a national holiday." Over the next several years Trotter and the NERL pressed for annual proclamations and exercises marking the day. These usually involved speeches, a procession from the site of the massacre to Faneuil Hall, and exercises at the martyrs' grave site.[22]

In the first formal proclamation honoring the date in 1926, Governor Fuller concocted a brand new story connecting Attucks with Boston's white patriot leadership, which William Trotter interpreted as a denial of Attucks's race and later refuted. "The beloved Paul Revere," Fuller began his moving narration,

> arriving too late to prevent the terrible tragedy, turned to his friend Crispus Attucks lying in the snow crimsoned by his life's blood and said: "Ah, Crispus, if only reason could have tamed that mad heart of thine. None truer ever beat. Freedom has lost an ardent friend this day. God grant that this blood has not been spilled in vain."

Whether or not he intended to imply that Attucks was white, Fuller clearly went a bit overboard in evoking the "stirring times" and the "inspiring lesson[s]" of the Revolutionary era, as he continued the tradition of exercising a very casual regard for historical accuracy when dealing with Crispus Attucks.[23]

Despite the governor's special attention to Attucks, it is significant that this first formal recognition of March 5 designated it Boston Massacre Day rather than Attucks Day, even though the governor and the ceremony paid little attention to the other massacre martyrs. Trotter and his allies contin-ued their push for a more specific official recognition of Crispus Attucks. In 1932, with Carter Woodson and other Attucks advocates up in arms over the martyr's omission from the George Washington Bicentennial, lobbying began for bills at both state and national levels declaring Attucks Day an offi-cial holiday. In Massachusetts, activists were "all astir" over the commission's slight, and their push for Attucks Day resulted in the holiday's being officially sanctioned by the state in 1933. In gearing up for the first official celebration and trying to spread national interest, a Boston correspondent to the *Chicago Defender* created yet another piece of inaccurate Attucks lore, with the claim that "General Washington oft cited [Attucks's death] to spur his troops to valor against the British."[24]

As the Massachusetts drive succeeded and the Attucks mythology expanded, two white Democratic politicians introduced bills in the House and Senate to make Crispus Attucks Day a national holiday. In the transfor-mational election year of 1932, Democrats saw an opportunity to draw black voters away from the Republican Party—the party of Lincoln—by calling attention to the failures of current Republicans to live up to Lincoln's legacy and touting their own concern with the well-being of their black constitu-ents. A joint resolution calling for the president to designate March 5 Crispus Attucks Day was introduced in the Senate by Massachusetts senator David I. Walsh, and in the House by Congressman Joseph A. Gavagan of New York. Gavagan used a mass rally a week before Election Day to remind his Harlem constituents that he had introduced both the Attucks Day bill and another that would compensate black North Pole explorer Matthew Henson. That both bills failed he hoped would not dampen voters' enthusiasm for support-ing his reelection.[25]

Upon William Monroe Trotter's death in 1934, the revival of Attucks Day was singled out as the most significant of the race leader's "recent accom-plishments." While the national holiday bill did not pass in Washington, the Massachusetts success and the attention generated by Negro History Week and public debate over black history in the schools was stimulating renewed interest in Attucks Day around the nation. Over the next several years Attucks Day celebrations were held not only in Boston but also in Chicago; New York; Berkeley, California; Washington, DC; Gary, Indiana; Springfield, Illinois; and Harrisburg, Pennsylvania, among other locales. Black barbers in Harlem, negotiating a new union labor contract in 1938, demanded "the recognition of Crispus Attucks Day as a workers' holiday." According to the barbers' spokesman, "all the other holidays specified in contracts between organized workingmen and their employers relate to individuals who were not working men." As a "sailor and ex-slave," Attucks exemplified "the contribution of the Negro in the struggle for economic and social liberty."[26]

On occasion, some African Americans would challenge Attucks's status as the race's greatest Revolutionary hero, as with the commentator, subsequently chastised by Carter Woodson, who had referred to Attucks as the "first national fool" for sacrificing his life for a slaveholding nation. In 1933, Joseph C. Coles advanced a similar sentiment and suggested a different sort of black hero who should supersede Attucks and most other well-known figures. Coles noted the many clubs and organizations named for Attucks as well as for other race heroes like Booker T. Washington, Frederick Douglass, Paul Laurence Dunbar, and Phillis Wheatley. Coles seemed to have no serious complaint with honoring those figures, but he was pleased the most by the existence of a "militant" Detroit organization "named in honor of Nat Turner, the great Negro revolutionist." For Coles, Turner was "the greatest figure in all American Negro history," since Turner, "unlike Attucks was a martyr for his own enslaved people" rather than for colonies that held "black brothers" in bondage. Yet even this critique of Attucks acknowledged his pervasive presence in the minds of African Americans and the speeches of "Negro orators."[27]

Along with all the other forms of attention he was receiving in the 1920s and 1930s, Crispus Attucks might have been surprised to see his name attached to organizations and institutions of amazing variety, from schools and churches to hotels and housing projects. In 1925, the Crispus Attucks Press Association purchased a house in Washington, DC, to serve as the office for black journalists from thirty-four newspapers.[28] Indianapolis's Crispus Attucks High School opened its doors in 1927, joining earlier Attucks schools in Kentucky and Missouri; by the end of the 1930s, Attucks schools welcomed African American students in Clayton, Missouri; Dania, Florida; Vinita and Oklamogee, Oklahoma; East St. Louis, Carbondale, and Colp, Illinois; Detroit, and other communities.[29] Need a place to stay in Philadelphia, Atlantic City, Baltimore, or Washington, DC? Each city boasted an Attucks Hotel. Those looking to settle down might consider the Attucks Court "low-cost housing project for Negroes" that opened in Pensacola, Florida, in 1940.[30] Black veterans in Grand Rapids, Michigan, and Pittsburgh and Philadelphia, Pennsylvania, honored Attucks's martial legacy with Crispus Attucks American Legion posts, while another post in Newark, New Jersey, boasted an Attucks Guard drill company. Columbus, Ohio, had a Crispus Attucks division of the Army-Navy Union veterans' organization

FIG. 5.3 "Photo of Band at [Crispus] Attucks [American Legion] Post [59] ca. 1940." Grand Rapids History & Special Collections, Archives, Grand Rapids Public Library, Grand Rapids, Michigan.

(see Fig. 5.3).[31] Those in the New York City area with fraternal affiliations might join the Attucks Masonic Lodge or the Attucks Lodge of the Order of the Eastern Star. Residents of Dawson, Georgia, could attend the Attucks African Methodist Episcopal Church. And for entertainment, Norfolk's Attucks Theatre was still going strong, featuring some of the most popular black entertainers of the era. One commentator praising the Norfolk venue in 1929 claimed that "most of the colored theatres in the country, incidentally, are named Attucks Theatre."[32] It seems that fewer parents after 1920 chose to honor the first martyr of liberty through the names of their children, though examples still can be found, including Crispus Attucks Chambliss (1925 Virginia) and Attucks Kelly (1921 Texas).[33]

One of the most active of all organizations bearing Attucks's name was Brooklyn's Crispus Attucks Community Council (CACC). Founded in 1933, the CACC was the only Negro organization affiliated with New York's Community Councils, Inc., and quickly took the lead in fighting for city services, civil rights, cultural development, and political empowerment for blacks in the Brooklyn area. The president and prime mover in the organization's early years was George E. Wibecan, a "prominent civic, political and fraternal leader" who was forced to retire from his position as foreman at the Brooklyn post office in 1933 after forty-six years of service. Wibecan's life was said to be "an active one of fighting for rights guaranteed the Negro." He was active in state Republican politics and well known for organizing numerous "meetings to protest injustices," which at times drew the ire of local officials and nearly cost him his job a few years earlier. He founded the CACC in May 1933 to serve as a "clearing house" for any issues facing Brooklyn's black community.[34]

The CACC pursued a cultural agenda by supporting a "movement to build a $1,000,000 Civic Center for Brooklyn's Negro population," lobbying to have a local playground named for Crispus Attucks, forming a junior league for local youths, sponsoring musical and dramatic programs, and hosting a monthly lecture series on historical topics. In one of its earliest events in 1933, Arthur A. Schomburg traced "the history of the Negro from his importation from Africa to the day when Crispus Attucks fell as the first martyr to American freedom." The same meeting featured several musical presentations; a reading of James Weldon Johnson's poem "Fifty Years," celebrating the semicentennial of emancipation; and a reading on the life of Toussaint Louverture. The next meeting featured a lecture on the life of John Brown. The CACC had such popularity and connections that Negro League baseball teams, featuring stars like Satchel Paige, Josh Gibson, and "Cool Papa" Bell, held fundraising games at Ebbets Field benefiting the organization in 1934 and 1935.[35]

Wibecam and the CACC, whose active leaders included numerous women, also pushed for the protection of blacks' civil and political rights. During one brief period in 1934 the group tackled numerous grievances on behalf of local blacks, including "the 'farming out' of a 16-year-old schoolgirl to a white family, the alleged railroading of a mother to the insane ward in King's County Hospital and the assaulting of another mother by a white policeman." The council supplied lawyers who successfully represented a black man who was "brutally assaulted" by police officers who arrested him after an altercation he had with a white man. The CACC joined the Brooklyn Urban League and the National Association for the Advancement of Colored People (NAACP) in protesting hotel housing discrimination when two black players from a visiting college football team were required to stay at a black YMCA when the team was in town to play Manhattan College. During the 1930s the council helped double black employment in local businesses and launched a campaign to prosecute a "white merchant" for the "sordid rape" of a young black girl. By the early 1940s the CACC had earned a reputation as a "militant civic organization" that would likely have pleased its namesake.[36]

The CACC also joined the increasing numbers of organizations and communities that sponsored Attucks Day celebrations during the 1930s, culminating in the designation of a special Crispus Attucks Day at the 1939 New York World's Fair. Attucks Day's appearance on that global stage likely benefited from the fact that CACC president George Wibecan had been named president general of the committee established to oversee the fair's "exhibit of the achievement of the Negro race in America."[37]

By the end of the decade, Attucks represented black citizenship and patriotism in a variety of other national venues. Blacks in Philadelphia participated in the city's "elaborate celebration" of the Constitution's Sesquicentennial by "presenting a drama of Crispus Attucks ... the first man to sacrifice his life for American freedom." When Boston hosted the national American Legion convention in 1940, black participants urged attendees to visit the Crispus Attucks monument, one of "the nation's most venerated shrines." In 1938, the *Chicago Defender* may have exaggerated a bit in saying that "we all know the story of Crispus Attucks," but the statement reflected the optimism that some African American leaders felt regarding the nation's inevitable acceptance of its black citizens. In an Independence Day essay that same year—recognizing that "the shadows of another World war loom[ed] with ominous significance"—veteran black journalist Nahum Daniel Brascher envisioned the emergence of a "new America" with a "new vision of economic opportunity and political justice" for all its citizens. The "deep thinking" Americans, black and white alike, who shared this vision, Brascher believed, all "know and pay tribute to the first blood shed for American freedom: Crispus Attucks, a black man."[38]

Many black activists wanted to see Attucks's renown expand further into white Americans' consciousness, and they suggested commemorative vehicles to spread his name and his image. As early as 1933 Postmaster General and Democratic Party leader James A. Farley was being lobbied to authorize a memorial postage stamp honoring Crispus Attucks. This was "the least that could be done for him," since written "histories have almost completely overlooked him." Columnist Cliff Mackay similarly observed that such a stamp was both important and necessary, since "white authors in recording the history books that are used as texts by American children conveniently forget to take note of the shining and glorious acts performed by black men in the building of a nation." In 1937, with recent stamps memorializing Robert E. Lee and Stonewall Jackson—"two rebel generals ... who once shot holes in the U.S. flag"—the *Chicago Defender* urged African Americans to "write Mr. Farley" to issue a stamp honoring either Attucks, Frederick Douglass, or Booker T. Washington. Thanks largely to the "tenaciousness and persistence" of Major Richard R. Wright Sr., a prominent black educator, banker, and Republican insider, Farley announced a Booker T. Washington stamp as part of the "Famous Americans" series in 1939. Wright had first issued his call for a stamp in 1933, preferring one "signalizing some great historical event, like the passage of the 13th amendment or the fall of Crispus Attucks at Boston Commons." The accommodationist Washington apparently proved more palatable for postal administrators, though Wright did eventually succeed in establishing both a stamp and an official national holiday celebrating the Thirteenth Amendment abolishing slavery. After the issuance of the Washington and Thirteenth Amendment stamps, black commentators continued to call for "two or three more stamps" recognizing the race. "The first one," argued journalist Roscoe Simmons, "ought to be one with Crispus Attucks on it."[39]

Though no Attucks stamp ever appeared, the call to expand Attucks Day continued to be sounded. In 1940, editor Roy Wilkins of the NAACP monthly, *The Crisis*, complained that African Americans' failure to celebrate important anniversaries and race heroes suggested that blacks had "absorbed completely the propaganda of white America that we do not amount to anything." Such events, he argued, "should mean so much to us and ... could be invaluable in educating our youngsters, to say nothing of educating white America." Crispus Attucks was foremost on his list of worthy black Americans to revere:

It took years of hammering before the story of Crispus Attucks was fairly well known, and yet there are today thousands of young Negroes and millions of whites who know nothing of Attucks. We should have been celebrating the death of Crispus Attucks on Boston Common generations ago. It would have impressed upon white America that we, too, had a share in building and dying for this country. Every white speaker invited to such a celebration, every notice in a daily newspaper would have helped uncover the truth that the histories have hidden so completely: that a black man was the first to die in the war for American independence.[40]

A year later, popular historian J. A. Rogers more pointedly called for the designation of the March 5 anniversary of Attucks's death as the most suitable date for a "National Negro Day." Rogers noted that for generations, African Americans had held celebrations on Emancipation Day but had been unable to "unite on a date" that was agreeable to all. Moreover, some argued that "the sooner the negro forgot about Emancipation, with its memories of slavery, the better." Rogers believed Attucks provided a symbol all blacks could rally around. He argued that "had [Attucks] been a white man, his name would have ranked next to George Washington in our histories. It is our duty to make it so."[41]

While an Attucks Day national holiday was not to be, the first martyr of liberty became ever more present in American public life between the World Wars. Nahum Daniel Brascher, "inspired by the martyrdom of Crispus Attucks," formed the Crispus Attucks Legion, "dedicated . . . to spreading the truth of this martyrdom," "telling the story of our founding fathers," and pursuing "fair play for all." During the 1930s, Crispus Attucks Political Clubs— both Democratic and Republican—were formed in Long Island, Harlem, Boston, Mt. Vernon, New York, and other cities. The Crispus Attucks News Service sponsored four black journalists' trip to cover the 1934 Chicago World's Fair. New Jersey artist Lorenzo Harris regularly used the NAACP's *Crisis* magazine to advertise his "suitable for framing" drawing of Attucks's martyrdom, which he said "should be in every home and school," and the Crispus Attucks Book Company ran its own ads in the race journal. Juvenile biographies continued to celebrate the exploits of Attucks and other race heroes, as with Evangeline Harris's 1940 *Stories for Little Tots*, which also featured "charming" illustrations by noted black artist Lois Maillou Jones. And Attucks remained omnipresent among the black heroes featured in pageants, plays, skits, or talks at local Negro History Week celebrations, like those in Colorado, New Orleans, California, and New York in the mid-1930s.[42]

As early as 1913 Attucks was featured theatrically in W. E. B. Du Bois's monumental pageant, *The Star of Ethiopia*, which celebrated the fiftieth anniversary of emancipation by chronicling the accomplishments of the race from the ancient Egyptians, through slavery and emancipation, and into the twentieth century. The elaborate and expensive three-hour spectacle, with its cast of hundreds, was presented in New York in 1913; Washington, DC, in 1915; Philadelphia in 1916; and Los Angeles in 1925. Du Bois hoped that the pageant would "teach . . . the colored people themselves the meaning of their history" while also introducing white Americans to the long history of black achievements, struggles, and contributions to the nation.[43] Much of Du Bois's pageant was designed to illustrate the distinctive glory of African cultures, but Attucks is used to establish the black contribution to the American nation and, indeed, to Western civilization. After identifying himself as "an Ethiopian," Attucks goes on to claim that "my blood was the first to flow for American freedom. When, on Boston Commons, the first blow was struck to break the chain of English tyranny, I fell as a martyr to the cause of civilization in the western world."[44]

Attucks also made appearances in other theatrical productions like Edward J. McCoo's 1924 pageant, *Ethiopia at the Bar of Justice*, and pioneering black playwright Willis Richardson's 1934 play, *Attucks, the Martyr*. Richardson also contributed to the further development of Attucks's invented personality and biography. The playwright, who as a youth experienced the racial terrorism of the Wilmington, North Carolina, pogrom of 1898, used theater to combat racial prejudice and build race pride. He is generally considered "the first proponent and practitioner of the black folk play, which challenged the white stereotypical portrayal of blacks." He firmly believed that black theater should be used as an educational tool "for the purpose of changing the opinion of the people." As with previous Attucks biographers, comments by Richardson's characters presented an Attucks who was "one of the boldest of rebels" and whose "intelligence . . . makes him [even] more dangerous." Attucks was also "fearless and inclined to leadership," a point proven by the admiring comments of his fellow martyrs. Portrayed as a group of patriots conspiring to provoke the British into firing on them, Caldwell, Gray, and Maverick were proud to follow "a man who carries himself as Crispus Attucks does, who is intelligent, brave, and born to leadership." When a fictional British officer threatens Caldwell in a shop, Attucks bursts onto the scene, declares himself a "desperate black man," and subdues the villain. Attucks explains to the loyalist shopkeeper that confronting British tyranny is the only patriotic course of action, and that "if reasoning fails, then the only way to get rid of these soldiers is to attack them. . . . I am here to risk my life or give it if necessary fighting against these invaders." The play ends with the death of Attucks and his fellows, and with vacillating townsmen like the shopkeeper seeing that Attucks was in the right.[45]

The new mass media of recordings, radio, and film also were put into service spreading Attucks's fame. In 1941, the Crispus Attucks Record Company was undertaking "a concerted effort to induce [clubs] catering to colored patrons and which have juke boxes to use their discs." A record album with a focus on heroic biography, *Cavalcade of the American Negro*, was produced in the same year by African American actress Mercedes Gilbert. It was to be distributed "to schools and colleges all over the country as a valuable aid in the teaching of Negro history." On Attucks Day in 1940, New York's WNYC featured a fifteen-minute radio spot with the city's assistant attorney general, Philip J. Jones, discussing the life of Crispus Attucks. The following year the station expanded its attention to black history with a thirteen-week series of half-hour biographical segments. In 1938, black columnist Al Moses praised the appearance of "Negro artists and performers" in a number of Hollywood films and suggested that blacks would "thrill a million times more to the dramatization and picturization of salient chapters of the lives" of black heroes like Frederick Douglass, Toussaint Louverture, Booker T. Washington, and, of course, Crispus Attucks. A year later, the Million Dollar Productions film studio "decided to produce a series of pictures built around actual facts of the Negro in history." Attucks was to be one of the biographical subjects, but there is no evidence that any films were made.[46]

Amid all these admiring images of the heroic black Founding Father, it still seems that Attucks was most frequently invoked when black leaders wanted to call attention to some injustice or denial of black citizenship rights. When white supremacist Mississippi senator Theodore G. Bilbo introduced a bill encouraging the "resettlement" of black Americans to Africa, blacks used the example of Attucks's and others' "sacrifices" of black "blood and bones" to suggest that "we are perhaps more an integral part of this civilization than is Senator Bilbo." Attucks was especially relevant in 1939, when the Daughters of the American Revolution (DAR) refused to allow black singer Marian Anderson to perform at the organization's Constitution Hall in Washington, DC. First Lady Eleanor Roosevelt was widely praised for resigning from the DAR in protest, and the organization was roundly condemned in the black press for its "discriminatory policy." One columnist noted that "Boston's patriots" had "welcomed Crispus Attucks to their ranks," and when he died "he did not fall as he would today on jim crow ground." He further observed that "many an ancestor of present-day members of the D.A.R. joined in tribute to black Crispus Attucks when his services were commemorated with a splendid monument on Boston's revered commons." The fact of Attucks's patriotism and heroism in the cause of the Revolutionary movement, wrote another, was "easily ignored if not forgotten" by the DAR members. Nahum Daniel Brascher commented with pride that "Crispus Attucks is being brought out of the archives of history and being given a high place on the pedestal of martyrdom of American history. Let the D.A.R. read and think."[47]

The occasion also provided the opportunity for yet another piece of Attucks misinformation to make its way before the public. The *Chicago Defender* passionately condemned Attucks's memory being "dishonored by [the] D.A.R." and its "prejudicial attitude." Blacks, the article maintained, had "proved our love for the flag" so that "we and our children have a heritage in America" based on loyalty and patriotism. But the writer went a step too far in saying that President John Adams had "eulogized" Crispus Attucks and praised his "glorious martyrdom." Displaying an increasingly typical lack of care in attributing comments about Attucks, the supposed Adams eulogy was actually an excerpt from George Washington Williams's 1883 *History of the Negro Race in America*. Misidentified quotes notwithstanding, the collective message of black critics was clear. Attucks was "the first martyr in the Boston Massacre whose death set aflame the spirit of the Revolutionary War." Yet "white America today 'honors' Attucks by jim-crowing his descendants, and disfranchising men of color." Another commentator summed up black America's disgust with the query, "What price patriotism?"[48]

With the era's intensifying global geopolitical crisis, that question became ever more pressing. As early as 1938, with many Americans anticipating "another war" on the horizon, one black journalist complained that African Americans were "tolerated, here and there," but for the most part the nation offered only "false allurements and promises." Both "Crispus Attucks, first to die for American liberty," and "the 500,000 black men who wore the uniform during the [First] World War" demonstrated that "we are for America." But in the "inevitable" world conflict to come, "black men cannot be expected to bare their breasts to shot and shell, unless, and until, the mighty forces of our great land deal with us in the spirit of truth and justice."[49]

The status of blacks in the military was particularly dismaying as the nation anticipated sending American soldiers into harm's way. As Hitler's armies claimed control over Europe, African Americans recognized the bitter irony of white America's continued disregard for black citizenship rights, even as most deplored the Nazi's "total war . . . to enthrone Racism and deny the fundamental human freedoms." Segregation in the American armed forces was especially galling, given "the loyalty and patriotism of the Negro throughout our history . . . from Crispus Attucks—the first American to be killed in our War for Independence—down to the present hour." Countless commentators in the black press echoed these sentiments between 1939 and 1941, with few failing to emphasize that "a Negro, Crispus Attucks, was the first one to give his blood for [the] freedom of this country." In the present crisis, blacks insisted, as "the Government is going to loosen its purse strings to build up the armed forces of the nation it is time that it scuttled its hateful policy of discrimination against citizens because of the color of their skin and permit Negroes to enlist in all branches of the service" in integrated units.[50]

Between the end of the First World War and America's entry into the Second, a "New Negro" had emerged as a cultural and political force. Organizations like the NAACP, Marcus Garvey's Universal Negro Improvement Association, the National Association of Colored Women, the National Negro Congress, and others challenged racial injustices in print, in the courts, in the halls of Congress, and in the streets. Novelists, poets, visual artists, and performers using the unprecedented reach of an expanding black press and the new mass media helped shape modern America's burgeoning popular culture. Carter Woodson's Association for the Study of Negro Life and History spearheaded a broad intellectual engagement with black history that infused the public media and innumerable schools with vital information about the integral role African Americans had played in the nation's past.

Crispus Attucks was hardly alone among the black heroes whose deeds were being lauded in black newspapers, books, and schools. Frederick Douglass, Phillis Wheatley, Booker T. Washington, Paul Laurence Dunbar, Toussaint Louverture, and others were widely praised and commemorated through the naming of schools and organizations. But Attucks's role continued to be a special one. In African Americans' eyes, he was the first black American hero. He was the first—black or white—to give his life in the cause of American freedom and independence. And his name deserved, above all others, to be honored by all Americans through textbooks, memorial stamps, monuments, holidays, and other commemorations. Yet despite Attucks's seemingly pervasive presence, in March 1941 *Chicago Defender* columnist Lucius C. Harper could still refer to Attucks as "the most neglected martyr in history." As the nation entered World War II, the legacy of Crispus Attucks would take on even greater meaning as modern black patriots prepared to make their own sacrifices to preserve American freedom.[51]

6

Crispus Attucks Meets Dorie Miller

BLACK PATRIOTISM AND ACTIVISM IN
THE WORLD WAR II ERA

Stop a soldier and ask him, "what are you fighting for?"
. . . If he is a Negro Soldier walking the Boston Commons
. . . the vision of Big Burley Magnificent Crispus Attucks,
a Negro,—the first American to shed his blood for freedom
. . . will float up in his soul and he'll look to see if you can
feel it—for that freedom is what he's fighting for.

C. LEROY HACKER, Chaplain, 366th Infantry
Atlanta Daily World (October 17, 1942)

There is no doubt about Negro Americans fighting Russia
or any other enemy who threatens our country. We'll not
even argue on that point. History speaks for itself from the
day Crispus Attucks fell at Boston until Dorie Miller lost
his life in World War II.

ARTHUR MOORE
New York Amsterdam News (August 6, 1949)

EVEN BEFORE THE Japanese attack at Pearl Harbor on December 7, 1941,
drew the United States fully into the new world war, African Americans
expressed concern about the meaning the global crisis would hold for black
citizens and soldiers. Blacks in the armed forces faced ill-treatment, segregation, and limited opportunities. In 1940, a black journalist acknowledged
the government's recent decision to "loosen its purse strings to build up the
armed forces of the nation" and called for an immediate end to the "hateful
policy of discrimination against citizens because of the color of their skin."[1]
This policy was especially poignant given that the military expansion was primarily directed toward confronting the threat of a "Nazi holocaust" which

amounted to a "total war to destroy democracy . . . to enthrone Racism and deny the fundamental human freedoms." To continue the "age-old pattern of anti-Negro prejudice," one commentator urged, "would endanger national unity" and "seriously impair the international influence and prestige of American democracy."[2]

Attention to the status of black men in the military expanded in 1941 after several violent clashes between black soldiers and white military police at Fort Bragg and Camp Davis, both in North Carolina. A *Chicago Defender* reporter spoke for much of the black community in blaming the army for allowing a hostile racial climate to develop throughout the military. The "resentment of colored soldiers to being bullied and assaulted while wearing their country's uniform" should have led any thoughtful observer to be "anticipating race trouble."[3]

One example of the government's response to the escalating racial tensions in the military was a radio address by Undersecretary Robert B. Patterson of the War Department and an accompanying "skit" drama-tizing black contributions during and after World War I. According to black columnist Frank D. Griffin, the skit "was supposed to be 'funny,' but instead it was insulting," incorporating the most demeaning black dialect and depicting black servicemen as uneducated, lazy, and essentially lucky to have the opportunity to serve in a Jim Crow military. Griffin called the August 26, 1941, broadcast a "slimy slander" which did little justice to "the honorable history of the American Negro from the day Crispus Attucks fell in Boston." "Negro Americans," he asserted, "hate Hitlerism and oppres-sion wherever it may be found" and "no people in the world . . . stand more fully behind the President's program of all-out-aid" to its European allies. Implicitly linking the bigotry of Nazi Germany with that of the Jim Crow United States, Griffin urged that only the nation's true commitment to "Freedom and Equality" would produce "the kind of morale that will stop Hitler, [Georgia] Governor [Eugene] Talmadge and the forces of oppression now."[4]

A. Philip Randolph, president of the Brotherhood of Sleeping Car Porters and arguably the nation's most influential black leader, used a more force-ful tactic than editorializing to challenge African Americans' marginaliza-tion within the defense buildup. In May 1941, Randolph proposed "that ten thousand Negroes MARCH ON WASHINGTON," pressuring the govern-ment to give blacks equal access to "jobs in National Defense" as well as "the integration of Negroes in the armed forces." While Roosevelt refused to act on the latter demand, he did issue Executive Order 8802, which created the

Fair Employment Practices Commission (FEPC) to oversee defense industries and, in theory, ensure that they end racial discrimination in hiring. This
modest step forward was not sufficient to mollify blacks' demands for equal
treatment. Barely two months after the United States entered the war, the
Pittsburgh Courier newspaper initiated its "double V" campaign, calling
for "a double victory for colored Americans": victory over blacks' "enemies
at home" as well as "our enemies on battlefields abroad." Black newspapers,
organizations, and individuals around the country rallied behind the double-
V slogan and made it clear that patriotic African Americans risking their lives
in yet another American war would accept nothing less than full and equal
citizenship rights in return.[5]

Such actions caused considerable anxiety for Franklin Roosevelt and
government officials who were enormously concerned with maintaining and projecting national unity in what was shaping up as a massive two
front war in Europe and Asia. The narrowly averted March on Washington,
the double-V campaign, and steady criticism in the black press caused the
newly created Office of War Information (OWI) to search for ways to boost
African Americans' morale. Theodore Berry, an African American lawyer
and NAACP leader from Ohio who served as liaison officer for the OWI,
identified "parades, rallies, glorified heroes, posters, radio and motion picture
appeals" as some of the OWI's tools to "stimulate and arouse patriotic fervor," "eliminate divisive interests and unite all people in the prosecution of the
war." Yet there were limits to how far the OWI would go to appease disqui-
eted blacks. Both Berry and William H. Hastie—former governor of the US
Virgin Islands, former Howard University Law School dean, and civilian aide
for Negro Affairs in the War Department—eventually resigned their respective posts out of frustration with the inadequate attention given to African
American concerns.[6]

Despite such frustrations, many African Americans embraced the propaganda opportunity provided by the war. As historian Scot French has
observed, their efforts in promoting black heroism were effectively restricted
to a certain type of African American hero who could prove viable for the
broader society during the war years. Black freedom fighters like Nat Turner
and Denmark Vesey had been a significant part of African Americans' reclamation of history and promotion of race pride over the preceding two decades.
But in the 1940s, French points out, "African Americans saw far more to be
gained by stressing their wartime patriotism, symbolized by the contributions of black defense workers and more than a million black soldiers, than by
invoking the insurgent spirit of the rebellious slave."[7] Historian Bell I. Wiley's

1938 review of Benjamin Brawley's book, *Negro Builders and Heroes*, supports this point. While he found Brawley's biographical sketches of "Revolutionary martyr Crispus Attucks" and other black literary and historical figures to be "impressive," Wiley condemned Brawley's inclusion of "such pillaging and murdering insurrectionists as Cato and Turner, such murder-bent characters as Gabriel and Vesey."[8] As black spokespersons looked back through the race's long history of military service, Crispus Attucks seemed an ideal candidate to place alongside the black heroes of the present.

After the outbreak of hostilities, Americans did not have to wait long before being introduced to contemporary black heroes and patriots. African Americans' wartime sacrifices for the nation may have begun before those of any other Americans, when a young black man from Birmingham, Alabama, was reported to be "the first member of the nation's armed forces killed in action during Japan's sneak attack on Pearl Harbor." With that sacrifice, twenty-one-year-old naval mess attendant Julius Ellsberry "became to Birmingham what Crispus Attucks is to the nation." The news report speculated that, after having already served for two full years, young Ellsberry might have risen higher than mess attendant first class, "but in the U.S. Navy colored boys can only go so high." Still, the reporter noted, "no man[,] not even an Admiral[,] can give more to his country than his life."[9]

Upon learning that the first casualty among United States forces in the Philippines was also a Negro, Chief of the Armored Forces Major General Jacob L. Devers did not deviate from his plan to name the main parade ground at Fort Knox, Kentucky, "in memory of this colored soldier." Devers quietly ignored the continuing segregation of the armed forces and the pervasive discrimination faced by black military men and women when he expressed the idealistic sentiment that "in this, the greatest democracy the world has known, neither riches nor poverty, neither creed nor race draws a line of demarcation in this hour of national crisis." The December 23, 1941, dedication of Brooks Field paid homage to Robert H. Brooks, "the son of Negro sharecroppers, [who] was the United States Armored Forces' first casualty" when he was killed at Clark Airfield, outside Manila, on December 8, 1941. In reporting on the dedication, *Chicago Defender* editor Lucius C. Harper emphasized that the present circumstances mirrored the American Revolution, in which "a Negro was first to shed blood in his country's cause." Harper echoed numerous black commentators in recognizing that from Crispus Attucks, through the War of 1812, the Civil War, the Spanish-American War, America's border conflict with Pancho Villa, and World War I, "the Negro soldier" had consistently risked all in "a battle to free others; a struggle for his own emancipation;

a fight for suffrage; a campaign for political patronage and prestige, and a challenge for true and real freedom." As he pondered "what will the harvest be" for this latest African American patriot martyr, Harper hoped that "it should settle at least the question of his place and his status as a citizen in this great American commonwealth."[10]

In February 1942, columnist Cliff Mackay complained that the American media still was failing to recognize African Americans' contributions to the war effort, but he noted that, "no doubt, through error, one fact was allowed to seep through the report on the Pearl Harbor attack."[11] One young man mentioned in the report, another son of Negro sharecroppers, became the most well-known African American hero of the war, though his name was not reported in the initial press release. The story involved "a Negro mess attendant who never before had fired a gun [who] manned a machine gun on the bridge until his ammunition was exhausted." In what was almost surely an unplanned coincidence, the US Navy finally revealed the serviceman's name on March 5, 1942—Attucks Day. If the black press did not appear to notice the date, they wasted no time connecting the new war hero, Mess Attendant Second Class Doris "Dorie" Miller, with that other heroic seafaring black patriot, Crispus Attucks. The *Pittsburgh Courier* praised the twenty-two-year-old Texas farmboy who "carried on at Pearl Harbor in the great tradition of Crispus Attucks ... and a host of other Negro warriors who had fought America's battles since the Revolutionary War." Miller's "fighting instinct and ... burning patriotism" established his place as "a real sailor, an American fighting man," and "a reincarnation of those Negro heroes of other years."[12] Miller's name remained in the black press's headlines, as African American leaders made him a larger than life symbol not only of black courage and patriotism but also of the military's unequal and unjust treatment of black servicemen and women.[13]

Miller's sudden fame awakened white political and military leaders to his symbolic potential as they charted a course through the nation's volatile racial tensions in a time of war. Two white Democrats—New York Senator James M. Mead and Michigan Congressman John W. Dingell—introduced parallel "bills in the Senate and House to secure the Congressional Medal of Honor for the Texas boy." While that honor eluded Miller, President Roosevelt took the unusual step of personally approving him for the highest naval honor, the Navy Cross. Shortly thereafter Miller was promoted to Mess Attendant, First Class—far short of his admirers' calls for officer training.[14]

Shortly before Miller received the Navy Cross, an aide to Assistant Secretary of the Navy Ralph Bard commented that Miller was "probably replacing [black heavyweight boxing champion] Joe Louis" as African Americans' most noteworthy hero and suggested that the military might exploit his "example of courageous fighting . . . [to] direct the emotions of thirteen million Negroes into the right channel and contribute to general unity." Miller was given leave to make public appearances, pose for photographs, and sign autographs; while he was at sea his mother made numerous public appearances in his stead. Sadly, Miller's status as a patriotic martyr was secured when his new ship, the USS *Liscome Bay*, was torpedoed in November 1943. Doris "Dorie" Miller was reported lost at sea and officially presumed dead in November 1944.[15]

From the moment his actions at Pearl Harbor made the news—and much like Crispus Attucks—myths about Miller competed with facts. College textbooks on African American history continue to repeat undocumented and fabricated information about Miller in the early twenty-first century.[16] Black writers insisted that he had been "forbidden to touch" the machine gun he manned that day, and that he had shot down numerous Japanese aircraft— some claiming as many as sixteen. Indeed, Miller was not trained on the gun, but other black messmen were. All messmen had specified battle stations which they were to man in the event of attack, but Miller's assignment on the USS *West Virginia* seems to have been supplying ammunition to the ship's anti-aircraft battery. Also, there is no unequivocal evidence that he shot down a single Japanese plane, though Miller himself was quoted at different times claiming that he had shot down either two or four. Most accounts even got his ship's name wrong, erroneously placing him on the most famous of Pearl Harbor's losses, the *Arizona*.[17]

Such exaggerations and distortions aside, Miller undoubtedly acted with courage and honor under enormously stressful conditions. After finding his battle station inoperative, Miller joined other enlisted men and officers topside, helping to move his mortally wounded captain to a safer position, then firing a fifty-caliber machine gun from the burning deck in the face of enemy strafing and bombing until his ammunition ran out and the order to abandon ship was given. Miller was one of only two enlisted men mentioned by name in the commanding officer's report for "unquestionably saving the lives of a number of people who might otherwise have been lost." Still, neither Miller nor any of the others involved were recommended for any commendation by the commanding officer. They were all doing their duty.[18]

Dorie Miller paralleled several key aspects of Crispus Attucks's story. Both men were physically imposing, with Miller being recorded as six feet, three inches tall and 225 pounds. Both men took to the sea and won fame by demonstrating courage in the face of enemy fire. One could say that both sacrificed their lives in the service of their country, but in Attucks's case that claim might venture more into the realm of myth. Yet the growth of myths, legends, and misinformation surrounding each man's life and exploits is itself significant. Black Americans, as well as some whites who were sympathetic to the race's struggles for equity and justice, made both Miller and Attucks poignant symbols of African Americans' patriotism, citizenship, and sacrifice.[19]

The construction of black American heroes during the World War II era was not limited to seafaring martyrs. Another powerful dark symbol of that time wore an army uniform but never saw actual combat duty. Ever since his 1938 rematch knockout of German Max Schmeling, heavyweight boxing champ Joe Louis was a truly national hero. Thanks to his carefully crafted soft-spoken and clean cut image as much as his pugilistic prowess, Louis was admired and lauded by blacks and whites alike. After Pearl Harbor Louis risked his title in a highly publicized charity bout for the Navy Relief Society, famously forgoing his paycheck with the comment, "Ain't fighting for nothing, I'm fighting for my country." On January 9, 1942, Louis easily defeated Buddy Baer, donated his $100,000 purse to the Navy Relief Society, and two days later enlisted in the US Army. After enduring the standard thirteen-week training, apparently with no special treatment, Louis declined a lieutenant's commission, instead entering service as a private assigned to the Morale Branch.[20]

Given these impeccably selfless and patriotic gestures, the War Department chose wisely in making Louis a centerpiece of their efforts to boost black morale and support for the war. According to one internal War Department memo, "To the rank and file of colored people he appears almost as a god. The possibilities for using him are almost unlimited." He was aptly described as a "tremendous propaganda asset." Louis's image appeared on posters and in pamphlets; he was a guest on radio programs; and he held boxing exhibitions and made appearances at American army camps across the United States and Europe. His victory over Schmeling was also featured in the 1944 propaganda film *The Negro Soldier*. While Louis made some behind the scenes efforts to confront discriminatory racial practices in the military, in the public's general perception he remained a humble symbol of racial harmony and black patriotism. In September 1945, he was awarded the Legion of Merit, solidifying his iconic status as a model American.[21]

While the attention heaped on Joe Louis and Dorie Miller stands out, the War Department also used the era's explosion in mass media in other ways to promote national unity, racial goodwill, and black morale. Radio and motion pictures were particularly powerful media that by 1940 were playing unprecedented roles in people's everyday lives. The majority of black and white Americans were steadily becoming part of a truly national media audience in which all had access to largely the same radio programming and the same films, making these media critical tools for the Office of War Information.[22]

In 1944, L. D. Reddick, African American historian, university professor, and curator of the New York Public Library's Schomburg Collection of Negro Literature, assessed the power of radio, motion pictures, and other media in "determining public attitudes" about race relations. According to Reddick, "traditional forms of 'education'" were "incapable of any major influence on the public mind." "If the main task of the educative process is the transmission of the culture of the society," he argued, "then the great educational agencies of the United States are not its schools and colleges; rather, its movie houses, newspapers and magazines, its radio broadcasting stations and its public libraries." Reddick feared that proponents of "the propaganda of race hatred" had successfully "appropriated the latest and most effective means of disseminating their message." He saw movies as the worst offenders in proliferating "anti-Negro" images. The historical blockbusters *Birth of a Nation* (1915) and *Gone with the Wind* (1939) were singled out as especially egregious, but even less overtly racial films regularly relegated blacks to insulting and stereotypical roles emphasizing "ignorance, superstition, fear, servility, laziness, clumsiness, petty thievery, untruthfulness, credulity, immorality or irresponsibility [and] a predilection for eating fried chicken and sliced watermelon," while generally eschewing "roles of heroism, courage and dignity." Demeaning stereotypes existed on radio as well, in popular programs like *Amos 'n' Andy*, *Molasses and January*, and *Aunt Jemima*. But Reddick noted that the scripts of *Amos 'n' Andy* had improved in recent years, and he found in radio considerable positive presentations of blacks in religious and musical and especially in the "outstanding" educational and cultural programs that had begun to appear around 1940.[23]

Especially after the establishment of the Armed Forces Radio Service (AFRS) in May 1942, the government made explicit efforts to increase the presence of black voices and black military contributions on the nation's airwaves. Perhaps the most popular radio show produced by the AFRS was *Jubilee*, a variety show featuring black musicians, singers, comics, and actors including Lena Horne, Duke Ellington, Eddie "Rochester" Anderson, Butterfly McQueen, and many others. While *Jubilee* offered uncontroversial entertainment rather than overt racial commentary, it did help establish

African Americans as a central part of American culture while reminding listeners of black troops' presence on the front lines in Europe and Asia.[24]

African Americans were often more explicit in using their limited access to radio broadcasts to challenge Jim Crow and highlight blacks' achievements and patriotism. Even before the United States entered the war, in May 1941, New York's WNYC began airing half-hour radio dramas "tracing [the] life and achievements of great Negroes who have made contributions to American culture." The thirteen-week *Native Sons* series differed from comparable programs during the war in that producers apparently felt no pressure to avoid controversial subjects like "Nat Turner (insurrectionist)" and "Denmark Vesey (slave rebel)." But the majority of individuals were less threatening notables like "statesman" Frederick Douglass, "woman liberator" Harriet Tubman, "inventor-mathematician" Benjamin Banneker, "scientist" George Washington Carver, and of course the "soldier" and "Revolutionary War hero" Crispus Attucks, who made his appearance on June 14.[25]

The *Native Sons* scripts, written by "Negro authors" Kirk Lord and Frank D. Griffin, provided fictionalized accounts of the lives of these "little known Negroes." The script for "Crispus Attucks: The First American Martyr," illustrates the authors' blending of historical research, mythology, and presentist propaganda to construct their narratives. Lord and Griffin's treatment repeated much of the by now standard fabrications and conjectures about Attucks's life. Attucks was presented as a favored slave, "well liked in Framingham," who still escaped bondage because, as the fictional Attucks put it, "if a man's a man he's got to be free." After fifteen years on a whaler, Attucks resided in Boston where he "devoted all his free time ashore to agitating for liberty and independence." Well before the Boston Massacre, Attucks was depicted as a close associate of fellow massacre martyrs Samuel Gray, Samuel Maverick, and Patrick Carr, with whom he "formed freedom clubs to combat the tyranny of the Prussian tyrant." Shortly before March 5, 1770, the authors had Gray, Carr, and Attucks assaulted by British troops, yet charged with "rioting" and taken before the magistrate, who chastised Attucks: "What has a black rascal like you to do with white men's quarrels?" Attucks responded with characteristic eloquence. "Liberty is the mother of all races and she does not deny herself to any. . . . When right is stricken the white and black are counted as one, not two. My blood is red like any man's. . . . Is tyranny white? Do the farmers and citizens under the yoke of a hessian despot suffer more than I, because of the fairness of their skins?" After their release the patriot "heroes of the day" headed for a "spontaneous protest meeting of the freedom clubs," where all clamored for Attucks to speak. He responded with a close

paraphrase of the 1773 John Adams diary entry warning that the governor—
"the king's agent here"—"will hear from us further hereafter." The events of
the massacre itself are even more grossly distorted as a vengeful confrontation
between Attucks and the same soldiers with whom he had tussled earlier. The
program closes with Attucks's voice from beyond the grave reiterating his earlier plea for the unity of races behind the banner of liberty: "Before our God
we are equals, and have fought for freedom until the blood in our veins grows
cold in death."[26]

The authors' characterization of George III as a "hessian despot" and a
"Prussian tyrant" who was not acting in accord with English principles
deflected blame from the British—who were now America's allies—and
reflected the growing American antipathy to Hitler's aggressive expansion-
ism in 1941. The comfortably biracial patriot "freedom clubs" and Attucks's
adamant call for American unity were very much in line with the Roosevelt
administration's efforts to promote national unity across race lines as the
nation inched ever closer toward direct military involvement in the global
conflict.

As the war wound down in early 1945, the Philadelphia Fellowship
Commission (PFC) launched the weekly radio drama series, *Within Our
Gates*, to "promote racial, religious and nationality understanding" in the
United States. The PFC had been founded in 1941 as a coalition of several
human rights organizations that eventually included the Philadelphia Anti-
Defamation League, the Race Relations department of the Philadelphia
Federation of Churches, the NAACP, and others. In addition to fighting
racial, ethnic, and religious discrimination in jobs, housing, and education,
the PFC in 1945 took to the airwaves on Philadelphia's WFIL with thirty-
minute biographical profiles of Americans representing the diversity of the
nation's peoples. One of its first productions, airing on February 11, 1945, was
"Crispus Attucks: First American Casualty."[27]

At a time when casualties in the current war were affecting thousands of
American families, the title of Attucks's story was sure to capture listeners'
attention and pull at their heartstrings. The episode was described explicitly
as a "radio play glorifying the heroism and participation of Negroes in every
war for democracy of our country." It pursued this mission with little regard
for historical accuracy. Unlike most Attucks tales, this one suggested that
Attucks was a troublemaker from childhood. Upon learning that Crispus had
run away, Deacon Brown's response was, "I might have known. I've had trouble with Crispus ever since he was born." Attucks was always arguing with
Brown about his sermons and reading too many inflammatory pamphlets,

but he was still "the best man we had. The biggest, strongest, hardest working one of them all." The fugitive Attucks finds work as a freeman on another farm, where his co-workers include future martyrs Caldwell, Maverick, and Gray, along with an Indian named Teecum, who seems to have been created to expand the patriots' diversity. Attucks impresses his colleagues with his reading, as when he tells them about the new pamphlet "Common Sense," by Tom Paine (which was actually published six years after the real Attucks's death). Attucks admits to having escaped slavery since "that's not right for a man. A man can't be himself unless he's free." When he learns that the farm's owner plans to turn him in for a reward, Attucks heads for Boston where he goes to work for Maverick's "good friend" Captain Folger. He and Folger become close on the whaler, where Crispus proves himself "a mighty demon of a man with a harpoon" who Folger says has "been doing the work of four men." Attucks was still reading and thinking and "tryin' to figure ways to make my people free."[28]

As he learns that British troops quartered in Boston were displacing families from their homes, Attucks knows he has to take action to preserve American liberty. Embodying both the postwar era's emergent American exceptionalism and the accelerating discourse of civil rights, Attucks declares that "America is the greatest hope any people has ever known," representing "the greatest promise of all the world . . . the promise that every single man and woman can have equal opportunity." With the threat of British actions "killing man's greatest opportunity," Attucks fears that "America is about to fail." Reunited in Boston with his fellow farmhand patriots—including the Indian Teecum—Attucks claims that British abuses prove "the time has passed for petitions." He explains to his comrades that "I saw and heard rough things . . . redcoats shoving and pushing people around. . . . AND IF THERE'S ONE THING I CAN'T STAND IT'S SEEING PEOPLE BEING PUSHED AROUND." The factually based abuse of a barber's apprentice by a British officer sparks the fatal confrontation at the Custom House, where Attucks hopes the patriots can "smoke them out for a show down." There, facing soldiers' rifles "armed with our people's weapons . . . stones and snowballs . . . sticks and clubs," Attucks dares the troops to fire. And of course they do. The program then segues through the playing of "Taps" to the Faneuil Hall funeral, where the "people of Boston . . . gathered . . . to pay deserving homage in public funeral services for Crispus Attucks." To top off the illogical performance, John Adams gives a eulogy pronouncing Attucks "the first American casualty within our gates" and claiming that "the English-speaking world will never forget the noble daring, the excusable rashness of Crispus

Attucks in the ever-lasting cause of Liberty. . . . We shall never forget that it was a Negro who came to the front and bore the burden of courageous leadership and inspiring victory."[29]

In 1948, Attucks was the subject of the inaugural broadcast of Richard Durham's radio series *Destination Freedom*, which aired in half-hour, Sunday morning segments on the National Broadcasting Company's Chicago affiliate WMAQ from 1948 to 1950. Durham, an African American born in Mississippi but raised in Chicago, wrote every script for the series to combat whites' negative presumptions about African Americans. "A good many white people," Durham stated in a 1949 interview, "have cushioned themselves into dreaming that Negroes are not self-assertive, confident, and never leave the realm of fear and subservience. . . . His role in society and history has been so distorted . . . that the first point of the series was to bring up some little known facts of history which would give the audience new insight on people in general." Durham could not have selected a better subject for his series premiere than Crispus Attucks. However, while media scholar J. Fred MacDonald asserts that *Destination Freedom*'s nearly one hundred programs "presented historical fiction crafted from careful research," the script for Crispus Attucks, at least—titled "The Knock-Kneed Man"—plays fast and loose with historical accuracy.[30]

The program maintains a casual relationship with the facts throughout, as when Attucks's owner in 1750 is presented as an industrial mill owner with a distinctly southern accent who offers a £100 reward for Crispus's return. He also notes the whipping scars Attucks bore on his back as a result of punishment after previous escape attempts. Durham gives the impression that the colonies remained on the brink of revolution against British tyranny from the time of Attucks's 1750 escape to his 1770 death—which is depicted as the decisive event that moved the Founding Fathers to call for independence. Attucks explicitly offers his life as leader of the Boston citizens, knowing full well that he would be killed and that his death would be the spark igniting the Revolution. As word of Attucks's death spread through the colonies, Patrick Henry called for liberty or death, George Washington left his plantation to join the struggle, and Thomas Jefferson "dreamed of declaring independence." But, listeners were told, "in Boston, Crispus Attucks and his fellows had already done it."[31]

Perhaps Durham's most audacious misstatement comes at the outset. The drama begins with the same quotation, ostensibly by John Adams, used at the end of the 1945 *Within Our Gates* broadcast: "The world will never forget the noble daring and excusable rashness of Crispus Attucks in the holy cause of liberty." Of course, Adams never said this. The passage is actually a close para-phrase of what black historian George Washington Williams wrote about Attucks in his 1883 *History of the Negro Race in America*, which was repeated a few years later in William Simmons's *Men of Mark*. The *California Eagle*, a black newspaper published in Los Angeles, had attributed the same quota-tion to Adams in a 1940 article covering dioramas presented at the American Negro Exposition at the Chicago Coliseum. Perhaps the *Eagle* reporter, Durham, and the *Within Our Gates* writers did not purposely mislead. More likely, they misread Williams or Simmons, each of whose works could easily be misconstrued to place Williams's commentary about Attucks's "excusable rashness" and unforgettability in Adams's mouth. Nonetheless, these 1940s misattributions unquestionably gave an incorrect impression of Attucks's influence on the Revolutionary generation. The error was persistent. Two decades later, Dharathula H. Millender reprised the false Adams quote in her popular Bobbs-Merrill fictionalized biography, *Crispus Attucks: Boy of Valor*, and again in the 1986 reprint, *Crispus Attucks: Leader of Colonial Patriots*. As recently as 2006, Oscar Reiss included the same misinformation in his adult-level book, *Blacks in Colonial America*.[32]

Attucks fabrications and appropriations of his name had been going on for years, of course, and the 1940s saw Attucks being represented and misrep-resented in ways both old and new. Just before Attucks Day in 1947, journal-ist Roscoe Simmons asserted that Attucks mixed regularly with antislavery "Boston whites, often people of eminence. . . . He attended church, picked up the alphabet, learned to read," and committed himself to opposing "British oppression" with "boldness and daring."[33] Some used Attucks to comment on current political questions. In 1947, W. E. B. Du Bois expressed his approval of African American workers' increasing involvement with union move-ments, looking back at earlier days when blacks "had forgotten the path that began with Crispus Attucks, who may have represented organized labor of his time, in his fight against the British."[34] Two years later popular historian J. A. Rogers complained about the exclusion of black West Indian immi-grants to the United States after the Immigration Act of 1924. This struck Rogers as unjust, since "this is as much a black man's land as a white man's." Rogers lauded the contributions of "foreign Negroes" and asserted that "the first American Negroes were West Indian. Crispus Attucks was very likely one."[35] Rogers had some basis for this claim, given that 1770 Boston newspa-pers had identified Attucks's home port as New Providence, in the Bahamas, even though his birthplace was clearly listed as Framingham, Massachusetts.

The last straw in Attucks inventions, according to a 1945 editorial by Carter G. Woodson in the *Negro History Bulletin*, came with the public unveiling of a portrait of Crispus Attucks at an Attucks Day celebration in Washington, DC, where Woodson had been seated next to the event's organizer. "Delighted to know that the likeness of this hero had finally been discovered, [Woodson] inquired how she had been so successful and where she happened to find it." The scholar was appalled to learn that the organizers had merely wanted some image to hold the audience's "concentration of attention" and had commissioned an artist "to use his imagination to supply this need." Even worse, Woodson claimed, "last year a Negro propaganda organization in order to secure money from gullible people had this painting reproduced and is now distributing it around the country as the picture of Crispus Attucks. Still more recently, a Negro author produced a popular book playing up as truth this spurious picture of Crispus Attucks. Evidently Negroes are learning from their traducers how to make history to order." Woodson expressed his outrage over the "bogus picture" again in his review of that "popular book"— *Unsung Americans Sung*, a collection of prose and poetry, images and songs, honoring Negro "makers of history," which was edited by the famous blues musician and composer W. C. Handy.[36]

Still, the dominant story line surrounding Attucks in the 1940s did not involve his likeness, birthplace, or working-class status but rather his symbolic importance as an African American patriot and citizen. In 1942, Harlem's Apollo Theatre hosted a "stirring, dramatic pageant" written by prominent black actor and theater director Carlton Moss entitled "Salute to Negro Troops." The review showcased black jazz musicians and other entertainers along with actors providing "fleeting appearances" of Attucks, Frederick Douglass, Sojourner Truth, Nat Turner, and others in a story "of struggle and of sacrifice, and of proud achievement."[37] In fact, Attucks made more than a fleeting appearance; his disembodied voice played a central role in the dramatic production, which opened with several black soldiers debating whether to fight or desert. The character "Buck" says to his friend, "Come on Shorty. We ain't got no business here. Let's out, out." Attucks's voice enters the scene:

ATTUCKS: Who speaks of blood?
BUCK: Who are you?
ATTUCKS: I am a Negro.
BUCK: What's your name?
ATTUCKS: I am Crispus Attucks.

One of the men, Alfonso, tells Attucks that "my grandfather used to talk about you all the time" and confirms that Attucks was "the first man killed in the Revolutionary War," but his comrades are skeptical. "Go on you're crazy," says Buck, "They ain't had no colored soldiers in that war." Upon the confirmation that many blacks had fought in the Revolution, Shorty is astounded: "Well tell me the news. Hip to the jive and straighten me out 'cause I don't know nothin'." Upon being queried as to why he fought and whether he was afraid, Attucks claimed that "I know why I died. I wanted freedom for you. I knew that my people would never be free unless my country was free. I wanted freedom for my country because I was proud of my country. I must make you proud. I must make you strong." Attucks wants these men to "know the names of our heroes" and proceeds to introduce Harriet Tubman, Nat Turner, Sojourner Truth, Frederick Douglass, and others, all of whom proclaim their own accomplishments and their devotion to the nation and its ideals. Attucks also lauds "the men and women standing behind us all, the dead without names . . . the dark faces, the heroes forgotten. . . . Their work is America, The work of their hands and the sweat of their backs, With the help of our people, America was made." Whites like Harriet Stowe, John Brown, Andrew Jackson, Abraham Lincoln, Thaddeus Kosciusko, and others lend their voices to the chorus praising blacks' contributions to the nation and decrying the wrongs done them. Finally, Shorty sees the light: "Boy, you know one thing, I'm beginning to think we got a history. Yes sir, yes sir! Attucks the first man to die for Old Glory. That ain't bad." Attucks challenges the men to fight for their own rights as well as for those of the white Europeans suffering under Nazi rule. As for America's problems, Attucks tells the men, "Fix them yourselves. This is your country. You have the right to fix its wrongs," just as "at Pearl Harbor—a Negro Mess Boy in an emergency became a gunner aboard the S. S. Arizona." "Yes," he concludes, "we are fighting this war."[38]

Langston Hughes wrote and produced another stage presentation of black heroism in his 1943 pageant, "For This We Fight," which J. A. Rogers called "the finest and most comprehensive pageant on Negro life and history I have ever seen." Paul Robeson, Duke Ellington, Canada Lee, and a number of white actors earned "tremendous applause" as they presented songs and scenes depicting African Americans' participation in the nation's wars "from the pre-Revolutionary War days when Crispus Attucks fell in defense of freedom" to the present. Attucks appeared in many smaller community events, including a Founders Day pageant at Morris Brown College in Atlanta; a Flag Day float in Clairton, Pennsylvania; and African American playwright

Thomas D. Pawley's play, "Crispus Attucks," an "experimental production" at the University of Iowa.[39]

Pawley's script differs from most fictionalized treatments in depicting Attucks as a family man motivated by patriotism, love of liberty, and vengeance against the English. And it distorts the historical record as much as any previous treatments of the subject. The opening scene has Attucks at home in Boston in February 1770, along with his wife Mary and their son Peter. Crispus puts down the Bible he was reading to start Peter's "spellin' lesson." After sending Peter out to play, Crispus tells Mary of his wish to send Peter to a real school where he could begin studying Latin. When Mary reminds him that people of color "can't go to school in the colonies," Crispus bemoans his status as a "mulatto freedman" and says, "I'd like to throw all these Tories into the Charles River. . . . Then we could set up a new country where everybody would be really free an' equal an' there wouldn't be no such thing as slaves and freedmen." Mary mildly scolds him, "You've been listening to Sam Adams again, haven't you?" Mary seems resigned to the way things were "jus' meant to be," but Crispus persists, hoping his son would "grow up free an' do something fo' his people some day."[40]

Attucks's close friend, a slave named Randolph, comes to ask Crispus to help him and several others to escape north into Canada. Crispus is tempted by Randolph's assertion that Peter could go to school there, but in the end he declines to take part in the plan, preferring to place his hopes in the colonists' overthrowing both English rule and slavery. Minutes later, the "foppish" British Captain Thomas Preston comes to Attucks's door and offers him a hefty fee to spy on Randolph and other slaves who are suspected of plotting an insurgency. Crispus replies with disdain, "All the silver in the world couldn't make me spy on my own people." Nonetheless, Randolph was arrested and since he was seen leaving the Attucks home, Preston leaves Crispus with a threat of possible arrest. Crispus is livid and rants about fighting back: "A man can stand only so much and it ain't natural for him to keep gettin' shoved around an' not do no shovin' back." To which Mary cautiously warns, "Crispus, you're a black man livin' in a white man's world. Won't you ever get that into your head?"[41]

Yet another knock at the door brings Attucks's employer, John Hancock, into the Attucks home, cordially greeting Crispus and "Mistress Attucks." Hancock tells Crispus of his plan to unload his ship's banned cargo of wine, even though the British officials have prohibited it. He knows Attucks and his other men, Carr, Maverick, and Caldwell, would gladly help but warns Crispus that their act "could even mean the beginning of armed rebellion."

He has noticed Attucks's hatred of slavery and love of liberty, and he promises that if the American colonies become free, "slavery will crumble." He calls Crispus "one of us," a "natural leader ... who could lead the attack when the right time came," and promises that he and his men would be "well armed." Attucks is skeptical: "I'm a black man." Hancock replies, "You're an American.... Believe me, your cause and our cause are one.—The cause of liberty. What do you say? Can I depend upon you?" Attucks asks for a day to consider.[42]

At that moment, Samuel Maverick bursts in the door, carrying young Peter. The boy had been running in the streets, taunting a drunk British soldier who had failed to pay his barber's debt and had been accidentally trampled by Captain Preston's horse. The arrogant Captain just rode on. The boy soon dies in his mother's arms, causing Crispus to exclaim, "It was the English— goddam them!" Sam Adams is called to the scene and barely restrains Attucks from going after Preston at that moment. Some days later, still mourning his son, Attucks plots with Carr, Maverick, and Caldwell to unload Hancock's contraband cargo—an act they recognize will be "striking the first blow" in the colonies' "break with England." The men succeed in unloading Hancock's ship, but all goes wrong when Preston and his men confront them. Hancock had held back the weapons he promised, fearing that they would be confiscated by the British. Most of the men back down and Attucks and a few close comrades go into hiding.[43]

After almost finding Attucks's hiding place, Preston is led out of town on a wild goose chase by Mary, while Attucks and Hancock convince a mass meeting at Faneuil Hall to march on the governor's residence with a petition denouncing British trade restrictions and demanding the removal of all British troops. Meanwhile, Preston discovers Mary's ruse and returns to Boston in time for the fatal confrontation with the mob. After the shootings, which take place off stage, Sam Adams comes to Mary to break the news of Crispus's murder. "Crispus was my friend and I was his," he comforts her. "I want you to lean on me now." When Mary asks what would be done next, Adams had a ready answer: "They were massacred, massacred in cold blood. Not a man of them was armed. From this day forward, there'll be no turning back. From this day forward, our destiny is sure. They shed the first blood, but we'll shed the last! The revolution has begun!" While its audience in the experimental Iowa production was likely limited, Pawley's idiosyncratic portrayal illustrates Attucks's symbolic potential for promoting not only a message of black patriotism and sacrifice but also an implicit demand that the white Founders' promise of racial equality be fulfilled.[44]

Away from the stage lights, tributes to Attucks and other Negro heroes appeared in various forms on the radio and in the recording industry. Boston's WMEX had musical programs featuring the Attucks Chorus through much of the 1940s, and black composer and promoter Perry Bradford established the Crispus Attucks Record Company, which was "entirely owned and operated by colored." Another company, the Asch Recording Studios, produced "'Cavalcade of the American Negro,' an album of records containing the story of the Negro in this country," including both spoken word and musical tributes to Attucks, Phillis Wheatley, Harriet Tubman, Frederick Douglass, Booker T. Washington, and others. The studio offered the album "to schools and colleges all over the country as a valuable aid in the teaching of Negro history."[45]

Attucks even entered the burgeoning motion picture industry, with a role in the 1944 War Department propaganda documentary, *The Negro Soldier*, which was written by Carlton Moss and directed by Frank Capra. The film used both authentic footage and actors to depict African Americans' long history of patriotic service in the nation's wars from the Revolution to World War II. Although the film was banned in parts of the South, it was well received among military audiences and across the rest of the country. The full-length, forty-minute film had played in approximately two thousand theaters by May 1944, and a shortened version reached another five thousand theaters, most with predominantly white clientele.[46] While most of the film focused on black participation in World War II, Attucks's death was the first example of black patriotism and sacrifice presented, accompanied by images of the Boston Common monument, the Granary Burying Ground, and the 1856 Champney print with its central image of Attucks confronting the British troops.[47]

Given the government's concern for maintaining racial harmony and the increasing presence of blacks in American popular culture, the time seemed ripe for an even more prominent role for African Americans in the movies. But blacks in major motion pictures were still mainly cast in demeaning stereotypical roles. Langston Hughes complained in 1943 that "for a generation now, the Negro has been maligned, caricatured, and lied about on the American screen" with "yes sir, yes ma'am, come seven, come eleven, praise-de-Lawd, whaw-whaw-whaw, boss, roles." Why not have talented black performers like Louise Beavers, Hattie McDaniel, and Clarence Muse play the likes of Sojourner Truth, Harriet Tubman, and Crispus Attucks, he wondered. In 1942, Frank Griffin, co-author of the *Native Sons* radio series, wrote to Metro Goldwyn Mayer studios to complain about the studio's glorification of Reconstruction-era president Andrew Johnson in the new film, *Tennessee Johnson*. This most recent "infamy and injustice" added to the "cankerous pile" of films like *Birth of a Nation* and *Gone with the Wind*. Rather than honor white supremacists like Johnson, Griffin urged studios to let "Americans ... learn of the men who fought against racial prejudices and bigotry; they should learn ... of Crispus Attucks, a Negro, the first to fall for American freedom." A 1941 editorial in the *Chicago Defender* similarly criticized the "incidental parts" played by blacks and called for film versions of the "great stories" of the Negro race, like that of "Crispus Attucks, the first man to die in the American Revolution."⁴⁸

Attucks's story seemed to be on the verge of reaching the American moviegoing public in late 1942, when it was reported that Earl Dancer, a longtime black entertainment entrepreneur, was "working night and day on a script for Warner Brothers around the life of Crispus Attucks." Dancer seemed the right man for the job. He had been instrumental in launching singer Ethel Waters into mainstream success, and he was the first African American to produce an all-black Broadway musical revue, with his 1927 production of *Africana*. Dancer moved to Hollywood in 1930, where he became the first African American to work as a dance director for a major studio, Warner Brothers. After surviving various professional and medical problems, Dancer was engaged in "perhaps the biggest job of his career"—fighting for "a better presentation of the Negro on the screen." In what appeared to be a major coup, Dancer reportedly secured Paul Robeson to play the part of Crispus Attucks. Robeson ostensibly called a draft of the screenplay "really magnificent in idea" and assured Dancer that he "would do much to play in such a film" and would offer his services for a "minimum" fee.⁴⁹

But it was not to be. In January 1943, Dancer published an "open letter" to Robeson and NAACP Executive Secretary Walter White, who himself had visited Hollywood twice in 1942 to lobby studios for more respectful and representative roles for blacks in the film industry. Dancer's letter explained that upon presenting his project to Warner Brothers, complete with assurances of the participation of Robeson, Lena Horne, and "two outstanding white motion picture stars ... the front office turned the whole idea down" even though they had initially "thought the idea, the script and the stars I had chosen were grand." Dancer expressed his great disappointment to his "Friends Paul and Walter" that "the men who control the motion picture industry in Hollywood are not interested in a motion picture story depicting a Negro character that possesses dignity, intellect and courage." He went on to express his befuddlement that "members of an oppressed group such as the Jews," who Dancer asserted "controlled" Hollywood, would countenance "the vicious [anti-black] propaganda that they send from Hollywood every day." Dancer felt that "Hollywood producers should resolve this year to produce scenes with Negroes as they are today, in our war industries, in the uniform of our armed forces."[50]

The studio also reportedly turned down the Attucks film "since it involves the story of America's fight against England" at a time when Britain was our key ally in the fight against Nazi Germany. J. A. Rogers pointed out the hypocrisy of silencing Attucks when treatments of Washington, Jefferson, and Patrick Henry would likely not be similarly suppressed. However, other black critics rejected Dancer's anti-Semitic insinuations and his general complaints about Hollywood. The *Pittsburgh Courier*'s theatrical editor Billy Rowe reported that many prominent black film actors—Hattie McDaniel, Clarence Muse, Louise Beavers, Mantan Moreland, and others—"were vociferous in their disapproval" of Dancer's statements. They believed that "the film industry is making an honest attempt to lift the status of the race in Hollywood." Indeed, the 1943 films *Sahara, Bataan*, and *Lifeboat* featured black actors Rex Ingram, Kenneth Spencer, and Canada Lee in positive roles as characters displaying courage, competence, and morality. While the actors found Dancer's Attucks script to be "fundamentally excellent," they asserted that any film showing "our early strife with England . . . is not only untimely but out of the question." Perhaps more to the point, they condemned Dancer's "attempt to implicate the Jewish race" as "most unwise."[51]

Several years after the war, another black actor hoped to enact Attucks on the silver screen. James Edwards had starred in the acclaimed 1949 Stanley Kramer production, *Home of the Brave*, playing a black soldier who loses the ability to walk as a result of psychological trauma from wartime encounters with racism and the horror of combat. The story unfolds in flashback as Edwards's character undergoes therapy with an army psychiatrist, who eventually shocks him out of his disability. Edwards had high hopes of translating the film's critical success into expanded professional opportunities for himself and for more serious black roles generally. During a press conference Edwards described his plans to open a drama school in California to help develop aspiring African American actors. He also indicated that another "of his immediate plans includes a role as 'Crispus Attucks' in a movie that would probably be named after this hero." Edwards asserted that "a picture on Crispus Attucks would do still more [than *Home of the Brave*] to foster a better relationship" between the races. Like Earl Dancer's project, Edwards's proposed Attucks film was never made.[52]

However, Crispus Attucks did slip into at least one major Hollywood film, the 1948 Spencer Tracy-Katharine Hepburn classic, *State of the Union*. Tracy's character, a wealthy but honest industrialist, is convinced to run for president and becomes corrupted during the course of his campaign before redeeming himself and his ideals in the end. Early in the film, while still contemplating whether or not to run, Tracy delivers a moving monologue in front of the White House, in which he praises all the great Americans who fought and died for the freedom that the presidential mansion symbolizes. Crispus Attucks made the list.[53]

If Attucks failed to become more visible in Hollywood's moving pictures, he at least found an increasing presence in still images, including one federal government venue. In late 1942, thanks to the activism and advocacy of Washington, DC's recorder of deeds, William J. Thompkins, the Works Progress Administration opened a competition for artists to create seven murals "depict[ing] the contribution of the Negro to America, [to] decorate the lobby and the library of the [new] Recorder of Deeds Building," which was completed in 1942. The location was selected because "the recorder of deeds office has traditionally been directed by Negroes." Art historian Sara A. Butler praises Thompkins for initiating and overseeing "the most ambitious, fully developed body of art of the period in the federal city dedicated to black activism and an important artifact of the early civil rights movement." Not surprisingly for the time period, slave rebels and insurrectionists were not among the murals' subjects, and much to the disappointment of Thompkins, only one of the murals would be painted by a black artist. The seven separate panels would feature Frederick Douglass, Benjamin Banneker, Matthew Henson, and Crispus Attucks, among others. The Attucks mural for the lobby's west vestibule was painted by the "young Philadelphia artist" Herschel Levit. According to Butler, Levit's social-realist depiction of Attucks at the Boston Massacre is "the most aesthetically daring" of the murals. "The canvas threatens to dissolve into a network of fractured shards." Attucks, clad in bold white and steely blue, is at the forefront of the sepia-toned mob, and his "anguished expression" and contorted body signify his distress as he awaits the fatal gunshots (see Fig. 6.1).[54]

Attucks appeared in another provocative eleven-by-seventeen-foot mural, painted in 1943 by African American artist Charles White, whose work was supported by a grant from the Julius Rosenwald Fund. *The Contribution of the Negro to Democracy in America* hangs in Wainwright Auditorium at the traditionally black Hampton Institute in Virginia. White spent six months researching African American history at New York's Schomburg Center

FIG. 6.1 *Crispus Attucks*, by Herschel Levit, mural at Recorder of Deeds Building, built in 1943. Library of Congress.

before traveling to Hampton to complete the work. An avid student of black history, White recognized the power of art to raise the historical consciousness of a broad public audience. He had recently produced two other historical murals depicting black historical figures and themes, but the Hampton project would be his masterwork. According to historian Erin P. Cohn, "White's highly complex mural depicts a series of historical episodes and important figures in order to explore three themes: the active participation of African Americans in developing American democracy and culture, resistance to oppression, and the importance of black labor." The spiraling overlapping images featured slave rebels like Vesey and Turner, along with less contentious figures like Revolutionary veteran Peter Salem, Harriet Tubman, Frederick Douglass, the 54th Massachusetts, and, interestingly, the contemporary blues singer Huddie (Lead Belly) Ledbetter. Crispus Attucks appears in the lower left center, collapsing backward in death, away from the British rifles, and initiating the mural's theme of blacks as "architects of American democracy, a message that would have particularly resonated with wartime viewers."[55]

Both these murals reflect the tendency among New Deal era artists to incorporate leftist social commentary in their work. Charles White was "a particularly enthusiastic member of the Graphic Art Workshop," formed during the 1940s by activist artists intent upon "creating a politicized people's art." Depicting African American history was central to the group's approach to the race and class struggle, as evidenced especially by folio publications like *Negro, U.S.A* (1949). This publication included twenty-six prints by fifteen artists and a foreword by historian (and communist) Herbert Aptheker. Like White's Hampton mural, *Negro, U.S.A*, whose cover White illustrated, addressed the themes of blacks' resistance to slavery and their role in shaping American history and culture. Along with depictions of plantation labor, the underground railroad, and individuals like Douglass, Turner, Salem, and others, white artist Jim Schlecker presented a stylized Attucks being cradled by his fellow revolutionaries in a print titled, *First to Fall*.[56]

African American artist William H. Johnson's "Crispus Attucks" (ca. 1945) presents a slain Attucks lying in a Christ-like pose, with arms spread wide, between the firing soldiers and distraught white colonists. One man holds his arm out as if to dissuade the soldiers from firing while three women in the background hold their hands over their breasts in lamentation. This painting was completed while Johnson was working in the New York Navy yards.[57]

In public performances and visual arts, Attucks often shared focus with other notable black heroes. Such was also the case during African Americans' expanding attention to honoring the race's history during Negro History Week. School and community programs tended to provide a broad overview of the black past, rather than concentrate on a single individual. Black newspapers and magazines like Carter G. Woodson's *Negro History Bulletin* similarly took advantage of the second week in February to call attention to the race's accomplishments, past and present, through articles offering thumbnail outlines of key events and individuals. Margaret T. Goss provided a typical example in the *Chicago Defender* in 1943, in a feature article presenting for the "boys and girls" of the race "a little story of the history of the Negro . . .

a story of a people's love of freedom, of a people's fight for freedom through the years." Mirroring the format of community programs and pageants, Goss then gave brief descriptions of heroes like Attucks, Vesey, Turner, Tubman, Douglass, and other "brave forefathers" in order to provide "shining examples [for Negro children] to follow today."[58]

While Attucks was one of many such examples during Negro History Week, he received plenty of individual attention during Attucks Day celebrations and through commemorative naming. Journalist Nahum Daniel Brascher had founded the Crispus Attucks Legion in 1939 to maintain a "program of patriotic information and justice to the American people" and to be "impartial and frank" in "telling the story of our founding fathers"—and especially black ones like the organization's namesake. Three years later, just months after America's entry into World War II, Brascher lauded Attucks as "America's First hero" and expressed his dissatisfaction that "sadly few name monuments" existed honoring Attucks; he called for the naming of "hundreds of others, as a symbol of our inheritance and faith in America's obligations." Brascher would have been deeply troubled, then, had he read the report a few weeks later that the New York City–based Crispus Attucks Mission Foundation had held a public meeting, decried in the press as a "pro-Axis" gathering, at which they "advocated refusal to fight [in the war] unless the Government insure justice under its Constitution for colored citizens." The organization's motto was, "Justice, like charity, begins at home. Remember Crispus Attucks."[59]

Most Attucks namesakes, however, remained either conventionally patriotic or more or less apolitical. Students at a black junior high school in Washington, DC, showed support for the war effort by selling nearly $7,000 in war bonds in 1943, "enough to give the Army seven new jeeps." The students honored past and present black patriots by christening two of the jeeps the "Crispus Attucks" and the "Dorie Miller." A year later African American artillerymen in France told a *Chicago Defender* reporter, "We've been mowin' the Nazis right and left," supporting an armored division's steady advance through occupied France with their batteries of howitzers. One of the guns in Able Company was nicknamed "Crispus Attucks." Shortly after the war, thirty black veterans, "most of whom held the Purple Heart for wounds sustained in combat," founded a Veterans of Foreign Wars post in Hampden County, Massachusetts, naming it "Crispus Attucks Post, VFW, in honor of the first Negro soldier killed in the Revolutionary War." Grand Rapids, Michigan, had its Crispus Attucks American Legion Post 59, and the Crispus Attucks Guard of Newark's American Legion Post 152 participated in both organizational and public events, like the parade preceding the opening game of the 1949 Negro American League baseball season, between the Philadelphia Stars and Kansas City Monarchs.[60]

Attucks's name also continued to be adopted by numerous other institutions, schools, and public facilities. Joining the many already established Attucks schools were facilities in Ponca City, Oklahoma; Washington, Missouri; and a proposed elementary school in Chicago, which would honor "the first American to die in the American Revolution." In the New York City area, Brooklyn's Attucks playground was joined in the 1940s by the Crispus Attucks Youth Center in Harlem and the Crispus Attucks Orphan Home. Perhaps to offset Harlem's Democratic Crispus Attucks Club, Black Republicans in the state founded the statewide Crispus Attucks League to pursue their political objectives. The Indianapolis Public Library opened an Attucks branch, which nicely complemented the city's Crispus Attucks High School. Though it had been established years earlier, the Attucks Hotel in Philadelphia garnered unwanted notoriety in 1947 when jazz vocalist Billie Holliday was arrested there on drug charges.[61]

These namesakes often were noticed only by people in the communities where they existed. Prominent journalist Lucius C. Harper suggested in 1944 that while "here and there a high school, a literary club, a dingy hotel, or probably a smelly tavern bears the name of Attucks . . . Boston alone keeps alive his memory in proper and appropriate fashion each year on the fifth of March." Harper seemed unaware of the popularity of Attucks Day celebrations in many black communities, complaining that the world outside Boston—and "Negroes especially—will regard March 5 as just another day." Harper believed that the Fifth of March was "one of the most memorable dates in the history of this country. To Negroes it should be a national holiday." Yet, "insofar as America as a whole is concerned, [Attucks] seems to have died in vain." Attucks may have been "first in war" and "first to die," but he remained "last in the hearts of his countrymen."[62]

Harper was certainly correct that Boston, where the official Massachusetts Attucks Day holiday had been established in the early 1930s, put on the most extensive commemorations. But in fact many black communities celebrated Attucks Day and even white Americans and governmental bodies began to take more notice during the 1940s. Springfield, Illinois, held an Attucks Day program in 1944 and all of Chicago's black churches held "memorial services" for Attucks the previous year. Gary, Indiana's St. Paul Baptist Church continued its tradition of annual Attucks Day celebrations that dated back to the early 1930s, and Indianapolis's Attucks High School students maintained their long-standing tradition of commemorating Attucks Day with a local observance and by sending a wreath to Boston to be placed on Attucks's gravesite. The *Chicago Daily Tribune*, a mainstream paper, regularly marked the occasion of Attucks's sacrifice during the late 1940s by noting local black celebrations and publishing articles informing readers that Attucks was "now honored as the first Negro to die in the cause of freedom." In 1953, a black spokesperson writing for the *Atlanta Daily World* urged blacks to continue calling special attention to Attucks and other black patriots, at least "until the day arrives when Mississippi finds itself, just as able and anxious to celebrate Crispus Attucks Day as does Mass[achusetts]."[63]

But Attucks Day celebrations seem to have been absent in the Deep South, and the most concentrated attention to Attucks remained in the Northeast, where Massachusetts' official state acknowledgment of Attucks Day was joined in 1943 by New York, thanks to a bill introduced by Harlem minister and city councilman, the Reverend Adam Clayton Powell Jr. Mayor Fiorello LaGuardia spoke at an Attucks Day event at Powell's Abyssinian Baptist Church in Harlem, where attendees enjoyed "the spectacle of seeing the Daughters of the American Revolution and delegations from other white patriotic societies honor this hero." Perhaps more important, the city council's resolution required that all the city schools "suitably observe this day so that all the students of our great city shall be further enlightened concerning the heritage of this Democracy."[64] In 1949, a New Jersey statute called for the annual celebration of "the first American patriot to give his life in our country's war of freedom," stipulating that "the fifth day of March, in each year . . . shall be known as Crispus Attucks Day."[65]

This increasing public attention to black history by visual artists, activists, organizations, and communities was paralleled by continuing attention in print publications. Ben Richardson included a brief and fairly typical biography of Attucks under the "military" heading of his *Great American Negroes* (1945), along with Brigadier General Benjamin O. Davis Sr. and Benjamin O. Davis Jr., commander of the Tuskegee Airmen. Among the twenty-one biographies of contemporary athletes, entertainers, educators, scientists, and other leaders, Attucks stands alone as the only pre-twentieth-century figure. Perhaps for the sake of consistency, Attucks was replaced with more contemporary figures like Dorie Miller in later editions of the book, which continued to appear until 1976. In 1942, the Langston Civic Club of America, based in Philadelphia, reprinted as a pamphlet nineteenth-century activist George L. Ruffin's popular oration on Attucks, which had previously appeared in

Alice Dunbar Nelson's *Masterpieces of Negro Eloquence* (1914). In 1948, Arna Bontemps's *The Story of the Negro* noted that for Daniel Webster, the Boston Massacre "marked the first break of the colonies away from the British Empire" and emphasized that "the first man to die in the War for American Freedom . . . happened to be a Negro." Bontemps described the massacre and the honor Boston paid to all the fallen martyrs before lamenting that, "despite the patriotic example of Crispus Attucks, the American colonies were slow to accept Negroes into the army." Langston Hughes testified to the broad appeal of Bontemps's book by recommending it as "one of the best presents you could give a boy or girl graduating from grammar school, or college this spring."[66]

Some of Attucks's appearances in books came in musical form. Evelyn LaRue Pittman's *Rich Heritage: Songs about American Negro Heroes* (1944) included "Crispus Attucks: Brave Soldier," which emphasized that Attucks "was the first to shed his blood . . . for America." The "Crispus Attucks" song in W. C. Handy's collection, *Unsung Americans Sung* (1943), provided a more comprehensive interpretation of Attucks's meaning for the nation. The verses by Andy Razaf told of the "angry citizens" rising against abusive soldiers led by "a man of dusky hue, Who was nonetheless a Yankee." But it was Razaf's chorus that proffered both a chastisement and challenge to white Americans: "More honor to this hero, And more justice to his race/Whose noble deeds like his, base men have striven to efface/Let those who steal their freedom/And begrudge them life as well,— Remember it was fully earned When Crispus Attucks fell."[67]

Significantly, for the first time in decades, white authors also began including Attucks in historical works. Edward Nicholas's *The Hours and the Ages* (1949) gave Attucks a prominent, if somewhat unflattering, place as the leader of the Boston mob, characterizing him as a "huge Negro-Indian half-breed" and "a veteran mob fighter." In 1945, Edith H. Mayer more pointedly addressed the problem of incorporating black Americans into the story of the nation's history and into the mainstream of current American life with her publication of the juvenile history book, *Our Negro Brother*. The Introduction by Anne Coolidge upbraided white Americans for having "not yet learned that the things that count in man are not tied up with the color of skin" and argued for the removal of all race-based restrictions in social and political life as well as in historical understanding. "History has been unfair in the things that it has *not* told about the Negro. It has been unfair in the things it has let people think about the Negro. In this book we tell a few stories everyone should know." Of course, they did not fail to tell the story of "the first man to fall" in "the first battle of the Revolution." Attucks was presented as "a tall, strong Negro" who "was well known in Boston as a leader of men" and who "had the courage to fight for what he thought were his rights and the rights of all the Colonists." As the mob assembled before the British troops, Attucks "stepped out before them and told them not to be afraid. . . . The crowd of Colonists were stirred by his words." Mayer thus repeated some of the same myths that black writers had been promoting for generations and signaled a shift in white attitudes that would become more pronounced during the coming decades of civil rights activism.[68]

Constance H. Curtis, book reviewer for the *New York Amsterdam News*, suggested that *Our Negro Brother* was overly simplistic in its presentation and criticized the illustrator for her "ineptness." Nonetheless, she recognized "the need for books of this type." "Books like *Our Negro Brother*," she declared, "are important, since they begin with youth to build up respect for other races. . . . [C]hildren's volumes along the same lines . . . are sorely needed in a country where too much of our education either forgets the Negro, or worse, paints him in a light that is far from truthful." The same reviewer was also unimpressed with the otherwise well-received book for young audiences, *North Star Shining: A Pictorial History of the American Negro*, with text by Hildegarde Hoyt Swift and illustrations by Lynd Ward, both highly regarded in their respective fields. Curtis declared Ward's illustrations "outstanding for both strength and beauty," but she found Swift's sparse free verse text too complex for young readers and too elementary and condensed for adults. In contrast, Annie L. McPheeters, writing for the *Atlanta Daily World*, found that the book's "few well chosen words" "gallantly sung" the race's noble past and that Ward's woodcuts "tell almost in illustration what the text does in words." She claimed that Swift researched the book for two years and submitted it to "several outstanding Negroes who unanimously endorsed its purpose and achievement." McPheeters concurred that "the book will be a welcome addition to the too limited supply of books which try to sincerely portray the Negro's record in an unbiased and realistic manner." The book was also favorably reviewed in mainstream newspapers, the *Christian Science Monitor* and *Chicago Tribune*, with the latter noting that "the courage of Crispus Attucks" was singled out in the book for "tribute." The book was widely collected by libraries and adopted as a guiding text for Negro history programs, school and church pageants, Negro History Week events, and theatrical performances from the 1940s into the 1970s.[69]

Despite steady progress in gaining public acknowledgment of black Americans' role in shaping American history and culture, the critical arena of public schools continued to resist the infusion of black heroes and black perspectives. In a 1944 letter to the editor, Philadelphian Jesse Dunson noted that some "courses in Negro History" were beginning to appear in schools "throughout the civilized areas of these United States above the Mason-Dixie line." But the fact remained that "when the jackpot question is asked 'Who Was Crispus Attucks?'" only a "favored few" might know the answer. Two years later, the *Chicago Defender* ran a twenty-week essay contest in which entrants were to write 750-word essays on "how to improve race relations in the South." Two submissions during the eighth week had the same solution: "Take the Notion of White Supremacy Out of American Textbooks." Puella R. Brigham, an Arkansas high school teacher, was conducting research on the topic for her master's degree at Tennessee A&M College in Nashville. She reported that "of one-hundred Tennessee state-adopted Social Studies books, only four spoke favorably of the Negro, 33 made no comment, and 63 made unfavorable comments." Brigham urged textbook authors to acknowledge that "the Negro has made great contributions to civilization, instead of picturing him as a vicious and backward savage." Upon winning the overall third place prize, Brigham noted that "the Negro . . . is portrayed as a shiftless, thriftless, ignorant, happy-go-lucky type" and complained that "our famous Negroes like Crispus Attucks [and others] are ignored."[70]

Indeed, Crispus Attucks seems not to have appeared in any mainstream history textbook at any grade level during the first six decades of the twentieth century. Typical was a 1943 college text by prolific textbook authors David Saville Muzzey and John A. Kraut, which called the Boston Massacre "a riot" in which "five men were killed," with no mention of Attucks. Similarly, a secondary school text in 1955 dispassionately described how "trouble flared" when "a group of young men threw snowballs and stones at the soldiers." The omission of Attucks from these accounts perpetuated what black politician and activist George W. Harris characterized as "the delusion, implanted in the mass American mind by history textbooks, that the black race played no vital part" in the nation's history. Journalist Lucius C. Harper declared that Americans as a whole "have been cheated by historians" who systematically omitted heroes like "Crispus Attucks, who shed the first blood in the American Revolution in the Boston Massacre in 1770."[71]

But change was coming. In 1940, poet and playwright Langston Hughes had challenged black writers to do more to promote and publicize the race's heroes. In an essay for the NAACP magazine, *The Crisis*, Hughes called attention to "the need for heroes," complaining that blacks themselves

> almost never honor the memories of our dead heroes with celebrations, songs, or programs. . . . It is the social duty of Negro writers to reveal to the people the deep reservoirs of heroism within the race. It is one of the duties of our literature to combat—by example, not by diatribe—the caricatures of Hollywood, the Lazy Bones of popular songs, the endless defeats of play after play and novel after novel—for we are not endlessly funny, nor always lazy, nor forever quaint, nor eternally defeated. After all, there was Crispus Attucks. There was Denmark Vesey. There was Harriet Tubman . . . Frederick Douglass . . . .

In particular, Hughes chastised "Negro writers," most of whom he argued, "seem unaware of the heroism, past or present, of the Negro people." Ordinary African Americans in the mid-twentieth century "need in our books and plays and on our screens and over the airwaves, Negro heroes and Negro heroines . . . who are courageous; straightforward; strong . . . whose words and thoughts gather up what is in our own hearts and say it clearly and plainly for all to hear."[72]

With his call to arms, his newspaper columns, and his 1943 Harlem pageant, Hughes had modeled the kinds of actions he called for. And during the World War II era many black writers, entertainers, and artists had answered his call. African Americans, growing numbers of sympathetic whites, and US government propagandists all used the era's expanding mass media—books, periodicals, plays, pageants, radio broadcasts, film, visual arts, school programs, and more—in order to make Crispus Attucks and other black heroes visible in American public culture as never before. Yet mainstream attention to black history, as well as advances in African Americans' ability to participate fully in American social and political life, was still slow in coming. The next two decades would bring the black freedom struggle into the center of American life. As it became more difficult for white Americans to ignore their black fellow citizens, attention to black history and black heroes entered a new phase. Hughes's "need for heroes" was beginning to be answered, and black literature and history was accelerating its mission to "come alive, speak, sing, and flame with meaning for the Negro people."[73]

7

Crispus Attucks and the Black Freedom Struggle, 1950s–1970s

*The Civil Rights program is as dead as Crispus Attucks. . . .
Nobody is going to save the Negro but himself, and he had
better get about the job and stop waving an empty gun
while walking hard and talking loud.*

GEORGE S. SCHUYLER
Pittsburgh Courier (March 26, 1949)

*That man who goes out and throws a brick at a white cop
is taking part in an uprising as Crispus Attucks, another
black man, was when he threw rocks in the American
Revolution at Boston.*

STOKELY CARMICHAEL
Chicago Daily Defender (September 20, 1966)

AFRICAN AMERICANS' STRUGGLE for both justice in the present and inclusion in the story of the nation's past had expanded dramatically during the 1940s. Nonetheless, by the end of that decade anyone interested in African American history still had to rely mainly on black-authored sources to learn about Crispus Attucks and other black heroes. In African Americans' ongoing efforts to incorporate black contributions into the nation's collective memory, Attucks Day commemorations continued to play a role during the 1950s, with Connecticut joining Massachusetts, New York, and New Jersey with a bill to create a statewide Attucks Day holiday, even though "many of the Senators and Representatives never heard of Crispus Attucks."[1]

And Negro History Week was still seen as a necessary vehicle for black communities to honor their own "great heritage," since "the facts of Negro history are still hidden from the general public . . . still omitted, distorted and ignored by the blind and the prejudiced."[2] Popular historian J. A. Rogers stressed the need for Negro History Week to counter the centuries of propaganda "that the black man has no history." "Those who would tell the truth," he noted, "are still on the defensive."[3] But some black commentators suggested that attention to the race's past heroes might be reconsidered. In 1948, the editor of the *Atlanta Daily World* recognized the need to honor those "departed saints . . . upon whose shoulders we have been able to climb," but he also counseled greater emphasis on "the efforts and achievements of living heroes."[4] Several years later a letter to the *Los Angeles Sentinel* concurred that black Americans simply did not "have the time" for "reminiscing." "If there must be a National Negro History Week," the writer argued, "the program should primarily look ahead and not backwards."[5]

In 1950, the last year of his accomplished life, Negro History Week founder Carter G. Woodson offered a somewhat different critique of his own creation. Though Woodson has himself at times been characterized as a "contributionist" who had a "predilection for reciting racial achievements," he expressed concern that the annual affairs too often tended toward "chauvinism" by neglecting white individuals who worked alongside blacks in seeking racial justice. Providing due attention to the broader context of blacks' struggles, he argued, would help "prevent the teaching of Negro history from descending to the level of the propaganda" found in most mainstream textbooks. "Let us note then," he urged in one example, "that Crispus Attucks was not the only martyr in the Boston Massacre."[6] Three years later, Roscoe C. Simmons, a black journalist whose long-running column for the *Chicago Tribune* consistently emphasized biracial cooperation, similarly noted that "what Attucks did was not done alone, for white men fought and died with him." While Simmons recognized that "a little bragging might be expected" and that historical black heroes and role models were important for contemporary African American youths, like Woodson he seemed more concerned that African American accomplishments be accurately and seamlessly integrated into the story of the American nation.[7]

This integrationist orientation helped define what historian John Hope Franklin called "the New Negro history" that emerged during the postwar era. Previous black historical writers often lacked academic credentials and many promoted African American history primarily to redress the omissions of white historians, call attention to black heroes and accomplishments, and instill race pride among black readers. The most prominent practitioners of the new approach, Franklin and fellow black historian Benjamin Quarles, were rigorously trained academic historians who used careful scholarship "to place the history of American blacks squarely in the mainstream of American history."[8] While Franklin's pathbreaking 1947 synthesis of African American history, *From Slavery to Freedom*, was criticized by some white historians for its "heroic lists" of black accomplishments and general "overemphasis on the Negro's role in American history,"[9] Franklin's main objective was to "integrate [the Negro] into the stream of American civilization."[10]

From Slavery to Freedom devoted a single page to Attucks and the Boston Massacre, stating that the mob in King Street was "led by Crispus Attucks, a runaway slave" and that "Attucks was the first to fall." The tone then became somewhat defensive, disputing John Adams's denigrating characterization during the soldiers' trial: as a forty-seven-year-old man, Franklin wrote, "Attucks could hardly be described as a saucy boy. Nor was he deserving of the other harsh things John Adams had to say about those who fell in the Boston Massacre." Franklin also inserted an unfounded presumption: "It was a remarkable thing, the colonists reasoned, to have their fight for freedom waged by one who was not as free as they."[11]

Given his narrower scope, Quarles, in his 1961 *The Negro in the American Revolution*, was far more thorough in discussing Attucks's identity, actions, and motivations. He incorporated the full range of the evidence and characterizations presented at the trial of the British soldiers and from selected later treatments. Quarles noted some debate regarding Attucks's racial identity, though he seemed convinced Attucks was "a Negro of obscure origin, with some admixture of Indian blood." He also offered conflicting eyewitness accounts as well as John Adams's assertions of Attucks's "prominent role," concerning whether or not Attucks had aggressively provoked the troops. Regardless of Attucks's actions, Quarles argued, his "one impulsive act wrote his name in the annals of American history." He went on to note the annual massacre commemorations and the judgments of later writers, particularly George Washington Williams's characterization of Attucks as a "true martyr." But Quarles also entertained the possibility that "Attucks was simply an unruly spirit who was looking for trouble." Ever the careful historian, Quarles concluded that "what vision moved Crispus Attucks can only be surmised." But he ultimately asserted that Attucks may well have been a patriot who, "probably no less than his companions in the riot . . . was motivated by principle."[12]

While not an academically trained historian like Franklin and Quarles, Lerone Bennett Jr., senior editor at the popular black monthly *Ebony*, offered an influential survey of African American history with his 1962 book, *Before the Mayflower*. The bulk of the book was drawn from Bennett's previously published *Ebony* magazine essays on black history, written in vigorous prose.

Bennett had read broadly in both primary and secondary literature on African American history, and reviews in academic historical journals were generally positive, though he was criticized for some "special pleading." Benjamin Quarles, in his review in the *American Historical Review*, lauded Bennett's "substantial reading in the historical journals" and in both "vintage and contemporary" sources. While noting some bias in the book's "dramatic" retellings, he praised Bennett's fealty to the "essential facts" and his "unusual ability to evoke the tragedy and the glory of the Negro's role in the American past."[13]

Bennett strays from the evidence more than Franklin or Quarles, presenting Attucks as "an imposing man" who was "well known around the docks in lower Boston." He situates Attucks, "who seems to have been everywhere on this night," as the leader of an assault on British soldiers well before the actual confrontation at the Custom House. After he had "rallied [the crowd of Bostonians] and urged them to stand their ground," Attucks "led a group of citizens who drove the soldiers back to the gate of their barracks." "Needless to say," Bennett claimed, Attucks "was not a proper Bostonian, a fact that has pained numerous historians. He was instead a proper rebel, a drifter, a man who loved freedom and knew what it was worth." Like others before him, Bennett imposed personal qualities on Attucks that suited his purpose. The people followed Attucks, he claimed, because "he had that undefinable quality called presence. When he spoke, men listened. Where he commanded, men acted." Bennett is unequivocal that it was Attucks, "an oppressed American, born in slavery . . . who carried the American standard in the prologue that laid the foundation of American freedom." While Bennett's tone was at times combative, his Crispus Attucks was as fundamentally American as Quarles's or Franklin's.[14]

Black historians' integrationist treatment of Attucks was in keeping with the general momentum of civil rights activism during the postwar era, and perhaps most meaningfully with the implications of the Supreme Court's 1954 *Brown* decision calling for the end of segregation in America's public schools. *Brown* met with "massive resistance" in the South, including the formation of White Citizens' Councils and the issuing of the 1956 "Southern Manifesto" from ninety-six southern congressmen pledging to ignore the court's ruling and to maintain segregated schools at any cost. These forces of white supremacy muted more moderate southern voices that saw in *Brown* an opportunity to pursue a "meaningful and level-headed approach" toward fostering "racial brotherhood" in the region and the nation. A white PTA leader from Virginia wrote to the moderate Virginia politician and *Washington Post* columnist Benjamin Muse, asking for advice on how PTAs might help

"educat[e] parents and their children toward accepting the eventual imple-
mentation" of *Brown*. Muse agreed that PTAs might well "hold the key" to
instilling racial tolerance, observing that "the average white Virginian knows
little about the Negro race" and blacks' place in American history. "It might
be helpful," he suggested as one case in point, "to recall incidentally that a
Negro patriot, Crispus Attucks, was the first to fall in the Boston Massacre."[15]

As civil rights advocates defined their integrationist agenda, many
African American public presentations and historical writings became more
explicit in addressing both black leaders' calls for forward-looking programs
and sympathetic whites' desires for practical strategies to make integration
work. A few months before the *Brown* decision, a radio presentation in
Washington, DC, met the issue head-on. Kicking off Negro History Week
on February 7, 1954, station WOOK's "Americans All" program aired an
installment on the theme, "Negro History—A Foundation for Integration."
The program involved a skit, "Firm Foundations," written by an African
American teacher at Washington's Banneker Junior High School, which
was subsequently printed in the *Negro History Bulletin*, the newsletter of
Woodson's Association for the Study of Negro Life and History (ASNLH).
In the setting of a ninth grade social studies classroom, a teacher and her class
"are all ready to plunge into [a] discussion of Negro History." The students
had been asked to prepare questions, and "Michael" sets the tone with his
query: "I would like to know how a study of Negro History can contribute
to creating conditions in which integration will succeed." Other students
follow up with, "What part have Negroes played in the development of this
country?" and "Are Negroes and whites really ready for integration? What
does history teach us about this?" The remarkably astute students rattle off
a long list of relevant issues, most of which concern the popular "fallacies"
of the "much maligned Reconstruction periods," which were used "as justification of the Ku Klux Klan, the disfranchisement of Negroes in the South,
and the widespread practice of segregation practiced in America." The students were sent home with the assignment to research these questions in
local repositories like Howard University and in various ASNLH publications. The following day the students presented "authoritative information"
to support an assertion attributed to John Hope Franklin: "Negro history
must be relied upon to correct the fallacies in American history upon which
the justification of slavery—and segregation—have been based." Often citing articles from the *Journal of Negro History* and other ASNLH sources,
the students rattle off numerous black contributions to the nation, from
Crispus Attucks and Benjamin Banneker to Frederick Douglass and Harriet

Tubman to the political and educational leaders of the Reconstruction era and beyond. Their studies proved that much of the nation's understanding of Reconstruction was based on "propaganda, masquerading as history," and that, indeed, "the study of Negro History makes a firm foundation for integration!"[16]

This well-researched conclusion from the segregated Banneker classroom, however, seems to bear out black columnist Albert Barnett's 1956 observation that one of the great "imperfections" of American education remained "the fact that . . . the heroic deeds and achievements of Negro men and women . . . are entirely ignored in the 'white' history books of the integrated North and the lily-white schools of the South. It's a sad commentary . . . [that] the only Negro students familiar with Negro history are those attending Jim Crow schools below the Mason-Dixon Line."[17]

A mix of progress and obstruction continued to mark the era. As the civil rights movement accelerated and blacks made some headway in mainstream popular culture, white Americans were forced to think about African Americans' place in the nation as at no time since Reconstruction. In 1956, popular singer Nat "King" Cole became the first African American to host a national television variety show; yet a few months earlier the star had been assaulted onstage by white supremacists during a performance in Birmingham, Alabama. A month after the attack, Cole recorded "We Are Americans Too," a song he prefaced with a spoken introduction trumpeting "the story of the Negro's contributions to the progress of America . . . from Crispus Attucks to Ralph Bunche." The song was intended to honor the "glorious history . . . of the Negro in America" and was dedicated "to the youth of America, who are the inheritors of a great tradition."[18] Of course, events beyond the realm of popular entertainment were dominating headlines as well.

Perhaps as Cole composed his introduction, he was thinking not only of his own assault but also of the tragedy that had befallen one of those youths to whom he dedicated his song. In 1955, the brutal Mississippi murder of the black Chicago teenager Emmett Till horrified the nation. A few months later, African Americans in Montgomery, Alabama, initiated the year-long bus boycott that would capture national attention while overturning segregated seating in the city's public transportation. In 1957, President Dwight D. Eisenhower reluctantly called on the US military to enforce the integration of Central High School in Little Rock, Arkansas. With media attention increasing, the 1960s began with intensifying violence against direct action participants in sit-ins, freedom rides, and public demonstrations in numerous southern communities.

Over a few hot months in 1963 Americans watching these events unfold in newspapers and on television had to make sense of both progress and terror. In May, months of heated protests in Birmingham, Alabama, culminated in a resolution promising the desegregation of public facilities and jobs for black workers in downtown stores. In June, President Kennedy sent troops to enforce the integration of the University of Alabama and proposed the passage of meaningful civil rights legislation; early the next morning, in Mississippi, NAACP field secretary Medgar Evers was assassinated in his driveway. In August, James Meredith, the first black student at the University of Mississippi, received his degree and the massive March on Washington brought the power and promise of nonviolent social change into the American mainstream. In September, four young black girls were killed in the Klan bombing of Birmingham's 16th Street Baptist Church. At the burial of Carole Robertson, a fourteen-year-old victim of the bombing, one eulogist "prayed that 'Carole's blood may become like that of Crispus Attucks,'" and another hoped that "Carole's death will not be in vain."[19]

In this environment, the need for greater attention to teaching African American history was clear to civil rights leaders on both the local and national levels. Martin Luther King Jr. wrote in the preface of his 1964 call for justice, *Why We Can't Wait,* about two hypothetical black children in Harlem and Birmingham, and about the "pale history books" used in schools that ignored black accomplishments and contributions to the nation's past. While not taught about blacks in school, these two children learned from their churches, parents, and Negro History Week speakers:

> They know that the first American to shed blood in the revolution which freed this country from British oppression was a black seaman named Crispus Attucks.... The boy and girl knew more than history. They knew something about current events.... They knew that a great-great-grandson of Crispus Attucks might be ruled out of some restricted, all-white restaurant in a restricted, all-white segment of some southern town, his United States Marine uniform notwithstanding.[20]

King's book was an attempt to explain the current "Negro revolution" to a white audience and to make the case against patience and gradualism. He presented educational reform as a small but critical part of the changes needed to move the nation toward racial justice.

Attucks was regularly held up as a shining example of black patriotism and citizenship by major black civil rights leaders and spokespersons, including King, A. Philip Randolph, Benjamin Mays, Jackie Robinson, and many others.[21] Even whites who remained sorely in need of education about African American life and culture recognized Attucks's symbolic value. In 1962, John Fischer, white editor of *Harper's Magazine*, demonstrated his liberal credentials by calling for "first-class citizenship" for Negroes, even as he suggested that blacks themselves needed to reform their immoral behavior before whites would accept them as such; he used Attucks as an example of a man "who knew that citizenship is earned, not given." Black columnist Gertrude Wilson mocked Fischer's "misguided" remarks in part by noting that Attucks "earned it by getting a hole in his head."[22]

Historian Charles Harris Wesley expanded on the link between history education and civil rights activism in his 1963 ASNLH presidential address. His call to arms, titled "Creating and Maintaining an Historical Tradition," challenged the students and teachers of Negro history represented in the Association to create "an historical tradition" rooted upon "solid historical foundations," with the "support of documents, primary and secondary sources, and . . . no uncertainty about the facts." Wesley praised the numerous efforts already underway to incorporate black history into American classrooms, and he called on ASNLH members to ramp up efforts to challenge "the larger field of public education already occupied by textbook publishers." Those "books tell a false, ugly story and illustrate an all-white America instead of the integrated people we are." Black activists needed to push publishers toward "revising and re-writing their texts" to include African Americans in the nation's story. "The present Negro Revolution," Wesley urged, "needs this support."[23]

As the South continued to roil in protest and violence and many schools across the nation continued to ignore the black past, some communities recognized that sweeping changes in the nation's racial order were underway and made conscious efforts to move with the times, though typically in fits and starts and only when faced with the kinds of organized agitation called for by Wesley. One aspect of these efforts addressed Albert Barnett's earlier chastisement of most schools' neglect of the black past. As early as the 1950s, New York City schools had begun to take steps toward removing derogatory content and expanding attention to minorities in American history textbooks. In the early 1960s, community activists in Detroit forced the city's board of education to develop a supplemental fifty-two-page pamphlet, *Struggle for Freedom and Rights: The Negro in American History*, to address the deficiencies of the district's mainstream history texts.[24]

In 1963, leaders in Chicago's Catholic parochial schools advanced a plan calling for more black teachers and more attention to black accomplishments. Dr. Deton J. Brooks noted, "I sometimes feel that our educational systems are bringing up the most racially ignorant students in the world at a time when racial sophistication and knowledge are all important." He recommended, among other things, lessons devoted to the "life stories" of Frederick Douglass, Crispus Attucks, "and many other Negro leaders" in order "to counteract the concept of racial superiority which is still built into the American environment and is still having a strong educational effect."[25] In the same year, a community group protested the city's racially unequal educational system by organizing a boycott of the South Side's public schools and setting up alternative "freedom schools" where students learned about Attucks and other black Americans. For "Freedom Schools" set up in Mississippi by young activists of the Student Nonviolent Coordinating Committee (SNCC), a pair of college graduates developed a fifty-page publication, "Negroes in American History: A Freedom Primer," which was "laced throughout with profiles on such Negro historical figures as Crispus Attucks," Toussaint Louverture, Denmark Vesey, and Nat Turner, among others. This "freedom fighting history book" was designed to "motivate Negro children," instill "racial pride," and connect "the young reader to the civil rights movement."[26]

Community activists in Los Angeles and Washington, DC, also moved their respective school systems toward incorporating African American history into the curriculum.[27] In January 1963, a special meeting of the curriculum committee of the District of Columbia public schools determined that "the contributions of American Negroes to progress in the United States have too long been neglected" and announced that "plans for a scheme to teach students about the Negro's heritage have been completed." According to the acting director of the city schools' history department, "history books" consistently excluded "the exploits of such outstanding colored Americans as Crispus Attucks" and others, and the district's new policy of inclusion would serve both to "give white students 'a different image' of the colored American, and also inspire pride among colored students." A study guide on Negro history for fifth, eighth, and eleventh grade American history classes was made available for fall 1963 classes. In 1965, the city recruited returning Peace Corps volunteers and recent liberal arts college graduates to work with teachers and community members to create a new educational model at several elementary, junior high, and high schools. At predominantly black Cardozo High School, teaching teams used African American novels and mimeographed handouts to overcome the "built-in bias" of traditional textbooks' "Jim Crow version of the American past." One intern showed his class two films on the Boston Massacre: "In one, Crispus Attucks, the Negro hero . . . was only a blur in an early scene. In the other, Attucks played a leading role." Students pondering Attucks's role were encouraged to engage historical narratives critically while also "discuss[ing] the commitment of a Negro in a society that degrades him."[28]

The latter "film" may well have been one of two filmstrips produced in 1964 and 1965. The first was the work of Negro History Associates (NHA), a company founded in New York in 1964 by Middleton A. "Spike" Harris to promote the teaching of African American history. Harris's filmstrip on the Revolutionary era, complete with twenty-page teacher's study guide, was "not intended as an eulogy to the long neglected black heroes of the Revolutionary period" but rather emphasized "the interdependence of Americans, one upon another." Its purpose was "to supplement text book material by presenting in proper context persons of varying degrees of greatness" and "to promote mutual respect and regard among all Americans." The opening scene presented Attucks leading "a crowd of Americans" to the Boston Custom House "to protest British rule over the colonies." Another filmstrip series from the same era, "The History of the American Negro, 1619–1865," was produced by popular textbook publisher McGraw-Hill, with John Hope Franklin as historical consultant. In its coverage of the Boston Massacre, the narrative text similarly indicates that "Crispus Attucks, an escaped slave, led the revolt." The event was said to have "ushered in the Revolutionary War."[29]

If mainstream publishers like McGraw-Hill were beginning to respond to market forces, some local situations required boots on the ground to spur change. In Los Angeles, the local NAACP chapter and a newly formed United Civil Rights Committee rallied one thousand people to march across downtown to present their demands at a June 1963 board of education meeting. They pressed for greater integration through redistricting or busing, more equitable class sizes across schools, and more jobs for black teachers. They also demanded, in the words of one placard carried by the marchers, that the schools "Teach Negro History." Board member J. C. Chambers responded to the last demand with the argument that "there is so little Negro history that it isn't worth teaching" and that, in any case, "there are no adequate textbooks." When the example of Crispus Attucks was suggested, Chambers countered that "Attucks was an innocent bystander during the Boston massacre." The crowd's boos turned to cheers when marcher Dr. Marcus McBroom schooled Chambers. Carrying Franklin's *From Slavery to Freedom*, Bennett's *Before the Mayflower*, and other black history books with him to the podium, McBroom "straightened out the record ... on the significance of Attucks ... and the severance of U.S.-British ties." The "good doctor" then "offered [Chambers] a list of books on Negro history. A red-faced Chambers made no comment."[30]

By the following summer, Los Angeles schools' social studies curriculum formally incorporated "the contributions Negroes, Mexican-Americans and other minorities have made to America's growth." Attucks would be introduced as a "patriot" to fifth grade students "studying national heroes," along with "slave poet" Phillis Wheatley, "abolitionist" Harriet Tubman, and other African American figures. Mrs. Gloria Curtis, the wife of city councilman Tom Bradley's administrative assistant, was charged with "doing the research and writing the biographies for incorporation into textbooks." Mrs. Curtis found the research "exciting" and "quite challenging," as she crafted stories about how these individuals overcame adversity in the hope that "children will be able to identify with these persons, and learn through self-esteem to change their negative self-image to a more positive one." A year later, black state representative Mervyn Dymally of Los Angeles gained the support of the Los Angeles city schools and the California School Board Association in passing a bill making California "the first state in the Union to require by law the teaching of Negro history." Dymally, a former educator who had unsuccessfully proposed the bill in 1963, expressed great satisfaction that "future generations [would] know the achievements of such Negroes as Crispus Attucks and George Washington Carver." Despite conservative opposition, in 1966 the pathbreaking racially inclusive text, *Land of the Free: A History of the United States*, co-authored by John Hope Franklin, was approved for use in California's public schools. This apparent movement toward racial equity in California was belied just two months after the bill's passage, when, in August 1965, rioting in Los Angeles' Watts neighborhood left death, destruction, and a period of martial law in the city.[31]

These community-based movements represent the growth of a broader national discussion, as both classroom activities and the content of secondary- and college-level history textbooks became sites of revision and reaction. During the early 1960s, Crispus Attucks began to reappear in mainstream American history texts, albeit largely as a simplistically inserted "token." David Saville Muzzey's immensely popular textbooks, published under several titles between 1911 and 1965, arguably "gave [Muzzey] perhaps as much influence as any modern writer on the American conception of history." Not surprisingly for the author of what has been called "one of the most unapologetically racist [textbooks] on the market," Muzzey excluded Attucks from all editions of his texts until 1963, when *Our American Republic*, at this point co-authored with historian Arthur S. Link, indicated in its discussion of the Boston Massacre that "the first to fall was a Negro, Crispus Attucks." In 1965, a "first revised edition" of *Our Country's History*, another popular Muzzey text newly co-authored with Link, also acknowledged that "Crispus Attucks [was] killed in the 'Boston Massacre.'"[32]

Another good measure of the change can be found in a popular high school text by Henry Graff and John Krout, *The Adventure of the American People*. The 1960 edition refers to a "mob of ruffians" taunting the troops, and revolutionaries using the memory of the event "to keep the flames of discontent fanned high." Identical language appeared in the 1970 edition, but it also noted that "one of the victims was Crispus Attucks, a runaway slave, who was the leader of the mob." The authors also pointed to the "irony of a black who was less than free becoming a martyr to the cause of freedom."[33] Graff's solo-authored 1967 text, *The Free and the Brave*, provided extensive, and somewhat more consistently sympathetic, coverage, while noting that "Crispus Attucks, a Negro, seems to have been the leader of the mob. Attucks and his fellow victims had become the first martyrs in the American struggle against Britain. . . . [They] became public heroes."[34]

Graff, like Muzzey, was a well-respected history professor at Columbia University; but Graff better reflects the mainstream history profession's transformation regarding the relevance of African American history. Commenting in a 1968 interview on *The Free and the Brave*, Graff observed that, until recently, "most white Americans" had been content with the "unreal view of the world" contained in conventional history textbooks, which "have been written, for the most part, about white Anglo-Saxon Protestants." He specifically noted that "missing from many standard texts is mention of Crispus Attucks, a Negro who was among the first men to die in the American Revolution." Graff had come to believe that "the failure to recognize the Negro as a historical figure" was detrimental to the education of "not only black young people but also white young people." Graff's ideas echoed those presented by prominent black spokespersons, including James Baldwin and Jackie Robinson, at a recent congressional subcommittee hearing. They also cited Attucks, among others, in their complaint that "textbooks had slighted the role of Negroes in the country's development and that the Negro consequently was deprived both of his heritage and his heroes."[35]

But other historians took issue with this movement to integrate blacks into the nation's story. Thomas A. Bailey, in his 1968 presidential address to the Organization of American Historians, complained that many teachers tended to uncritically "perpetuate the hallowed myths" of American history and chastised textbook writers for being "among the most active preservers of hoary myths." However, while warning against the "pitfalls of apotheosis" regarding traditional white American political and military leaders, he also argued that "pressure-group history of any kind is deplorable, especially when significant white men are bumped out to make room for much less significant black men in the interests of social harmony." One case of "this distortion get[ting] completely out of hand," in Bailey's mind, was the "apotheosis of Crispus Attucks." Attucks "and his fellows were guilty of hooliganism," not heroism. Moreover, "we do not even know for a certainty whether he was a Negro or an Indian or even a runaway." According to Bailey, promoting Attucks as a significant patriotic hero demonstrated a "determination to stand American history on its head" which was "characteristic of minority groups." Inserting Attucks into the curriculum "may stimulate pride among Negroes," he concluded, "but it can win little support from true scholarship." Garden City, New York, social studies teacher Alan L. Benosky similarly rejected the "historical juggling" involved in the "attempt to prescribe an orthodox inter-pretation of Negro history" meant to feed blacks' "search for status." He also questioned the notion that a "faulty teaching of history has contributed to the Negroes' plight." While he expressed hope for improved conditions for African Americans, Benosky believed that "the elevation of Negroes to his-toric heroes won't buy a Negro a hamburger in Harlem. The whites get the money" from authoring inclusive textbooks, he claimed, "and the blacks get Crispus Attucks. The Negroes need hamburgers, not heroes."[36]

As the 1960s came to a close—and the bicentennial of the Boston Massacre loomed—legal historian Hiller B. Zobel undertook the task of giving the massacre its first extensive historical analysis which would meet Bailey's criteria for "true scholarship." Zobel provided a thorough and dis-passionate analysis of the Boston Massacre, including a balanced description of what the evidence suggests about Attucks and his role in the affair. Zobel's three hundred pages provided what multiple reviewers considered the "defin-itive" study of the massacre, analyzing the Anglo-American political context, colonial legal culture, government documents, witness testimony, newspaper accounts, personal reminiscences, and a hefty dose of other primary and sec-ondary sources. Yet Zobel's ultimate conclusion was that "no one yet knows what really happened" on that fateful March evening.[37]

In acknowledging the many unresolved questions surrounding the Boston Massacre, Zobel also recognized the event's symbolic importance and its sus-ceptibility to distortion. In Americans' popular understanding of the nation's story, the massacre was "an old friend among the historical residue we all carry." People typically embraced the story, corroborated by Revere's famous depiction, of "helpless citizens" being assaulted with a "deadly volley" fired with "military precision" by heartless British soldiers. The most memorable name among the dead in this telling was "Crispus Attucks, the first American to die for liberty, [who] lies an innocent martyr at the feet of his butchers." A second component of this tale involved the "Birth of American Justice" theme, in which John Adams's sense of duty led him to defend the soldiers, and Boston's citizens' "nobility of soul" caused them to set aside their outrage and see that right was served in the soldiers' acquittal. Well before the study of collective memory captured the historical profession's attention, Zobel saw the massacre as "a part, not only of our national history, but of our national mythology," which "fills a need in our national historic memory." He noted how both abolitionists and modern activists used Crispus Attucks to serve their interests, observing that "the complex myth that rose from the bloody snow of King Street needs no factual support."[38]

Zobel thus seemed well aware that Americans would continue to construct the Boston Massacre—and the Crispus Attucks—they needed to suit their varied interests. In reviewing Zobel's book, *New York Times* book critic Thomas Lask noted that the Boston Massacre had "created a folk hero in the person of the presumably black Crispus Attucks, whose participation in the fracas has somehow been turned into a 20th-century battle for civil rights."[39] While Lask's comment suggests the extent to which some version of Attucks had entered at least superficially into the American scene, Zobel remained mindful that the evidence and arguments of academic scholarship filter only slowly and incompletely into popular understanding. Zobel's allusions to the power of historical myths and historical memory suggest that textbooks and school curricula were limited in reach and that public commemorative activity might play a significant role in shaping a nation's understanding of its past. Some black activists during the civil rights era shared this recognition and took appropriate action.

One of those actions challenged perhaps the most conservative and exclusionary bastion of the Revolutionary heritage, the Daughters of the American Revolution (DAR). The DAR had been targeted during the World War II era, largely in reaction against its refusal to allow African American singer Marian Anderson to perform at the organization's Constitution Hall. In 1966, an organization calling itself the Society for Crispus Attucks Women to join the DAR (SCAWDAR) claimed to have "certified 164 descendants of good old Crispus Attucks" who qualified for membership. In promoting SCAWDAR's cause, black journalist Harry Golden asserted that "it is a matter of record that at his death Attucks was survived by five nephews and seven nieces." SCAWDAR had taken "many years" of research to track down these "lineal descendants of Crispus Attucks," and Golden hoped that the DAR would "certify the Attucks women for membership" at its next meeting. In fact, the DAR criteria for membership included only descendants of those who served between April 19, 1775 (Lexington and Concord), and November 23, 1783 (British Evacuation of New York City). The dubious claims of the ostensible Attucks nieces, nephews, and other descendants were moot, and in any case there appears to be no evidence other than Golden's newspaper column to corroborate the SCAWDAR claims, or even the society's existence.[40]

Other actions had greater substance and public presence. In early 1963, as civil rights protests expanded in Greenwood, Mississippi; Birmingham, Alabama; and other communities in the South, a group of black Chicago business organizations "voiced enthusiastic approval" for an initiative from the Chicago Metropolitan Mutual Assurance Company (CMMAC) to "have President John F. Kennedy proclaim a national holiday commemorating the heroism of Crispus Attucks." The CMMAC declared March 5 an annual holiday for all its employees, and the move was supported by the interracial Cosmopolitan Chamber of Commerce and several black real estate, mortgage, and insurance organizations. Chicago Metropolitan president George S. Harris emphasized that "this observance is not intended to become a 'segregated' holiday" since "the Boston Massacre represents an all-American sacrifice and it deserves recognition by all Americans." Ernest R. Rather, president of the Chicago Committee of 100, pushed further for "the national adoption of a holiday in honor of Attucks." Several months later, two days before the historic March on Washington, the African American National Insurance Association linked its support for "the Kennedy civil rights program" with a "resolution call[ing] for a national holiday commemorating the martyrdom of Crispus Attucks."[41]

The Chicago-based movement also argued for a "greater emphasis on the Negro's role in American history in school textbooks" while maintaining its push for a national Attucks Day holiday over the next several years. In 1965, the organizers succeeded in gaining the support of Chicago mayor Richard Daley and Illinois governor Otto Kerner, each of whom issued a proclamation declaring March 5 Crispus Attucks Day in the city and state, respectively. The 1965 commemoration featured the participation of over one thousand school students and addresses by the Reverend Wyatt T. Walker, formerly chief of staff to Martin Luther King Jr., with the Southern Christian Leadership

Conference (SCLC), and the noted black history writer and *Ebony* magazine senior editor, Lerone Bennett. No white political leaders appear to have
attended.[42]

The proclamations by Mayor Daley and Governor Kerner were likely mere
token gestures to assuage a black population increasingly dissatisfied with
being ignored as important components in the nation's history. Not coincidentally, the mid-1960s saw increasing black frustration with the slow pace of
change in African Americans' quest for equal rights and racial justice. Despite
the momentous changes represented by the passage of the 1964 Civil Rights
Act and the 1965 Voting Rights Act, most black Americans saw little if any
change in their material conditions or their prospects for equal opportunities in the United States. Between 1964 and 1965, murders, burnings, and
bombings continued across the South; members of the Mississippi Freedom
Democratic Party were excluded from the Democratic National Convention
in Atlantic City; voting rights marchers from Selma to Montgomery, Alabama,
were brutally beaten by police; urban ghettoes seethed with tension; and the
nation's schools were just as separate and unequal as they had been prior to
the 1954 *Brown* decision. Little wonder that many blacks were attracted by
the empowering calls of black nationalism and black power as they sought to
claim their constitutional rights while also reasserting and redefining black
American identity.

A 1968 *Christian Science Monitor* editorial, titled "Crispus Attucks and
Swahili," captured part of the challenge they faced. The writer began with an
imagined conversation in which a sympathetic white man questions a black
man about the relative lack of upward mobility among African Americans.
He points out that Irish, Italian, Polish, Jewish, and even Chinese immigrants to the United States had "made it" while blacks, who had been in the
country far longer than the Chinese, had not. "What do the Chinese have
that the Negroes haven't?" The black man's response: "Dragons!" The editorial pointed out that non-black ethnic groups arrived with "a family unit,
a social cohesion and a deeply rooted cultural background and history." In
contrast, "the black American" had arrived "forcibly stripped of his identity"
and "reduced to chattel status," and so needed to construct new and empowering traditions, symbols, and historical narratives in the American context.
The editorialist saw this need as central to the recent inclusion of courses in
Swahili in a predominantly black New York City secondary school and the
declaration of Crispus Attucks Day in Newark, New Jersey. The "historical
accuracy" of Attucks's ostensible heroism and the practical value of learning Swahili were irrelevant in a nation "striving still to deny the black man

his identity." Both acts represented "an understandable step forward toward acquisition by blacks of the dragons so long denied them."[43]

Newark's Attucks Day movement was consistent with similar steps taken in Chicago, Boston, and elsewhere. But Newark in the 1960s was also a focal point for African American urban rebellion, cultural nationalism, and political power. The city's Negro Historical Society first organized an Attucks Day parade and awards dinner in 1966, as part of the city's 300th anniversary observances. The 1967 event was expanded to Crispus Attucks Week and was organized by the Crispus Attucks Society, which appears to have been formed in the wake of the previous year's event. The week culminated with an integrated parade of some four thousand marchers, including school groups, marching bands, government officials, floats, and "contingents of police, fire, nurses, Elks, Masons, churches, political and civic groups," as well as the Polish Falcons drum and bugle corps from nearby Elizabeth and several Gold Star Mothers who had lost sons in the Vietnam War. The awards banquet the same evening, sponsored by Ballantine Brewery and limited to members of the Attucks Society, honored a local black reporter and photojournalist and presented awards to various marching units, floats, bands, and several businesses that provided financial support. A few months later, Newark's biracial alliances became more strained as the city exploded in one of the largest urban uprisings of the era, with significant deaths, property damage, and arrests.[44]

Subsequent years nonetheless saw an expansion of Newark's Attucks Week festivities. The 1968 parade dwarfed previous events with a reported 20,000 marchers and between 50,000 and 100,000 spectators. Another 100,000 were estimated to have seen a film of the festivities, titled *A Tribute to Crispus Attucks*, made by the Prudential Insurance Company. Perhaps more significant than the parade was the Newark Board of Education's designation of March 5 as Crispus Attucks Day, making Newark the first major city to create an officially sanctioned school holiday honoring a black American. Board member Stanley A. Stolowski was one of two dissenters, arguing that the holiday was "a good proposal," but it "discriminates against other groups." The NAACP and the Attucks Society were active in pushing for the holiday, but much of the credit went to Central High history teacher and Attucks society leader John Thomas, who also sponsored the high school's Afro-American club, which promoted the study and appreciation of black culture and history. The new school holiday, Thomas said, "gives the Negro a hero to identify with, like the Italians and Columbus Day." He also made clear that "we're not teaching separatism or anything like that. . . . We want the kids to take pride in being both black and American." Still, Thomas's intent for the holiday and for his school's Afro-American club was clearly in line with the goal of creating those "dragons" identified in the *Christian Science Monitor* editorial. Black city employees began a campaign for the city to make Attucks Day a holiday for all municipal workers, and Thomas expressed confidence that the city and even the state would follow through.[45]

While Newark and statewide workers did not get their paid holiday, over the next several years the city's Attucks commemorations expanded to other communities. In 1968, King's County, New York, assemblywoman Gail Hellenbrand submitted a resolution calling for the governor to declare Attucks Day in that state. In 1969, the New Jersey cities of Paterson and Plainfield created their own Attucks school holidays, and Chicago maintained its Attucks Day tradition with another large celebration. In 1970, Governor Ronald Reagan signed a bill designating March 5 as Black American Day in the state of California; originally the date was to be January 15, the birthday of Martin Luther King Jr., but the state senate amended the bill to honor Attucks instead. In that same year, Newark's Crispus Attucks Society honored both those fallen black heroes by holding an Attucks-King parade, which drew some 200,000 spectators and 50,000 marchers. In a sign of the city's changing political and demographic identity, speeches were given by current mayor Hugh Addonizio and Newark's soon-to-be-elected first black mayor, Kenneth Gibson. An Attucks Society spokesperson was gratified that the parade had "come into its own," with the march being "covered by all the major teevee channels and for the second year, broadcast in its entirety via radio station WNJR."[46]

The 1971 Newark Attucks-King parade exhibited more of a black power sensibility, in part thanks to the unanimous selection of Newark poet and nationalist leader Amiri Baraka as the parade's grand marshal. Baraka's selection was likely the reason "former financial contributors" from business and industry were reluctant to offer the support they had in previous years. Nonetheless, organizers refused to "negate the choice." One spokesperson was proud that the parade was "black geared and oriented"; while local white business and community support was welcome, that welcome did "not include the right of the white minority to select leadership for the black majority." The parade's theme was "Protest Plus Pride Equals Progress," and longtime Attucks Society member and local journalist Connie Woodruff expressed her view that the event would be "as big, colorful and prideful as it has ever been." The corporate pullouts were but "little annoyances" which merely meant that "the black community will be forced to greater input . . . and maybe that's as it really should be." The "six hour spectacle of music, color and precision" featured a surprise appearance by popular music sensation Stevie Wonder, and Grand Marshal Baraka "beam[ed] approval" as he returned a black power salute from one of the "Simba units representing the Committee for a Unified Newark [CFUN]."[47]

CFUN was a black nationalist organization spearheaded by Baraka in the wake of the 1967 uprising and was based on his adherence to Kawaida, a religio-nationalist philosophy dedicated to black political, economic, and cultural self-sufficiency.[48] The emergence of black nationalist leaders and organizations in the late 1960s represented a transformation in civil rights activism and black identity that had been underway for some time. As tensions between the poles of integrationism and separatism came into sharp relief among black Americans during this period, Crispus Attucks came to occupy a somewhat ambiguous status.

Attucks's name was invoked after the assassinations of both the Mississippi NAACP leader Medgar Evers and the nationalist icon Malcolm X.[49] In 1963, Jackie Robinson used Attucks, as had many others over the years, to exemplify the American Negro's "loyalty and patriotism" and love for America. The Pan-African intellectual Frederick H. Hammurabi's House of Knowledge, a Chicago black cultural center committed "to fus[ing] African consciousness with the study of the black past," honored Attucks alongside past and present "freedom fighters" like Martin Luther King Jr., Toussaint Louverture, and Congolese leader Patrice Lumumba, all of whom had lost their lives in pursuit of justice for their people.[50] New York congressman Adam Clayton Powell Jr. told a 1968 Los Angeles audience that Attucks died in a war fought for "a democracy that we don't have here any more."[51] In 1970, Jesse Jackson compared Attucks's "first blood shed for this land's liberty" with the "disproportionally large number" of black infantrymen dying on the front lines in Vietnam.[52]

Like Jackson, *Christian Science Monitor* columnist Joanne Leedom constructed meaning around Attucks by connecting him with critical events in the late 1960s. Writing on the two-hundredth anniversary of Attucks's death, Leedom described a visit to the Boston State House Museum, where she pondered the massacre as a "symbol of a revolt against tyranny." She then recounted hearing chants of "Power to the People" from outside the museum, as "young people . . . determined to have a say in their own history" seemingly took up Attucks's example in protesting the recent conviction of the Chicago Seven.[53]

Another commentator noted that the assassination of Martin Luther King Jr. had brought "the greatest outpouring of national mourning and flowery accolades and concern ever accorded a Negro in American history.... Yet, the country's 'first hero,' who happened to be a Negro, as was Dr. King, is not only forgotten but, more importantly, probably unknown to most Americans." Attucks's supposed erasure from Americans' knowledge of the past was "vitally important" because it "hits directly at the heart of the ills of a society which sees a Negro to be the first to die for 'freedom' and which 193 years later allows another Negro to be gunned down on the streets of one of its cities still in the quest for a freedom which the first man died for. In this one crystal clear example, one sees all of the wrongs, injustices, prejudices, despair, hopelessness, and frustration which have been heaped upon the Negro in America."[54]

Black Power spokesperson Stokely Carmichael illustrates the complexity of Attucks's place among African Americans' search for symbols and heroes. In 1966, Carmichael argued that African Americans should not condemn the participants in urban rebellions, saying that the black "man who goes out and throws a brick at a white cop is taking part in an uprising as Crispus Attucks, another black man, was when he threw rocks in the American Revolution at Boston."[55] But on the other hand, Carmichael also argued that Attucks exemplified blacks' fundamental problem of "always tr[ying] to be American first and black people all the way down the end. And that's why we catching hell the way we catching it today." After excoriating whites' attempts to systematically denigrate black cultural achievements, he listed a host of black heroes who should be a part of school curricula, including Denmark Vesey, Frederick Douglass, W. E. B. Du Bois, Alain Locke, J. A. Rogers, and Malcolm X. He mocked the fact that only "Toms" like Booker Washington and George Washington Carver received attention, and condemned Attucks as the archetypal example of integrationist blacks misplacing their priorities, telling an audience at a Seattle high school in 1967 that

> the very first man to die for the War of Independence in this country was a black man named Crispus Attucks! The very first man, yes! {Applause}
>
> He was a fool! Yeah! {shocked applause}
>
> He died for white folk country while the rest of his black brothers were enslaved in this country. He should've been fighting white folk instead of dying for white folk! But that's been our history as black people—we've always been dying for white folk![56]

In the month of the massacre's bicentennial, an editorial in the ASNLH monthly *Negro History Bulletin*, presumably written by editor Charles Harris Wesley, used 1770 newspaper sources to support a counterargument highlighting "the fact that [it] was an integrated massacre" in which Attucks gave his life, "with one black man and four white men as martyrs." The martyrs' funeral "was also an integrated one." With comments like Carmichael's apparently in mind, Wesley expressed "fear that some of us to justify our own acts today must become ashamed of the nation's forefathers who integrated this first shedding of blood for American independence."[57]

Varied versions of Attucks also began to appear more frequently in historical biographies for young readers. In 1965, Gary, Indiana, librarian and newspaper columnist Dharathula H. Millender published her fictionalized children's biography, *Crispus Attucks: Boy of Valor*, which presented the classic all-American Attucks who conformed to the integrationist ideal of sacrificing one's life in the name of loyalty, patriotism, and love of country. In constructing a set of experiences, personal attributes, religious sensibilities, and political convictions that are in no way supported by the scant historical record, Millender created an Attucks who was largely an idealized, pious, integrationist American patriot who looked beyond the superficialities of race and died in the cause of liberty for all Americans.

Another publication about Attucks targeting young readers appeared in 1967, in the third installment of the Golden Legacy Illustrated History Magazine (see Fig. 7.1). Essentially a historical comic book, Golden Legacy was the brainchild of a Harlem-born black history buff and New York State government employee named Bertram Fitzgerald. Fitzgerald had grown up frustrated by the treatment of blacks in children's reading materials, and he established Golden Legacy in 1966 to present the "worldwide achievements" of black historical figures that would "implant pride and self-esteem in black youth while dispelling myths" among all readers. Between 1966 and 1976, Golden Legacy published sixteen biographies or group biographies on subjects ranging from ancient African kingdoms, black cowboys, and black inventors to Toussaint Louverture, Harriet Tubman, and Martin Luther King Jr. *Crispus Attucks and the Minutemen* (1967) was the third in the series and the first to receive support from a major corporate sponsor, the Coca Cola Corporation. Fitzgerald experienced both financial and product quality issues in Golden Legacy's first two numbers, on Louverture and Tubman. Coke's interest in financing this venture is indicative of a growing recognition of black buying power among American corporations. Coke mass distributed copies of the issue "free to schools, libraries, and organizations such as the

FIG. 7.1 "Crispus Attucks and the Minutemen," *Golden Legacy*, Vol. 3 (1967). From the author's collection. Scan by Western Michigan University Libraries Digitization Center. Courtesy of Bertram A. Fitzgerald, Golden Legacy.

NAACP, the Urban League and [the federal] Reading is Fundamental programs." A&P food stores, McDonald's, and other major corporations sponsored subsequent Golden Legacy titles through full-page, back cover ads.[58]

The Attucks volume also was the first to feature the work of the up-and-coming black illustrator Tom Feelings. Feelings had written a full-length comic on Attucks in the late 1950s but was unable to find a publisher until interest in black-focused educational materials expanded in the mid-1960s. His story was included in a 1965 Negro heritage reader and appeared with essentially the same text and artwork in the Golden Legacy issue. While *Crispus Attucks and the Minutemen* listed historian Benjamin Quarles as a consultant, the text bore little resemblance to actual historical events. The story opens with Attucks befriending a young black cabin boy on a ship entering Boston harbor. Attucks and his friend are greeted by Crispus's good friend Patrick Carr, who took them to a patriot meeting. Egregious errors come fast and furious, as Attucks addresses the crowd, reminding them that he had spoken to them two years before and calling on them to fight for their freedom. We are told that Attucks's "enthusiasm and fervor ... stirred the citizens again, this time into acting." "Lead us and we will follow," they shouted in one speech bubble. "Lead on Attucks, we'll follow!" pronounced another. As Attucks and his followers confront the British troops, a hand-to-hand brawl ensues until Captain Preston asks one of his men to "capture the leader of the mob ... that tall dark fellow," in order to negotiate a peaceful solution. But alas, someone yells, "Fire!" and Attucks is slain with the "PFFLAM!" of a musket shot. Attucks's young friend sees that his death was not in vain, since "he has shown us the way to freedom."[59]

While Millender's *Boy of Valor* and other works from the 1960s also contain gross historical inaccuracies, the Golden Legacy version seems less informed by the wave of factual black history materials that emerged during the civil rights era. It is almost a throwback to the children's books from the 1920s in its simplicity and inattention to detail. And, also unlike Millender, Golden Legacy provided no discussion of Attucks's background and identity other than the dubious claim that he "was sold into slavery when [he] was just a young boy." Still, it fit the emerging dominant integrationist narrative: a brave and articulate black man who could not abide "one man owning another against his will" and who applied that same principle to the American nation as he became a leader of white patriots.[60]

Another illustrated historical magazine that appeared a year later fit less easily into that narrative. In 1968, a New York City organization calling itself Noble Heritage, Ltd., produced a thirty-three-page illustrated magazine for young readers that presented an Attucks who was just as loyal an American but who also reflected an Afrocentric sense of self. This text's dramatically different biography of Attucks certainly reached a much smaller audience than either Golden Legacy or Millender, but it suggests how a sketchy historical record might be filled in to suit a variety of agendas, particularly in a period of social and political upheaval like the 1960s.

Noble Heritage seems to have been affiliated with New York's Schomburg Center for Research in Black Culture, and the issue on Attucks (identified as "Volume 1, Number 1") appears to have been intended as the first in an ongoing series on black history; thus far no other issues have come to light. The authors described trade between Africa, the Caribbean, and North America while presenting the eighteenth-century world Attucks was born into. Rather than following the conventional understanding that Attucks was partly of Native American background, Noble Heritage asserted that he "was born of an African mother and an American father," making him "Afro-American in the truest sense of the word." His mother, Ola, and her brother Kwame were children of "a chief, Wantobo, a man much feared and respected all through the Guinean kingdom of Benin." Nonetheless, they were captured and endured the Middle Passage together. Separated at the dock in Newport, Rhode Island, in 1717, Kwame was taken away to be sold in Jamaica, but not before promising Ola that he would "come and find her" one day.[61]

Ola was sold to a Framingham, Massachusetts, farmer named Mayhew, learned English, adapted to the life of a domestic slave, and came to take charge of the household, all the while dreaming of the day Kwame would return and they would be free. A few years later "a new slave by the name of Ottobah" was brought to the farm as a skilled carpenter. He "was clearly of mixed black and white parentage" and "spoke English rather well, yet preferred the African dialect that he had learned from his mother." He and Ola fell in love and married, with "Otto" promising that when Kwame returned they would all go to Africa, since, he told her, "I want to go home one day as much as you do." Shortly before the birth of their child, however, Otto was thrown from a horse and killed. She decided to give her new son an "American" name since he would be able to "call himself an American" just as the white children did. Ola decided on "Christopher," but since she could not pronounce it correctly, everyone called him Crispus.

One evening, an Indian friend of Otto's, named Attucks, who worked on a whaler, brought news to their cabin that he had found Kwame, who was a maroon in Jamaica fighting against the British. Ola held out hope of being reunited with Kwame, and she taught young Cris the language, stories, and culture of her people, even as she made sure he learned to read English and became familiar with all the ways of the whites. Attucks returned from time to time to update them on Kwame's well-being. When Cris was a teenager, Ola died of scarlet fever and he was sold to William Brown, for whom he traveled around the region buying and selling livestock. In 1743, Kwame, who had led a successful revolt in Jamaica, found Cris and tried to take him to Africa. Cris, however, refused, since he saw himself as an American. He gave Kwame all the money he had been saving to buy his freedom. "Always remember that you are the grandson of an African chief," a grateful Kwame advised his nephew.

With no money, Cris decided to run away and take to the sea. To disguise his identity, he took on the name of their Indian friend and signed aboard a Portuguese whaler as Crispus Attucks. He spent much time in and around Portugal and learned that races might intermingle there more than among the English; in fact, the royal family there was presented as having mixed African and European blood. On one of his voyages to the Cape Verde Islands, Cris purchased the freedom of a young African woman and they married. He happened to be on shore leave in Boston on the evening of March 5, 1770, when he joined a crowd of colonists who were listing their grievances against the Redcoats. Attucks spoke his mind about the abuses of English slavery and claimed that "we can do nothing about this evil until we rid ourselves of the Redcoats." The crowd cheered him. "'Freedom,' Crispus continued, 'It must be that or nothing for each one of us.'" Later, when the soldiers saw Attucks in the crowd they taunted him, saying "a black man has no rights," calling him a slave and a dog, and telling him to go home to his master. Attucks responded, "This land is mine, I say. No man is my master." The soldiers fired and Attucks and four others were killed.

The Noble Heritage version of Crispus Attucks strayed even further from the historical record than Millender's. And it certainly lived up to the organization's name, exemplifying a deep identification with a virtuous and dignified African past as well as a dedication to the America of his birth, with its ideals of liberty and equality for all. But in the tumultuous 1960s, there emerged cultural commentators who could present yet another, far less respectful, portrait of Attucks and his role in America's history. The San Francisco Mime Troupe was not in the habit of showing much respect for any established traditions, and their 1965 satirical treatment of Attucks was no exception. Founded in the late 1950s, by 1965 the troupe had evolved into perhaps the first modern example of what founder R. G. Davis referred to as "guerilla theatre." Their outrageous performances in city parks and other public spaces addressed topical issues and were intended to be the vanguard of radical revolutionary change in American society. One of the earliest and most controversial of their guerilla productions, *A Minstrel Show, or Civil Rights in a Cracker Barrel* (1965), was characterized by the *New York Times* as "a sarcastic history of the American Negro" and "an outrageous pin-pricking of All We Hold Dear." *Cracker Barrel* used the minstrel format of white and black actors in blackface performing comical skits that traded on deep-seated stereotypes of black Americans. The troupe's radical subversion of minstrelsy's racist caricatures mocked the notions of racial progress and inclusion that comforted many white Americans in the wake of the 1964 Civil Rights Act and 1965 Voting Rights Act. As the *Times* reporter suggested in a very positive review of a 1966 New York performance, the show's primary target was America's "racial hypocrisy."[62]

Crispus Attucks made his appearance in the production about midway through the first act, as the performers used the vehicle of "Negro History Week [to] tell you all how it really happened" and to "trace back through the years and the ages the history of the colored race." Using standard, degrading minstrel show dialect, the players presented "de first man to be killed by de redcoats in de war for Independence: Crispus Attucks." As two blackface performers in periwigs debate joining with Sam Adams or Patrick Henry, Crispus enters sweeping the floor. One of the "revolutionaries" spits on the floor and addresses Attucks: ""Wanta take care o dat, nigger?" Upon being warned by a rider that "de redcoats is comin'," the following dialogue ensues among revolutionaries 1 and 2 and Crispus:

1: Crispus, do you believe in equality?
CRISPUS: Yeah.
2: Do you believe in justice?
CRISPUS: Yeah.
1: Do you believe in brotherhood?
CRISPUS: Sure!
2: Do you believe in taxation without representation?
CRISPUS: Yeah, yeah! I believe in everything. What's wrong with everybody?

After Attucks was shot by the redcoats, "God in heaven above was rewardin ol Crispus as he rewards all de heroes of American history, by grantin dem everlasting immortality in de grade school history books." As the scene shifts to heaven, the audience finds Crispus eating a watermelon and being praised: "Crispus, you're a hero, baby. Tell us your story—would you give your life again for the cause of freedom?" Crispus's response could have come from any of the obsequious "Sambo" characters from the minstrel tradition: "Lawzy, Mass'r, I'ze just mindin my own business, cleanin up, when dese two mothers throw me into de middle of de street and dem redcoated cats shoot me. Leave me alone, man, I'm eatin!"[63]

The Mime Troupe's Sambo-esque Attucks was as unique in its characterization as was Noble Heritage's Afrocentric version. Most accounts for young readers in the late 1960s and early 1970s, however, stuck with the more conventional integrationist hero. Eloise Crosby Culver's book of poems honoring more than fifty black heroes, illustrated by the prominent black artist Lois Mailou Jones, was published by the ASNLH in 1966. It expressed the familiar concern with books that "continue to frustrate little Negro children by giving them only heroes whom they can never see as images of themselves" while also "depriv[ing] white children of a fruitful knowledge of Negroes." Her Attucks poem presented the standard "mighty giant of manhood" who "died in the name of freedom." The NAACP-published *Black American Heroes of the American Revolution* (1969) relied on commentary from Harriet Beecher Stowe, George Washington Williams, John Hope Franklin, and the inscription on the massacre martyrs' gravestone to highlight Attucks's significance.[64]

The period's most extensive treatment of Attucks, other than Millender's *Boy of Valor*, was the 155-page historical novel by Edmund F. Curley, *Crispus Attucks: The First to Die* (1973). Curley claimed two purposes in writing the book; the first was to "put to rest the never proven, often stated allegation that the Boston Massacre of 1770 was caused by rabble bent on mischief, having fortified themselves at local taverns." Rather, for Curley the massacre represented "the great mass of common people" whose support was essential for the "men of education" who planned the Revolution to "realize any [of their] aims." The second purpose was "to establish the truth that the first man to shed blood by an English bullet in America's fight for liberty was a black man." Curley argued that "will-o'-the-wisp evidence" surrounding Attucks had caused others to have "greatly exaggerated his life and lineage." Curley completely rejected as "strictly supposition" the widely held idea that Attucks may have had Indian or white ancestors:

> He was called a mulatto, a term applied by whites to lighter-skinned black people, even though they possess full blood of the black race. The white man is dividing the heroism of Attucks by claiming part of him. There is no definite basis of his having anything but so-called black blood. . . . Crispus Attucks in this book is asserted to be a full-blooded

black man ... a hero to whom black Americans should be allowed to
point with pride and ownership ... a black man who was the first to
die for our love of liberty.

Curley asserted that his presentation of the "historical incidents" was based
on "complete historical research of the period," but clearly he took extensive
liberties in crafting his image of Attucks, as had many others before him. His
definition of the term "mulatto" was inaccurate and his assertion of Attucks's
"full-blooded" blackness was, to say the least, inconsistent with the most
suggestive evidence. Curley also ignored evidence placing Attucks as a slave
in Massachusetts, as he traced Attucks's escape from slavery "in the South,
through his desperate escape northward." He displayed similar disregard for
the known facts in presenting Attucks as an insider among Boston's patriot
leaders, particularly close to Sam Adams and Joseph Warren. At the book's
end Adams claimed that Attucks's "greatness will grow with the years" while
Warren called him "the flame that started the real revolution." Curley's post-
script even asserted that, due to Attucks's sacrifice, the "colonists now openly
disavowed slavery. With the memory of Attucks there could be little else but
that feeling."[65]

Previous writers had made similar—or similarly unsupportable—claims
about Attucks, including the recent publications by Millender, Golden
Legacy, and Noble Heritage. But unlike those works, Curley's appeared several years after the publication of Hiller Zobel's highly credible study of the
massacre and Attucks's role in it. That the book was published through a
vanity press may help explain the lack of basic fact-checking, but it attracted
enough attention to have been advertised in a major mainstream newspaper
and to reach the shelves of nearly one hundred fifty American libraries. It was
even reissued in 1998.

Editorial oversight also seems to have been lacking at the *Negro History
Bulletin*. One hopes that Charles H. Wesley—a well-respected black historian who had been director of the ASNLH and editor of the *Bulletin* since
1965—had nothing to do with a March 1971 editorial that reverted to the
worst practices from nearly a century of unreliable Attucks biographies.
Lifting, without citation, some of the most blatant fabrications from George
Washington Williams's 1882 *History of the Negro Race*, the writer then made
his own claim that "one has but to read [Attucks's] letters and speeches to realize that he could and did write beautifully, and wisely"—as if any evidence of
Attucks's literacy, let alone letters or speeches, actually existed. The writer then
lifts, again without citation, passages from the 1942 Pulitzer Prize–winning

biography, *Paul Revere and the World He Lived In*, by acclaimed popular history writer Esther Forbes. Forbes's well-researched yet somewhat fictionalized account of the massacre was presented in the *Bulletin* as the actual eyewitness reportage of Paul Revere himself.[66]

As the bicentennial of Crispus Attucks's death passed and the nation began to look forward to the bicentennial of American independence, questions about Attucks became more complicated. Especially due to attempts to incorporate African Americans into the nation's public schools, Attucks was being introduced to more Americans than ever before. Black spokespersons still lamented the absence of Attucks and other black heroes from school curricula, but by 1974, according to historian Lois Spear, university professors could be confident that "the average college freshman" could be expected to have been taught "some version of the following: 'Crispus Attucks, a black man, was the first person to die for American independence.'" Spear echoed the concerns Thomas Bailey voiced in his 1968 presidential address to the Organization of American Historians, suggesting that Attucks may merely have been seeking "wanton amusement" by harassing the soldiers, and expressing her "hope that educators and students will carefully re-think the Negro's role and find better leaders with which to identify."[67]

The age-old questions about who Crispus Attucks was and what meanings should be attached to him remained, and commentators continued to debate varied aspects of Attucks's identity. Was he black, white, or Indian? Massachusetts-born, a West Indian, or a southerner? A sailor or a soldier? A patriot, rabble-rouser, or unlucky passerby? One writer even claimed he died on April 19, 1775, at the Battle of Lexington and Concord.[68] But in the wake of the upheavals of the 1960s—civil rights, black power, the New Left and counterculture, the beginnings of government action to enforce desegregation and racial justice—those and other questions were framed in new and distinctive ways.

Attucks was now more present than ever in the nation's public schools and popular culture, but whose agenda did he serve? Was he the first martyr of liberty and a legitimate hero of the American Revolution? Was he a mere token who was largely irrelevant to the nation's history and who was added to textbooks, curricula, and the commemorative calendar to appease an increasingly vocal and influential black minority? Did he represent the integrationist ideal of black and white standing shoulder to shoulder in the fight for freedom and the American way? Was he the quintessential Uncle Tom who gave his life to serve the needs of his white superiors, rather than rallying with his black brothers and sisters to confront racial injustice? Or was he the embodiment of black solidarity and pride? As the nation adjusted to the fallout from Vietnam and the rights revolution, it became enmeshed in energy crises, presidential scandals, and yet another transformation of American culture. The period leading toward the celebration of America's two-hundredth birthday was fraught with confusion and discord. Attucks's place in the emerging bicentennial narrative provides an interesting starting point from which to assess African Americans' place in the nation's historical imagination and collective memory during the last quarter of the American century.

8

Crispus Attucks from the Bicentennial to the Culture Wars, 1970s–1990s

First man to die for the flag we now hold high was a black man.

STEVIE WONDER, "Black Man" (1976)

There are images and echoes of black heritage almost every-where today. . . . There are sights and sounds on TV. There are lesson plans in the schools and courses in colleges. . . . Black heritage sells soap, whiskey, and detergent. It sells everything, in fact, except the meaning of black heritage and the humanity of black people.

LERONE BENNETT JR. (1976)

NEAR THE END of Alice Walker's 1976 novel, *Meridian*, the title charac-ter, a young, black civil rights activist who had continued her struggle into the 1970s, speaks idealistically about her 1960s Freedom School experiences and the intellectual energy that had fueled her radical politics. Her longtime friend, the artist and fellow black activist Truman Held, mocked what he saw as nostalgic romanticism:

Do you realize no one is thinking about these things anymore? Revolution was the theme of the sixties: Medgar, Malcolm, Martin, George [Jackson], Angela Davis, the Panthers, people blowing up buildings and each other. But all that is gone now. I am, myself, making a statue of Crispus Attucks for the Bicentennial. We're here to stay: the black and the poor, the Indian and now all those illegal immigrants from the West Indies who adore America just the way it is.[1]

By the mid-1970s Alice Walker, through her character, could use Crispus Attucks not as a symbol of revolutionary action but as just the opposite—a repudiation of the kind of radical confrontation that had informed the postwar black freedom struggle and, two centuries earlier, had cost Attucks his life.

As the nation's bicentennial approached, Attucks had become more a part of the American mainstream. He was appearing as a standard figure in most popular American history textbooks and even featured more visibly in mainstream culture outside the classroom. In fact, in 1976 a memorial sculpture dedicated to Attucks by British-born white artist Reginald Beauchamp, the "Whispering Bells of Freedom," was erected outside Philadelphia's African American Museum.[2] Of all the competing versions of Attucks then circulating, it was the taken-for-granted Revolutionary token that seemed most prominent in the nation's collective memory; for many, he was a bland symbol of a romanticized American Revolution and an unthreatening black patriotism. Walker's choice to have Truman Held create an Attucks statue for the bicentennial perfectly represented her character's acquiescence to an American racial order that preferred a limited and superficial integration over radical social transformation.[3]

Much of the discussion relating to Attucks during the 1970s took place within a broader consideration of the meanings of the American Revolution, as the nation geared up to celebrate its two-hundredth birthday. Another British native and naturalized American citizen, Alistair Cooke, established his credentials as a great admirer and popular interpreter of American history through his 1972–73 documentary history television series, *Alistair Cooke's America*. In a 1975 op-ed on the bicentennial, Cooke warned against the emerging "orgy of self-congratulation that will make us look very foolish around the world, since we are now at the nadir of our power and our glory." Disdainful of both the glorification and the commodification of the American Founders, Cooke called on the nation to eschew all that was "gaudy, childish, frivolous, vulgar, [and] idiotic," especially since most of it "has already been done." Instead, he suggested legislation or public projects that would "get on with the business in hand"—improving Americans' lives and reestablishing the nation's greatness. One project he suggested was to "build a bicentennial park in every slum" and "sound the anniversary note" by naming these parks after Crispus Attucks. But most of all, Cooke "eagerly await[ed]" January 1, 1977, when he hoped the "orgy" would end.[4]

Commemorating the bicentennial brought to light some of the fundamental tensions in American society that had emerged during the post–World War II era. On one hand were organizers and celebrants who saw the bicentennial as an opportunity to venerate all that was good and true and just in the American experience and to reclaim some of the luster that had been dulled through recent years of radical protest; civil unrest; and the economic, military, and political embarrassments that shook the nation's confidence during the early 1970s. As America was entering what memory scholar Barry Schwartz has termed a "post-heroic era," many Americans believed the nation needed heroes more than ever.[5] Their bicentennial was a moment for recalling infallible Founders and their ideals of liberty and justice; America was still that shining city on a hill providing a beacon to guide the rest of the world. This view was presented to a mass audience in *Swing Out, Sweet Land*, a 1970 ninety-minute NBC television comedy/variety special on America's history, hosted by Hollywood's embodiment of American patriotism, John Wayne. The show opened with Wayne swaggering onto the stage behind the iconic Revolutionary fife, drum, and flag trio and telling the audience,

> Well, I guess you're all saying, "Here it comes. Just put John Wayne and a show about America together and you're in for a lot of preaching about what a great country this is, and how we should all be patriotic and love our flag, and be glad we live in the good old USA, problems and all." Well, that's about the size of it, except it'll be short on preaching.[6]

Wayne acknowledged, at the height of America's anti–Vietnam War protests, that "some folks have the idea that patriotism's gone out of fashion," but a series of "comedy vignettes, musical production numbers and dramatic sketches," featuring a star-studded cast, proceeded to illustrate the nation's high ideals and steady progress toward a more perfect union, from the purchase of Manhattan island through the "family fight" of the Civil War to the Wright Brothers at Kitty Hawk. The Boston Massacre had its moment, with actors portraying the martyrs identifying themselves as Americans who had died for the cause of liberty. Last to speak was Crispus Attucks, portrayed by Greg Morris, a black actor from the popular television show, *Mission Impossible*: "My name is Crispus Attucks, American. I died in 1770 fighting for freedom. I hope it was worth it." Wayne replied, "So do I, Mr. Attucks, so do I." In his concluding remarks, Wayne trumpeted his belief in decency, freedom, and doing good for one's country, insisting that "this country . . . is man's best chance to make a go of it for humanity." He also singled out

Attucks as an example to those contemporary Americans "pushing fifty" who might be "complaining that the country is goin' to hell"; Attucks, he reminded them, "was in his forties when he died on State Street in Boston, fighting for the freedom that we share."[7]

On the other hand were those who recognized that the turmoil of recent decades laid bare how far the nation had fallen short of its founding ideals and that, along with a set of all-too-human Founders, there were long lists of others—minorities, women, immigrants, workers—who had contributed to an ongoing American experiment, in part by challenging the nation to live up to its promise of liberty and justice for all. Leaders the Afro-American Bicentennial Corporation (ABC) took issue with the unproblematic celebratory approach of the official government-sanctioned planning commission, pointing out that African Americans, at least, had "experienced the Revolution in our own lives. We know it is a continuing thing. And we believe much of the leadership for continuing the American Revolution in recent decades has come from Black Americans."[8] Another organization of activists calling itself the People's Bicentennial Commission (PBC) also challenged the official commission's approach. "The White House and Corporate America," it claimed, "are planning to sell us a program of plastic Liberty Bells, red-white-and-blue cars and a 'Love It or Leave It' political program." Like the ABC, the PBC wanted the bicentennial to stand for more than mere nostalgic back-patting on the nation's greatness, insisting instead on a meaningful movement toward "the fulfillment of the revolutionary promise of America."[9]

Both groups were committed to shaping the meaning of the bicentennial. But while the ABC sought to incorporate black perspectives into the celebration, other African American spokespersons debated whether they should participate at all. As historian Tammy S. Gordon has noted, "The bicentennial was a complicated issue for African Americans."[10] Historian Benjamin Quarles assumed that "bicentennial blacks will . . . have much to contribute to the forthcoming celebrations," concurring with the ABC position that "Black Americans will certainly give attention to the revolution as an ongoing process." Dr. Joseph Jackson, president of the National Baptist Convention, USA, also believed blacks "should and must participate" so as not to "deny their own history and their contribution to the life of this great nation." The accomplished historical writer and *Ebony* magazine senior editor Lerone Bennett Jr., however, voiced "an adamant 'No'" on the question of black participation, since "two hundred years have passed and we're not free." Black Americans, he argued, "have no time for fun and games." National Urban

League executive director Vernon Jordan maintained that participation was "imperative," but only so long as blacks "use the occasion of the Bicentennial to press our uncompleted revolution." New York state senator H. Carl McCall emphasized the Revolution's "hypocritical underpinnings" but also argued that black Americans had to "keep the spirit of true patriotism alive," not by "celebrating old lies and re-enacting old myths," but by "work[ing] toward the revolution and renewal which is yet to come."[11]

When *Ebony* published essays by Bennett, Jordan, and Jackson in its August 1975 special issue on blacks and the bicentennial, readers wrote letters challenging or championing their varied views. Most of the printed letters endorsed Bennett's argument against celebrating two hundred years of slavery and racism; blacks, wrote one, "surely are not free and we don't have anything to celebrate." Some found Jackson's position "archaic and misleading," though others "heartily agree[d]" with him that "black people have played a major role in the building of this country" and that past and present heroes "justly deserve[d] to be commemorated." Yet the contributions of one of the most widely known heroes remained problematic for some. "When we hear the name of Crispus Attucks," wrote Reginald A. Barnett of Chicago, "should we rejoice or weep? For it seems to me that two hundred years after the 'Revolution,' the descendants of Crispus Attucks can't walk some areas of Chicago safely."[12] The consensus seemed to be that the work was not done and that the Revolution, especially for black Americans, was still being fought.

The notion that Attucks would be dismayed by the continuing oppression of his figurative descendants two hundred years after his death was expressed consistently during the bicentennial years, perhaps never more directly than in a June 1976 *Ebony* photo-editorial titled "The Bicentennial Blues." Centered on the white antibusing violence in Boston then dominating much of the national news, the editorial focused on a particularly poignant assault on African American lawyer Ted Landsmark, who was on his way to "a City Hall meeting to discuss minority hiring practices when he and other blacks were attacked" by a mob of white antibusing demonstrators. The attack took place "within sight and sound of Faneuil Hall," where Crispus Attucks had lain prior to his martyr's burial. "One wonders," the editorial intoned, "what Crispus Attucks, the black who became the first martyr of the Revolution and the hero of the Boston Massacre, would have made of it." The accompanying photo of a white attacker attempting to impale Landsmark with a large American flag spoke volumes, as did the short poem within the editorial, which conjured images of "stoning black children on Bunker Hill" and "whipping black men with pieces of the liberty tree." Lines from its final two stanzas summed things up:

> *If you see Crispus Attucks and the blacks who died to make us free.*
> *Tell 'em it's business as usual in Boston and the land of liberty.*
>
> *Got the Bicentennial Blues, blue as I can be. . . .*
> *And after 200 years, there ain't no freedom for me.*[13]

Not surprisingly, Boston was the center of considerable bicentennial attention, which generated what one scholar has termed "a deep and challenging moment of self-examination" regarding "the city's . . . historical inheritance." Pulitzer Prize–winning journalist J. Anthony Lukas emphasized the importance of Boston's many "re-enactable events," which he described as "the building blocks of the national myth, the American ABC's chalked on the blackboard of our collective memory." Black Bostonians seized the opportunity presented by bicentennial fervor to create a Black Heritage Walking Trail, which of course included a stop at the Attucks monument. The Boston Equal Rights League held its 1975 Attucks Day ceremony without incident, but a reenactment of the Boston Massacre the same evening was disrupted by protestors from the white antibusing organization, ROAR (Reclaim Our Alienated Rights). Some four hundred ROAR members attended the massacre reenactment, carrying signs saying "Boston Mourns Its Lost Freedom" and, more ominously, "You Think This Is a Massacre, Just Wait." No violence marred the event, though when the British soldier reenactors fired the fatal shots, all four hundred ROAR protestors fell to the ground, apparently unaware of the irony in their assuming the roles of the integrated massacre martyrs.[14]

Attucks remained a key symbol of the black bicentennial outside Boston and even outside the United States. In 1975 and 1976, respectively, the Caribbean nations of Grenada and St. Christopher Nevis Anguilla commemorated the American Bicentennial with a series of stamps, each of which included one depicting Attucks and the Boston Massacre.[15] In 1969 a group of Brooklyn stamp collectors lobbied unsuccessfully for a commemorative postage stamp featuring Attucks, as had others since the 1930s. In the same year the American Negro Commemorative Society, whose founding had been inspired by the assassination of Martin Luther King Jr., met with greater success when they contracted with the Franklin Mint to produce 1,380 medals featuring a bust of Attucks on one side and a depiction of the Boston

Massacre on the other, with the inscription, "First Martyr to American Independence." The medal was the thirteenth of fifty sterling silver medals produced to honor significant African Americans. The official bicentennial organizers did not take formal or extensive strides to identify black heroes, though they did attempt to incorporate African Americans through token gestures, like the distribution of buttons with an image of Attucks declaring him a "Black American Patriot" who was the "first man to die for American freedom" (see Fig. 8.1).[16]

By and large, any earnest commemorative acts were overwhelmed by the crass commercialism surrounding the bicentennial, prompting the PBC to dub it the "buycentennial," a term that could not help but catch on. According to Tammy Gordon, the buycentennial approach to commemoration reflected several related processes in postwar American culture: the growth in Americans' identification with individualistic lifestyles, the related emergence of a consumerist mentality, and a resulting shift in marketing practices since the 1950s. Americans had unprecedented access to consumer

FIG. 8.1 Crispus Attucks bicentennial pin. From the author's collection. Photo: Western Michigan University Libraries Digitization Center.

goods, and mass media provided businesses with unprecedented access to consumers through radio, television, movies, billboards, and print media. The advertising industry moved away from broad mass marketing in favor of a targeted marketing approach that tailored both products and advertisements to appeal to specific ethnic, regional, and lifestyle groups in American society. Bicentennial promoters embraced these changes.[17]

As Lerone Bennett Jr. observed in the bicentennial year, "images and echoes of black heritage [were] almost everywhere," from classrooms to mass media. But the black presence in mainstream culture was both superficial and exploitative. "Black heritage," Bennett explained, "sells soap, whiskey, and detergent. It sells everything, in fact, except the meaning of black heritage and the humanity of black people."[18]

The use of black history in targeted marketing campaigns had begun in the 1960s, as evidenced by full-page Coca-Cola advertisements appearing on the back cover of *Crispus Attucks and the Minutemen* and other issues of Golden Legacy's historical comic series. In 1969, the Seagram Distillers Company began producing an annual Negro History Calendar highlighting key dates in African American history. Beginning in 1974, the calendar was illustrated by Jerry Pinkney, a black artist acclaimed for his illustrations in numerous children's books. The 1976 calendar highlighted "important contributions of black patriots to America's struggle for freedom." Pinkney's twelve-by-twenty-inch painting for March, titled *Heroes and Fighters*, featured Attucks as "a young black sailor" who was "spokesman for a crowd of angry Bostonians" and "the first American to give his life in the confrontations between the colonies and England." The calendar was advertised for sale in popular black magazines like *Jet* and *Ebony* as well as black newspapers from coast to coast.[19]

Advertisers in the year leading up to Independence Day 1976 used those same magazines to attract black consumers, with some ads making a point to encourage black heritage tourism. United Airlines offered special "Bicentennial fares" and American Airlines recommended specific destinations, including the Attucks monument in Boston. The Attucks monument also appeared on a map prepared for tourists preferring ground travel, who were encouraged to "Take Amtrak to Black History." Greyhound Bus Lines did not specify particular destinations, though its ad depicted modern black Americans wearing tricorn hats and other Revolutionary era garments while manning an eighteenth-century cannon. Black readers who would rather just stay home might still get into the black buycentennial spirit by sipping on some 100-proof Jim Beam bourbon, poured from a commemorative decanter honoring the "American hero Crispus Attucks who was the first colonial to fall in the Boston Massacre, March 5, 1770" (see Fig. 8.2). They might even do so while wearing one of the four Ametco "Black Bicentennial T-shirts" commemorating the "Great Black Americans" Jean Baptiste Point Dusable, George Washington Carver, Sojourner Truth, and of course Crispus Attucks. These shirts' "stunning designs" would allow African Americans to "join the Bicentennial celebration with style and dignity."[20]

While bicentennial commercialism threatened to trivialize any public attention to history in this era, the commemoration of Attucks and black history could still serve genuine symbolic purposes pertaining to African

FIG. 8.2 Jim Beam bicentennial commemorative decanter. From the author's collection. Photo: Western Michigan University Libraries Digitization Center.

Americans' collective identity and place within the nation. The bicentennial also marked the fiftieth anniversary of Negro History Week, which by the 1970s was becoming Afro-American History Week and ultimately Black History Month. This expansion and renaming had been evolving for some time. As early as the 1940s, African Americans in the state of West Virginia had adopted a month-long format, and in the mid-1960s the Chicago black nationalist group, the House of Knowledge, held "Freedom Month" celebrations, albeit in July.[21] A 1971 Pepsi-Cola Company "public service" ad in an Atlanta black newspaper, highlighting Attucks and other black heroes, was as commercial as they come; but its "recognition of Afro-American History Week" and its emphasis on "Discovering a Black Past" at least reflected the emerging shift in terminology. The Kent State University student organization, Black United Students, is credited with having held the first Black History Month celebration in February 1970. Younger members of the Association for the Study of Negro Life and History (ASNLH) also had been calling for expanding and renaming Negro History Week. The transition in both terminology and duration was complete by 1976, the same year the Association replaced "Negro" with "Afro-American" in its name.[22]

President Gerald R. Ford provided national sanction for the change in 1976 when he "urg[ed] Americans to join in observing February as Black History Month" by "honor[ing] the too-often neglected accomplishments of black Americans in every area of endeavor throughout our history." In 1984, President Ronald Reagan gave a Black History Month address in the East Room of the White House to leaders of the Association for the Study of Afro-American Life and History, in part to unveil a new commemorative postage stamp honoring the organization's founder, Dr. Carter G. Woodson. Reagan singled out numerous black accomplishments, including the fact that "the first American to die in [the Revolutionary] war was named Crispus Attucks." The president also added a detail that his audience was already well aware of: "he was black."[23]

While Ford had acknowledged the "significant strides" toward "the full integration of black people into every area of national life," his and Reagan's token gestures made it clear that African Americans remained tangential to the mainstream history of America that the nation continued to tell itself. During the last quarter of the century, artists, activists, scholars, and educators all attempted to move beyond tokenism toward a fuller incorporation of Attucks and black Americans generally into American history. As multiculturalism became more of a watchword during the 1980s, those efforts met continued resistance from other Americans who were unwilling to revise their understanding of the cherished myths that had occupied America's collective memory for generations.[24]

During and after the bicentennial era, references to Attucks began to find their way into various popular cultural forms, including recorded music. The theme of Stevie Wonder's funky 1976 song "Black Man," from his wildly popular *Songs in the Key of Life* album, was that "this world was made for all men." Emphasizing the contributions of black, red, yellow, brown, and white to the nation's history, Wonder gave Crispus Attucks his turn in the opening line: "First man to die for the flag we now hold high was a black man." Wonder's embrace of the bicentennial spirit of harmonious pluralism was shared by longtime Chicago radio host John Doremus, whose self-released spoken word album, *The Spirit of '76*, contained tributes to Americans from Crispus Attucks to football coach Vince Lombardi.[25] In the late 1980s, leftist folk singers Charlie King and Martha Leader released "The Ballad of Crispus Attucks," which presented an idealized martyr who was "the first to die for freedom, though his people were still slaves."[26] While the meanings in jazz saxophonist Ricky Ford's 1989 instrumental "Ode to Crispus Attucks" are harder to discern, the 1990s alt-country artist Bruce Smith's "Crispus Attucks" was clear. Smith offered a sharp condemnation of the failed war on drugs and the nation's push to "build more jails" rather than providing playgrounds, better schools, and decent wages. Also invoking martyrs John Brown, Martin Luther King Jr, and Malcolm X, Smith presents an Attucks who was "bleedin', but no one hears him screamin.'" Around the same time a group of high school classmates from Maryland learned about Attucks in their history class and named their hardcore thrash punk band "Crispus Attucks" in homage to his rebellion against oppressive authority. The band remained popular in the Washington, DC, area until it disbanded in the early 2000s.[27]

In keeping with earlier efforts to present Attucks's story on stage and screen, *Jet* magazine reported in 1973 that "plans for a film to honor Crispus Attucks, Black hero of the American Revolution, were disclosed recently by Crispus Film Production Co. Inc., and Professional Pictures International." A 1974 report indicated that the film project, scripted by white former television actor Mark Weston, had a $1.2 million budget and was scheduled to be shot on location in Massachusetts. The producers appear to have made some effort to promote the film, commissioning a striking publicity poster from noted illustrator Robert C. Frankenberg (see Fig. 8.3). *Jet* reported that the film was said to be "scheduled for release within a year," but it never went into production.[28]

FIG. 8.3 Promotional artwork for the proposed film *Crispus*. By Robert C. Frankenberg, ca. 1973. Reproduction courtesy New York Public Library, Schomburg Center for Research in Black Culture, Photographs and Print Division. Courtesy of Mr. Elliott Geisinger, Professional Pictures International.

The "screenplay titled Crispus" was Mark Weston's very first writing effort, and it seems he did not give up on it.[29] Though it never appeared on screen, a seventy-two-page Weston script with the same title, dated 1987, may represent his attempt to revive the project; but like the earlier film, no stage production appears to have reached the public. Weston's story presents a young Attucks who, according to his mother Phyllis, "never gets tired with his book learnin.'" His kindly master, Silas Brown, "the best tutor in all of Massachusetts," instructs him in Shakespeare, the fine points of English grammar, and a host of other subjects. Silas's death makes his abusive son Crispus's master, prompting Attucks to flee to Boston, where he quickly develops a love interest before evading pursuit by taking to the sea. He becomes a skilled sailor and on one voyage meets Benjamin Franklin, who backs him in a boxing match against the English champion. Attucks turns down Franklin's offer to manage his pugilistic career in order to return to Boston, where various heroic exploits—saving a family from an Indian attack, aiding a runaway slave, protecting a girl from being raped by a British soldier—make him "a symbol even to the young." He already "had become a legend" in the colony. In order to secure Attucks's support, John Hancock and Paul Revere assure him that "the

Sons of Liberty are sworn to the abolishment of slavery." With black freedom on the table, Attucks delays his planned escape to the Bahamas with his sweetheart. Upon meeting an old friend of his kindly Framingham master, Attucks finally learns the truth: that master, Silas Brown, was in fact his father, and the papers he had hidden freeing Crispus had been found. Barely had he received this news when the streets erupt in violence, with soldiers "cutting and slashing everyone" and "attacking children." Attucks "grabs a cordwood stave" and is shot dead as he confronts the soldiers. The off-stage voice of John Adams echoes: "ON HIS BLOOD . . . THE WAR HAS STARTED."[30]

Another playscript from the 1980s presented very different details about Attucks's life but took similar license with historical evidence. In Willie Thomas Harris's "A Lantern for Crispus," Attucks's childhood goes unexplored, and all the action takes place on March 4 and 5, 1770. Attucks has no interactions with patriot leaders but is well acquainted with three other Boston Massacre martyrs, Maverick, Gray, and Carr. He is also romantically involved with a black woman named Peggy, who was known as the British soldiers' "whore." One loyalist character calls Attucks a "trouble maker" for "talking against the crown," but Carr and Maverick back him, with the latter saying, "I feel the same as Crispus!" Attucks is also "well known in Boston" among the British troops. His most vocal critic is a fictional loyalist named Hill, who denounces him as the product of an "uncivilized, uncultivated black continent" and "shiftless, indigent Indians." Attucks proudly claims that heritage as justification for his strong "opinion about the future direction of this country." Most of the script involves conversations among these characters regarding whether there is either justice or sense in provoking a confrontation with the British. Attucks's position is that the British imposed slavery on both blacks and whites in the colonies, and that colonists must fight until "all the slaves are free" and "the colonies [are] free to make their own destiny." "We—blacks and whites—owe it to ourselves and to each other to make this a free land," Attucks urges, "and it shall be free." The ultimate clash with the troops is vaguely presented as a pitched battle, with soldiers marching down the streets to their drummers' beat and a small but steadfast band of colonists sallying forth to meet them. It ends with Attucks's death and a silent crowd forming around the bodies of the martyrs.[31]

The playwright, Willie Thomas Harris, had written several plays that had been produced in the United States and in France, where he lived from 1965 to 1978. Harris's curiosity "about a black man who charged British soldiers with only a club" led him to spend considerable time researching Attucks in various New York and Boston repositories. Though he "came up with very little material concerning Attucks' life," he was able to "glean enough facts to put together a play." In 1985 Harris wrote to the agency representing actor James Earl Jones, whom Harris claimed to have "made the acquaintance of" several years earlier. "Mr. Jones," he wrote, "is the one actor I know with the stature and the maturity capable of doing justice to Attucks." While Harris hoped that Jones would read the script, it is not clear whether that occurred or if the agency ever responded to Harris. The play does not seem to have been published or produced.[32] Differences aside, both these plays present Attucks as a noble and heroic martyr whose commitment to liberty and justice in a multiracial America helped inspire and unify the American independence movement.

In the realm of academic scholarship, one significant work from the bicentennial years that tried to redress blacks' marginalization in the nation's history was Sidney Kaplan's 1973 *Black Presence in the Era of the American Revolution*. Kaplan was thorough in his account of the Boston Massacre and even discussed nineteenth-century Attucks Day commemorations and the 1888 monument. The author acknowledged that "little is known of his [Attucks's] personal life" and was deliberate in describing Attucks tentatively, using phrases like "probably," "it is possible," "seemed," and "in local lore" when suggesting the possible details of his life and background. He relied upon lengthy quotations from the trial transcript and from period newspapers to flesh out a thoughtful overview of Attucks's real and symbolic importance. Kaplan's overall assessment of Attucks's role in the Revolution, drawing upon a famous quote from Thomas Jefferson, moved away from evidence and into the realm of speculation. "The blood of Attucks," he wrote, "nourished the tree of liberty . . . in two ways." First, Kaplan suggested that "the spirit of Attucks doubtless spurred New England blacks openly to question" their status as slaves in a society rooted in liberty; second, he claimed that Attucks's name "was still green in the memory of the minutemen—black and white— who took their stand at Lexington and Bunker Hill." Both these claims rested more on supposition than documentation.[33]

Given the expanded attention to African American history and heroes during the bicentennial era, surprisingly few juvenile biographies of black heroes were published. The most popular work by far was Burke Davis's *Black Heroes of the American Revolution*. Davis was a prolific and respected writer of historical fiction and nonfiction for both juvenile and adult audiences. The bicentennial provided an opportunity for him to draw attention to African Americans' contributions to the nation's founding, and Attucks occupied about eight of the book's eighty pages. His narrative covered the standard ground fairly accurately, with the "burly black man named Crispus Attucks" taking a leading role. Davis made it clear that "the people of Boston knew almost nothing about" Attucks. Even though "little is known of his early life," Davis sketched out timeworn speculation about his family background and his skill "as a trader of horses and cattle." The only glaring error in the account is Davis's casting Thomas Jefferson as an Attucks admirer: "As Thomas Jefferson said, the blood of Crispus Attucks nourished the tree of liberty." Jefferson, of course, never said any such thing and likely had never heard of Attucks. Davis probably misconstrued the reference to Jefferson's "tree of liberty" quote in Sidney Kaplan's 1973 book. Davis also noted, accurately, John Adams's 1773 diary entry warning Governor Hutchinson, "You will hear further from Us hereafter," as well as Daniel Webster's view of the Boston Massacre as "the turning point" for American independence. "The reckless bravery of Crispus Attucks," Davis concluded, "had helped change the course of history."[34]

Attention to the place of African Americans in the nation's story also got a boost from one of the signal mass cultural phenomena of the bicentennial era: the publication of the book and subsequent 1977 television miniseries *Roots*. Based on author Alex Haley's genealogical research into his own family's history, *Roots* chronicled the fictionalized—some argued over-romanticized—lives of several generations of an African American family from a young boy's eighteenth-century abduction in Africa through the period of antebellum southern slavery. The extent to which *Roots* altered people's opinions about black history or race in American society is open to debate, but there is no denying its impact in placing black history squarely before the American public imagination as at no time since emancipation. With a viewership well in excess of 100 million, *Roots* represented a uniquely powerful shared experience of black history for Americans of all races. Along with the bicentennial itself, *Roots* also helped stimulate a broader "heritage project" in which Americans of all backgrounds were inspired to investigate their family trees and their ancestors' place in American history. This multiracial ethnic revival carried on well after the bicentennial decade and informed many Americans' sense of their place in the nation's saga.[35]

Another indicator of African Americans' persistent struggle to incorporate their story into that of the nation was the ongoing development of more inclusive curricular materials for use in the public schools. The Los Angeles School District continued its efforts from the previous decade to give teachers the tools they needed to incorporate black perspectives into their lesson plans. In 1970 the district helped develop a Scholastic Black Literature Series to complement standard textbooks with "good literature written by Black

Americans, for all students in that city's schools." The series included six texts, one each for grades seven through twelve. The tenth grade text, *The Black Hero*, used a collection of prose and poetry to identify key themes defining the black hero in literature and to give students an "opportunity to look for people and ideals to respect." Neither Crispus Attucks nor any other actual historical figure appears to have been represented in the volume's selections since the series criteria were literary rather than historical. But the volume's emphasis on black heroism's relevance in American history and culture, past and present, was consistent with a broader social movement that sought to move beyond a merely integrationist agenda and toward the embrace of a more thorough multiculturalism that would animate the coming generation. *The Black Hero* articulated increasingly popular views about the significance of African American heroism as a central component of the American experience.[36]

Historian Tammy Gordon observes that the bicentennial in the 1970s served as a vehicle through which minorities, women, the new left, and others pursuing "movements for social justice" attempted to maintain continuity among the activism of the 1960s, the coming multiculturalism debates of the 1980s, and the full-fledged "culture wars" of the 1990s.[37] These issues gained particular traction in the area of American public education. In the bicentennial year, black teachers continued to complain about textbooks' inattention to "black contributors to our country's early history."[38] Blacks were showing up far more consistently in classrooms, but educational scholar James A. Banks noted that American school curricula during the "ethnic revival movements" of the 1960s and 1970s typically took an unenthusiastic "additive" approach to acknowledging non-whites' presence in American history. Teachers and curricular materials tended to present "fragmented ethnic content" without altering the dominant Anglocentric narrative and ideology. Rather than "infus[ing] the curriculum with new perspectives, frames of reference, and values" and fundamentally reorienting the narrative to reflect the nation's pluralistic history and culture, Banks pointed out that "ethnic heroes such as Crispus Attucks and Martin Luther King, Jr., were inserted into the curriculum along with bits and pieces of content about ethnic cultures and traditions." As proponents of a truly multicultural curriculum pushed their agendas during the 1980s, they met with staunch opposition from traditionalists who perceived any proposed changes as "un-American" threats that would "undercut American patriotism" and "create ethnic Balkanization."[39] The multiculturalism debates of the 1980s intensified during the 1990s as a proposed new set of national standards for teaching American history embroiled scholars, activists, teachers, parents, students, and pundits in heated debates over the content and meaning of the past.[40]

A 1987 study of eleven widely used junior high school American history textbooks found that "outstanding black figures such as Crispus Attucks, Phyllis [*sic*] Wheatley, Booker T. Washington, Martin Luther King, and Jesse Jackson" were mentioned in "the overwhelming majority" of such texts, and that "the accuracy of historical information about blacks found in history texts has also improved." Indeed, while the study's author claimed that there was "nothing wrong" with bolstering group identity through such inclusion, he mildly criticized this "ethnocentric" approach for emphasizing "cultural diversity" as an overarching theme at the expense of traditional "major themes in American studies" and "common bases of group experiences and interests that transcend ethnic lines." The article also explained a good reason for textbooks' overall conformity: "All, to sell effectively and to be on the adoption lists of all major states, must be in the mainstream of all the others and not be singled out as being unique or different in any way that may be considered unorthodox or promoting a controversial viewpoint." They had to avoid making waves in order to sell.[41]

So it should be no surprise that a 1992 analysis of public school curricula by multicultural education scholar Ellen Swartz found that the mainstream "master script" in all fields of study was still firmly "grounded in Eurocentric and White supremacist ideologies."[42] In her study, Swartz offered an interesting assessment of Crispus Attucks's treatment in American history textbooks, which suggests how difficult it was to incorporate African Americans into mainstream narratives without rocking the boat of conformity. Swartz used Attucks to illustrate how history textbooks maintained merely "compensatory approaches" that offered "decontextualized lessons" about African American individuals while avoiding "comprehensive, accurate portrayals of African Americans' collective struggle" and that struggle's central place in American history and culture. She criticized textbooks in which "information on Crispus Attucks is included only to tell students that he was a former slave who died in the Boston Massacre, rather than tell them that he was a symbol of African American leadership and liberation." Swartz specifically called out a 1991 fifth grade textbook that presented Attucks both "simplistically" and, she argues, dismissively:

> Crispus Attucks was a runaway slave who worked on the docks of Boston. He was about 50 years old when he was killed in the Boston Massacre."

This statement, according to Swartz, was flawed for portraying Attucks "foremost as a slave—and a runaway slave at that." Swartz made an interesting argument that "the prior enslavement of Attucks and its significance could be alternatively stated in a way that would draw a stronger connection between his personal experiences of achieving freedom from chattel slavery and his efforts as the leader of the colonial rebels who charged up King Street to confront British soldiers in 1770." She suggested the following revision:

> Crispus Attucks was a dock worker in Boston who believed deeply in freedom. In 1750 he took his freedom by escaping the system of slavery. In 1770, at the age of almost 50 years, he showed how much he still believed in freedom when he led colonial patriots in a demonstration against British soldiers in Boston. Attucks was one of five men to be killed in what was later called the Boston Massacre.

"This revision of the master script," she argued, "pulls Attucks away from the margins of the patriotic struggle" and places his experiences and ideals—as well as those of other self-liberated blacks—appropriately at the center of the American independence movement. Such a revision, for Swartz, was not merely "grist for the mill of multiculturality"; it reflected a "more accurate, nonhegemonic, and nonracist" representation of the past.[43]

Swartz was surely correct that American history textbooks—then and now—generally present uncomplicated narratives that tend to maintain what she called "White, patrician, and patriarchal privilege."[44] Textbooks still fail to fully incorporate African American experiences into the "master script" of American history. And her critique of this textbook's characterization of Attucks as an individual is compelling. In one sense, defining Attucks primarily by his status as a fugitive slave does him the same disservice as would defining Benjamin Franklin as a runaway indentured servant. However, far more is known about Franklin's "experiences and ideals," both before and after his self-liberation, than can ever be known about Attucks's. Swartz's conclusion that Attucks "believed deeply in freedom" might be inferred from the evidence that he likely liberated himself from bondage in 1750. But Swartz also made problematic assertions both about Attucks's status as "the leader of the colonial rebels" and about his mindset and motivations on the evening of March 5, 1770. Characterizing the colonists as engaged in a "demonstration" rather than as an out-of-control mob placed them in the same positive light that was then enjoyed by nonviolent 1960s civil rights protestors. And while Attucks may well have worked on Boston's docks, both Swartz and the textbook went beyond the scant evidence in stating this as a proven fact. Most significantly, Swartz did not seem aware that Attucks's place as "a symbol of African American leadership and liberation" was hardly a given; rather, it was the result of a conscious manipulation of history by black activists in the nineteenth and twentieth centuries.

Presenting American history in textbooks was complicated. Textbook publishers at the end of the twentieth century were under increasing pressure from economic market forces, driven by both those who cherished the traditional narrative and those who demanded greater attention to previously marginalized or ignored groups. The "compensatory" approach was a solution that failed to fully satisfy either camp, and publishers seemed reluctant to include potentially controversial symbolic narratives like those that had grown around Crispus Attucks. Treatments of Attucks in textbooks since the 1980s usually present him the way many Americans today remember him, if they remember him at all—the black guy from the Revolution.

My examination of twenty middle and high school textbooks published between 1985 and 1998 found both consistency and idiosyncrasy in the ways Attucks and the Boston Massacre were presented.[45] The massacre itself was generally treated in a balanced way, with some texts taking a mildly pro-British slant that emphasized the size and aggressiveness of the mob, the trial's "not guilty" verdict for the British soldiers, and the distortions in Paul Revere's engraving and Sam Adams's written propaganda. The size of the crowd in different accounts varied from fifty to five hundred, and virtually all the texts mentioned their aggression in taunting, jeering, and throwing projectiles at the beleaguered soldiers. All but one of the accounts that included an image featured the Revere engraving, and many made a point of discussing the use of propaganda to stir up anti-British sentiment. Regarding its place in the buildup toward Revolution, the massacre's relevance lay in its representing the "rising tensions" in the colonies after the 1767 Townshend Duties and being the last significant colonial confrontation until the 1773 Boston Tea Party. Some texts claimed that word of the event spread rapidly throughout the colonies, greatly expanding colonial resistance to perceived British tyranny, while several minimized its impact. One, for example, argued that the massacre was "a major conflict," and another stated that it played "a major role in whipping up colonial fury against the British." Others, however, asserted that it "drew little reaction outside Massachusetts" or that "no massive protests resulted."[46]

Seventeen of the twenty texts mentioned Attucks in their discussions of the Boston Massacre, but only five explicitly ascribed any significance to his ostensible heroism or martyrdom. A 1985 high school text noted that "it is ironic that a black American who had been deprived of his freedom became one of the first martyrs of the American Revolution," and another pointed out that while Attucks "was among the first to die in the struggle over colonial freedom," he "did not share the same degree of freedom as other citizens of Boston."[47] Only one identified him unambiguously as "the leader of the throng" and singled him out as the "first to die"; others equivocated, saying that Attucks "has been called 'the first casualty of the American Revolution'" or that he "has become, in the opinion of many, one of the first heroes of the American Revolution."[48] The seventeen textbooks mentioning Attucks were fairly consistent in describing him racially, with thirteen calling him "black" and the 1998 text calling him "African American." The other three books mentioning Attucks suggested no racial category, but all of them identified him as an escaped slave, thereby implying his racial identity.

Five books used the exact term "runaway slave," and six used the phrase "black sailor," with three other texts identifying his occupation as "sailor." It is not surprising that Attucks's race, status, and occupation were the main forms of identifying him, given the paucity of evidence regarding his life. Ellen Swartz might have argued that such descriptions marginalized Attucks, and by extension all black Americans, from the story of the Boston Massacre. But given the realities of the textbook publishing industry and the limitations imposed by the historical evidence, it seems reasonable that authors conformed to safe language. Other noncontroversial terms were used to describe Attucks. One text called him a "tall man" who may have come from the "West Indies"; two others made note of his being "tall" or even of "giant stature"; and a third referred to him as a "colonist." Some still repeated old fabrications or speculations, as when one author stated that Attucks was "active in the Sons of Liberty" or another said he was "well-known in the Boston dock area." The latter text also noted Attucks's "courage" but still played to the same racialized characterization favored in 1770 by John Adams, claiming that "a friend said of him that 'his very looks were enough to terrify any person.'" The "friend" in question must have been Adams himself, since that phrase came directly from his closing statement at the soldiers' trial. This was the only late twentieth-century textbook examined that presented a negative, racialized comment about Attucks.[49]

One 1990 textbook included a half-page "American Profiles" box in each chapter providing biographical information on one key individual; in apparent response to pressures for diversity, more than half of these profiles featured either a woman or a person of color. The Attucks profile included a detail from the 1856 Bufford image of an aggressive and heroic Attucks wielding a club and seizing a bayonet. The authors exercised some care by emphasizing that "little is definitely known about Attucks." They speculated that this "mulatto with Natick Indian ancestry" had "apparently" worked as a sailor and dock-worker after escaping slavery and was "in the forefront" of the massacre mob. The final paragraph, however, allowed some inaccuracy to filter in. Attucks's name, students were told, "became a symbol for black and white Patriots. During the Revolutionary War, black military companies called themselves Attucks Guards, and Crispus Attucks Day was celebrated in Boston."[50] Of course, Attucks hardly became a symbol during the war, since his name and those of the other victims were quickly forgotten. While Revolutionary-era Bostonians did hold solemn commemorations of the massacre, Attucks Day celebrations and the Attucks Guards military companies were products of the 1850s, not the 1770s.

While misinformation about Crispus Attucks still abounded, by the end of the twentieth century, more than two hundred years after his death, Attucks was more widely known than he had ever been. Not only had his name and story—or some version of it—finally become firmly ensconced in the nation's history textbooks but they had also found a broader airing in popular culture. The last several decades had reinforced Attucks's place in the nation's collective memory. The successes of the civil rights move-ment played their role, as had the nation's appetite for all things bicenten-nial during the 1970s. Changes in advertising and targeted marketing helped spread the word, and the powerful surge of multiculturalism after the 1980s sealed the deal. Not only was Attucks more widely known but he was also more likely than ever before to be characterized in a positive light. Few voices could be found denigrating him as merely an unsavory, drunken rowdy who was hell-bent on destroying the social order. Almost as hard to find was the hapless sailor who was in the wrong place at the wrong time. He received accolades or at least acknowledgment from American leaders and patriotic icons from John Wayne to Ronald Reagan. During the 1990s, President Bill Clinton and his wife Hillary Rodham Clinton unveiled a White House Christmas tree that was adorned with a Crispus Attucks ornament.[51]

Attucks's entry into the pantheon seemed to be sealed by the 1990s when the United States Mint issued a commemorative coin honoring African American veterans of the Revolution, the front of which featured a famil-iar likeness of Crispus Attucks (see Fig. 8.4). "The Black Revolutionary War Patriots Silver Dollar," Mint Director Philip N. Diehl announced, "will recall and commemorate history by focusing on Crispus Attuck's [sic] sacrifice as

FIG. 8.4 Black Revolutionary War patriots silver dollar. United States Mint. 1998. From the author's collection. Photo by the author.

a symbol of the commitment of all Black American patriots." The coin was issued in 1998 to mark the 275th anniversary of Attucks's birth, and proceeds from the sale of the planned striking of 500,000 would go toward funding a monument memorializing black patriots on the National Mall.[52]

The Black Revolutionary War Patriots Memorial was first proposed in Congress in 1984, in part to publicize a recent decision by the Daughters of the American Revolution (DAR) to deny membership to the descendant of a black veteran. The bill approving the memorial and establishing the Black Revolutionary War Patriots Memorial Foundation was passed in 1986, and a 1988 bill approved a location on the National Mall between the Lincoln Memorial and the Washington Monument. As with most such monuments, the foundation was responsible for meeting planning and fundraising goals within strict deadlines. Despite several extensions, those goals were not met, and the congressional authorization for the memorial expired in 2005. However, when the Black Patriots Memorial Foundation disbanded, a new group, the National Mall Liberty Fund, DC, was established to continue working for a memorial to black Revolutionary veterans. In December 2012, Congress passed legislation approving the National Liberty Memorial on a site near the mall. The new backers have until 2019 to confirm an appropriate site and raise the necessary funds. Proponents of a memorial for black veterans of the American Revolution would have to wait.[53]

By the end of the twentieth century, Attucks had, to a large degree, become what black activists had promoted since the 1850s: he was a black American hero of the Revolution. Yet, for historian Kristin Haas, the Black Revolutionary War Patriots Memorial represented the limits of this recognition. The stalled memorial was "a failed attempt . . . to redraw primary boundaries of national inclusion" and demonstrated the "tenacity with which the Daughters of the American Revolution" and others committed to an exclusive national narrative "fought to maintain these boundaries." African American artist Ed Dwight, who was contracted to design the ill-fated memorial, complained, "They wanted it to be abstract. In this city, our nation's capital, there was an issue with putting black faces on the National Mall." Similarly, Haas maintains that the difficulty faced by those advocating a Black Patriots memorial "reveals how an obvious but, for some, untenable truth—that African Americans served in the Revolutionary War and that they are both figurative and biological creators of the nation—is repressed in the maintenance of these boundaries" demarcating who was truly a part of the American nation and who was not. The obstacles impeding the incomplete Black Patriots Memorial signaled that controversy, confusion, and denial would continue to haunt the memory of Crispus Attucks into the next century.[54]

9

Crispus Attucks in
Twenty-First-Century America

As long as history is told, the first fallen fighter in America's
struggle for independence will be remembered. . . . Crispus
Attucks gave his life for the cause of freedom. And in doing
so, he gave the freedom he loved to a nation. His was the
first sacrifice for liberty, and after it was made, there would
be no looking back.

homeofthebravejournal.wordpress.com (January 8, 2009)

Attucks is said to have gone out into the street waving a
cordwood stick about the thickness of a man's wrist, leading
a crowd of about 20 or 30 soldiers. Sounds like a thug to me.

PAULINE MAIER (*Boston Globe*, February 9, 2000)

IN 2003, HISTORIAN Allison Dorsey attended a screening of a moving documentary featuring African American actors reading excerpts from the recollections of former slaves, thousands of which had been collected by the New Deal Federal Writers Project in the 1930s. After the screening, Dorsey was puzzled by a conversation she overheard among a group of thirty-something, "college-educated, professional black women," none of whom had been aware of the slave narratives' existence. The women seemed "stunned" by these powerful black voices recounting their historical experiences and irate that those stories had for so long "been hidden away from us." Dorsey, as a scholar of African American history, was equally stunned that these otherwise well-educated women were ignorant, not only of the slave narratives' existence but of the vast scholarship on the black past that was widely available by the early twenty-first century. "If [these] middle-class and rising black women did not know their history," Dorsey pondered, "what might that mean for other people of color or whites in the larger society?" Dorsey's "troubling" realization about historical scholarship's negligible impact on Americans' historical consciousness left her determined that none of her college students, at least, "would leave school without knowing the history of African-descended people in the United States and that this history is readily accessible and belonged to all Americans."[1] Despite the efforts of scholar-teachers like Dorsey as well as the expanding presence of black history in the nation's schools and in popular culture, far too many Americans remained ignorant of blacks' central place in the American story.

While the new century saw continued nods to African American figures and experiences in American history textbooks and curricula, blacks still remained mostly on the margins of those mainstream accounts' master narrative. Generally, treatments of Crispus Attucks and the Boston Massacre in twenty-first-century textbooks adhered to many of the same patterns found in those from the late twentieth century.[2] For example, of the seven texts I examined from the period between 2003 and 2009, only one failed to mention Attucks and all included some discussion of the propaganda uses of the Boston Massacre. But several twenty-first-century texts showed a significant shift in the presentation of Attucks's race, identity, and character. His presentation was becoming more problematized. A few accounts still referred to him simply as "black" or "African American," but others now also acknowledged his probable Native American ancestry. Two texts by the same team of authors called Attucks "part African, part Native American" (in a 2009 middle school text) and a "man of African and Native American descent known as both Michael Johnson and Crispus Attucks" (in a 2010 high school text).[3] The mention of "Michael Johnson" seems to serve no particular purpose, though one would think it might have stimulated students' curiosity about why the man was known by two different names.

The presentation of a mixed-race Attucks, however, complicates the time-honored story—crafted initially in the 1850s by William C. Nell—of an unequivocally black man who had been the first to give his life in the cause of American liberty. While Native Americans had not done much to claim Attucks over the years, in 1995 the editor of the American Indian Society's newsletter argued that "to be correct in today's complicated society, Crispus Attucks should be referred to as an Indian-African American." By the twenty-first century, the Natick Praying Indian Tribe was collaborating with the Boston Equal Rights League in its annual reenactments of the Boston Massacre, with a tribe member often playing the role of Attucks.[4] Attucks's blackness continued to serve a clear purpose for African Americans, as it had since the time of the antebellum abolitionists. In the twenty-first century, however, Attucks's mixed heritage helped expand his symbolic relevance in a postmodern American society increasingly given to seeing itself as inclusive and multicultural.

One highly unflattering characterization of a mixed-race Attucks in another textbook illustrates that vetting statements supposedly made about him could be challenging. A 2007 text that identified Attucks as the "best-remembered" of the massacre victims (though without suggesting why that might be the case) also dredged up James R. Gilmore's old and obscure description of him. The text noted that the slain colonists included the "sailor Crispus Attucks . . . 'half Indian, half negro [*sic*], and altogether rowdy,' as he was called."[5] The textbook wisely omitted Gilmore's judgment that Attucks "should have been strangled the day he was born." Still, the passive voice phrase—"as he was called"—implies that it was Attucks's eighteenth-century contemporaries who deemed him a mere half-breed rowdy. While many surely did, it is far more likely that this particular pejorative assessment was crafted by Gilmore amid the widespread criticism of Attucks in the wake of the 1888 Attucks monument controversy.

What is interesting is that this disparaging characterization of Crispus Attucks found its way into a twenty-first-century textbook. One possible recent source for the Gilmore quotation was the 1998 book *Slavery, Propaganda, and the American Revolution*, by historian Patricia Bradley. In adding to the growing scholarship on the role of slavery and race in the nation's past, Bradley also raised important questions about Attucks's potential usefulness to the patriot cause: "Was Crispus Attucks to be a hero, one of the innocents cut down in King Street? Or a rowdy who helped provoke the attack? Could there be an innocent with a tawny skin? Should he be remembered at all? And at what cost?" She correctly notes the early identification of Attucks as a "molatto" and in subsequent newspaper references as "Mr. Attucks," which masked his racial identity and would have led readers outside Boston to "assume the courtesy title indicated Attucks was white." But Bradley veers from the evidence by asserting that Attucks was "an easily recognizable figure in the city, although probably more known by his free name, Michael Johnson." This statement implies that Attucks was in fact known in Boston and also assumes more than can be substantiated about his possible use of the Michael Johnson pseudonym. She goes on to use Nathanael Emmons's supposed statement to support this impression. First, Bradley incorrectly identified Emmons as a minister in nearby Franklin, Massachusetts, when he did not assume that position until 1773. She then suggested that Emmons was well acquainted with Attucks since he "had no problem recalling him

[Attucks] by his old slave name." Bradley then used the Gilmore quotation to emphasize that "Attucks elicited no sympathy" from Emmons, despite the minister's being "a lifelong opponent of slavery." Bradley's unproblematic acceptance of Gilmore's characterization leaves her readers with the dubious impression that Emmons was a knowledgeable local and that Attucks was both well known and little respected in the area.[6]

Several other works of African American history published after 1990, some by academic historians and others by uncredentialed scholars, discuss Attucks and his place in early American history. Some of these works exhibit care in presenting contingent accounts of Attucks that stay within the bounds of the available evidence. Some perpetuate inaccuracies that date to the nineteenth century. And some put forward fresh interpretations to fit the mood of the nation as it moved into the twenty-first century.

In their book on free black Americans before 1860, historians James Oliver Horton and Lois E. Horton make important and valid points about the life and political attitudes of the era's seafaring men and the "interracial nature" of mobs like the one Attucks joined in March 1770. While their broader interpretations reflect the cutting edge of historical scholarship at the time and much of their analysis is well supported, they distort the timeline of events and use unequivocal language in identifying Attucks as a "part Nantucket Indian" who was both a ropemaker and "a seaman on a whaling crew generally sailing out of Boston harbor." Those particular details are based on conjecture from nineteenth-century sources but still remain fairly close to Attucks's probable experiences. The authors err in one detail by indicating that Captain Preston gave the order to fire on the mob when the trial showed that he probably did not. But in another case, the authors place too much faith in one of their sources, leading to their mistaken assertion that Attucks "wrote to Governor Thomas Hutchinson" prior to the Boston Massacre. When Sidney Kaplan mentioned the "You will hear further from Us hereafter" threat (in both the 1973 original and 1989 reissue of his *Black Presence in the Era of the American Revolution*), he correctly attributed it to John Adams's 1773 diary entry; but the Hortons, relying on an erroneous statement by nineteenth-century historian George Washington Williams, put the pen into Attucks's hand.[7]

Historian Marcus Rediker exercised the historian's prerogative to interpret sources relating to Attucks in order to advance broader arguments. In a 2004 essay, Rediker discussed how a book he had recently co-authored with Peter Linebaugh presented Attucks as "an emblematic figure" representing the multiracial working classes whose participation in "the cycle of rebellion" of the late-eighteenth century helped "create movement from below toward revolution" in the Atlantic world. In his essay, Rediker wrote about the ways in which "conservative elements" among the American revolutionaries "shoved people like Attucks aside" and "thereby sealed the victory of affluent artisans like [Paul] Revere over and against proletarians like Attucks, who largely disappeared from the national picture until rescued by radical historians and activists . . . beginning in the 1960s." Rediker juxtaposed Revere and Attucks to "reflect on some of the issues now facing early American and labor history." While he was largely on target in his description of Attucks and his role in the massacre, his emphasis on Attucks as a "proletarian" served his particular intellectual agenda as surely as black activists' emphasis on Attucks's race served theirs.

Both those choices are certainly within the bounds of valid historical interpretation, but Rediker did make some assertions that push beyond what the historical record allows. First he identified Attucks as "almost surely a descendant of John Attuck," the Indian hanged in 1676. Then, even after acknowledging that Attucks was a "stranger" in Boston, he speculated that "chances are good" that Attucks and Revere "were acquainted." Most problematic was his misidentification of the 1856 Bufford/Champney image showing an aggressive Attucks as the central figure in the massacre; Rediker mistakenly identified it as the 1770 Pelham drawing on which Revere based his engraving. His main point was to argue that Revere purposely excised a central and heroic Attucks from his own image because he "apparently did not want the American cause to be represented by a huge half-Native American, half-African American stave-wielding, street-fighting sailor." While Revere may have considered such a figure ill-suited to his purpose, there was no such figure in the Pelham image for him to erase.[8]

The last years of the twentieth century also brought a number of new textbooks on African American history, many geared toward university classes and written by trained academic historians. Not surprisingly, these texts tended to give considerable attention to Attucks; however, they too perpetuated some of the misinformation that had become entrenched in popular understanding through years of repetition. Several pre-collegiate textbooks also appeared on the market, one as early as 1978. This text said very little about Attucks, identifying him as a "runaway slave who worked as a seaman and a laborer" who was "the first person killed."[9] A very brief middle school text from 1989 featured Attucks in a "Spotlight on People" section, which also remained fairly close to the facts, though it did misleadingly suggest that "people remembered Attucks long afterward" and, oddly, that "Augustus Saint-Gaudens made a statue of Crispus Attucks" that students could "see . . .

if you visit Boston." Students making that trip might be confused upon finding no statue of Attucks by Saint-Gaudens or anyone else in the city.[10] A 1992
high school text mistakenly stated that the "runaway African American slave
Crispus Attucks . . . was well known in Boston as a strong opponent to British
rule," but otherwise stayed within the realm of the probable.[11]

The main text used in college African American history classes during the
late twentieth century was John Hope Franklin's *From Slavery to Freedom*,
which had been in print continuously since its publication in 1947 and by
2000 was in its eighth edition. That edition retained almost the exact language of the original, calling Attucks a "runaway slave" who was "first to fall,"
and who did not deserve to be called a "saucy boy . . . [or] the other harsh
words John Adams had to say about those who fell." The "significance of
Attucks's death" was also the same: "Here was a fugitive slave who, with his
bare hands, was willing to resist England to the point of giving his own life.
It was a remarkable thing, the colonists reasoned, to have their fight for freedom waged by one who was not as free as they." This reasoning may have been
apparent to many in both the mid-twentieth and early twenty-first centuries, and surely many whites of the Revolutionary generation recognized the
inconsistency between their rhetoric of liberty and their practice of human
bondage. But there is no clear evidence that Attucks in particular had such an
impact on his contemporaries.[12]

A welcome new wave of college-level textbooks on African American history provided more options in a market that had been dominated by John
Hope Franklin since African American history courses began to be offered in
significant numbers in the early 1970s.[13] Regarding Attucks, the texts were a
mixed bag. Most stuck with a fairly standard and mostly accurate description
of the Boston Massacre and Attucks's background, although with some of the
more common conjectures slipping in, like his supposed "Nantucket Indian"
heritage or his being based in Boston. But some significant errors also found
their way into a few texts, especially those offering extended commentary on
Attucks and his significance.

James and Lois Horton's 2000 *Hard Road to Freedom* is similar to
Franklin's volume in that it provides a concise narrative history of African
Americans. The authors' several page section on Attucks and the Boston
Massacre repeats some of the description from their 1997 book. "Attucks's
role," they argue, "was central to the event and is crucial for the understanding
of the social and political relations of the eighteenth century." They particu-
larly call attention to the lack of "racial distinctions" at the martyrs' funeral.
The authors also corrected their earlier error by indicating that it was John

Adams who wrote in Attucks's name in his 1773 diary. They do argue that "it is likely that Adams wrote the letter and signed Attucks's name recognizing the former slave as a revolutionary symbol and acknowledging the important role blacks played in the cause of American freedom." This reading projects a not unreasonable, but perhaps overly wishful, gloss on Adams's possible thinking, since the future president never clearly articulated such thoughts about either Attucks or blacks' role in the Revolution.[14]

Another 2000 textbook, the team-authored *The African-American Odyssey*, includes a full-page "profile" of Crispus Attucks to supplement the brief mention of the massacre in the main text. Much of the profile provides a fairly detailed and even-handed account and interpretation of the key events, but it contains several errors. A statement that Attucks "lay in state for three days with the other victims" at "Faneuil Hall . . . the 'Cradle of Liberty,'" incorrectly implies that all the martyrs' bodies were there to be viewed and honored by the citizens, when in fact only Attucks's and James Caldwell's bodies were kept there before the funeral, not for public tribute, but primarily because they were strangers with no home in which to be prepared for burial. Similarly, a mention of "the monument raised to commemorate the martyrs" fails to include a date, thereby implying that it was erected by contemporary eighteenth-century Bostonians rather than those from the 1880s. Readers are also told that "Bostonians celebrated the anniversary of the massacre annually until the 1840s" when those commemorations ended in 1783. Finally, the authors note that in 1967 the city of Newark "made March 5 an annual holiday," but they incorrectly state that it was "the first holiday to recognize an African American"—that distinction belongs to the state of Massachusetts, which formally established Attucks Day in 1933.[15]

A familiar error came in Joe William Trotter Jr.'s 2001 *The African American Experience*, which repeats the old canard that Attucks had written the letter to Governor Hutchinson warning, "You will hear further from us hereafter."[16] Even a 2007 text that says very little about Attucks presents him in language that crafts an interpretation for its readers based more on presumption than evidence: Attucks was a "black patriot" who was "the first to lose his life in the Americans' bid for Independence" and who "became a symbol of American resistance to the hated British occupation of Boston."[17]

Other works from the early 2000s barely touch on Attucks. Nell Irvin Painter's innovative survey, *Creating African Americans* (2006), focuses largely on black Americans' artistic production. Attucks is mentioned as "the first martyr to the American cause" and one of several "eighteenth and nineteenth century individuals with one African and one Indian parent [who] appeared in American history as 'black.'" He is also noted for being included in one of painter Charles White's Hampton University murals.[18] Perhaps Thomas C. Holt made the most intriguing choice in his 2010 narrative exploration of African American history by omitting Attucks altogether. But for most textbook authors Attucks proved too enticing a symbol of black patriotism and black agency to ignore.[19]

Textbooks necessarily have to rely on numerous secondary sources to inform their narratives and do not typically include notes to cite those sources. Nonetheless, they are often accepted as the True Story of the past by the students who read them. Authors' decisions about whether or not to include Attucks, and if included what to say about him, are based on the kinds of stories they set out to tell. Even texts that reject hagiography and stick close to the facts still use Attucks, albeit cautiously: as a token black presence to satisfy market demands; to illustrate relationships among Africans and Native Americans in colonial America; to represent African Americans' active presence in the life of the eighteenth-century colonies; to show that blacks—or sailors—participated in the radical politics of the Revolution. Holt's choice to exclude Attucks altogether seems to be explained by his decision not to write a typical textbook. Holt rejected "historians' conventional divisions of historical time" in order to emphasize the experiences of black women and men whose lives were not bound by neat periods like "the Revolutionary era" or "the Civil Rights Movement." Because his emphasis was on conveying real experiences of real people across those chronologies, perhaps Attucks's story was simply too incomplete to be included. Given the inaccuracies contained in many textbooks, one has to wonder whether the best approach regarding Crispus Attucks in that genre might be "the less said the better."[20]

Academic historians and textbook authors have hardly been the only writers to interpret Crispus Attucks for public audiences. He is at least touched on in most books about blacks' service during the Revolution or in the United States military more generally, with varying degrees of accuracy. Many are content merely to mention Attucks and sketch out the basics of his involvement in the massacre. Those authors who decide to offer greater detail or to impose meaning on Attucks's actions often wander into error or speculation. Robert Edgerton's *Hidden Heroism* claims that Christopher Snyder, not Attucks, was the first African American to be killed by a British soldier. Snyder (or Seider or Snider) was actually the child of white German immigrants, and he was killed in February 1770 by a fellow Bostonian, not British troops. Like several other works, Catherine Clinton's book for young readers on blacks in the Revolution mentions John Attuck, but not as a maternal ancestor—here he was Crispus's African father. Historian Douglas R. Egerton cites Linebaugh and Rediker to support his reasonable characterization of Attucks as fighting for "workingman's rights," but he repeats several minor distortions from other secondary works in his description of Attucks and the events leading to the massacre.[21]

One African American historical writer without an advanced degree in history was passionate in telling readers what Attucks meant to him. After his retirement as a basketball superstar, Kareem Abdul-Jabbar attained recognition as an author and public intellectual, particularly regarding issues pertaining to race in American society. His 1996 book, *Black Profiles in Courage*, was written because history books tended to be "focused on white people's concerns" and usually "don't convey black people as fundamentally 'American.'" All Americans, he felt, needed to know more about "black people whose contributions to American history have been distorted, stereotyped, or ignored."[22] In a conversational book with ardent discussions of dozens of courageous black people, Attucks stood out as "the first real American martyr." Even though he had majored in history at UCLA and "read voraciously," Abdul-Jabbar claims he had never heard of Attucks until 1970 when he asked his professional teammate Oscar Robertson about the name of Crispus Attucks High School in Indianapolis, where Robertson had helped win the Indiana state basketball championship in 1955. From that point, he wrote, "I started reading everything about Attucks that I could find."[23]

Abdul-Jabbar says his first instinct was to place Attucks on a pedestal: "I imagined him as larger than life: leader of men, noble freedom fighter, combination of Jefferson, Washington, Paine. The classic American hero, only black." But his reading led him to recognize that "history only recorded fragments of his life" and that some portrayed Attucks as "ordinary" or even "unsavory"—which for Abdul-Jabbar ultimately "made him seem all the more courageous." He became "obsessed" with Attucks. Investigating this ordinary man's story, he claimed, "mattered more to me at the time than winning an NBA championship." Abdul-Jabbar's account of the events leading to the Boston Massacre repeated much of the same somewhat problematic narrative presented in Lerone Bennett's now-classic *Before the Mayflower*, whose sixth edition had appeared in 1993. That narrative included Attucks being "known around the lower Boston docks as a tough customer" and leading the "mob [that] drove the soldiers back to their barracks gates" in a conflict ostensibly preceding the fatal one on King Street.[24]

But if much of his information about Attucks's role in the massacre came from Bennett, Abdul-Jabbar drew his own personal meaning from Attucks's story. Like all historical interpretations, it emerged to a large degree from his own time and place. John Adams's closing arguments, he wrote, had characterized Attucks as "a low-life thug" whom the soldiers were "justified in shooting." Writing just a few years after an all-white jury acquitted Los Angeles police officers of any wrongdoing in their beating of black motorist Rodney King, Abdul-Jabbar observed that Adams's vilification of Attucks "sounds like he's defending the Los Angeles Police Department." Abdul-Jabbar saw Attucks as "a hard man who led a hard life" and the mob he led as a violent one—"they were trying to *hurt* people." As for intentions, "Maybe Crispus Attucks had no business being in that square," he wrote. "Maybe he didn't care about taxes or the British boot. He was not politically active; we don't know if he could even read." But even though "we don't know his motives . . . Crispus Attucks will always be an American hero. Say he *was* engaged in thuggery. Fortunately for him, it was thuggery *for the right side*." He "aligned himself with the downtrodden." "What counts," for Abdul-Jabbar, "is, a black man was in the first group of patriots to bite the dust, for *whatever* reason." Attucks "stood up and was counted when it mattered." Abdul-Jabbar wanted his version of Attucks and other black heroes to inspire young people to develop "a moral center and character" and to "shine a brighter light" on heroic virtues that transcend racial divisions.[25]

These goals of improving upon existing history books and presenting empowering and inspiring heroes to the nation's youth, across the lines of race, motivated many writers of the new millennium. Of the many books for younger readers that discussed Attucks and the Boston Massacre, most took this approach. As with other genres, juvenile literature—both fiction and nonfiction—did not always adhere to the highest standards of historical accuracy, and many works continued to rely on compensatory tokenism rather than a serious rethinking of America's master narrative.

Numerous collected biographies of black Americans for young audiences as well as individual juvenile biographies of Attucks appeared in the late twentieth and early twenty-first centuries, with most following what had become a fairly standard storyline of Attucks's heroism and significance. He was typically presented as a mixed-race man who seized his own freedom, worked as a sailor and laborer, and took a leadership role in the confrontation with the British on March 5, 1770. Most included some speculation (often presented as fact) about Attucks's parentage, his cattle-trading skills, his views of British policy, his connections with the Sons of Liberty, and his commitment to the cause of American liberty. Some of the individual Attucks biographies repeated details of his early life apparently drawn from Dharathula

Millender's 1965 volume (which was reprinted by a different publisher in 1986) or invented friendships and conversations between Attucks and real or fictional Bostonians. Aside from those literary inventions, a few of these works also produced true doozies of misinformation.

Two books from the 1990s made an identical error by falsely adding George Washington to the list of Founders who praised Attucks. "When the Colonists were staggering wearily under the cross of woe," both texts had the first president intone, "a Negro came to the front and bore the cross to the victory of glorious martyrdom." They were close. It was not the first president but early black historian George Washington Williams who had made this flowery declaration in the 1880s. The theme of one unusual volume appears in its title: *More Dirty Little Secrets about Black History, Its Heroes and Other Troublemakers.* Here, Attucks was said to be "not the first person killed in the Revolutionary War. Apparently, a Black youngster named Christopher Snyder had been killed by the British a few days earlier." As mentioned above, Snyder (or Seider) was white and was killed by a fellow Bostonian. Nonetheless, the authors noted that "Black Americans honored Crispus Attucks as a national hero and patriot, while Whites labeled him a criminal outsider."[26]

While that stark division between black and white assessments of Attucks is exaggerated, some writers did dispute his status as an American hero. Joy Hakim is a case in point. A "teacher and journalist who studied elementary and middle school textbooks, found them boring, and decided to do something about it," Hakim wrote a ten-volume American history series, *The History of US*, for elementary and middle school students. In her coverage of the Boston Massacre, Hakim briefly describes the events of March 5 and declares, "None of them was a hero. The victims were troublemakers who got worse than they deserved. The soldiers were professionals . . . who shouldn't have panicked." Attucks is only mentioned in the caption under the Revere engraving, which Hakim criticizes, in part, because "it doesn't show Crispus Attucks, a black laborer, who was killed." For Hakim, what was worth emphasizing was the propaganda value of Revere's depiction, which "helped start a war." The only real hero was John Adams, whose defense of the soldiers illustrated his commitment to "a totally new kind of government: a government based on fair play and self-government."[27]

A historical novel for juvenile audiences written around the same time offered a more problematic assessment of Attucks. Ann Rinaldi's *The Fifth of March* (1993) was the story not of Attucks but of a teenage girl whose position as a servant of John and Abigail Adams placed her in the thick of debates about British troops and colonial resistance. Rinaldi claims she had studied

"Colonial America for years" and reviewers praised *The Fifth of March* as a "painstakingly researched tale" that presented a "vivid picture of colonial life." Indeed, many historical details and Rinaldi's depiction of the "lifestyle of the people of the times" hold up fairly well. While Crispus Attucks appears only sporadically through the novel, Rinaldi's treatment of this minor character departs dramatically from the available sources.[28]

Crispus Attucks, writes Rinaldi, was one of the "new names . . . spoken in whispers" after British troops arrived in Boston in 1768. He was a muscular, mixed-race "giant" who had been "sent for" by Boston's Sons of Liberty because they "know he's an agitator." Rinaldi's Attucks gathers crowds around him and urges them to violence against the troops. "Tonight," he whispers to one group, "we'll see to it that a soldier accidentally falls off a bridge into the water. . . . Tonight, a sentry will have his face cut with an oyster shell." When approving members of the mob volunteer to act against specific targets, Attucks—the hired outside agitator whose "real name is Michael Johnson"—asserts his control: " 'I name who it is and I name who does it,' the mulatto said. They fell silent."[29]

Rinaldi's description of the massacre itself incorporates a good amount of eyewitness testimony, though she does put a rather anti-mob spin on the account. Some men in the streets spotted Attucks and followed him because "He'll do what has to be done." Soon after, the protagonist saw Attucks throw a club at a soldier, "who then fell down. Attucks came forward and the two of them scrambled for the soldier's musket." Within seconds a shot rang out and the young protagonist "saw Attucks on the ground, bleeding." The only sympathy shown for Attucks came from "Sukey, the nigra girl," a dialect-speaking character who cooked and cleaned for the Adamses: " 'He wuz a slave,' she said. 'But he done somethin'. He stood fer somethin'. People, they looked up to him. They respected him.' "[30]

In her Author's Note, Rinaldi discusses both her sources and her depiction of the massacre. "As with many movements or rebellions or causes," she says, "there were those who were involved in the massacre for the violence of it, or to avenge personal grievances. And there were those brought in to act as 'antagonists.' " She "learned that Crispus Attucks was one of these, an agitator brought in from elsewhere to help move the mob to action." She claims to have found that tidbit by "reading Hiller B. Zobel . . . the acknowledged authority on the event," but I have not found anything resembling that characterization of Attucks in Zobel's 1970 book or in any other credible source.[31]

Rinaldi's historical novels often address issues of race in American history and her interpretation of the Boston Massacre was shaped by her views on the racial violence of the 1990s. "When I started my research," she says, "I could not help likening the massacre to the Los Angeles riots in 1992. There were many similarities." In contrast to Kareem Abdul-Jabbar, who also read the massacre in part through the lens of the Rodney King incident, Rinaldi never clearly explains what those similarities are, beyond suggesting that the Boston Massacre was "as unavoidable, perhaps, as the L.A. riots, and as was true of the L.A. riots, no one actually knows whom to blame, who was responsible."[32]

Compared with Rinaldi, the inflammatory conservative radio talk show host Rush Limbaugh is a relative newcomer to the realm of children's literature. Assuming the persona of substitute history teacher "Rush Revere," Limbaugh's illustrated books for young readers promise them "time travel adventures with great Americans." The three books in the series to date transport modern students back to the colonial and Revolutionary eras. In his 2014 *Rush Revere and the First Patriots*, Rush and his students (along with a talking horse named Liberty) encounter Sam "the Samuelator" Adams just after the Boston Massacre. Adams urges his fellow patriots to "never forget the horrid massacre" and to "honor Crispus Attucks, who was first to fall, struck twice in the chest by bullets." When one student admits to never having heard of Attucks, Rush fills him in: "History tells us that Attucks was of African and Native American descent and had fled to Boston after escaping his enslavers. In fact, he has a monument in Boston that hails him as a hero of the American Revolution, the first Patriot to give his life for the cause." When another student wonders whether Attucks would have gone up King Street if he knew what awaited him there, Rush explains that "a hero does what needs to be done and says what needs to be said despite the consequence, even if it means giving your life." Attucks thus met Limbaugh's criteria to qualify as an American hero and patriot.[33]

Attucks also continued to make appearances outside the printed word in twenty-first-century popular culture, with varied interpretations. Acclaimed hip-hop artist Nas's 2008 song, "You Can't Stop Us Now," mentions Attucks as part of a complex critique of the continuing oppression of black Americans in the twenty-first century. The "critically praised" untitled album, released just after the Democratic National Convention selected Barack Obama as the party's presidential candidate, was described as "the most intelligent hip-hop album that confronted race issues in this country." Speaking of the album's content, Nas pointed out that "Americans want their independence and they celebrate it," but "America still got a lot of growing up to do. . . . I love this country," he claimed, "but . . . we have to fix up a lot of things." The album included a track titled "Black President," which expressed guarded optimism

that with the hoped-for election of Obama, "yes we can, change the world."
"You Can't Stop Us Now" is more critical, featuring references to historical
eras from "pyramids to cotton fields to Wrigley Fields," and nods to Betsy
Ross, Willie Lynch, Aunt Jemima, James Baldwin, Sammy Davis, and nameless "so-called coons, shines and darkies." "Crispus Attucks the first blast"
is mentioned alongside "forgotten men who didn't get killed," and it is not
completely clear what Nas thinks of him. Other compositions mentioned
Attucks, at times with similarly unclear meanings. Especially cryptic was
the rap group Prophetix's 2002 release, "Crispus Attucks," which randomly
inserts Attucks's name several times in a narrative that seems to have no connection with him at all.[34]

In 2005, Virginia composer Adolphus Hailstork's "Crispus Attucks," a
classical cantata incorporating "African-American musical styles," was explicit
in praising the "resolute" Attucks for leading patriots who "were the voice
of liberty." The cantata was performed to mark the reopening of the recently
renovated Attucks Theatre in Norfolk. The libretto, written by poet Herbert
W. Martin, tells Attucks's story in two parts, the first dealing with his life
leading up to the Boston Massacre and the second covering the soldiers' trial.
When John Adams, in the second section, challenges Attucks's legitimacy
with the query, "How can people allow themselves to be led by a runaway
slave?" the chorus responds with a passionate defense of Attucks against
Adams's "vitriolic outburst." Other parts of the book celebrate Attucks's willingness "to strike a blow for freedom" and "the joy of liberty which resides
in the blood of all free men." Hailstork hoped the forty-minute piece would
attract black audiences to the "historically important" Attucks Theatre. The
same venue presented the "Attucks Nutcracker" during the Christmas season
in 2011.[35]

Rapper, actor, and activist Common gave a shout out to Attucks in "Pops
Belief," the closing track on his 2011 release, *The Dreamer, the Believer*. The
spoken word benedictory poem opens with a dedication "to two very outstanding people . . . Gentleman Crispus Attucks and Mr. Marcus Garvey."[36]
A little-known rapper in 2014 was preparing to release a song with a less laudatory message. "I don't teach my baby about no Crispus Attucks," Indiana-
based artist Merc Versus rapped. "Crispus Attucks was the one the first to
die in the American Revolution. The nigga shouldn'ta died." Five years into
Obama's presidency, this artist observed that "they're prejudice [*sic*] and racist against the first black president." As "another young boy's head is split,"
Merc Versus saw little change in the plight of African Americans. Better to
teach one's children, one sampled section of the song advised, about Denmark

Vesey, Toussaint Louverture, and Nat Turner than about Attucks. Merc implied with his lyric, "got to shoot them Crispus Attucks," that both Attucks and slain blacks in the singer's own day should have been more forceful and proactive in asserting their rights and protecting their lives.[37]

In 2012 a parodic music video on the "Funny or Die" comedy website used rapper Ice Cube's 1992 video for the song "It Was a Good Day" as the vehicle for a humorous reenactment of Attucks's final hours. The original video follows a Los Angeles gangsta through a "good day" of cruising, sex, basketball, craps shooting, no friends killed, and no hassles from the police until he is confronted by a full swat team and arrested upon his return home in the evening. The parody begins with a clock-ticking "60 Minutes"-style intro, and a serious commentator discussing the lack of historical certainty about this black dockworker and his role in "the events of that fateful day which led to the most important of American wars." Attucks then follows a similar sequence as the Ice Cube video, altered in lyric, costume, and context to evoke the eighteenth century. The video ends with Attucks being ambushed and shot down on his doorstep by several British soldiers. As he prepares to meet his fate, Attucks reflects on his place in history: "I'm just as important as those other black history figures, you know what I'm sayin'? Marcus Garvey, Sojourner Truth, who that dude who make peanuts? I'm Crispus Motherfuckin' Attucks. Yeah."[38]

Along with these references in popular music and video, Attucks appeared sporadically in mainstream television programs, including several documentaries and educational programs. The 1997 PBS documentary, *Liberty! The American Revolution*, presented the Boston Massacre in the first of its six, hour-long episodes. The interpretation notes that Revere's "wildly inaccurate illustration" of "innocent civilians" being gunned down "galvanize[d] people throughout the colonies" but does not mention Crispus Attucks. In 2006, the History Channel's thirteen-episode documentary miniseries, *The Revolution*, gave the massacre more coverage and also emphasized the role of propaganda. While it "was not remotely a massacre," the narrator explains, "the Patriot spin machine roar[ed] into high gear" and a "tragic accident is recast as a murderous crime against the colonial people." Attucks is mentioned only in passing as "a sailor and runaway slave" who is "widely viewed as the first martyr of the American Revolution."[39]

Attucks also made occasional appearances in non-documentary television programs. He was all but absent in the 2006 HBO dramatic miniseries, *John Adams*. While the massacre and Adams's central role in the subsequent trial received attention, Attucks made only a brief and uncredited appearance as an anonymous black corpse Adams was shown inspecting at the massacre scene. The heavily fictionalized 2015 History Channel miniseries *Sons of Liberty* treated him similarly. Attucks was never named and appeared on screen merely as a black victim of the massacre, this time cradled in death in the arms of the series' central character—John Adams's handsome and dashing cousin Sam. Attucks was even mentioned in popular situation comedies. In a 2003 episode of the Disney Channel series *Lizzy McGuire*, we learn that African American character Lanny Onasis (Christian Copelin) is related to the "American patriot" Crispus Attucks. And on the hit NBC comedy *30 Rock*, black character Tracy Jordan (Tracy Morgan) visits Boston's Freedom Trail and complains to a John Hancock interpreter that the Revolution did not mean independence for all Americans. "Hancock" later introduces Tracy to "Crispus Attucks" (another interpreter) to demonstrate that he has black friends. But when Hancock says he met Attucks in 1775—five years after Attucks's death—Tracy indignantly calls out his error.[40]

A 2002 animated PBS children's series on the Revolution, *Liberty's Kids*, failed to even mention Attucks, but it offered an emphatically disapproving interpretation of the Boston Massacre. In the third of forty total episodes, titled "United We Stand," one of the young protagonists meets John Adams and dismissingly identifies him as the man "who defended the British troops who fired on our Patriots . . . who simply stood up for what they believed." Adams justifies his actions by pointing out that the jury acquitted the soldiers and by asserting that "the men involved in the so-called massacre were not patriots, they were a drunken mob spoiling for a fight." When the young man maintains that had he been there, he "would have been with the Patriots," Adams calmly counsels the lad: "You must learn to distinguish between a patriotic act of protest and mob rule. The tyranny of the people can be just as brutal as the tyranny of the Crown." Though Attucks is not mentioned, the story's interpretation implicitly delivers a blow to his status as an American patriot and hero.[41]

Quite the opposite intent was in the mind of Cheo Hodari Coker, creator of the 2016 Netflix series "Luke Cage," which is based on a Marvel Comics Blaxploitation-style hero from the early 1970s, updated for the twenty-first century. Cage acquired superhuman strength and impenetrable skin through experiments performed on him while imprisoned for a crime he did not commit. On gaining his freedom, the Netflix version of Cage settles in Harlem, where he reluctantly uses his powers to protect the good people of the community from wrongdoers. One of the main villains is a criminal boss named Cottonmouth, whose base of operations is the fictional Crispus Attucks

Complex. In a pivotal scene that solidifies Cage's commitment to fight for a good cause, Cage gazes at the Attucks Complex from a park across the street, where he is called a "nigger" by a young black mugger. Without averting his gaze he lays a little perspective on the youth:

> You see a nigger standing in front of you? Across the street from a building named after one of our greatest heroes? . . . Do you even know who Crispus Attucks was? A free black man, the first man to die for what became America. He could have acted scared when those Brits raised their guns, blended into the crowd, but he stepped up. He paid with his life, but he started something.[42]

Showrunner Coker told *TV Guide* that he quite consciously had the series' bulletproof hero idolize Attucks in order to reacquaint a new generation with the first African American hero:

> I wanted to talk about the first person to die for a revolution and what that meant, and what he sacrificed. We used Crispus Attucks for that because half of these kids haven't even heard of Crispus Attucks. . . . You get to tell stories and history that people have not really thought about in a long time.[43]

While Attucks has made some inroads on the small screen, film producers since the 1940s have consistently failed to complete a major motion picture based on Attucks's life. But they do keep trying. In 2013, actor and director Gabriel Bologna was listed as writer for a film project entitled *A Man Named Crispus*, touted as "the epic story of Crispus Attucks, the first martyr of the American revolution. His name may not ring a bell today," the online plot summary claims, "but his very name was the battle-cry of our soldiers in our Great War of independence." We also learn that "Paul Revere, John Adams, Samuel Adams, and Thomas Paine, carried Crispis' [*sic*] coffin on their shoulders four miles" during the funeral—even though Paine would not arrive in the colonies for several years. Attucks is described as "America's only Martyr . . . a fugitive slave, who died for a country that wouldn't outlaw slavery for another hundred years." No further details about this film project have been found, but the online summary augurs a storyline as implausible as other scripts that have appeared over the years.[44]

It is worth noting here that Attucks's presence in twenty-first-century popular culture has been magnified by the Internet. A google search for crispus attucks (without quotation marks) in April 2015 delivered 398,000 hits, the first page of which included a Wikipedia entry; links from the University of Massachusetts online Crispus Attucks Museum; the Library of Congress online exhibit, "The Murder of Crispus Attucks"; a PBS website for the *Africans in America* documentary series; brief biographies from factmonster.com and biography.com; the website of the Boston Massacre Historical Society; and the homepage of the Crispus Attucks Association, an eighty-plus-year-old nonprofit community service organization in York, Pennsylvania. Subsequent pages of the search results offered a wide range of websites, videos, and images relating to Attucks, including academic and pseudo-academic writing; news and media items; local and racial heritage pieces; websites of various schools or organizations named for Attucks; political commentary; elementary school student reports; and more. Some of the information on these sites is presented cautiously, with caveats about how little can be known with certainty about Attucks's life. But most repeat as fact the assorted fabrications and myths that have graced more traditional print and broadcast media for generations.[45]

African American newspapers have been as guilty as other media in disseminating questionable information about Attucks. One 2002 newspaper story recounted details that had appeared in Dharathula Millender's fictionalized life of Attucks, presenting them as fact and without attribution: his African father Prince, his Native American mother Nancy, his siblings Phebe and "Little Brother," and everything down to his "well received" speech in Boston, which "triggered unity amongst the colonists to fight for their freedom." With his sacrifice "Attucks showed [twenty-first-century readers] how loyal someone can be to his country and become an inspiration, at the same time encouraging others to stand up for what is fair, just, and true."[46] Another short news story said that Attucks "resented and hated the unjust laws and political restrictions" imposed by the British and that his "zeal for freedom, justice and equality for the human race" helped lay "the foundation for a United America."[47] Another misleadingly asserted that March 5 was designated Crispus Attucks Day during the 1770s, and that "Attucks Day remained the chief American anniversary until independence was won." As for that victory itself, the story's assertion that "it is indisputable that African Americans provided the balance of power that brought America independence" would be seen as disputable by many historians of the Revolution.[48]

Some accounts in the black press added new fictions. In one odd story that chastised those who "don't know our Black history and how long we have been fighting for freedom," the reporter likely misheard the "highly respected historian" who was said to have claimed that Attucks "took charge of a group of Black men and confronted the British soldiers" on March 5 and that "over 500,000 African Americans were counted among the 2.5 million revolutionary forces from 1775 to 1783." There is no evidence that the group Attucks led contained any other blacks, and the stated numbers of the "revolutionary forces" actually reflects the total population figures for the colonies during the war.[49]

In another account, the oft-repeated image of a "tall and brawny" "black man with some Indian blood" who was a "well-known and well-respected figure in Boston," was augmented by the news that "Attucks also loved children for their free and open nature; and he was adored by them. Contemporary accounts," readers are told, "relate the sight of Attucks on the grass surrounded by scores of children held spellbound by his tales of the sea and far-off lands." One wonders if more harm than good was done by well-intentioned columnists and reporters bent on expanding awareness of African American history who were so careless with facts that even their accurate descriptions of black accomplishments might be called into question. Perhaps the last story's attempt to connect Attucks with children was intended to explain why the Boston neighborhood of Roxbury had named a new daycare facility the Crispus Attucks Child Care Center in honor of "this great American hero." Years later children from the center participated in the Boston Equal Rights League's annual Attucks Day celebration, which also featured a speech by Roxbury's congressman, who praised Attucks as "a role model for our times."[50]

While some black journalists went overboard in crafting Attucks into a quintessential American hero, others questioned whether he was the kind of role model twenty-first-century African Americans needed. Echoing views other black critics had expressed over the years, one commentator argued, "Blacks breed disrespect for themselves and their ancestors by pointing with pride to the 5,000 misguided men like Crispus Attucks who joined and served the American cause in a war that was being fought in large measure to keep Africans in bondage." While "white historians gleefully proclaim that 5,000 of our ancestors fought for the American side," the writer asserted, "they do not tell us that 20 times that number sought their own liberty from slave-owners like George Washington." Another writer was likely unaware of the arguments articulated in 1860 by black abolitionist John S. Rock, when he reiterated Rock's suggestion that perhaps Nat Turner should "be heralded the same way that Attucks is." Was Attucks "really fighting for 'his' freedom in that war?" he pondered. Was he "right in his fight?" It was Turner, not Attucks, who "was 'really' fighting for 'his own' freedom."[51]

By the late 1990s, academic historians were beginning to emphasize that black American colonists did often side with the British during the Revolution, implicitly, if not always intentionally, calling into question Attucks's status as a hero.[52] Historian Simon Schama's 2006 *Rough Crossings*, for example, highlighted "the story of thousands of blacks in the 13 American colonies who rallied to the British lines during the Revolutionary War because they believed that it is where freedom lay." An American journalist commenting on Schama's book found himself wondering why "Crispus Attucks, who fell to British bullets in the Boston Massacre of 1770 is celebrated here while Newton Prince, a Boston barber who testified on behalf of the British soldiers who shot Attucks, is not." Rather, Prince "was tarred and feathered by ignorant Bostonians. When the war came, Prince, not surprisingly, joined the British side." This journalist wondered whether Americans might "glorify our Founding Fathers too uncritically. . . . Do Americans, in these morally ambiguous times of Abu Ghraib, Guantanamo, and the secret prisons into which our prisoners disappear without trial or hope, long for heroes and heroic times?"[53]

Yet another journalist mused about the meanings that Crispus Attucks might hold for the present on Attucks Day 2001—several months before the September 11, 2001, terrorist attacks upended Americans' sense of stability and morality. "I've often wondered," wrote Michael P. Quinlan, "if Crispus Attucks and Patrick Carr knew each other before their fates were entwined?" The two men were menial laborers and outsiders—one a mixed-race fugitive slave and the other "an expert in rioting from growing up in seditious Ireland." These men, along with the other martyrs with whom they share a common grave, had been "brought together by history and by the passion and idealism of a single night." Quinlan wondered what lessons the possible acquaintance of Carr and Attucks might hold for contemporary Boston, "a city that often struggles to be one in spirit and thought when it comes to matters of race."[54]

A somewhat unconventional twenty-first-century lesson about Attucks's significance came in the form of "a snarky little Web site" called *Urban Exposé*, which emerged in 2001 and quickly drew attention for "skewering" American media companies geared toward "urban" or African American markets, "from hip-hop oriented Web sites and magazines to Black Entertainment Television." The founder, a young African American hacker from Brooklyn named John Lee, reveled at the time in maintaining his "mystery man" status by using the pseudonym "Crispus Attucks" and wearing a white, colonial-style wig in his rare public appearances. While other staff members adopted names like Harriet Tubman, Sojourner Truth, and George Washington

Carver, Lee chose Attucks because he "set off the revolution—took a bullet for something he didn't have a stake in." Lee was introduced to Attucks, as were so many others, through a history textbook that had Attucks's picture on the cover. "I guess students were supposed to feel good that Crispus got shot," he figured, "so his family could be enslaved real quick after the revolution." Lee exposed sometimes "scandalizing" insider gossip about his media targets and saw his use of the Attucks moniker as an "inside joke": he saw his position in the emerging tech world as similar to Attucks's—acting as a "deus ex machina" who "sparked the events and set the foundation for what you see around you."[55]

Others found different meanings in Attucks, some predictable and some perhaps a bit counterintuitive. It was not surprising for the progressive black Newark mayor (and later New Jersey senator) Cory Booker to invoke Attucks just after Barack Obama's 2008 election during his appearance on the satirical comedy-news show *The Colbert Report*. "One nation, under God, indivisible, with Liberty and Justice for all: Those values," Booker professed, "which we haven't fully achieved yet, those values have been fought for by our nation for generations. The first person to take a bullet for this country was Crispus Attucks, an African American man." A few years into Obama's first term, *Atlantic* magazine columnist and blogger Ta-nehisi Coates used Attucks explicitly to characterize the first black president's approach to healing the nation's racial rifts:

> Obama offered black America a convenient narrative that could be meshed with the larger American story. It was a narrative premised on Crispus Attucks, not the black slaves who escaped plantations and fought for the British; on the 54th Massachusetts, not Nat Turner; on stoic and saintly Rosa Parks, not young and pregnant Claudette Colvin; on a Christlike Martin Luther King Jr., not an avenging Malcolm X.

Coates titled his essay "Fear of a Black President" in part because much of the nation refused to accept that integrationist narrative. Recalling the confrontational rhetoric of Obama's erstwhile Chicago minister, Coates observed that for many white Americans "Jeremiah Wright's presence threatened to rupture that comfortable narrative by symbolizing that which makes integration impossible—black rage."[56]

Other groups also distanced Attucks from black rage by attaching his name to right-wing political movements. In 2006, a black Los Angeles activist named Ted Hughes founded a Crispus Attucks Brigade of the so-called

Minuteman movement, which had emerged to urge both government and civilian action to secure America's border with Mexico. The Crispus Attucks Brigade embraced "the first black to die in defense of the American nation" as an inspiration for twenty-first-century African Americans to "take their rightful and dutiful role to stop illegal immigration into the United States of America." Blacks' particular stake in this movement stemmed from the perception that undocumented immigrants "are not only stealing our jobs, housing, health care, and education, but our Civil and Constitutional Rights as well." Unlike the illegal immigrants, "American Blacks and others," the group's website proclaimed, "fought, suffered and gave their lives" for those rights. Supporters of the undocumented were likened to "present day slave proponents" and "betrayers of the ideals of the founding fathers," since "illegal immigrants work for slave wages and many are forced into squalor [sic] living conditions."[57]

Another African American group aligning itself with a far-right political movement devoted to the ostensible ideals of the nation's founders was the Crispus Attucks Tea Party, established in Houston, Texas, in early 2011. The Texas group's "primary objective is to break the cycles of dependency and decay that continue to anesthetize and hold captive too many Black families and neighborhoods" and "to help Blacks fully assimilate into and be competitive in American society." They also aspired "to teach all Americans the fullness of the history of Blacks in America and to help Blacks gain control of their lives and the destiny of their children. Only by understanding our full and true history will we all [sic] of America be liberated." The group invoked another African American icon by holding its inaugural meeting in January 2011 in conjunction with its "celebration of Martin Luther King's birthday and his leadership." The group sought to align both King and Attucks with the Tea Party movement's ideals of limited government by helping "lead the way" into "a period in time where 'Content and Character are indeed more important than Color' for those who prepare themselves to be competitive."[58]

Other recent attempts to honor Crispus Attucks in the public landscape avoided tying him to an explicit political agenda but nonetheless generated discord. In 2002, a white resident of St. Charles, Missouri, tried to attract support for the erection of a Crispus Attucks statue in a prominent St. Louis public park. Don Smith, described in one news account as "a man on a mission," had first learned about Attucks from a black friend he served with in the navy during the late 1960s. Smith wrote hundreds of letters to St. Louis government officials and civic leaders, mounted a local radio and newspaper campaign, and even recruited a sculptor and several financial donors. He assumed that "no one could oppose Crispus Attucks" as a subject for public tribute, imagining "the pride of a young black dad" sitting with his children at an Attucks statue and relating a key moment in the race's "proud history." "How could anybody—black or white—find fault with this?" While Smith did find some supporters, the project never gained much traction. Some simply saw little value in directing limited human and financial resources toward public memorials while others objected to Smith's apparently abrasive personality. And many, as always, questioned whether Attucks was a legitimate American hero or merely a drunken rabble-rouser.[59] This last question was also at the center of another commemorative project that brought Attucks and the controversy that surrounded him back to where it all began.

Conclusion

From Crispus Attucks to Michael Brown 245 years later,
two things remain clear: We never know what sparks a
revolution. And black lives matter.

AMY GOODMAN (*truthdig.com*, March 4, 2015)

QUESTIONS ABOUT CRISPUS Attucks's heroic credentials remain central to Americans' understanding of who he was and how—or if—he should be remembered. These debates—among government officials, academic historians, and interested citizens—all came together in the early 2000s in Crispus Attucks's old stomping ground of Framingham, Massachusetts. Reminiscent of nineteenth-century controversies over raising an Attucks monument in Boston and the more recent St. Louis debate, heated arguments arose over whether Attucks should be commemorated in the public landscape as an American hero. The landscape in question was a small Framingham bridge that allowed traffic on the Old Connecticut Path to cross Cochituate Brook. The movement to rename the bridge to honor Crispus Attucks was initially proposed to the Framingham Historical Commission in the late 1990s by Stephen Herring, the commission's chair and the town historian at the time. Herring believed that since Attucks had achieved the status of "a prominent national figure in Afro-American history, it seemed appropriate that his background as a runaway slave from Framingham should be recognized in some visible public manner." Members of the commission agreed, as did the Framingham Historical Society, the African American Heritage Commission, and several local spokespersons. The Crispus Attucks Bridge project received financial support from corporate, governmental, and private donors.[1]

But there were critics. Foremost among them was a Framingham bus driver and amateur local historian named Joe Rizoli, who argued that "naming this bridge after Crispus Attucks is like naming it after [convicted Mafia boss] John Gotti. . . . What Attucks did would be like going to the Salvation

Army and rounding up all the drunks and saying, 'Hey, let's go protest at the town hall.'" African American Heritage Commission member Edwina Weston-Dyer suggested that Rizoli "should go back to the [history] books" to learn the truth about Attucks's heroic actions, also intimating that Rizoli's objections might be racially based. That particular argument is weakened by the fact that Rizoli proposed that the bridge instead be named after Peter Salem, a black Framingham Revolutionary soldier whose patriotic bona fides are more clearly documented, and less controversial, than Attucks's. The local reporter who first wrote about Rizoli's concerns conducted an informal poll, whose early responses weighed against naming the bridge for Attucks. The *Boston Globe* editorialized on Attucks's behalf, suggesting that Attucks should be commemorated not so much because he was a heroic patriot but because his life represents "American complexity" and is therefore "symbolically important." Attucks "probably wasn't a saint," and his "rough life" may well have "lacked the high gloss" his champions often accorded him. But Attucks "did what the country still asks citizens to do every day: When the American experiment fails—slavery, segregation, discrimination—continue to struggle." Attucks's actions at the massacre were far less important for the *Globe* writer than the symbolic meaning of his presumed "faith in the cause of independence," despite the obstacles that hindered his personal pursuit of life, liberty, and happiness.[2]

Respected academic historians of the Revolutionary era entered the fray on both sides. Pauline Maier characterized Attucks and his comrades as "thugs looking for a fight" who "weren't much interested in political ideals." "The massacre wasn't led by the patriots," she argued. "Attucks was of a different crowd." But Maier's assessment assumes a fairly narrow view of who might be considered a patriot. Historian Alfred F. Young argued throughout his career that Americans must expand their view of who the Revolutionaries were and what the Revolution was. "We Americans like the result of the Revolution," he noted when interviewed about the bridge-naming controversy, "but we often don't like to acknowledge the radicals like Attucks who brought it about." Even Joe Rizoli acknowledged that Attucks might at least have had "an economic grievance" against the occupying British soldiers, who often took jobs away from colonists. For Rizoli, this "economic grievance" was not a sufficient basis for true patriotism; for historians like Young, Crispus Attucks and others of his lowly social position must be seen "as historical actors with aspirations of their own" and must be incorporated into the nation's understanding of its complicated revolutionary beginnings.[3]

The controversy surrounding the Framingham Bridge brings Crispus Attucks's story full circle. Arguments about Attucks in the twenty-first century have much in common with the views articulated during the 1770 trial of the British soldiers; with debates in both the 1850s and 1880s over the appropriateness of honoring Attucks's aggressive actions with a public monument; and with the conflicting interpretations about Attucks and the massacre expressed by historians, educators, politicians, journalists, and the general public for some two and a half centuries. Ultimately, the Crispus Attucks Bridge in Framingham was dedicated as planned on Attucks Day, March 5, 2000. A plaque informs passersby that an enslaved Attucks "escaped in 1750 in search of his own freedom" and that he "was the first to die in the Boston Massacre, an event which initiated America's struggle for independence from British rule."[4] That inscription provides the most fundamental and widely agreed upon understanding of who Attucks was and what he did.

The success of Framingham's advocates for the Crispus Attucks Bridge dedication demonstrates the extent to which Attucks had become a part of the nation's Revolutionary heritage and an accepted local hero in his presumed hometown. But Framingham claims another black Revolutionary hero in Peter Salem. Anita C. Danker, in her essay on the Framingham bridge controversy, offers some thoughtful observations about the town's decision to honor Attucks rather than Salem. There is much to recommend Salem for commemoration. Like Attucks, Salem had been born a slave in Framingham, probably around 1750—the year Attucks took his own freedom. Salem seems to have earned his freedom by enlisting as a Minuteman in Framingham and later reenlisting in the Continental army. In making this conscious decision to fight formally for American independence he differed from Attucks, who Danker describes as "an accidental hero." Salem saw action in the first pitched battle of the Revolution at Concord in 1775 and also fought at Bunker Hill, where many contend he fired the shot killing British Major John Pitcairn. He served as a body servant for a Colonel Nixon in a Massachusetts regiment and saw action in numerous battles until his discharge from duty in 1780. After the war Salem lived a quiet life, eking out a living weaving baskets and caning chairs in Leicester, Massachusetts, where he was said to be "well liked in the community and popular among children," whom he entertained with "colorful stories of his service in the war under 'Massa Nixon.'" When he could no longer support himself he returned to Framingham, where he died in 1816.[5]

Salem did receive some commemorative acknowledgment after his death. In 1882, Framingham declared June 17—the anniversary of the Battle of Bunker Hill—"Peter Salem Day" and marked his grave with a headstone bearing the inscription: "Peter Salem. A Soldier of the Revolution. Died August 16, 1816. Concord. Bunker Hill. Saratoga. Erected by the Town, 1882." The town of Leicester later named the road on which Salem lived "Peter Salem Road," and the Daughters of the American Revolution marked the spot where his cabin was thought to have been located with a plaque reading, "Here lived Peter Salem, a Negro soldier of the Revolution." Salem also garnered a commemorative honor that has eluded Crispus Attucks. In 1968 the United States Postal Service issued a commemorative stamp depicting a detail from John Trumbull's famous 1786 painting *The Death of General Warren at the Battle of Bunker's Hill, June 17, 1775.* The stamp featured the wounded and wavering American soldier Thomas Grosvenor, and behind him a black man who is thought by some to represent Peter Salem.[6]

   Peter Salem, then, had not been completely ignored in Framingham's public memory of the Revolution. But, as Danker observes, the selection of Attucks over Salem for the Framingham bridge raises intriguing questions about who gets commemorated and why. Stephen Herring, the local historian who initially proposed renaming the bridge for Attucks, in fact, later suggested that another Framingham bridge be named for Salem, but that idea never gained any momentum. Herring explained that "Attucks received priority attention from the commission due to his national stature in the Black History movement, and the fact that no memorial existed in the town to show its connection." While the absence of any prior Attucks memorial in Framingham provides some explanation, Herring's comment about Attucks's "stature in the Black History movement" raises other questions. The phrase implies that black history is in some sense a special cause that requires a "movement" in order to gain public recognition. Was Framingham's commemoration of Attucks merely an attempt to appease proponents of black inclusion in the nation's narrative? To what degree are commemorative acts, the construction of heroes, and the crafting of historical narratives driven by public perceptions or political motives?

   In her own assessment of why the bridge might have been named for Attucks, and not Salem, Danker points to key differences in how the two black Revolutionaries' stories might be viewed. She argues that "the rebellious Crispus Attucks ... [represented] an empowering hero for the twenty first century" in a way that "the dutiful Peter Salem," with his deferential service and postwar life—including his stories of serving "Massa Nixon"—could not. Peter Salem was a harmless black hero who kept his place and didn't make trouble, before, during, and after the Revolution. Attucks clearly was a more problematic hero, yet, in Danker's eyes, for that very reason a more suitable hero for post–civil rights America.[7] But Attucks's motives and goals remain unclear. For all we know he may have been just as committed an American patriot as Peter Salem. Was his action at the forefront of the mob on March 5, 1770, an extension of his love for freedom, which had caused him to liberate himself from bondage twenty years earlier? Or do his actions in both 1750 and 1770 mark him as little more than a violent threat to the social order? Was he more like Peter Salem or Nat Turner?

Considering Turner along with Attucks and Salem suggests an interesting continuum of masculine black heroism. Over the years, many black Americans—nineteenth-century abolitionists, twentieth-century black nationalists, and twenty-first-century journalists and rappers—have compared Attucks unfavorably with Turner as an appropriate model of black heroism. Attucks, in this view, was basically an Uncle Tom who died for whites' benefit while his own people remained enslaved. Turner, on the other hand, led a revolt to impose a righteous, if brutal, justice on white enslavers in order to secure black liberty. Several scholars have examined Nat Turner's place in American memory and have found him to be a "troublesome property"—both as an enslaved man in antebellum Virginia and as a historical figure vying for inclusion in the nation's story. Nat Turner was as willing as Attucks, perhaps more so, to die for a cause, but his use of revolutionary violence in the cause of black liberation led to the death of dozens of white Americans, including women and children. Between these two, Crispus Attucks seemed the safer choice. There is no monument to Nat Turner, and his treatment in public media from historic sites to textbooks to literature to movies has been fraught with controversy.[8] Considering how the individual stories of Peter Salem, Crispus Attucks, and Nat Turner intersect with ideas about black patriotism, manhood, violence, revolution, and race pride offers an interesting point of departure for contemplating African Americans' efforts to incorporate their experiences into the story Americans tell themselves about the nation's past.

Since the early years of the republic, African American spokespersons exercised great care in crafting the race's historical narratives and its heroes. They typically highlighted Crispus Attucks as strong, manly, and assertive in defending his rights, his people, and his nation. This image of patriotic black manhood willing to do and die for a just cause—in this scenario for freedom and the independence of the nation—was a powerful statement in African Americans' struggle for citizenship, equality, and belonging.[9] But the black man as a violent threat to the social order was always the dangerous flip side of the coin. Over two and a half centuries, Attucks's champions have played a careful balancing act, reading the country's mood and especially the mood of the white American public and the white-dominated American power structure. Assertive and brave and loyal are acceptable attributes, but a perceived threat of unchecked black violence tends to fuel white fears and incite backlash.

This is as true in the early twenty-first century as it was in Attucks's or Turner's days. When political journalist Amy Goodman linked the death of Crispus Attucks with the 2014 shooting of Michael Brown, she was attuned to the white fears about black male violence that are deeply embedded in the American fabric.[10] Brown was an eighteen-year-old black man who was killed after an altercation with a police officer in Ferguson, Missouri, in the summer of 2014. Brown's death was one of numerous highly publicized cases of black men being killed under dubious circumstances by law enforcement officers or white vigilantes around the same time. These killings called attention to the ongoing controversy in American society over issues of race, violence, and the criminal justice system and gave rise to the "Black Lives Matter" movement, with its telling slogan, "hands up, don't shoot." Goodman's suggestion that Brown's death might lead to a social revolution as significant as that which followed Attucks's might seem overstated; still, her comparison of Attucks and Brown is not without basis. Both were physically imposing black men whose confrontations with official authorities led to their deaths. The killing of both men gave rise to enormous public outcries about the abuse of state power against innocent civilians, even as many characterized each man as nothing more than a brutish thug. And after official inquiries were concluded, the killers of each man went free. As for long-term legacy, Michael Brown's death is far too recent to assess. Even after two and a half centuries, Crispus Attucks's saga is still being written.[11]

For some who crafted Attucks's story over the years, especially those highlighting his working-class status or revolutionary fervor, it didn't matter if he were a rough and rowdy, illiterate, mixed-race fugitive slave. As Kareem Abdul-Jabbar suggested, he may have been a thug, but he was a thug for the right side. But for many, those attributes seemed to detract from his suitability as an American hero. An aggressive Attucks who used violence, however just the cause, also had to be sanitized. In addition to being loyal and brave and willing to make the ultimate sacrifice in doing what was right for the American nation, he also had to be respectable. A heroic Attucks who could be widely accepted as a black Founder had to be educated, Christian, temperate, courteous, clean-cut. He had to associate with the better sort of people. Sometimes this translated into the need for Attucks to have friendships with Paul Revere or Samuel Adams or other patriot leaders, or for others who did not know him personally, like George Washington and Thomas Jefferson, to praise him after his death as an exemplary citizen and symbol. Even if they were of a lower social class, Attucks's allies, family, and friends had to be of the highest moral character. Whether in "historical" accounts, speeches, plays, poems, textbooks, children's literature, or websites, this idealized Attucks was often presented as a model American who maintained his integrity and honor and did his patriotic duty, even as a self-emancipated slave who was ever under the threat of reenslavement.

Of course, not everyone set out to aggrandize Attucks and make him into a model citizen. Others sought to ignore him, vilify him, impugn his character, question his motives, deny his actions, dispute his identity, trivialize his contribution, or reject his relevance and significance. That malleability—in the absence of much concrete evidence to support Attucks as a hero, a villain, or an Uncle Tom—is a big part of what makes Crispus Attucks so intriguing.

In popular culture and mass media, one can still find many versions of Crispus Attucks. Fortunately, school textbooks in the twenty-first century have grown a bit more circumspect in their depictions of Attucks, his role, and his significance. In textbooks at least, the wild claims of earlier years have, for the most part, been replaced with more equivocal language. And academic historians writing about Revolutionary-era African Americans have become much more careful in recognizing the fine line separating convenient myth from verifiable fact and in resisting the temptation to imbue Attucks with qualities, meanings, and significance he may not deserve. Several works published since 2010 have mostly succeeded in avoiding misstatements about Crispus Attucks while also adding to our understanding of the contexts in which blacks like Attucks, Salem, and others made their choices and lived their lives in the era of the Revolution. Still, one widely praised 2016 history of American abolitionism perpetuated the tale of Attucks writing to Thomas Hutchinson.[12]

For more than a century-and-a-half African Americans have used a heroic characterization of Crispus Attucks to revise and reshape the master narrative of American history. For an even longer period—going back to John Adams's arguments in 1770—others have portrayed Attucks as an outlaw who was the antithesis of the heroic ideal. While Adams's 1773 diary suggests that he may have revised his assessment after the trial, his courtroom rhetoric characterized Attucks as a racial outsider and a symbol of disorder. Proponents of his vilification ever since have rejected Attucks's heroism on similar grounds—perhaps as much for his representing a violent threat to the political order as for his race. Among African Americans, proponents of black solidarity have objected to Attucks on the grounds that he was not pursuing a black-centered agenda. Was he a patriot or a thug? Freedom fighter or drunken brawler? Revolutionary citizen or Uncle Tom? Black Founder and first martyr of liberty or just some irrelevant nobody who got shot?

In the early twenty-first century Attucks can be found everywhere, yet he is still invisible to many. While most schoolchildren learn something about him as part of classes on the Revolution or during Black History Month, many soon forget his name. Several years ago I conducted an informal poll on Facebook, asking the following: "Without googling, in one short sentence or phrase, tell me something you know about Crispus Attucks—anything from a specific detail, to a vague memory, to 'never heard of it.' This is a contribution to scholarship, so don't cheat!" I excluded from the results all responses by historians and African Americans. One response was from a twenty-year-old college student, and the others were from middle-aged white men and women, all with at least undergraduate degrees. Responses included the following:

- Boston Massacre?
- File this under "vague memory": "Black guy involved in the Revolutionary War."
- Never heard of it, but from interpreting the Latin I'd say it describes the situation when the potato chips go on a rampage.
- I was thinking 1st black killed for the U.S. in some war, wasn't sure of the war.
- Um, that I like to eat mine with milk, and [my spouse] likes his plain? Sorry.
- first black man to be killed in some battle . . . no clue the year. maybe boston?
- My 4th grade recollection (ca. 1962) is that he was one of the first colonists to be shot by British soldiers and that he was . . . a black man!
- First man killed in the American revolution. Boston. African American.

One acquaintance who provides musical programming for public schools wrote this: "I wrote a song with 4th graders back in March '09 (they're studying the American Revolution) and here's their opening verse":

> *Hey—look over there, it's the British soldiers*
> *King George-the-3rd must've sent them over*
> *Colonists didn't pay their taxes,*
> *Look what happened to Crispus Attucks . . .*

Outside cyberspace, in the real face-to-face world, when people ask me about my research, I begin with the question, "Have you ever heard of Crispus Attucks?" The variety of responses I receive mirrors this informal poll, except that African Americans are considerably more likely to be familiar with the basics of Attucks's story. These admittedly nonscientific results suggest something about the range of Americans' recognition of Attucks's name. For some the name means absolutely nothing; for those who do remember him, he is most often simply "the black guy from the Revolution."[13]

Does Crispus Attucks deserve to be treated as an American hero? Should he be enshrined as the First Martyr of Liberty? I have my doubts. We simply do not know enough about his experiences, associations, mindset, or motives before or during the Boston Massacre to make any such judgment. Even many of his actions on that day remain unclear. But does he deserve to be included in the nation's story? Absolutely. It does not matter whether or not he was a leader, or a friend of Revere and Hancock, or well-read in political philosophy, or a good Christian, or active in the Sons of Liberty, or merely a drunken dockworker. His very presence in that mob on March 5, 1770—along with the other blacks and sailors and workers and immigrants who were in the streets with him that day—embodies the diversity of colonial America and the active participation of workers and people of color in the public life of the Revolutionary era. The strong likelihood that Attucks was a former slave who claimed his own freedom and carved out a life for himself in the colonial Atlantic world adds to his story's historical significance. The lived realities of Crispus Attucks and the many other men and women like him must be a part of Americans' understanding of the nation's founding generations.

That, of course, is one historian's interpretation. Other thinkers and indeed each new generation will offer alternative readings of the contested meanings surrounding Attucks's story and their implications for our understanding of both the Revolutionary era and African Americans' relationship to the larger narrative of American history. Considering Attucks's place in American history and memory also raises broader questions about Americans' engagement with the past and about the interplay between academic history and a society's collective memory. Academic historians are sometimes charged with "revisionism"—advancing new interpretations that challenge time-honored understandings of the past with which people have become comfortable. The opposition to Attucks's insertion into the public school curriculum after the 1960s is one example of many Americans' resistance to changes in the nation's story and its cast of characters. Decades of historical research on previously neglected groups in American society—minorities, immigrants, women, workers—have provided alternative perspectives that often point toward America's failure to fulfill its promises of liberty and justice for all. Also, as representative figures from those groups began to find their way into textbooks and classrooms, less class time and fewer pages could be devoted to the traditional elite white male protagonists. And even the traditional heroes who remained were tarnished—Columbus and the Pilgrims destroyed native societies; Washington and Jefferson owned slaves; Carnegie and Rockefeller exploited workers. Historians and teachers who call attention to these historical realities face a backlash from parents, school boards, and politicians who believe the proper story of American exceptionalism—of the nation's greatness and unique mission for the world—is threatened by unpatriotic ivory tower academics who take pleasure in highlighting the nation's faults over its triumphs.

"Revisionism" has become a dirty word, signifying the distortion of the past by mean-spirited intellectuals bent on tearing down cherished Heroes and sacred Truths. Some of these criticisms are valid. At times the pendulum of interpretation can swing too far toward the dismantling of myths and the vilification of iconic figures. Yet revision is what historians do. We examine new sources, ask new questions of old sources, and continuously try to refine and deepen our understanding of the past and its implications for the present and future. Indeed, modern historians generally reject the very idea of immutable Truths. It has been half a century since historian Hayden White challenged his colleagues to recognize the contingency of historical narratives and embrace ambiguity and irony. White's ideas are problematic and have been widely criticized, but they have had a profound influence on the cohorts of historians trained since the 1970s, ushering in new ways of thinking about sources, analysis, language, and the very nature of the historian's craft.[14]

In a series of publications beginning in the mid-1960s, White argued that historical inquiry itself was "historically conditioned," and that historians must stop thinking about their facts "as though they were 'given'" and accept that "they are not so much 'found' as 'constructed' by the kinds of questions which the investigator asks." When historical questions and even the facts themselves are seen as changeable or unstable, the historian must "recognize that there is no such thing as a *single* correct view of any object under study but that there are *many* correct views." White argued that history must be written in the ironic mode, in the sense that it must not commit dogmatically to any single one of the many ways the past might be interpreted.[15]

Irony, for White, reflects "the imperfect and fragmentary nature of any given comprehension of the world." But history written in the ironic mode cannot address White's concern with what he termed "the burden of history." One scholar has characterized that burden as "the existential 'terror' instilled by [history's] apparent meaninglessness, absurdity, and formlessness." Even history written in the ironic mode must necessarily impose some form and meaning on the past, but not the kind of mythic meaning that a society needs to create a coherent shared identity for its members. White recognized this social need for heroic myths that academic history simply cannot provide. Historical "stories cast in the Ironic mode," he noted, "gain their effects precisely by frustrating normal expectations about the kinds of resolutions provided by stories cast in other modes." In other words, written history must be contingent; it must equivocate; it must embrace ambiguity. But an ironic, contingent, ambiguous history does not fill a society's need for a clear resolution and an empowering story to tell itself.[16]

Filling that need is the task of a society's collective memory. Collective memory cannot be ironic; it cannot be contingent; it cannot be ambiguous. It must create myth and reinforce heritage. Theorist Edward Said described collective memory as "a field of activity in which past events are selected, reconstructed, maintained, modified, and endowed with political meaning."[17] If White is correct that the lack of inherent meaning in history is in some sense a burden that must be borne, then collective memory is the tool with which societies shape their shared understandings of the past to make that burden more manageable.

One of the important outgrowths of the shift in historical thinking that White helped initiate has been historians' movement toward analyzing cultural traditions, myths, and commemorations to understand how shared popular historical narratives take shape. Over the past several decades the study of "history and memory" has provided useful approaches for understanding how and why people and societies construct and become attached to particular versions of the past. The multifaceted intersections of memory and history can involve both individual and collective memories; constructions of national identities; the invention of traditions; public commemorations, holidays, and monuments; museums and archives; cultural and national heroes; formal written histories; material culture and landscape; and popular culture. Historian Wulf Kansteiner neatly summarizes the construction of collective memory "as the result of interaction among three types of historical factors: the intellectual and cultural traditions that frame all our representations of the past, the memory makers who selectively adopt and manipulate those traditions, and the memory consumers who use, ignore, or transform such artifacts according to their own interests." Scholars studying these interactions remind us that "history" is not the mere collection of facts that speak for themselves but rather a continual process in which each generation constructs its own understanding of the historical record, and reevaluates its significance for that time.[18]

And so it is with the narratives that have taken shape around Crispus Attucks. There have always been widely divergent opinions about Attucks and the meanings that Americans should attach to him. By the start of the twenty-first century, access to those opinions had been magnified by the wide and rapid reach of mass media. For every voice in education, print, entertainment, and cyberspace dismissing or vilifying Attucks, there are others intent on enshrining him in the American pantheon. Many of the same inaccuracies that have circulated for years still frequently mar accounts of all kinds. Attucks remains a convenient blank slate upon which Americans continue to inscribe a wide variety of cultural meanings. This study of how Americans have debated Crispus Attucks's place in the nation's history and memory engages the paradoxes and politics involved with remembering and forgetting. It helps illuminate the contested terrain upon which we construct our understandings of American heroes, American patriotism, the American historical narrative, and, most important, the idea of who "belongs" as a part of the American nation and its story.

Notes

INTRODUCTION

1. Trailer, *We the People: From Crispus Attucks to Barack Obama*, Internet Movie Database, http://www.imdb.com/video/wab/vi1062311961/, accessed March 13, 2012.

2. Several historians examining Attucks's symbolic use in the antebellum era include Mitch Kachun, "From Forgotten Founder to Indispensable Icon: Crispus Attucks, Black Citizenship, and Collective Memory," *Journal of the Early Republic* 29:2 (Summer 2009), 249–86; Stephen Kantrowitz, *More than Freedom: Fighting for Black Citizenship in a White Republic, 1829–1889* (New York: Penguin, 2012), esp. ch. 5; Margot Minardi, *Making Slavery History: Abolitionism and the Politics of Memory in Massachusetts* (New York: Oxford University Press, 2010); Tavia Nyong'o, "'The Black First': Crispus Attucks and William Cooper Nell," in *Slavery/Antislavery in New England*, ed. Peter Benes, *Annual Proceedings of the Dublin Seminar for New England Folklife*, Vol. 28 (Boston: Boston University Press, 2005), 141–52; and Elizabeth Rauh Bethel, *The Roots of African-American Identity: Memory and History in Free Antebellum Communities* (New York: St. Martin's Press, 1997). A recent master's thesis examines the memory of Attucks in twentieth-century Boston: Maureen McAleer, "The Legacy of Crispus Attucks in Boston in the Twentieth Century: How Activists, Politicians, and the Public Have Remembered, Commemorated, and Used His Name," master's thesis, Harvard University, 2014. While not explicitly dealing with the memory of Crispus Attucks, two recent works on the Boston Massacre include thoughtful discussions of the ways in which narratives of that event and Attucks's role in it have taken shape: Robert J. Allison, *The Boston Massacre* (Beverly, MA: Commonwealth Editions, 2006); Neil L. York, *The Boston Massacre: A History with Documents* (New York: Routledge, 2010).

3. H. W. Brands, "Founders Chic," *Atlantic* (September 2003), http://www.theatlantic.com/magazine/archive/2003/09/founders-chic/302773/, accessed November

20, 2016. Representative popular biographies of the Founders include Joseph J. Ellis, *American Sphinx: The Character of Thomas Jefferson* (New York: Alfred A. Knopf, 1997); David McCullough, *John Adams* (New York: Simon & Schuster, 2001); H. W. Brands, *The First American: The Life and Times of Benjamin Franklin* (New York: Anchor Books, 2000); Richard Brookhiser, *Founding Father: Rediscovering George Washington* (New York: Free Press, 1996); Ron Chernow, *Alexander Hamilton* (New York: Penguin, 2004).

CHAPTER 1

1. J. Hector St. John Crèvecoeur, *Letters from an American Farmer* (New York: Fox, Duffield, 1904), 54. University of Virginia American Studies Hypertexts, http://xroads.virginia.edu/~HYPER/crev/letter03.html, accessed May 27, 2009.

2. Vincent N. Parillo, *Diversity in America*, 3rd ed. (Thousand Oaks, CA: Pine Forge Press, 2009), 45–49.

3. *Boston Chronicle*, March 8, 1770; *Boston News-Letter*, March 8, 1770; *Boston Gazette*, March 12, 1770; *Essex Gazette*, March 13, 1770; *Boston News-Letter*, March 15, 1770. The autopsy report was reprinted in the *New England Historical and Genealogical Register*, Vol. 44 (Boston: David Clapp & Son, 1890), 382. A very useful summary of the materials relating to Attucks can be found in J. L. Bell, "On the Trail of Crispus Attucks: Investigating a Victim of the Boston Massacre," *Readex Report*, http://www.readex.com/readex-report/trail-crispus-attucks-investigating-victim-boston-massacre, accessed February 21, 2017. Extensive material relating to Attucks, the Boston Massacre and indeed most aspects of Revolutionary Boston can be found on Bell's fascinating website and blog, *Boston 1775*, http://boston1775.blogspot.com/. The use of aliases by fugitive slaves was widespread in the eighteenth century. See, for example, Barbara J. Mitnick, *New Jersey in the American Revolution* (New Brunswick, NJ: Rutgers University Press, 2005), 125; Mechal Sobel, *The World They Made Together: Black and White Values in Eighteenth-Century Virginia* (Princeton: Princeton University Press, 1989), 159; and numerous advertisements in the website, *The Geography of Slavery in Virginia*, http://www2.vcdh.virginia.edu/gos/, accessed June 17, 2009.

4. C. James Taylor, ed., *The Adams Papers Digital Edition*. Charlottesville: University of Virginia Press, Rotunda, 2008, http://www.upress.virginia.edu/content/adams-papers-digital-edition, accessed May 20, 2009, original source: Legal Papers of John Adams, Volume 3, Cases 63 and 64 (Cambridge, MA: Belknap Press, 1965), pp. 192, 269, 312; *Oxford English Dictionary*, 2nd ed., http://dictionary.oed.com, accessed February 21, 2017. The fact that virtually every reference to Attucks in the trial proceedings calls him "the Molatto" suggests that he may have been the only person of color in this large mob. However, since three witnesses at the trial were people of color, we know the crowd was mixed; the use of the specific article in references to Attucks may merely indicate that he was the only person of color among the principal participants and victims.

5. *Boston Chronicle*, March 8, 1770; *Boston News-Letter*, March 8, 1770; *Boston Gazette*, March 12, 1770.

6. C. James Taylor, ed., *The Adams Papers Digital Edition*, Charlottesville: University of Virginia Press, Rotunda, 2008, http://www.upress.virginia.edu/content/adams-papers-digital-edition, accessed February 22, 2017, original source: Legal Papers of John Adams, Volume 3, Cases 63 and 64, 269.

7. *Boston Gazette*, October 2, 1750.

8. *Boston Chronicle*, March 8, 1770; *Boston News-Letter*, March 8, 1770; *Boston Gazette*, March 12, 1770. The height of British soldiers is noted in Hiller B. Zobel, *The Boston Massacre* (New York: Norton, 1970), 191. A very useful summary of the materials relating to Attucks can be found in J. L. Bell, "On the Trail of Crispus Attucks: Investigating a Victim of the Boston Massacre," *Readex Report*, http://www.readex.com/readex-report/trail-crispus-attucks-investigating-victim-boston-massacre, accessed February 22, 2017. Extensive material relating to Attucks, the Boston Massacre, and indeed most aspects of Revolutionary Boston can be found on Bell's fascinating website and blog, *Boston 1775*, http://boston1775.blogspot.com/.

9. See, for example, James H. Sweet. "Mistaken Identities? Olaudah Equiano, Domingos Álvares, and the Methodological Challenges of Studying the African Diaspora," *American Historical Review* 114:2 (April 2009), 279–306; and W. Jeffrey Bolster, *Black Jacks: African American Seamen in the Age of Sail* (Cambridge, MA: Harvard University Press, 1997), 35–37.

10. Life aboard ships is vividly described in Bolster, *Black Jacks*, 7–43; and Peter Linebaugh and Marcus Rediker, *The Many-Headed Hydra: Sailors, Slaves, Commoners, and the Hidden History of the Revolutionary Atlantic* (Boston: Beacon Press, 2000), 143–73. On race and racism on ships, see Bolster, *Black Jacks*, esp. 93–101.

11. Linebaugh and Rediker, *Many-Headed Hydra*, 212–17, quoted at 213; Bolster, *Black Jacks*, 27–31, quoted at 27.

12. Bolster, *Black Jacks*, 5–7, 13, 26–43; Linebaugh and Rediker, *Many-Headed Hydra*, 143–73.

13. Benjamin L. Carp, *Rebels Rising: Cities and the American Revolution* (New York: Oxford University Press, 2007), 37; Linebaugh and Rediker, *Many-Headed Hydra*, 216; Alfred F. Young, *The Liberty Tree: Ordinary People and the American Revolution* (New York: New York University Press, 2006), 33–34, 118–19, 351; Jesse Lemisch, "Jack Tar in the Streets: Merchant Seamen in the Politics of Revolutionary America," *William and Mary Quarterly*, 3rd Series 25:3 (July 1968), 371–407.

14. Young, *Liberty Tree*, 333–38; Zobel, *Boston Massacre*, 87–106; Lemisch, "Jack Tar in the Streets"; Zobel, *Boston Massacre*, 133–36; J. L. Bell, "Edward Montgomery: Private, Family Man, Defendant," *Boston 1775*, http://boston1775.blogspot.com/2007/03/edward-montgomery-private-family-man.html, accessed June 14, 2009.

242   *Notes to pages 12–20*

15. Zobel, *Boston Massacre*, 134–39, 143–81.

16. Zobel, *Boston Massacre*, 180–84, quoted at 182.

17. The preceding overview of the events of the Boston Massacre is based on several primary and secondary sources, including Zobel, *Boston Massacre*, 183–205, quoted at 185; Taylor, *The Adams Papers Digital Edition*; Frederick Kidder, *History of the Boston Massacre* (Albany, NY: Joel Munsell, 1870); John Hodgson, *The Trial of William Wemms . . . for the Murder of Crispus Attucks . . . .* (Boston: J. Fleeming, 1770); *The Trial of the British Soldiers, of the 29th Regiment . . . for the murder of Crispus Attucks. . . .* (Boston: William Emmons, 1824); and various entries related to the Massacre in J. L. Bell, *Boston 1775*, http://boston1775.blogspot.com/, accessed June 11–14, 2009.

18. *Essex Gazette*, January 1–8, 1771; Zobel, *Boston Massacre*, 191; Kidder, *Boston Massacre*, 137–42, 197.

19. Kidder, *Boston Massacre*, 139, 205.

20. Hickling and Goddard depositions reprinted in Kidder, *Boston Massacre*, 93–95.

21. *The Trial of the British Soldiers*, 116.

22. *The Trial of the British Soldiers*, 116, 114.

23. Regarding racial identification, the *Boston Gazette*, March 12, 1770, printed an account referring to all the victims as "Mister" except Attucks, who was described as a "mulatto man." Salem's *Essex Gazette* (March 13, 1770) was probably not the only paper to have reprinted the story. Several months later the *Boston News-Letter* (June 21, 1770) announced the publication of a quarto edition of a sermon by John Lathrop, which was "Occasioned by the horrid Murder of Mess. Samuel Gray, Samuel Maverick, James Caldwell, and Crispus Attucks, with Patrick Carr, since dead . . ." In 1771, the *Essex Gazette* (January 8, 1771) provided a description of the events leading to the massacre, including the statement that "Mr. *Attucks*, it is said, was at supper when the bells rang." On the propaganda uses by contemporaries, see Patricia Bradley, *Slavery, Propaganda, and the American Revolution* (Jackson: University Press of Mississippi, 1998); Stephen H. Browne, "Remembering Crispus Attucks: Race, Rhetoric, and the Politics of Commemoration," *Quarterly Journal of Speech* 85:2 (1999), 169–87; and Zobel, *The Boston Massacre*. Henry Pelham's engraving, titled "The Fruits of Arbitrary Power, or the Bloody Massacre," likely preceded Revere's better known image but was not nearly as widely distributed and reproduced. See the March 29, 1770, letter from Pelham to Revere, accusing the latter of plagiarism, in *Letters and Papers of John Singleton Copley and Henry Pelham, 1739–1776* (New York: Kennedy Graphics, 1970), 83.

24. Zobel, *Boston Massacre*, 214–15; *Boston Post Boy*, March 12, 1770; David Ramsay, *The History of the American Revolution* (Dublin: printed for W. Jones, 1795), 80–81.

25. "Boston Orations" as reprinted in Hezekiah Niles, *Principles and Acts of the Revolution in America . . .* (Baltimore, 1822), 1–59. Parenthetical citations in the text refer to the orator, year of oration, and page number in Niles. The other Boston

Massacre orators used comparably evocative language. Niles, *Principles and Acts of the Revolution*, 1–59.

26. K. G. Davies, ed., *Documents of the American Revolution, 1770–1783*, Vol. II: *Transcripts 1770* (Shannon, Ireland: Irish University Press, 1972), 51, 70, 128; *Gentleman's Magazine*, 40 (April 1770), 146, 189–90; Alfred F. Young, *The Shoemaker and the Tea Party: Memory and the American Revolution* (Boston: Beacon Press, 1999), 96.

27. *The Trial of the British Soldiers* (Boston: William Emmons, 1824 [first published in 1770]); Ephraim Chambers, *Cyclopædia; or, an universal dictionary of arts and sciences* (1728), as cited in the entry for "mulatto," *Oxford English Dictionary* online, http://dictionary.oed.com, accessed June 24, 2009; *Boston Gazette*, October 2, 1750.

28. William Barry, *A History of Framingham, Massachusetts, including the Plantation, from 1640 to the Present Time* (Boston: James Munroe and Company, 1847), 21, 358.

29. A Bostonian [B. B. Thatcher], *Traits of the Tea-Party; being a Memoir of George R. T. Hewes* (New York: Harper and Brothers, 1835), 103–4; "From the *Liberator*: Crispus Attucks Once a Slave in Massachusetts," *National Era* (Washington, DC), August 18, 1859. According to the records of the Boston Custom House, a George Folger, master of the Brigantine Lucretia of London, brought his ship into Boston harbor in May (not March) 1770; rather than a whaler, the ship was a merchant vessel carrying a typically eclectic cargo of silk, linen, nails, wrought iron, lead, shot, and hemp. See John Mein(?), *A State of importations from Great-Britain into the port of Boston. From the beginning of January 1770. To which is added an account of all the goods that have been re-shipt from the above port for Great-Britain, since January 1769. The whole taken from the Custom-House of the Port of Boston. 1770* (Boston: John Fleeming(?), 1770), 38–41.

30. J. H. Temple, *History of Framingham, Massachusetts . . . 1640–1880* (Framingham: Published by the Town of Framingham, 1887), 255; "From the *Liberator*: Crispus Attucks Once a Slave in Massachusetts," *National Era* (Washington, DC), August 18, 1859; "Talking Teapots: What Treasures Tell Us about History," *The World Lecture Project*, http://www.world-lecture-project.org/lecture/?id=57345207c8b74, accessed August 12, 2009; Nancy Carlisle, *Cherished Possessions: A New England Legacy* (Boston: Society for the Preservation of New England Antiquities, 2003). Brown family descendants' later claim that Attucks "returned after his runaway excursion" and was in Boston on family business prior to the massacre does not fit with accounts from 1770. See "Remarks of William C. Nell," *Liberator*, March 16, 1860.

31. "Description" of George E. Stanley, *Andrew Jackson, Young Patriot* (New York: Aladdin Books, 2003), http://www.simonandschuster.com/books/Andrew-Jackson/George-E-Stanley/Childhood-of-Famous-Americans/9780689857447, accessed February 22, 2017.

32. Dharathula H. Millender, *Crispus Attucks, Boy of Valor* (Indianapolis: Bobbs-Merrill, 1965), 15, 19. Page numbers for subsequent quotations are indicated

parenthetically in the text. Well-reasoned assessments of what we can know about Attucks and his family are presented in J. L. Bell's blog, *Boston: 1775,* http://boston1775.blogspot.com/, especially entries from May 22, 23, 24, 25, 26, and 27, 2015; February 5, 2009; and February, 24, 25, and 28, 2008.

33. Library holdings are derived from the books' listings in the WorldCat digital library catalog, https://www.worldcat.org/, accessed February 10, 2016.

34. Dharathula H. Millender, *Crispus Attucks, Black Leader of Colonial Patriots* (New York: Aladdin Books, 1986). Internet searches conducted on www.google.com, September 20, 2009.

35. Millender, *Boy of Valor,* 123 (almost to recklessness), 148 (daring harpooner); Temple, *History of Framingham, Massachusetts,* 255. See also, *Traits of the Tea Party,* 103–4.

36. Barry, *History of Framingham,* 200, 65 (footnote).

37. Barry, *History of Framingham,* 64–65 (footnote), 200; Temple, *History of Framingham,* 237, 668.

38. Barry, *History of Framingham,* 64–65 (footnote), 200; Temple, *History of Framingham,* 237, 668. Oral tradition from antebellum Natick held that Attucks had siblings named Sal, Sam, and Peter, all fathered by Jacob Peterattucks. See "Remarks of William C. Nell," *Liberator,* March 16, 1860.

39. Barry, *History of Framingham,* 64.

40. Temple, *History of Framingham,* 254–55; Kidder, *History of the Boston Massacre,* 29, n.3; Barry, *History of Framingham,* 64 (footnote).

CHAPTER 2

1. Letter in Adams's diary in *Adams Family Papers, An Electronic Archive,* Massachusetts Historical Society. http://www.masshist.org/digitaladams/archive/doc?id=D19&bc=%2Fdigitaladams%2Farchive%2Fbrowse%2Fdiaries_by_number.php, accessed May 3, 2015. The entry is also reproduced in Sidney Kaplan and Emma Nogrady Kaplan, *The Black Presence in the Era of the American Revolution* (Amherst: University of Massachusetts Press, 1989), 10. See also, Robert J. Allison, *The Boston Massacre* (Beverly, MA: Commonwealth Editions, 2006), 57.

2. *The Trial of the British Soldiers* (Miami, FL: Mnemosyne Publishing, 1969 [1807]), 100.

3. Letter from Adams to Matthew Robinson, March 2, 1786, in *The Works of John Adams, Second President of the United States: with a Life of the Author, Notes and Illustrations, by his Grandson Charles Francis Adams,* Volume VIII (Boston: Little, Brown, 1853), 384.

4. William Gordon, *The History of the Rise, Progress, and Establishment of the Independence of the United States of America: Including an Account of the Late War; and of the Thirteen Colonies, from their Origin to that Period* (New York, 1789). Discussion of the Boston Massacre on 200–210, quoted at 202.

5. David Ramsay, *The History of the American Revolution* (Dublin, 1795), 80–81. Among other histories that gave some attention to the massacre, Attucks was not mentioned, nor was there any reference to the racial composition of the mob, in the accounts of Charles Stedman (1794), David Ramsay (1795), Abiel Holmes (1805), Mercy Otis Warren (1805), Roger Lamb (1809), Stanley Griswold (1813), Noah Webster (1813), W. D. Cooper (1818), Paul Allen (1819), Hezekiah Niles (1822), Jedidiah Morse (1824), Timothy Pitkin (1828), William Shepherd (1834), James Grahame (1845), or Robert Sears (1845). Other accounts neglected the Boston Massacre altogether, including those by John Lendrum (1795), Jonathan Boucher (1797), Bernard Hubley (1805), Alexander Garden (1822), Sylvester Judd (1842), Elizabeth Fries Ellet (1850), and Benson John Lossing (1860). Many of the histories borrowed liberally from earlier publications (some with attribution, some without), with Ramsay's 1795 *History* (which did not mention Attucks) providing an especially well-used font of information. Charles Stedman, *The History of the Origin, Progress, and Termination of the American War* (London, 1794); Abiel Holmes, *American Annals; or a Chronological History of America* . . . (Cambridge, MA, 1805); Mercy Otis Warren, *History of the Rise, Progress and Termination of the American Revolution* (Boston, 1805); Roger Lamb, *An Original and Authentic Journal of Occurrences during the late American War, from its Commencement to the Year 1783* (Dublin, 1809); Stanley Griswold, *The Exploits of Our Fathers, or a Concise History of the Military Events of our Revolutionary War. An Oration* (Cincinnati, 1813); Noah Webster, *Elements of Useful Knowledge*, Vol. II (Hartford, 1813); W. D. Cooper, *The History of North America* (Albany, 1816); Hezekiah Niles, *Principles and Acts of the Revolution in America* . . . (Baltimore, 1822); Paul Allen, *A History of the American Revolution* (Baltimore, 1822); Jedediah Morse, *Annals of the American Revolution* (Hartford, 1824); Timothy Pitkin, *Political and Civil History of the United States of America*, Vol. I (New Haven, 1828); William Shepherd, *A History of the American Revolution* (Columbus, OH, 1834); James Grahame, *The History of the United States of America*, Vol. IV (Boston, 1845); Robert Sears, *The Pictorial History of the American Revolution* (New York, 1845); John Lendrum, *A Concise and Impartial History of the American Revolution* (Boston, 1795); Jonathan Boucher, *A View of the Causes and Consequences of the American Revolution* (London, 1797); Bernard Hubley, *The History of the American Revolution Including the Most Important Events and Resolutions of the Honourable Continental Congress during that Period* (Northumberland, PA, 1805); Alexander Garden, *Anecdotes of the American Revolution* (Charleston, 1828); Sylvester Judd, *A Moral Review of the Revolutionary War, or Some of the Evils of that Event Considered. A Discourse* (Hallowell, ME, 1842); Elizabeth Fries Ellet, *Domestic History of the American Revolution* (New York, 1850); Benson John Lossing, *The Pictorial Field-Book of the Revolution* (New York, 1860).

6. "Bunker Hill Monument," *Boston Statesman*, July 17, 1823; "Twenty-Second of February," *National Philanthropist* (Boston), March 7, 1828; Michael Kammen,

A Season of Youth: The American Revolution and the Historical Imagination (New York: Alfred A. Knopf, 1978), 41–45, 78–81; Len Travers, *Celebrating the Fourth: Independence Day and the Rites of Nationalism in the Early Republic* (Amherst: University of Massachusetts Press, 1997); David Waldstreicher, *In the Midst of Perpetual Fetes: The Making of American Nationalism*, 1776–1820 (Chapel Hill: University of North Carolina Press, 1997); Andrew Burstein, *America's Jubilee* (New York: Alfred A.Knopf, 2001); "Boston Massacre," *Salem Gazette*, March 30, 1824; *The Trial of the British Soldiers* (Boston: J. Fleeming, 1770); *The Trial of the British Soldiers* (Boston: Belcher and Armstrong, 1807); *The Trial of the British Soldiers* (Boston: William Emmons, 1824).

7. "Republican Jubilee," *Independent Chronicle* (Boston), March 7, 1803; "Celebration of the Fourth of March, 1802," *Independent Chronicle* (Boston), March 11, 1802; "National Register," *Columbian Centinel* (Boston), March 5, 1803; *Independent Chronicle*, March 7, 14, 1803. Indeed, Republican Fourth of March celebrations continued well beyond Jefferson's tenure, though his political ascendancy remained a central focus of the affairs for some time. In 1820, Republicans in Boston hailed "the recurrence of the anniversary of that important era in the political history of our country, when sound and healthful republicanism arose superior to the machinations of its enemies, and placed at the head of our Republic a statesman and philosopher, of whom our country will long be proud" ("4th of March," *Independent Chronicle and Boston Patriot*, March 4, 1820). Similarly, in 1824, the *Boston Statesman* noted that cannon-firings and toasts marked "the Anniversary of the *glorious triumph of Republicanism* by the election of THOMAS JEFFERSON" ("The Fourth of March," *Boston Statesman*, March 8, 1824). Proponents of John Quincy Adams claimed the day in 1825, but "true Republicans of the Jackson stripe" rejoiced in the "triumph of Democracy over Aristocracy" in 1829 ("4th of March," *Boston Statesman*, March 5, 1825; "Fourth of March Celebration," *New Hampshire Gazette*, February 24, 1829). By the 1840s, new political alignments had displaced the centrality of Jefferson's republican spirit, and the anniversary seems to have been marked only upon the actual inauguration of a president, with either Democrats or Whigs celebrating the day, depending on the outcome of the preceding election. See, for example, "Appropriate!" *New Hampshire Patriot and State Gazette* (Concord, NH), March 26, 1841; "Fourth of March," *Barre Gazette* (Barre, MA), February 28, 1845.

8. *Independent Chronicle and Boston Patriot*, March 5, 1807; "History of the War in America," *Vermont Gazette or Freemen's Depository* (Burlington), July 12, 1784; *New Jersey Magazine and Daily Advertiser*, February 1787, 78; *Boston Gazette*, March 12, 1770. The name of Boston's King Street, where the Boston Massacre occurred, was changed to State Street after the Revolution, reflecting another way in which the nation's collective memory and identity might be influenced.

9. *New-Jersey-Journal*, March 18, 1795; *City Gazette and Daily Advertiser*, April 4, 1795; "Standing Army, No. 4," *Constitutional Telegraph*, October 19, 1799; "Republican

Celebration" and "Be it Remembered," *Independent Chronicle* (Boston), March 6, 1806; Daniel Webster, "An Anniversary Address Delivered by Daniel Webster before the Federal Gentlemen at Concord and its Vicinity, July 4th, 1806" (Concord, NH: George Hough, 1806), reprinted in *Granite Monthly: A New Hampshire Magazine Devoted to History, Biography, Literature and State Progress*, Vol. 5 (Concord, NH: Evans, Sleeper & Woodbury Printers, 1882), quoted at 10.

10. "Fifth of March—or Boston Massacre," *Independent Chronicle* (Boston) March 5, 1810; "5th of March—or, BOSTON MASSACRE!" *Independent Chronicle and Boston Patriot*, March 5, 1812; "Efficiency of Militia," *Salem Gazette*, September 23, 1814.

11. *The Scourge* (Boston), October 9, 1811. Information on the paper and its editor from Frank Luther Mott, *A History of American Magazines, 1741–1850*, Vol. 3 (Cambridge, MA: Harvard University Press, 1958), 170; and "Early American Newspapers: Selected Newspaper Descriptions by State," Readex, http://www.readex.com/early-american-newspapers-place-publication, accessed February 21, 2017. John Adams was on a diplomatic mission in the Netherlands in the early 1780s, but the *Scourge* piece clearly states that the "late worthy patriot" it referred to "died in New York, in 1803." Adams was very much alive at that time.

12. Charles Elihu Slocum, *A Short History of the Slocums, Slocumbs, and Slocombs of America* (Syracuse, NY: published by the author, 1882), 86; Lamont D. Thomas, *Paul Cuffe: Black Entrepreneur and Pan-Africanist* (Urbana: University of Illinois Press, 1988), 3–6; Brock N. Cordeiro, "Paul Cuffe: A Study of His Life, and the Status of His Legacy in 'Old Dartmouth,'" master's thesis, University of Massachusetts, Boston, 2004, 10–14.

13. Thomas, *Paul Cuffe*, 3–6. New Bedford was formally established as a separate town, adjacent to Dartmouth, in 1787.

14. On early histories, commemorations, and the emphasis on elites rather than ordinary people in the public memory of the Revolution, see Alfred F. Young, *The Shoemaker and the Tea Party: Memory and the American Revolution* (Boston: Beacon Press, 1999); Sarah J. Purcell, *Sealed with Blood: War, Sacrifice, and Memory in Revolutionary America* (Philadelphia: University of Pennsylvania Press, 2002); Lester H. Cohen, *The Revolutionary Histories: Contemporary Narratives of the American Revolution* (Ithaca: Cornell University Press, 1980); Margot Minardi, *Making Slavery History: Abolitionism and the Politics of Memory in Massachusetts* (New York: Oxford University Press, 2010), 10, 73–76.

15. James Hawkes, *A Retrospect of the Boston Tea-party, with a Memoir of George R. T. Hewes, a Survivor of the Little Band of Patriots who Drowned the Tea in Boston Harbour in 1773* (New-York, 1834), 28–32; B. B. Thatcher, *Traits of the Tea Party: Being a Memoir of George R. T. Hewes, One of the Last of its Survivors: with a History of that Transaction, Reminiscences of the Massacre, and the Siege, and other Stories of Old Times* (New York, 1835), 103–4. On Hewes's emergence as a figure of note in the 1830s, see Young, *Shoemaker and the Tea Party*.

16. Charles Botta, *History of the War of the Independence of the United States of America*, Vol. 1, trans. George Alexander Otis (Philadelphia, 1820), 159–60; Sparks quoted in Michael Kammen, *A Season of Youth: the American Revolution and the Historical Imagination* (New York: Alfred A. Knopf, 1978), 282–83 n83. Botta's 1820 US publication was a translation from an earlier Italian edition.

17. Samuel Goodrich, *The First Book of History for Children and Youth, by the Author of Peter Parley's Tales* (New York, 1831), 104–5. The popularity of Goodrich's various texts is noted in Charles Carpenter, *History of American Schoolbooks* (Philadelphia: University of Pennsylvania Press, 1963), 200–202, and Ruth Miller Elson, *Guardians of Tradition: American Schoolbooks of the Nineteenth Century* (Lincoln: University of Nebraska Press, 1964), who estimates that the 170 textbooks Goodrich had written or supervised by 1876 had "sold seven million copies in the United States" (406). Another text, *The Story of the American Revolution* by "Lambert Lilly" (a pseudonym for Frances L. Lister), appeared in editions from 1831, 1833, and 1839. The narration of the Boston Massacre in the 1839 edition is almost identical to, and likely based on, Goodrich's. Goodrich is listed as copyright holder in the 1839 edition.

18. Frances FitzGerald, *America Revised: History Schoolbooks in the Twentieth Century* (New York: Holiday House, 1979), 48–49.

19. On the changing view of mobs, see Paul A. Gilje, *The Road to Mobocracy: Popular Disorder in New York City, 1763–1834* (Chapel Hill: University of North Carolina Press, 1987).

20. Elson, *Guardians of Tradition*, 288–89, 257.

21. Alfred F. Young, *Liberty Tree: Ordinary People and the American Revolution* (New York: New York University Press, 2006), 300, 307. See also, Minardi, *Making Slavery History*, 10, 73–76.

22. *Peter Parley's Common School History*, 6th ed. (Philadelphia, 1839), 345; J. E. Worcester, *Elements of History, Ancient and Modern* (Boston, 1836), 262; Noah Webster, *History of the United States* (New Haven, 1833), 202. The first edition of the *Common School History* appears to have been published in 1837, with subsequent editions into the 1850s containing the same rendition of the massacre.

23. "The Boston Massacre," *Connecticut Courant* (Hartford, CT), November 11, 1837; "Relics of the Olden Time," *Southern Literary Messenger* (Richmond, VA) 4:3 (March 1838), 163–65. Other newspaper mentions may exist, but extensive research in microfilm and searchable digitized databases has brought to light only two.

24. An Aethiopian, *A Sermon on the Evacuation of Charlestown* (Philadelphia, 1783), in Early American Imprints, Evans Series 18182, Massachusetts Historical Society.

25. "Triumph of Mobocracy in Boston," *Liberator*, November 7, 1835; Lydia Maria Child, *The Rebels; or, Boston before the Revolution* (Boston: Phillips, Sampson & Co., 1850); "Oration of A. H. Francis," *North Star* (Rochester, NY), August 17, 1849.

26. Purcell, *Sealed with Blood*, 76–77; "A Black Whig," *A sermon, on the present situation of the affairs of America and Great-Britain. Written by a black, and printed at the request of several persons of distinguished characters* (Philadelphia, 1782), 8,

10; Russell Parrott, *An Oration on the Abolition of the Slave Trade* (1808), in *Two Orations on the Abolition of the Slave Trade Delivered in Philadelphia in 1812 and 1816*, ed. Maxwell Whiteman (Philadelphia: Rhistoric Publications, 1969), 8; Hosea Easton, *A Treatise on the Intellectual Character, and the Civil and Political Condition of the Colored People of the United States* (Boston, 1837), 30–34, in *Black Abolitionist Papers* (hereafter *BAP*) (mfilm) 1:972–74; Robert Purvis, *Appeal of Forty Thousand Citizens, Threatened with Disfranchisement, to the People of Pennsylvania* (Philadelphia, 1838), 13, in *BAP* (mfilm), 2:425; Henry Scott, letter, *Liberator* (Boston), December 14, 1838, in *BAP* (mfilm), 2:672.

27. William P. Powell, "Coloured Seamen—Their Character and Condition, No I," *National Anti-Slavery Standard*, September 14, 1846; William P. Powell, "Coloured Seamen—Their Character and Condition, No II," *National Anti-Slavery Standard*, October 8, 1846; J. G. W., "The Black Men of the Revolution and the War of 1812," *National Era* (Washington, DC), July 22, 1847; Nell, *The Colored Patriots of the Revolution* (Boston, 1855), 9.

28. "The First of August in Boston," *Colored American* (New York), August 31, 1839 [reprinted from the *Liberator*]. Biographical information on Beman in *The Black Abolitionist Papers*, Vol. 3, C. Peter Ripley et al., eds. (Chapel Hill: University of North Carolina Press, 1991), 455–56.

29. William C. Nell to Wendell Phillips, April 15, 1841, Wendell Phillips Papers, Houghton Library, Harvard University, bMS Am 1953, folder 924: letters from William C. Nell (hereafter Phillips Papers). Nell's presence at the celebration is confirmed by his letter, William C. Nell to Wendell Phillips, August 21, 1839, Phillips Papers. One other possible reference to Attucks among African Americans is intriguing but as yet unverified. In a 1978 essay on William P. Powell, black activist and founder of New York City's Colored Seamen's Home, Philip S. Foner claimed that Powell "frequently stressed the role black seamen had played in the anti-impressment riots of the colonial period . . . [and] kept a portrait of Crispus Attucks in the main room of the Colored Seamen's Home." Subsequent scholars discussing Powell repeat this claim, always citing Foner's essay as its source. Unfortunately, the several specific sources cited by Foner in the footnote most proximate to the claim about the Attucks portrait contain no relevant documentation to verify the existence of a portrait. If verifiable, the presence of an Attucks portrait at the Colored Seamen's Home suggests that there may have been an underground oral tradition about Attucks among black sailors. However, if the portrait did exist, it is entirely possible that it did not appear in the Home until after the appearance of Nell's work. Even if we accept the presence of an Attucks portrait as early as the Home's founding in 1839, we must consider that the knowledge about Attucks among black seamen might not have been obtained through their own oral traditions but rather through the Botta and Hewes texts, which had appeared by that time. See Philip S. Foner, "William P. Powell: Militant Champion of Black Seamen," in Foner, *Essays in Afro-American History* (Philadelphia: Temple University Press, 1978), 94.

See also *The Black Abolitionist Papers*, Vol. 5, C. Peter Ripley et al., eds. (Chapel Hill: University of North Carolina Press, 1992), 235n1, 236n2.

30. Richard S. Newman and Roy E. Finkenbine, "Black Founders in the New Republic: Introduction," *William and Mary Quarterly*, 3rd Series, 64:1 (January 2007), 92. The index to the *Black Abolitionist Papers* is housed at the Black Abolitionist Archive at the University of Detroit Mercy, of which Finkenbine is director.

31. "From the Liberator: Crispus Attucks Once a Slave in Massachusetts," *National Era* (Washington, DC), August 18, 1859; Nyong'o, " 'The Black First.' " Perhaps not surprisingly, while Attucks's Native American ancestry was generally accepted by black activists, they rarely mentioned this aspect of his identity while seeking to develop close ties in the public mind between African Americans and the nation's founding.

32. See, for example, Young, *The Shoemaker and the Tea Party*; Purcell, *Sealed with Blood*; Burstein, *American Jubilee*; Kammen, *A Season of Youth*; Travers, *Celebrating the Fourth*; Waldstreicher, *In the Midst of Perpetual Fetes*; Simon P. Newman, *Parades and the Politics of the Streets: Festive Culture in the Early American Republic* (Philadelphia: University of Pennsylvania Press, 1997); Paul C. Nagel, *This Sacred Trust: American Nationality, 1798–1898* (New York: Oxford University Press, 1971).

33. Waldstreicher, *In the Midst of Perpetual Fetes*, 324.

34. On the shifting attitudes toward mob action in the early republic, see Gilje, *The Road to Mobocracy*, and David Grimsted, *American Mobbing, 1828–1862: Toward Civil War* (New York: Oxford University Press, 1998). Numerous recent works have emphasized the importance of "respectability" among nineteenth-century black leaders. See, for example, Patrick Rael, *Black Identity and Black Protest in the Antebellum North* (Chapel Hill: University of North Carolina Press, 2001).

35. Young, *The Shoemaker and the Tea Party* and *Liberty Tree*.

36. Joanne Pope Melish, *Disowning Slavery: Gradual Emancipation and Race in New England, 1780–1860* (Ithaca: Cornell University Press, 2000), 5–6; Minardi, *Making Slavery History*, 8–11.

37. Mitch Kachun, *Festivals of Freedom: Memory and Meaning in African American Emancipation Celebrations, 1808–1915* (Amherst: University of Massachusetts Press, 2003), esp. 39, 49–50, 69–70, 90–91; quotations from 69, 91. On antebellum African Americans commemorations, see Kachun, *Festivals of Freedom*, esp. chaps. 1 and 2; Elizabeth Rauh Bethel, *The Roots of African American Identity: Memory and History in Antebellum Free Communities* (New York: St. Martin's Press, 1997); Waldstreicher, *Perpetual Fetes*, 323–48; William B. Gravely, "The Dialectic of Double Consciousness in Black American Freedom Celebrations, 1808–1863," *Journal of Negro History* 67 (Winter 1982), 302–17; Patrick Rael, *Black Identity and Black Protest in the Antebellum North* (Chapel Hill: University of North Carolina Press, 2002), chap. 2; and Leonard I. Sweet, "The Fourth of July and Black

Americans in the Nineteenth Century: Northern Leadership Opinion within the Context of the Black Experience," *Journal of Negro History* 61:3 (1976), 256–75.

CHAPTER 3

1. Biographical information on Nell can be found in George Forbes, "Biographical Sketch of William Cooper Nell," Ms. Am. 282 (18), Antislavery Collection, Boston Public Library, copy in Black Abolitionist Archive (BAA), University of Detroit Mercy.

2. William C. Nell, *Services of Colored Americans in the Wars of 1776 and 1812* (Boston, 1851); William C. Nell, *The Colored Patriots of the Revolution* (Boston, 1855); Forbes, "Biographical Sketch of William Cooper Nell."

3. W. C. N., "Communications: The Morning Dawn," *North Star* (Rochester, NY), May 5, 1848.

4. "Address of H. W. Johnson," *North Star* (Rochester, NY), August 21, 1848; "First of August," *North Star* (Rochester, NY), August 11, 1848. Nell had been resident in Rochester since late 1847 and was working with Frederick Douglass in publishing the *North Star*. While the connection between Nell and Johnson is unclear, it is likely that they had some contact before the celebration. Johnson was a well-known regional activist and was known to Douglass; it seems reasonable that he and Nell at the very least had met. With the exception of mistaking Attucks's first name, Johnson's historical description of black patriotism is thorough and well contextualized; he may have developed his understanding in the weeks or months before the celebration through conversation with Nell, who at this point was well along with his research on black military service.

5. Nell, *Services*, 7–9; Nell, *Colored Patriots*, 13–18.

6. Martin Delany, *The Condition, Elevation, and Destiny of the Colored People of the United States* (Philadelphia: King and Baird, 1852), 68–70.

7. *Liberator*, October 11, 1850.

8. Higginson quoted in Stephen Kantrowitz, "Crispus Attucks among the Abolitionists, 1842–1863," unpublished manuscript, cited with permission; "Crime against Humanity," *Frederick Douglass' Paper*, June 16, 1854; "Our Military Operations," *Frederick Douglass' Paper*, December 22, 1854. See also Stephen Kantrowitz, *More than Freedom: Fighting for Black Citizenship in a White Republic, 1829–1889* (New York: Penguin, 2012), esp. ch. 5.

9. "A Decade of the Slave Power," *National Era* (Washington, DC), March 20, 1856; Nell, *Colored Patriots of the Revolution*, 18. Bowditch quoted in Kantrowitz, "Crispus Attucks among the Abolitionists."

10. "Equal School Rights," *Frederick Douglass' Paper*, August 25, 1854.

11. "African Colonization—the Other Side," *Frederick Douglass' Paper*, September 25, 1851.

12. *Memorial of the Thirty Thousand Disfranchised Citizens of Philadelphia* (Philadelphia, 1855) copy in BAA 3477:16135; letter from George A. Johnson to *Douglass' Monthly*, October 1860.

13. Frontispiece, n.p., Nell, *Colored Patriots*. The Nell image's similarity to the Trumbull painting is also discussed in Margot Minardi, *Making Slavery History: Abolitionism and the Politics of Memory in Massachusetts* (New York: Oxford University Press, 2006), 142–45.

14. "Boston Massacre, March 5, 1770. Copy of chromolithograph by John Bufford after William L. Champney, circa 1856., ca. 1936–ca. 1942." National Archives and Records Administration at College Park, MD.

15. Minardi, *Making Slavery History*, 148–49; Nell, *Colored Patriots*, 15, 18.

16. Ethiop, "Afric-American Picture Gallery," *Afro-American Magazine*, February 1859, in the Black Abolitionist Archive, University of Detroit Mercy, vertical file "Ethiop," 10826, 20227–20229.

17. William J. Watkins, *Our Rights as Men: An Address Delivered in Boston before the Legislative Committee on the Militia* (Boston, 1853), copy in BAA 3235:13921–13933; "To the White Citizens of Franklin County, from the Colored Convention held in Columbus, December 28, 1855," *Anti-Slavery Bugle* (Salem, OH), January, 19, 1856.

18. Frederick Douglass and Henry Highland Garnet each had one unit named for them, while the ancient North African military leader Hannibal had two. Nell letter to William Lloyd Garrison, *Liberator*, November 21, 1856; Jeffrey R. Kerr-Ritchie, "Rehearsal for War: Black Militias in the Atlantic World," *Slavery and Abolition* 26:1 (April 2005), 1–34, quoted at 3.

19. *The Campaign Union* (Boston), October 9, 1860; "Wide-Awake Meetings," *New York Times*, August 23, 1860; "The Wide Awakes," *Chicago Tribune*, April 4, 1860; "Wide Awakes Disbanded—Patriots Enrolled," *Chicago Tribune*, April 19, 1861. Wide Awakes carried no firearms but often carried small batons that at times were used in violent melees with opponents who harassed them on the streets. Part of their function was to monitor the polls on Election Day to prevent any tampering by Democratic opponents. For more on Wide Awakes and other antebellum political marching clubs, see Jon Grinspan, "'Young men for War': The Wide Awakes and Lincoln's 1860 Presidential Campaign," *Journal of American History* 96:2 (September 2009), 357–78, and Glenn C. Altschuler and Stuart M. Blumin, *Rude Republic: Americans and Their Politics in the Nineteenth Century* (Princeton: Princeton University Press, 2000), 60–64. On the 1860 activities of Wide Awakes, see "Wide Awake Demonstration," *New York Times*, October 3, 1860; "Impromptu Wide Awake Parade—They are Attacked by Armed Men," *New York Times*, November 7, 1860.

20. "Address of William C. Nell," *Liberator*, March 12, 1858.

21. William C. Nell, "Commemorative Meeting in Faneuil Hall," *Liberator*, February 26, 1858; "Program of Boston Massacre Commemorative Festival," Fred Landon Papers, University of Western Ontario, copy in BAA, 3902:19526–19529; Bethel,

The Roots of African American Identity, 1–24, quoted at 15, 4, 2. Boston's Civil War–era celebrations of Attucks Day are documented, among other sources, in *Liberator*, March 16, 1860; March 29, 1861; February 28, 1862; March 20, 1863; April 1, 1864; March 24, 1865. Nell biographer George Forbes observes that Attucks Day "continued to be an occasion of great interest till the end of [Nell's] life in 1874, finally culminating a few years later [in 1888] in a monument to [Attucks's] memory on the Boston Common." Forbes, "Biographical Sketch," Section 4, p. 2.

22. "Crispus Attucks Once a Slave in Massachusetts," *Liberator*, August 5, 1859.

23. *Weekly Anglo-African*, December 17, 1859.

24. Osborne P. Anderson, *A Voice from Harpers Ferry* (Boston, 1861), 60; "Ninetieth Anniversary of the Boston Massacre," *Liberator*, March 2, 1860; *Liberator*, March 16, 1860; "Speech of Dr. John S. Rock," *Liberator*, March 16, 1860.

25. "Rev. J. W. Loguen on the Position of Colored Men," *Weekly Anglo-African*, September 14, 1861, copy in BAA, 24420:14226. On Loguen's militancy, see Fergus M. Bordewich, *Bound for Canaan: The Underground Railroad and the War for the Soul of America* (New York: HarperCollins, 2005), 325.

26. "The Call for Colored Soldiers. Will They Fight? Should They Fight?" *Christian Recorder* (Philadelphia), February, 14, 1863; Senah, "Do Colored Men Make Good Soldiers?" *Christian Recorder*, August 27, 1864; George W. Potter, "Our Honor's Bright All o'er the Land: an original poem commemorative of heroic deeds and loyalty of colored patriots" (MA: s.n., ca. 1870), Broadside, Massachusetts Historical Society (Bdses-Sm 1870).

27. Letter from "Ivanhoe," *Weekly Anglo-African*, October 19, 1861; Benson J. Lossing, *A Primary History of the United States for Schools and Families* (New York, 1860), 115; John J. Anderson, *A School History of the United States, Arranged on the Catechetical Plan* . . . (New York, 1864), 115; John Bonner, *A Child's History of the United States*, Vol. 1 (New York, 1866), 266.

28. S. G. Goodrich, *A Pictorial History of the United States* . . . *for the Use of Schools and Families* (Philadelphia, 1868), 176–77.

29. John Gilmary Shea, *A School History of the United States from the Earliest Period to the Present Time* (New York, 1858), 129–30; A. B. Berard, *School History of the United States* (Philadelphia, 1863), 113.

30. Earlier historical writing by African Americans includes Robert Benjamin Lewis, *Light and Truth: From Ancient and Sacred History* (Portland, ME: D. C. Colesworthy, 1836); and J. W. C. Pennington, *Text Book of the Origin and History, &c. &c. of the Colored People* (Hartford: L. Skinner, 1841). Black historical writing in this period is discussed in depth in Stephen G. Hall, *A Faithful Account of the Race: African American Historical Writing in Nineteenth-Century America* (Chapel Hill: University of North Carolina Press, 2009); and John Ernest, *Liberation Historiography: African American Writers and the Challenge of History, 1794–1861* (Chapel Hill: University of North Carolina Press, 2004).

31. William Wells Brown, *The Black Man: His Antecedent, His Genius, and His Achievements* (Boston: R. F. Wallcut, 1863), 6, 31–34.

32. Brown, *The Black Man*, 37, 106–10.

33. Frederic Kidder, *History of the Boston Massacre* (Albany: Joel Munsell, 1870), "Preface," n.p.; 29n.3.

34. "The Boston Massacre," *American Historical Record* (Philadelphia) 1:3 (March 1872), 114–15, 123–24.

35. "Who Was Crispus Attucks?" *American Historical Record* (Philadelphia) 1:12 (December 1872), 531–33.

36. "Current Notes," *American Historical Record* (Philadelphia) 2:14 (February 1873), 90; "Crispus Attucks Again," *American Historical Record* (Philadelphia) 2:15 (March 1873), 128–29. See the Brown family claims in "Remarks of William C. Nell," *Liberator*, March 16, 1860.

37. US Freedmen Bank Records, 1865–1874, Series M816, Roll 27, p. 778; US Freedmen Bank Records, 1865–1874, Series M816, Roll 23, p. 344; *Miscellaneous Documents of the House of Representatives for the Second Session of the Forty-sixth Congress, 1879–80*, Vol. 6, no. 40, Part 2 (Washington: Government Printing Office, 1880), 1388–89; 1880 US Federal Census, Norfolk, Norfolk County, Virginia, p. 57; 1900 US Federal Census, Tanners Creek District, Norfolk County, Virginia, p. 12.

38. Thomas Carlyle, *On Heroes and Hero Worship and the Heroic in History*, cited in William L. Van Deburg, *Black Camelot: African-American Culture Heroes in the Times, 1960–1980* (Chicago: University of Chicago Press, 1997), 1; Van De Burg, 2–3, 38.

CHAPTER 4

1. 1880 US Federal Census, Norfolk, Norfolk County, Virginia, p. 57; 1900 US Federal Census, Tanners Creek District, Norfolk County, Virginia, p. 12; 1910 US Federal Census, Tanners Creek District, Norfolk County, Virginia, p. 8 (all census records from HeritageQuest online database); National Archives and Records Administration. US World War II Army Enlistment Records, 1938–1946 [database on-line]. Provo, UT, USA: The Generations Network, Inc., 2005. Original data: Electronic Army Serial Number Merged File, 1938–1946 [Archival Database]; World War II Army Enlistment Records; Records of the National Archives and Records Administration, Record Group 64; National Archives at College Park, College Park, MD.

2. Ancestry.com. World War I Draft Registration Cards, 1917–1918 [database on-line] (Provo, UT, USA: The Generations Network, Inc., 2005), original data: United States, Selective Service System, World War I Selective Service System Draft Registration Cards, 1917–1918 (Washington, DC: National Archives and Records Administration), M1509, 4,582 rolls; 1920 US Federal Census, Norfolk City, Norfolk County, Virginia, p. 5; 1930 US Federal Census, Norfolk City, Norfolk County, Virginia, 21st Precinct, Block 1638, p. 7B; Ancestry.com.

US Rosters of World War II Dead, 1939–1945 [database on-line] (Provo, UT, USA: The Generations Network, Inc., 2007), original data: United States. Army. Quartermaster General's Office. Rosters of World War II Dead (all services) (Washington, DC: US Army); National Archives and Records Administration, US World War II Army Enlistment Records, 1938–1946 [database on-line] (Provo, UT, USA: The Generations Network, Inc., 2005), original data: Electronic Army Serial Number Merged File, 1938–1946 [Archival Database]; World War II Army Enlistment Records; Records of the National Archives and Records Administration, Record Group 64; National Archives at College Park, College Park, MD.

3. 1870 US Federal Census, Norfolk City, Norfolk County, Virginia, p. 91. On racial uplift ideology, see Kevin K. Gaines, *Uplifting the Race: Black Leadership, Politics, and Culture in the Twentieth Century* (Chapel Hill: University of North Carolina Press, 1996). On black families after slavery, see Elizabeth Regosin, *Freedom's Promise: Ex-Slave Families and Citizenship in the Age of Emancipation* (Charlottesville: University of Virginia Press, 2002).

4. Eric Foner, ed., *Freedom's Lawmakers: A Directory of Black Officeholders during Reconstruction* (Baton Rouge: Louisiana State University Press, 1996); *Lynchings in America: Statistics, Information, Images*, http://www.law.umkc.edu/faculty/projects/ftrials/shipp/lynchingyear.html, accessed April 17, 2010.

5. The best overview of the process of postbellum white reconciliation is provided in David W. Blight, *Race and Reunion: The Civil War in American Memory* (Cambridge, MA: Belknap Press, 2001). See also Mitch Kachun, *Festivals of Freedom: Memory and Meaning in African American Emancipation Celebrations, 1808–1915* (Amherst: University of Massachusetts Press, 2003); John R. Neff, *Honoring the Civil War Dead: Commemoration and the Problem of Reconciliation* (Lawrence: University Press of Kansas, 2005); William Alan Blair, *Cities of the Dead: Contesting the Memory of the Civil War in the South, 1865–1914* (Chapel Hill: University of North Carolina Press, 2003); and W. Fitzhugh Brundage, *Where These Memories Grow: History, Memory, and Southern Identity* (Chapel Hill: University of North Carolina Press, 2000).

6. FitzGerald, *America Revised*, 51; John Bach McMaster, *A School History of the United States* (New York, 1897), 118–19; Susan Pendleton Lee, *A School History of the United States* (Richmond, 1895), 143; Albert Bushnell Hart, *Essentials in American History, from the Discovery to the Present Day* (New York: American Book Company, 1905), 142.

7. Samuel G. Goodrich, *The American Child's Pictorial History of the United States* (Philadelphia, 1881), 125; FitzGerald, *America Revised*, 47–48.

8. Laurie F. Maffly-Kipp, "Mapping the Race: The Negro Race History, 1874–1915," *Church History* 64:4 (December 1995), 622.

9. George Washington Williams, *History of the Negro Race in America, 1619–1880*, 2 vols. (New York: G. P. Putnam and Sons, 1883); William Simmons, *Men of*

Mark: Eminent, Progressive and Rising (Cleveland: G. Rewell & Co., 1887). For a thoughtful discussion of black historical writing during this period, see Stephen G. Hall, *A Faithful Account of the Race: African American Historical Writing in Nineteenth Century America* (Chapel Hill: University of North Carolina Press, 2009), 151–87.

10. Williams, *History of the Negro Race*, Vol. 1, 330–32.

11. Williams, *History of the Negro Race*, Vol. 1, 332–33.

12. Simmons, *Men of Mark*, 103–6.

13. Edward A. Johnson, *School History of the Negro Race in America* (Raleigh, NC: Edwards and Broughton, 1891), 63–65.

14. J. W. Gibson and W. H. Crogman, *Progress of a Race: or the Remarkable Advancement of the American Negro* (Harrisburg, PA: Minter Company, 1902), 62–63.

15. John Stephens Durham, *To Teach the Negro History: A Suggestion* (Philadelphia: David McKay, 1897), 1–9, 32.

16. John W. Cromwell, *The Negro in American History: Men and Women Eminent in the Evolution of the American of African Descent* (Washington, DC: American Negro Academy, 1914), 50; John Daniels, *In Freedom's Birthplace: A Study of the Boston Negroes* (Boston: Houghton Mifflin, 1914), 9–11.

17. *A Memorial of Crispus Attucks, Samuel Maverick, James Caldwell, Samuel Gray and Patrick Carr* (Boston: City of Boston, 1889), 11.

18. Stephen H. Browne, "Remembering Crispus Attucks: Race, Rhetoric, and the Politics of Commemoration," *Quarterly Journal of Speech* 85 (1999), 176–77; Nelson's comments from the *North American Review* quoted in Browne, 177. Browne also argues that the monument represents a "rhetorical expropriation" in that the original 1851 monument proposed by Nell was completely ignored in the 1880s and transformed Attucks from an oppositional figure of resistance to racial injustice into a "unified, homogenous, and altogether optimistic trope of national identity" (169, 171). I disagree with this interpretation primarily on the grounds that it misrepresents Nell's use of Attucks during the 1850s and 1860s. Rather than a symbol of opposition and resistance, Nell presented Attucks as the embodiment of black Americans' patriotism and national belonging. As he wrote in 1851, "the colored man, ATTUCKS, was *of* and *with* the people, and was never regarded otherwise" (*Services of Colored Americans*, 7).

19. *A Memorial of Crispus Attucks*, 27–28.

20. *A Memorial of Crispus Attucks*, 28–35.

21. *A Memorial of Crispus Attucks*, 36–37, 46–47.

22. *A Memorial of Crispus Attucks*, 60, 80–84, 87, 89.

23. John Boyle O'Reilly, "Crispus Attucks," *Liberty (Not the Daughter but the Mother of Order)*, December 1, 1888, American Periodical Series Online.

24. "The 'Boston Massacre,'" *Christian Union*, June 2, 1887 (reprinted from the *New York Sun*); Kammen, *Mystic Chords*, 122; Nora Perry, "Boston Letter," *Independent*, December 6, 1888; *Boston Globe*, November 15, 1888, cited in Browne, "Remembering

Crispus Attucks," 182. See also Dale H. Freeman, "The Crispus Attucks Monument Dedication," *Historical Journal of Massachusetts* 26:2 (1997), 125–38. Popular lore held that the Great Chicago Fire of 1871 had started when a cow kicked over a lantern and set the O'Leary barn ablaze.

25. "Crispus Attucks's Grave," *New York Freeman*, June 5, 1886.

26. "Colored Troops in the Struggle for Liberty," *New York Freeman*, March 12, 1887. I discuss Fortune's attention to history and memory in Mitch Kachun, *Festivals of Freedom: Memory and Meaning in African American Emancipation Celebrations, 1808–1915* (Amherst: University of Massachusetts Press, 2003), esp. 158–59, 165–67, 171–72, 176–77, 192–203. See also Shawn Leigh Alexander, ed., *T. Thomas Fortune, the Afro-American Agitator: A Collection of Writings, 1880–1928* (Gainesville: University Press of Florida, 2010).

27. "The Afro-American League," *New York Freeman*, June 4, 1887.

28. Significant pieces on Attucks the monument in *New York Freeman*, April 16 (with image), May 28, 1887; *New York Age*, December 10, 1887; March 24, September 29, November 17 (with image), and December 8, 1888.

29. Goodell quoted in Browne, "Remembering Crispus Attucks," 180, 182.

30. Arlo Bates, "They Must Not Marry, Flaws on a Martyr," *Chicago Daily*, March 19, 1890.

31. The "black brute" stereotype is discussed in George M. Frederickson, *The Black Image in the White Mind: The Debate on Afro-American Character and Destiny, 1817–1914* (New York: Harper and Row, 1971). Contemporary proponents of the stereotype include Charles Carroll, *The Negro a Beast* (St. Louis: American Book and Bible House, 1900) and Thomas Dixon, *The Leopard's Spots: A Romance of the White Man's Burden* (New York: Doubleday, Page, 1903).

32. John Douglas Lindsay, "The Boston 'Massacre,'" *National Magazine*, January 1893, 239–50; "Lindsay, John Douglas," in *New York University: Its History, Influence, Equipment and Characteristics*, Vol. II, ed. Joshua J. Chamberlain (Boston: R. Herndon, 1903), 327–28.

33. James R. Gilmore, "Nathaniel Emmons and Mather Byles," *New England Magazine* 16 (March 1897–August 1897), 735.

34. Gilmore, "Nathaniel Emmons," 733, 734.

35. Gilmore, "Nathaniel Emmons," 735.

36. J. L. Bell, "Mather Byles, Sr., and 'three thousand tyrants,'" March 11, 2007, *Boston 1775* blog, http://boston1775.blogspot.com/2007/03/mather-byles-sr-and-three-thousand.html, accessed January 3, 2015.

37. J. L. Bell, "Mather Byles, Sr., and 'three thousand tyrants,'" March 11, 2007, and blog comment by J. L. Bell, November 6, 2014, *Boston 1775* blog, http://boston1775.blogspot.com/2007/03/mather-byles-sr-and-three-thousand.html, accessed January 3, 2015.

38. Vernon G. Miles, "Gilmore, James Roberts," *American National Biography Online* (February 2000), http://www.anb.org, subscription database, accessed January 3, 2015.

39. City of Boston, *A Memorial of Crispus Attucks, Samuel Maverick, James Caldwell, Samuel Gray and Patrick Carr* (Miami, FL: Mnemosyne, 1969 [1889]), 11–12.

40. "Ninetieth Anniversary of the Boston Massacre, March 5, 1770," *Liberator*, March 16, 1860, as cited in google books version of William Cooper Nell, *William Cooper Nell: Nineteenth-Century African American Abolitionist, Historian, Integrationist, Selected Writings, 1832–1874*, ed. Dorothy Porter Wesley and Constance Porter Uzelac (Baltimore: Black Classics Press, 2002), 583.

41. George Livermore, *Opinions of the Founders of the Republic on Negroes as Slaves, as Citizens, and as Soldiers* (Boston: A. Williams, 1863), 92.

42. James Spear Loring, ed., *The Hundred Boston Orator* (Boston: John P. Jewett, 1852), 20 [emphasis added]; Frederic Kidder, *The Boston Massacre* (Albany, NY: Joel Munsell, 1870), 30n1 [emphasis added]. Several twenty-first-century writers have perpetuated belief in the existence of this inscribed gravestone, and some have even attributed the verse to the Revolutionary-era black poet Phillis Wheatley. While it is possible that Wheatley did author the lines of verse, which appeared without title or attribution in the March 12, 1770, issue of Boston's *Fleet's Post*, it seems unlikely that those particular lines ended up marking Attucks's grave, however meaningful and desirable such a congruence of early African American icons might be for later generations. Writers implying the existence of an original gravestone, with the lines of poetry, include Margot Minardi, *Making Slavery History: Abolitionism and the Politics of Memory in Massachusetts* (New York: Oxford University Press, 2010), 46, 185n8; and Jill Lepore, *The Whites of Their Eyes: The Tea Party's Revolution and the Battle over American History* (Princeton: Princeton University Press, 2010), 64. Wheatley's authorship of a poem entitled "On the Affray in King Street, on the Evening of the 5th of March," has been accepted by many scholars. That title was listed in a 1772 call for subscribers in the newspaper, the *Boston Censor*, to finance the publication of a volume of Wheatley's poems. The volume apparently was never published, and no confirmed text of "Affray" exists. See Vincent Carretta, *Phillis Wheatley: Biography of a Genius in Bondage* (Athens: University of Georgia Press, 2011), 80–84. Some scholars argue that Wheatley's "Affray" was the poem that appeared in *Fleet's Post*: William H. Robinson, *Phillis Wheatley and Her Writings* (New York: Garland, 1984) notes the poem's similarity to Wheatley's "style, sentiment, and vocabulary" (455); Antonio Bly, "Wheatley's 'On the Affray in King Street,'" *Explicator* 56 (1998), 177–80, asserts that the poem was "unquestionably" written by Wheatley (177); Carretta, however, seems less certain, referring to Wheatley's "Affray" as "now-lost" (72).

43. J. L. Bell, "Samuel Adams and the Massacre Victims' Grave," *Boston 1775* (blog), March 6, 2014, http://boston1775.blogspot.com/2014/03/samuel-adams-and-massacre-victims-grave.html, accessed April 25, 2015; Kidder, *Boston Massacre*, 30n1; Robert J. Allison, *The Boston Massacre* (Beverly, MA: Commonwealth Editions, 2006), 63. Carr's burial with the other massacre victims is reported in numerous contemporary newspapers, including the *Boston Evening-Post*, March

19, 1770; Supplement to the *Boston Gazette*, March 19, 1770; and the *Pennsylvania Chronicle and Universal Advertiser*, April 2, 1770. As Bell notes in the blog cited above, the *Massachusetts Spy* (March 7, 1771), in reporting on a massacre commemoration at Paul Revere's house a year after the event, mentions Seider and states that the massacre victims were "all interred in the same grave with him." However, I have not found any primary evidence corroborating that Seider's remains were ever placed with those of the massacre victims; in particular, neither the accounts of the first four massacre victims' burial nor those reporting the burial of Patrick Carr with them mention Seider's remains being moved. The *Boston Gazette* (March 5, 1770) was quite clear in stating that Seider was buried "under the Tree of Liberty," several blocks from the Granary Burying Ground. The *Gazette* article's author also promised that "a Monument will be erected over the Grave of young Snider [*sic*]" and that any money collected beyond the monument's cost "will be given to the Parents" of the slain youth. A year later, a letter to the *Massachusetts Spy* from "Trifler" (March 21, 1771) commented on "a collection made some time ago by a Gentleman . . . for the professed purpose of erecting a Monument over the grave of young SEIDER." Trifler's 1771 complaint was that money had been collected but no monument had appeared, but the letter also implied that Trifler, at least, still believed Seider to occupy an individual grave. I would be grateful to learn of any evidence that might shed further light on where the bodies are buried. My understanding of the location of the Liberty Tree comes from Alfred F. Young, *The Liberty Tree: Ordinary People and the American Revolution* (New York: New York University Press, 2006), 297, 327–28.

44. "Cemetery Department Annual Report, 1906–1907," *Documents of the City of Boston for the Year 1907*, Vol. I (Boston: Municipal Printing Office, 1908), 9.

45. "Anniversary of the Boston Massacre," *Trenton* (NJ) *Times*, March 6, 1894; "Terse Tales of the Town," *Kansas City* (MO) *Times*, April 12, 1893; "Missouri," *Chicago Defender*, June 1, 1918; "Tennessee," *Chicago Defender*, March 2, 1918; "Crispus Attucks Light Guard," *Los Angeles Times*, June 8, 1904; "Denies They Are for Taft," *Washington Post*, February 25, 1908.

46. *Directory . . . of the Crispus Attucks Relief Association, and Annual Report of the Board of Directors* (Washington, DC: Record Printing, 1904), "Preamble" (n.p.), 24, Schomburg Center for the Study of Black Culture, New York Public Library, Sc Micro R-5906, doc. 24; "Crispus Attucks Relief Association," *Washington Post*, September 25, 1903; "The Crispus Attucks Smoker," *Colored American* (Washington, DC), October 24, 1903; "Will Escort Ladies Association," *Washington Post*, October 4, 1905; "Portrait of Crispus Attucks," *Washington Post*, January 14, 1904; "Crispus Attucks Relief Election," *Washington Post*, September 10, 1913; Preston H. Harris, "Under the Capitol Dome," *Chicago Defender*, May 17, 1919.

47. Wayne D. Shirley, "The House of Melody: A List of Publications of the Gotham-Attucks Music Company at the Library of Congress," *Black Perspective in Music*

15:1 (Spring 1987), 79–112; "Cleveland Colts Win," *Chicago Defender*, June 23, 1917; "The Empire State," *Chicago Defender*, May 19, 1917; "Chancellor Commander J. H. Johnson in City," *Chicago Defender*, June 18, 1910; Fred H. Lester, "Down in Tennessee," *Chicago Defender*, July 1, 1916; "Negro Fellowship League," *Chicago Defender*, July 17, 1915; Lloyd L. Brown, "Orphans and Old Folks Revisited, with a Story," *Minnesota History* 57:7 (Fall 2001), 368–79; "Crispus Attucks Old Folks Home and Orphanage," *Chicago Defender*, August 23, 1913; "Apartment Houses for Negro Tenants," *New York Times*, July 11, 1917; Virginia Historic Landmarks Commission Staff, Attucks Theatre National Register of Historic Places nomination form, http://www.dhr.virginia.gov/registers/Cities/Norfolk/122-0074_Attucks_Theatre_1982_Final_Nomination.pdf, accessed April 21, 2015.

48. "Negroes Order Bust of Attucks for City," *Chicago Defender*, January 20, 1912; *Chicago Defender*, November 20, 1915; Booker T. Washington, *The Story of My Life and Work* (Naperville, IL: J. L. Nichols, 1900), 263–64; W. E. B. Du Bois, ed., *The Negro Artisan: Report of a Social Study Made under the Direction of Atlanta University* (Atlanta: Atlanta University Press, 1902), 153.

49. "Want Attucks Statue," *Afro-American Ledger* (Baltimore), March 30, 1907; "Was Crispus Attucks Negro or Indian?" *Afro-American Ledger* (Baltimore), May 25, 1907.

50. "Reception for the Eighth," *Chicago Tribune*, March 21, 1899.

51. Cyrus Field Adams, letter, "Another Contribution for Parker," *Washington Post*, September 12, 1901; "Tennessee Mob Bent on Lynching Foiled When Members of the Race Show the Courage to Fight," *Chicago Defender*, October 28, 1916.

52. "No Opportunity for Colored Soldiers," *Baltimore Afro-American Ledger*, December 28, 1912.

53. "Nebraska," *Chicago Defender*, December 29, 1917; "Company B Adopted," *Chicago Defender*, August 4, 1917; J. H. Gray, "Pennsylvania," *Chicago Defender*, June 22, 1918; Preston H. Harris, "Under the Capitol Dome," *Chicago Defender*, May 17, 1919.

54. James W. Johnson, "Views and Reviews," *New York Age*, February 15, March 29, 1917.

55. Herbert Kauffman, "To the American Negro," *New York Age*, August 2, 1917 (reprinted from the *New York American*); Ralph W. Tyler, "To the American White Man," *New York Age*, August 2, 1917; W. F. Cozart, "To the White American," *Chicago Defender*, July 14, 1917. Sign in parade is clearly visible in the photograph, "The Women's Section of the Parade," *New York Age*, August 2, 1917.

56. Nahum Daniel Brascher, "Here's to the Memory," *Chicago Defender*, May 31, 1919.

57. Mitchell Kachun, "The Shaping of a Public Biography: Richard Allen and the African Methodist Episcopal Church," in *Black Lives: Essays in African American Biography*, ed. James L. Conyers (Armonk, NY: M. E. Sharpe, 1999), 44–63.

58. Samuel A. Green, "The Boston Massacre," *American Antiquarian Society, Proceedings* n.s.:14 (October 1900–October 1901), 45–46.

59. "World War I Draft Registration Cards, 1917–1918," "U.S. World War II Draft Registration Cards, 1942," "Social Security Death Index," "U.S. World War II Army Enlistment Records, 1938–1946," all at www.ancestry.com, accessed October 2007.

60. Excerpt from Du Bois, "Returning Soldiers," *The Crisis* 18 (May 1919), 13, reprinted at *The Gilder Lehrman Center for the Study of Slavery, Resistance and Abolition*, http://glc.yale.edu/returning-soldiers, accessed February 22, 2017; excerpt from McKay, "If We Must Die," from James Weldon Johnson, ed., *The Book of American Negro Poetry* (1922), reprinted at *Bartleby.com*, http://www.bartleby.com/269/74.html, accessed July 8, 2010.

CHAPTER 5

1. Arthur A. Schomburg, "From 'Racial Integrity': A Plea for the Establishment of a Chair of Negro History," excerpted in *Negro: An Anthology*, ed. Nancy Cunard (New York: Continuum International, 1996 [1934]), 77–78.

2. Michael Kammen, *Mystic Chords of Memory: The Transformation of Tradition in American Culture* (New York: Vintage Books, 1991), 242–53. Jonathan Zimmerman, " 'Each "Race" Could Have Its Heroes Sung': Ethnicity and the History Wars in the 1920s," *Journal of American History* (June 2000), 92–111, quoted at 94. Historian Elizabeth Pleck offers an interesting analysis of how public schools' Thanksgiving holiday programs connected with the immigrant Americanization process in "The Making of the Domestic Occasion: The History of Thanksgiving in the United States," *Journal of Social History* 32:4 (Summer 1999), 773–89.

3. Elizabeth Ross Haynes, *Unsung Heroes* (New York: Du Bois and Dill, 1921), 228–31.

4. Bessie Landrum, *Stories of Black Folk for Little Folk* (Atlanta: A. B. Caldwell Publishing Company, 1923), Preface (n.p.), 70–72.

5. Arthur Huff Fauset, *For Freedom: A Biographical Story of the Negro* (Philadelphia: Franklin Publishing and Supply Co., 1934 [1927]), 14–20, quoted at 14, 16–18.

6. Arthur A. Schomburg, "The Negro Digs Up His Past," in *The New Negro: Voices of the Harlem Renaissance*, ed. Alain Locke (New York: Simon and Schuster, 1992 [1925]), 231–37.

7. Stephen G. Hall, *A Faithful Account of the Race: African American Historical Writing in Nineteenth-century America* (Chapel Hill: University of North Carolina Press, 2009), 218–22. See also Jacqueline Goggin, *Carter G. Woodson: A Life in Black History* (Baton Rouge: Louisiana State University Press, 1993). The journal is still in publication, now named the *Journal of African American History*.

8. Goggin, *Carter G. Woodson*, 84; "Notes," *Journal of Negro History* 14:3 (July 1929), 359–60.

9. "Notes," *Journal of Negro History* 14:3 (July 1929), 359–60. Responding more passionately to blacks' sense of racial inferiority, Woodson's 1933 screed, *The Mis-education of the Negro*, expanded his critique of educated middle-class blacks—who he

believed had the responsibility to lead and empower the race—for wallowing in race inferiority and preying upon the black masses for their own profit.

10. Michael Kammen, *Mystic Chords of Memory*, 299–527; Washington Bicentennial on 455–56, quoted at 455.

11. *Journal of Negro History* 17:2 (April 1932), 119–23; Carter G. Woodson, "Vital Suggestions on the Washington Bicentennial," *New York Amsterdam News*, December 9, 1931.

12. *Journal of Negro History* 17:2 (April 1932), 119–23; Woodson, "Vital Suggestions on the Washington Bicentennial"; *Journal of Negro History* 22:2 (April 1932), 119–23.

13. Carter G. Woodson, "Bicentennial Eliminates Crispus Attucks' Day," *New York Amsterdam News*, December 30, 1931.

14. Carter G. Woodson, *The Negro in Our History*, 4th ed. (Washington, DC: Associated Publishers, 1927 [1922]), 121–22; "Woodson Hits Defamers of Race Patriot," *Chicago Defender*, December 18, 1937; "Must Negro Despise His Glorious Past, Noted Historian Queries," *Pittsburgh Courier*, December 18, 1937.

15. Drusilla Dunjee Houston, "Why Negroes Reject Negro History," *Atlanta Daily World*, September 2, 1934. Houston (1876–1941) was author of *Wonderful Ethiopians of the Ancient Cushite Empire* (Oklahoma City: Universal Publishing, 1926). Biographical information on Houston from Peggy Brooks-Bertram, "Drusilla Dunjee Houston," online *Encyclopedia of Oklahoma History and Culture* (Oklahoma Historical Society), http://digital.library.okstate.edu/encyclopedia/ entries/H/HO038.html, accessed September 15, 2008.

16. Josephine T. Washington, "Know Thyself!" *Pittsburgh Courier*, December 18, 1937; "Letters Pour in on Du Bois Argument," *Chicago Defender*, April 14, 1934.

17. "Listen, My Children," *New York Amsterdam News*, November 30, 1935.

18. Melvin B. Tolson, "Dark Symphony," reprinted in *The Norton Anthology of African American Literature*, ed. Henry Louis Gates and Nellie Y. McKay (New York: W. W. Norton, 1997), 1331. Tolson's poem was presented at Chicago's American Negro Exposition in 1939 though it was not published until 1944. The epigraph that begins this chapter is from the same poem. See Gates and McKay, 1328–34.

19. Garvey quoted in Scot French, *The Rebellious Slave: Nat Turner in American Memory* (New York: Houghton Mifflin, 2004), 187; George S. Schuyler, "Views and Reviews," *Pittsburgh Courier*, September 22, 1934.

20. Thabiti Asukile, "J. A. Rogers: The Scholarship of an Organic Intellectual," *Black Scholar* 36:2/3 (Summer/Fall 2006), 35–50; W. Burghart Turner, "J. A. Rogers: Portrait of an Afro-American Historian," *Black Scholar* 6:5 (January 1975), 33–39; A. Wellington Clarke, "Crispus Attucks and the American Revolution," *Chicago Defender*, May 4, 1935; Arturo A. Schomburg, "Crispus Attucks—Free Patriot," *New York Amsterdam News*, August 24, 1935.

21. "Trotter Lauded as Modern Atlas as 3,500 Mourn Boston Publisher," *New York Amsterdam News*, April 14, 1934; *A Memorial of Crispus Attucks, Samuel Maverick, James Caldwell, Samuel Gray and Patrick Carr* (Boston: City of Boston, 1889),

15, 36–37; Stephen R. Fox, *The Guardian of Boston: William Monroe Trotter* (New York: Atheneum, 1970).

22. "Call for Attucks Day," *Chicago Defender*, March 3, 1923; "State Proclamation for Crispus Attucks," *New York Amsterdam News*, March 10, 1926; "First Boston Massacre Day Proclamation," *New York Amsterdam News*, March 17, 1926; "Bostonians Honor Memory of Attucks," *New York Amsterdam News*, March 13, 1929.

23. "First Boston Massacre Day Proclamation," *New York Amsterdam News*, March 17, 1926; "Submits Proof of Attucks' Race," *New York Amsterdam News*, March 24, 1926.

24. "Boston Astir as Day to Honor Attucks Nears," *New York Amsterdam News*, February 24, 1932; "New Bill Will Honor Attucks," *New York Amsterdam News*, March 16, 1932; "Mass. Governor Signs Attucks Day Bill," *New York Amsterdam News*, May 25, 1932; "Push Drive for 'Crispus Attucks Day,'" *Chicago Defender*, February 25, 1933.

25. "Harlem Democracy Hails O'Brien," *New York Amsterdam News*, November 2, 1932; "Mass. Senator Would Honor Crispus Attucks," *New York Amsterdam News*, April 13, 1932.

26. "Trotter Lauded as Modern Atlas as 3,500 Mourn Boston Publisher," *New York Amsterdam News*, April 14, 1934; "Berkeley, Calif.," *Chicago Defender*, March 23, 1935; "Notables Will Mark 'Crispus Attucks Day,'" *Washington Post*, March 10, 1935; "Noted Orator to Honor Race Hero," *New York Amsterdam News*, February 29, 1936; "Barbers Union Makes Demand for a Holiday," *New York Amsterdam News*, July 16, 1938; "Dr. Leslie P. Hill on Attucks Day Program," *Chicago Defender*, March 14, 1931.

27. Joseph C. Coles, "Laud Nat Turner's Memory," *Pittsburgh Courier*, August 12, 1933.

28. "Colored Writers Buy House," *Washington Post*, June 21, 1925.

29. "Oklahoma News," *Chicago Defender*, February 25, 1933; "Weddings," *New York Amsterdam News*, April 9, 1930; "Florida," *Chicago Defender*, May 6, 1933; "Sigma Gamma Rhos' Educational Week Interests Sorors," *Pittsburgh Courier*, November 30, 1940; "East St. Louis Schools Crowded by Race Migration," *Chicago Defender*, August 14, 1937; "Colp, Ill." *Chicago Defender*, January 19, 1935; "Bias in Teaching Practice Ended," *Chicago Defender*, December 21, 1940; J. A. Rogers, "Rambling Ruminations," *New York Amsterdam News*, July 15, 1931.

30. "3-Week Trip," *New York Amsterdam News*, September 21, 1940; Dan Burley, "Confidentially Yours," *New York Amsterdam News*, May 3, 1941; Oscar O. Thomas, "Baltimore, Md.," *New York Amsterdam News*, November 2, 1927; "National Directory, Hotels and Guest Houses," *Pittsburgh Courier*, July 6, 1940; "Low-Cost Housing Project Named," *Pittsburgh Courier*, August 26, 1939; "Attucks Court Nearing Completion," *Atlanta Daily World*, January 27, 1940.

31. "J. M. Burrell Is Made Head of Vets Post," *New York Amsterdam News*, July 23, 1938; "Crispus Attucks Post Plans Radio Program Sunday," *Pittsburgh Courier*, February

18, 1933; "Elect Purnell as Historian," *Atlanta Daily World*, December 5, 1940; "Crispus Attucks Post No. 151," *Chicago Defender*, March 28, 1936; Hazel M. Taylor, "Grand Rapids, Mich.," *Chicago Defender*, June 2, 1934.

32. Charles T. Magill, "Fraternal World," *New York Amsterdam News*, May 26, 1934; Charles T. Magill, "Do You Know the Password?" *New York Amsterdam News*, December 18, 1929; "Georgia," *Chicago Defender*, November 10, 1923; "Attucks Theatre," *sevenvenues*, http://www.sevenvenues.com/venues/detail/attucks-theatre, accessed February 22, 2017; C. A. Leonard, "Negro Histrionism in U.S.," *New York Amsterdam News*, May 8, 1929.

33. California Death Index, 1940–1997 (online database); Social Security Death Index (online database), *Ancestry.com*, accessed July 8, 2010.

34. "Mayor Expected to Make Speech," *New York Amsterdam News*, May 31, 1933; "Wibecan Is Retired from the Post Office," *New York Amsterdam News*, January 3, 1934; "Negro Must Prove Self, Says Jurist," *New York Amsterdam News*, July 12, 1933.

35. "Brooklynites Split over New Center," *New York Amsterdam News*, March 14, 1936; "Groups Fight Naming Park in Honor of Colonial Hero," *New York Amsterdam News*, December 8, 1934; "Junior League Formed by Community Council," *New York Amsterdam News*, August 25, 1934; "Will Observe Death Of Crispus Attucks," *New York Amsterdam News*, February 28, 1934; "Schomburg Talks on Negro's Role in U.S.," *New York Amsterdam News*, October 4, 1933; "Imes Will Address Community Council," *New York Amsterdam News*, October 25, 1933; "Great Dihigo to Play Every Position in Charity Game Here; Paige Is Coming for Big Contest," *New York Amsterdam News*, September 7, 1935; "When Grays Met Dodgers," *New York Amsterdam News*, October 20, 1934.

36. "Grievances Arouse Council's Protests," *New York Amsterdam News*, July 14, 1934; "Principal in Police Assault Case Held," *New York Amsterdam News*, July 14, 1934; "Hotel Denies Bias Charges," *New York Amsterdam News*, November 3, 1934; "Local Group Plans a New Job Campaign," *New York Amsterdam News*, August 20, 1938; Marvel Smith, "Brooklyn," *New York Amsterdam News*, February 12, 1938; "Seek Rape Case Reopening," *New York Amsterdam News*, June 25, 1938.

37. "Race Achievement to Get Spot at Exposition," *New York Amsterdam News*, May 27, 1939; "To Show Race Achievem'nts at N.Y. Fair," *Chicago Defender*, June 24, 1939.

38. "Constitutional Celebration Will Honor Crispus Attucks," *Chicago Defender*, June 18, 1938; Monroe Mason, "Legionnaires Will View Monument to Crispus Attucks," *Chicago Defender*, September 14, 1940; "We Are Thankful," *Chicago Defender*, November 26, 1938; Nahum Daniel Brascher, "Views and Reviews: There Is a New America," *Chicago Defender*, July 2, 1938.

39. "Attention Mr. Farley," *Chicago Defender*, September 29, 1934; "Wouldn't This Look Fine on a Postage Stamp?" *Chicago Defender*, March 10, 1934; "Write Mr. Farley and Ask Him about the Stamp Issue," *Chicago Defender*, April 10, 1937; "Wright Again Honored," *Atlanta Daily World*, October 11, 1940; Cliff Mackay,

"The Globe Trotter: The Washington Stamp," *Atlanta Daily World*, July 30, 1939; "Charleston Club Wants a Stamp Dedicated to an Outstanding Negro," *Pittsburgh Courier*, July 15, 1939; Roscoe Simmons, "The Week," *Chicago Defender*, April 20, 1940. On Wright's role in the creation of National Freedom Day (February 1), see Mitch Kachun, "'A beacon to oppressed peoples everywhere': Major R. R. Wright, Sr., National Freedom Day, and the Rhetoric of Freedom in the 1940s," *Pennsylvania Magazine of History and Biography* 128:3 (July 2004), 279–306.

40. Roy Wilkins, "Watchtower," *New York Amsterdam News*, June 29, 1940.
41. J. A. Rogers, "Rogers Says: Negroes Should Unite on a National Holiday—Suggests Attucks' Birthday," *Pittsburgh Courier*, October 11, 1941.
42. "Random Thoughts," *Chicago Defender*, February 4, 1939; "'Crispus Attucks Legion Will Carry On;' Brascher," *Chicago Defender*, April 8, 1939; "On Way to World's Fair," *Chicago Defender*, June 2, 1934; "Ozone Park, L.I.," *New York Amsterdam News*, June 23, 1934; "Directing Attucks Club," *New York Amsterdam News*, March 20, 1937; "Westchester Politicos Stir," *New York Amsterdam News*, October 5, 1940; "Out of Beanpot Boston," *Chicago Defender*, October 22, 1938; "La Junta, Colo.," *Pittsburgh Courier*, February 19, 1938; "Dillard to Celebrate History Wk.," *Chicago Defender*, February 8, 1936; "Jamaica Branch in History Week," *New York Amsterdam News*, February 18, 1939; "San Francisco," *Pittsburgh Courier*, June 11, 1938; "The Death of Crispus Attuck" (adv.), *The Crisis* 44:2 (February 1937), 36; "Textbooks Direct from All Publishers" (adv.), *The Crisis* 45:1 (January 1938), 3; "Lives of Seven Famous Negroes Told in Book," *Chicago Defender*, December 14, 1940; "Dillard to Celebrate History Wk.," *Chicago Defender*, February 8, 1936; "Jamaica Branch in History Week," *New York Amsterdam News*, February 18, 1939; "San Francisco," *Pittsburgh Courier*, June 11, 1938.
43. David Krasner, "'The Pageant Is the Thing': Black Nationalism and *The Star of Ethiopia*," in *Performing America: Cultural Nationalism in American Theatre*, ed. Jeffrey D. Mason and J. Ellen Gainor (Ann Arbor: University of Michigan Press, 1999), 106–22, Du Bois quoted at 108.
44. Quoted in William H. Wiggins Jr., *O Freedom! Afro-American Emancipation Celebrations* (Knoxville: University of Tennessee Press, 1987), 59.
45. "Ethiopia at the Bar of Justice," in *Plays and Pageants from the Life of the Negro*, ed. Willis Richardson (Washington, DC: Associated Publishers, 1930); May Miller and Willis Richardson, eds., *Negro History in Thirteen Plays* (Washington, DC: Associated Publishers, 1935); Emmanuel Sampath Nelson, ed., *African American Dramatists: An A-to-Z Guide* (Westport, CT: Greenwood Press, 2004), 361.
46. "Launch New Record Firm," *New York Amsterdam News*, December 13, 1941; "Mercedes Gilbert Making Records of Negro History," *New York Amsterdam News*, March 1, 1941; "On the Radio," *New York Amsterdam News*, March 5, 1940; "Depict Lives of Notables," *New York Amsterdam News*, May 3, 1941; "Portray Race Greats in Moving Pictures, Al Moses Suggests," *Pittsburgh Courier*, January 8, 1938; "Black

Heroes Film Subject," *New York Amsterdam News*, May 6, 1939; D. G. Gibson, "West Coast Jottings," *Chicago Defender*, March 22, 1941.

47. "Senator Bilbo's Bill," *Chicago Defender*, May 6, 1939; David Ward Howe, "The Observation Post: Mrs. F.D.R. Delivers Smarting Blow to Intolerance," *Chicago Defender*, March 11, 1939; "Topics of the Week: Crispus Attucks vs. D.A.R.'s," *New York Amsterdam News*, May 20, 1939; Nahum Daniel Brascher, "Random Thoughts," *Chicago Defender*, March 18, 1939.

48. "Crispus Attucks Eulogized by President John Adams, but Later Dishonored by D.A.R.," *Chicago Defender*, March 11, 1939; *Chicago Defender*, March 11, 1939; "In Memory of Crispus Attucks," *Chicago Defender*, March 4, 1939.

49. "Black America Takes an Inventory," *Chicago Defender*, September 24, 1938;

50. "Democracy in National Defense" (reprinted form the *Interracial Review*), *Chicago Defender*, April 19, 1941; "Our Armed Forces," *New York Amsterdam News*, June 1, 1940. A few examples of essays expressing similar sentiments include, "Thrilling Military History of U.S. Negroes Recounted: Attucks First to Die," *Atlanta Daily World*, August 18, 1940; "Negro Air, Naval Base Is Urged," *Atlanta Daily World*, December 3, 1940; "Lieutenant Osceola McKaine Delivers Ringing Address," *Atlanta Daily World*, November 21, 1941; and "Paul V. McNutt Stresses Negro's Loyalty," *New York Amsterdam News*, March 8, 1941.

51. Jucius C. Harper, "Dustin' Off the News: Crispus Attucks, the Most Neglected Martyr in History," *Chicago Defender*, March 8, 1941.

CHAPTER 6

1. "Our Armed Forces," *New York Amsterdam News*, June 1, 1940.
2. "Democracy in National Defense," *Chicago Defender*, April 19, 1941.
3. "Blame Army Policy for Race Clashes in Two Camps," *Chicago Defender*, August 16, 1941.
4. Frank D. Griffin, "War Department Broadcast Is Feeble Effort at Appeasement," *New York Amsterdam News*, August 30, 1941.
5. A. Philip Randolph, "Call to Negro America to March on Washington for Jobs and Equal Participation in National Defense," *Black Worker* 14 (May 1941), n.p.; "The Courier's Double 'V' for a Double Victory Campaign Gets Country-Wide Support," *Pittsburgh Courier*, February 14, 1942; Thomas J. Ward, "Double V Campaign," *The Jim Crow Encyclopedia: Greenwood Milestones in African American History*, Vol. 1, ed. Nikki L. M. Brown and Barry M. Stentiford (Westport, CT: Greenwood Press, 2008), 247–49.
6. Lauren Rebecca Sklaroff, *Black Culture and the New Deal: The Quest for Civil Rights in the Roosevelt Era* (Chapel Hill: University of North Carolina Press, 2009), 135–37.
7. Scot French, *The Rebellious Slave: Nat Turner in American Memory* (New York: Houghton Mifflin, 2004), 217.

8. B. I. Wiley, review of Benjamin Brawley, *Negro Builders and Heroes* (Chapel Hill: University of North Carolina Press, 1937), *Journal of Southern History* 4:3 (August 1938), 405–6. The Nat Turner insurrection and the Denmark Vesey and Gabriel conspiracies are well known; Cato was a leader of the 1739 Stono Rebellion in South Carolina.

9. Emory O. Jackson, "Jap Bombs Claim Life of Birmingham Youth," *Atlanta Daily World*, December 20, 1941. It is not clear what evidence the newspaper used to determine that Ellberry was the first to die, but the apparent desire to claim that status for the race and to make the connection with Crispus Attucks, is noteworthy.

10. Lucius C. Harper, "Shoulder Arms for Freedom," *Chicago Defender*, September 26, 1942.

11. Cliff Mackay, "The Globe Trotter: Black Heroes Unsung," *Atlanta Daily World*, February 8, 1942.

12. Navy Secretary Commends Dorie Miller for Bravery," *Pittsburgh Courier* (City Edition), April 11, 1942; "'Messman Hero' Identified," *Pittsburgh Courier*, March 14, 1942.

13. Richard E. Miller, *The Messman Chronicles: African Americans in the U.S. Navy, 1932–1943* (Annapolis, MD: Naval Institute Press, 2004), 298–301.

14. "Navy Secretary Commends Dorie Miller for Bravery," *Pittsburgh Courier* (City Edition), April 11, 1942; Miller, *The Messman Chronicles*, 285–317.

15. Miller, *The Messman Chronicles*, 286, 298–309.

16. See, for example, Darlene Clark Hine et al., *The African American Odyssey* (Upper Saddle River, NJ: Prentice-Hall, 2000), 476; James Oliver Horton and Lois E. Horton, *Hard Road to Freedom: The Story of African Americans* (New Brunswick, NJ: Rutgers University Press, 2001), 263.

17. Miller, *The Messman Chronicles*, 285–317.

18. Miller, *The Messman Chronicles*, 285–317, quoted at 311.

19. Miller, *The Messman Chronicles*, 287–88.

20. Sklaroff, *Black Culture and the New Deal*, 144–46.

21. Sklaroff, *Black Culture and the New Deal*, 146–56.

22. By 1940, more than 90 percent of all urban households and nearly 70 percent of all rural households owned radios, though these numbers were somewhat lower among African Americans and in the South. Similarly, motion picture theaters had become an ever-expanding presence. One contemporary analyst estimated that by 1944, ninety million people attended movies each week and thirty million homes contained radios. See, for example, Steve Craig, "How America Adopted Radio: Demographic Differences in Set Ownership Reported in the 1930–1950 U.S. Censuses," *Journal of Broadcasting and Electronic Media* 48:2 (June 2004), 179–95; L. D. Reddick, "Educational Programs for the Improvement of Race Relations: Motion Pictures, Radio, the Press, and Libraries," *Journal of Negro Education*, 13:3 (Summer 1944), 367–89, quoted at 367; Sklaroff, *Black Culture and the New Deal*; Lizbeth Cohen, *Making a New Deal: Industrial Workers in Chicago, 1919–1939* (Cambridge, UK: Cambridge University Press, 1990).

23. Reddick, "Educational Programs for the Improvement of Race Relations," 367–89, quoted at 367, 369, 384.

24. Sklaroff, *Black Culture and the New Deal*, 159–92.

25. "Depict Live of Notables," *New York Amsterdam Star-News*, May 3, 1941; Reddick, "Educational Programs for the Improvement of Race Relations," 384–86.

26. "Depict Live of Notables," *New York Amsterdam Star-News*, May 3, 1941; playscript, "Crispus Attucks: The First American Martyr," Schomburg Center for Research in Black Culture, New York Public Library, Radio Transcripts Collection, Box: 5, Folder: Native Sons A-E.

27. Playscript, "Crispus Attucks: First American Casualty," *Within Our Gates*, February 11, 1945, Schomburg Center for Research in Black Culture, New York Public Library, Radio Transcripts Collection, Box: 2, Folder: 5—Within Our Gates, January–March, 1945; "Background," Fellowship Commission Records, 1941–1994, Temple University Libraries Urban Archives Collections, http://library.temple.edu/collections/urbana/fell-626.jsp?bhcp=1, accessed August 14, 2011.

28. "Crispus Attucks: First American Casualty," n.p.

29. "Crispus Attucks: First American Casualty," n.p.

30. J. Fred MacDonald, ed., *Richard Durham's Destination Freedom: Scripts from Radio's Black Legacy* (New York: Praeger, 1988), both Durham and MacDonald quoted at 4.

31. Richard Durham, "The Knock-Kneed Man," audio recording, "Destination Freedom," *The Internet Archive: Radio Programs*, http://www.archive.org/details/DestinationFreedom, accessed September 22, 2011.

32. Durham, "The Knock-Kneed Man"; Williams, *History of the Negro Race in America*, Vol. I (New York: G. P. Putnam and Sons, 1883), 333; William Simmons, *Men of Mark: Eminent, Progressive and Rising* (Cleveland: G. Rewell & Co., 1887), 106; "Dioramas at Expo Give Short Course in Negro History," *California Eagle*, August 1, 1940; Dharathula H. Millender, *Crispus Attucks: Boy of Valor* (New York: Bobbs-Merrill, 1965), 186; *Crispus Attucks: Black Leader of Colonial Patriots* (New York: Aladdin, 1986), 186; Oscar Reiss, *Blacks in Colonial America* (Jefferson, NC: McFarland, 2006), 232–33.

33. Roscoe Simmons, "The Untold Story," *Chicago Daily Tribune*, March 2, 1947.

34. W. E. B. Du Bois, "The Winds of Time: Union Labor," *Chicago Defender*, November 22, 1947.

35. J. A. Rogers, "Rogers Says," *Pittsburgh Courier*, August 13, 1949.

36. "Mis-Directed Effort," *Negro History Bulletin* 8:7 (April 1945), 165; Woodson review of *Unsung Americans Sung*, *Journal of Negro History* 30:2 (April 1945), 228–30, quoted at 228–29.

37. "'Salute to Negro Troops' Apollo Offering," *New York Amsterdam News*, March 28, 1942.

38. "Salute to Negro Troops," Radio Transcripts, Box 6, folder: Miscellaneous Broadcasts (1937–1947), Schomburg Center for Research in Black Culture, New York Public Library.

39. J. A. Rogers, "Rogers Says," *Pittsburgh Courier*, June 19, 1943; "'For This We Fight' Drama Records Age-Old Battle," *New York Amsterdam News*, June 12, 1943; "Dudley Will Be MBC Founders' Day Speaker," *Atlanta Daily World*, March 10, 1942; "Clairton Takes Part in Impressive Flag Day," *Pittsburgh Courier*, June 28, 1941; "Virginian Has Play Staged at Iowa University," *Chicago Defender*, March 27, 1948.

40. Thomas D. Pawley, *Crispus Attucks*, Department of Special Collections, University of Iowa, electronic edition by Alexander Street Press, http://alexanderstreet.com/, subscription database, accessed June 8, 2012.

41. Pawley, *Crispus Attucks*.

42. Pawley, *Crispus Attucks*.

43. Pawley, *Crispus Attucks*.

44. Pawley, *Crispus Attucks*.

45. "Radio Timetable," *Christian Science Monitor*, September 20, 1943, July 15, 1947; "Launch New Record Firm," *New York Amsterdam Star-News*, December 13, 1941; "Mercedes Gilbert Making Records of Negro History," *New York Amsterdam Star-News*, March 1, 1941; "Big Names: Recordings of Famous Folk to Be Done by New York Group," *Chicago Defender*, March 1, 1941.

46. Sklaroff, *Black Culture and the New Deal*, 236–37; Thomas Cripps and David Culbert, "*The Negro Soldier* (1944): Film Propaganda in Black and White," *American Quarterly* 31:5 (Winter 1979), 616–40.

47. *The Negro Soldier*, Motion Picture, Sound, and Video Records Section, Special Media Archives Services Division (NWCS-M), National Archives at College Park, ARC Identifier 35956 / Local Identifier 111-M-6022; *The Negro Soldier*, http://www.youtube.com/watch?v=XRUeOObzY4o, accessed March 8, 2012.

48. Langston Hughes, "Here to Yonder," *Chicago Defender*, March 13, 1943; Frank Griffin, "Lauds Thaddeus Stevens in Attack on Film," *New York Amsterdam Star-News*, October 10, 1942; "Under the Lash," *Chicago Defender*, November 22, 1941.

49. "Earl Dancer Doing Script for Crispus Attucks Film," *Pittsburgh Courier*, October 3, 1942; "His Eye Is on the Sparrow," *Washington Post and Times Herald*, April 25, 1954; Earl Dancer, "Flo Zeigfeld Sees, Is Conquered by Ethel; Earl Arrives as Star Maker," *New York Amsterdam News*, March 18, 1950; "Star Maker Dancer Back at Old Stand," *New York Amsterdam News*, October 22, 1949; "Robeson May Come Back to Movies," *Pittsburgh Courier*, October 10, 1942.

50. "Movie Moguls Reject Script for Dignified Race Screen Play," *New York Amsterdam Star-News*, January 9, 1943; "Rowe's Notebook," *Pittsburgh Courier*, January 16, 1943; Cripps and Culbert, *The Negro Soldier* (1944): Film Propaganda in Black and White," 622.

51. J. A. Rogers, "Rogers Says," *Pittsburgh Courier*, March 6, 1943; Sklaroff, *Black Culture and the New Deal*, 222–31; Billy Rowe, "Artists Assail Dancer's Article as Thoughtless," *Pittsburgh Courier*, January 30, 1943.

52. National Board of Review Awards, http://www.nationalboardofreview.org/award-years/1949/, accessed February 22, 2017; "*Home of the Brave* Plot Summary, Internet Movie Database," *Wikipedia*, http://en.wikipedia.org/wiki/Home_of_

the_Brave_%281949_film%29, accessed March 13, 2012; "James Edwards, "Home of the Brave" Star, on Palace Stage," *Atlanta Daily World*, October 21, 1949; Lilian Scott, "Along Celebrity Row," *Chicago Defender*, July 17, 1948.

53. *State of the Union*, directed by Frank Capra (1948, Metro-Goldwyn-Mayer, Culver City, CA).

54. "Murals to Honor Negro in America," *New York Times*, December 3, 1942; J. W., "Seven Winning Mural Designs for Federal Building Displayed," *Washington Post*, April 25, 1943; Sara A. Butler, "Groundbreaking in New Deal Washington, DC: Art, Patronage, and Race at the Recorder of Deeds Building," *Winterthur Portfolio*, 45:4 (Winter 2011), 277–320, quoted at 281, 300.

55. "Negro Paints Story of Race in America," *New York Times*, June 27, 1943; Erin P. Cohn, "Art Front: Visual Culture and Race Politics in the Mid-twentieth Century United States," Doctoral Dissertation, University of Pennsylvania, 2010, 137, 138.

56. Cohn, "Art Front," 156–63; *Negro, U.S.A.* (New York: Graphic Art Workshop, 1949).

57. Brittany Rose Rogers, "Johnson, William Henry (1901–1970)," *BlackPast. org: Remembered and Reclaimed*, http://www.blackpast.org/aah/johnson-william-henry-1901-1970, accessed April 21, 2015; "William H. Johnson: His Story," in *A Journey through Art with W. H. Johnson*, Smithsonian American Art Museum (online exhibit), http://americanart.si.edu/education/johnson/hisstory.html, accessed April 21, 2015.

58. Margaret T. Goss, ""Negro History Week Enough to Make Billikens Proud," *Chicago Defender*, February 13, 1943. See also "Lest We Forget—Negro History Week 1948," *Chicago Defender*, February 14, 1948; "Negro History Week Program of the Halsey Junior High School, New York City," *Negro History Bulletin*, 13:3 (December 1949), 60, 70–71; "Girls High School Negro History Week Program," *Negro History Bulletin*, 13:7 (April 1950), 160–64; "Negro History Week," *Atlanta Daily World*, February 5, 1950.

59. "'Crispus Attucks Legion Will Carry On'; Brascher," *Chicago Defender*, April 8, 1939; Nahum Daniel Brascher, "Thoughts To-Day," *Chicago Defender*, March 7, 1942; J. Robert Smith, "Objectors Aid Pro-Axis Work," *New York Amsterdam Star-News*, March 28, 1942.

60. "Victory Sidelights," *Washington Post*, May 8, 1943; Edward Toles, "Negro Vets Tell Toles, We Mowed Down Nazi," *Chicago Defender*, September 9, 1944; "Mass. County Gets First Negro Vets' Post," *Chicago Defender*, February 9, 1946; "Monarchs Play Stars on May 8," *Chicago Defender*, May 7, 1949.

61. "Strollin' with the Billikens," *Chicago Defender*, January 22, 1949; Gladys Gray Jones, "Attucks School Has Graduation," *Pittsburgh Courier*, June 14, 1947; "Ask Crispus Attucks for New School Name," *Chicago Defender*, December 6, 1947; "'New' Kid Center to Be Introduced Sunday, October 27," *New York Amsterdam News*, October 26, 1946; "Long Beach Host to 4,000 Orphans," *New York Times*, August 13, 1947; "GOP's Annual Convention," *New York Amsterdam News*, April

20, 1946; "100 Librarians Attend Confab," *Chicago Defender*, May 24, 1947; "Billie Holliday Face Prison," *New York Amsterdam News*, May 24, 1947.

62. Lucius C. Harper, "Dustin' Off the News: What Does March Fifth Mean to Colored America?" *Chicago Defender*, March 11, 1944.

63. "Springfield," *Chicago Defender*, March 35, 1944; "Attucks Students Send Annual Wreath to Revolutionary War Hero's Grave," *Indianapolis Recorder*, March 18, 1939; "Crispus Attucks Services," *Chicago Daily Tribune*, March 5, 1943; "Remember Crispus Attucks," *Chicago Defender*, March 18, 1944; "Six Days in March," *Chicago Daily Tribune*, March 4, 1949; Dr. O. B. Taylor, "It Seems to Me," *Atlanta Daily World*, April 9, 1953.

64. "3 States Honor Crispus Attucks," *New York Amsterdam News*, March 13, 1948; "Seeks Crispus Attucks Day," *Pittsburgh Courier*, February 27, 1943; "May Decree Attucks Day in Gotham," *Chicago Defender*, February 27, 1943; "Crispus Attucks Day to Be Marked March 7," *New York Amsterdam Star-News*, March 6, 1943; "NY City Council Proclaims Attucks Day for March 7," *Chicago Defender*, March 6, 1943; "City Council to Honor Attucks March 5," *New York Amsterdam Star-News*, February 20, 1943.

65. The prime mover in pushing for the New Jersey holiday was Mrs. Ella Barksdale Brown, a longtime activist, journalist, and community leader, who also organized Negro History Week programs for many years in Jersey City. "2013 New Jersey Revised Statutes—Title 36 Legal Holidays—36:2–1 Crispus Attucks Day," L.1949, c. 49, p. 336, s. 1, eff. April 25, 1949, http://law.justia.com/codes/new-jersey/2013/title-36/section-36-2-1/, accessed February 22, 2017; "Mrs. Ella B. Brown Is 92," *New York Amsterdam News*, August 4, 1962.

66. Ben Richardson, *Great American Negroes* (New York: Thomas Y. Cromwell Company, 1945); Alice Moore Dunbar Nelson, *Masterpieces of Negro Eloquence: The Best Speeches Delivered by the Negro from the Days of Slavery to the Present Time* (New York: Bookery Publishing Company, 1914); Arna Bontemps, *The Story of the Negro* (New York: Alfred A. Knopf, 1951), 93, 95; Langston Hughes, "Here to Yonder: The Story of the Negro," *Chicago Defender*, May 29, 1948.

67. Evelyn LaRue Pittman, *Rich Heritage: Songs about American Negro Heroes* (Oklahoma City: Harlow, 1944), 26–27; Handy, *Unsung Americans Sung*, 53–55.

68. Edward Nicholas, *The Hours and the Ages: A Sequence of Americans* (New York: William Sloane, 1949), 78, 81; Edith H. Mayer, *Our Negro Brother* (New York: Sandy Hill Press, 1945), Introduction (n.p.), 8–10.

69. Constance H. Curtis, "About Books," *New York Amsterdam News*, April 21, 1945; Constance Curtis, "About Books and Authors," *New York Amsterdam News* February 8, 1947; Annie L. McPheeters, "The Bookshelf," *Atlanta Daily World*, February 2, 1947; Agatha L. Shea, "Pictorial Tribute to U.S. Negroes," *Chicago Daily Tribune*, February 9, 1947; Harriet Ford Griswold, "Your World Grows as You Read," *Christian Science Monitor*, April 10, 1947; "JHS 178 Has Negro Program," *New York Amsterdam News*, May 14, 1949; "Evening School Notes

Negro History Week," *Atlanta Daily World*, February 11, 1953; "St. John Sets Negro History Observance," *Pittsburgh Courier*, February 10, 1962; "East River Players in 'North Star,'" *New York Amsterdam News*, June 4, 1966; "Race Relations Sunday Due at Wesley United Methodist," *Los Angeles Sentinel*, February 6, 1969; "East River to Compete at Festival," *New York Amsterdam News*, October 24, 1970.

70. Jesse Dunson, "Negro History Campaign," *New York Amsterdam News*, May 6, 1944; "Two Essay Contestants Ask Unbiased Textbooks," *Chicago Defender*, December 7, 1946; "Here Are Three Best Essays in Great Defender Contest," *Chicago Defender*, August 16, 1947.

71. David Saville Muzzey and John A. Kraut, *American History for Colleges* (Boston: Ginn, 1943), 76; Mabel B. Casner and Ralph H. Gabriel, *The Story of American Democracy* (New York: Harcourt Brace, 1955), 118; George W. Harris, "Expose Textbook Prejudices Used to Ballyhoo Phony 'Superior Group,'" *New York Amsterdam News*, March 27, 1948; Lucius C. Harper, "Dustin' Off the News," *Chicago Defender*, November 4, 1950.

72. Langston Hughes, "The Need for Heroes," *The Crisis* (June 1941), 184–85.

73. Langston Hughes, "The Need for Heroes," *The Crisis* (June 1941), 206.

CHAPTER 7

1. "3 States Honor Crispus Attucks," *New York Amsterdam News*, March 13, 1948; J. A. Rogers, "Rogers Says: March 5, Independence Day," *Pittsburgh Courier*, March 12, 1955.

2. "Lest We Forget—Negro History Week … 1948," *Chicago Defender*, February 14, 1948.

3. J. A. Rogers, "Rogers Says," *Pittsburgh Courier*, February 2, 1952.

4. "Negro History Week," *Atlanta Daily World*, February 8, 1948.

5. Leroy Gibson, "To the Editor," *Los Angeles Sentinel*, March 1, 1951.

6. August Meier, "Whither the Black Perspective in Afro-American Historiography?" *Journal of American History* 70:1 (June 1983), 101; Stephen G. Hall, "Black History and Historiography," *Encyclopedia of the Harlem Renaissance*, Vol. 1, A-J, ed. Cary D. Wintz and Paul Finkelman (New York: Routledge, 2004), 129–30; "Broader Knowledge of History Required," *Negro History Bulletin*, 13:6 (March 1950), 144.

7. Roscoe Simmons, "Telling the Untold Story," *Chicago Tribune*, February 18, 1951.

8. John Hope Franklin, "The New Negro History," *Journal of Negro History* 42 (April 1957), 89–97; Meier, "Whither the Black Perspective," 101.

9. William B. Hesseltine, review of Franklin, *From Slavery to Freedom*, in *American Historical Review*, 54:1 (October 1948), 155–56.

10. Lorenzo Greene, review of Franklin, *From Slavery to Freedom*, in *Journal of Negro Education*, 17:2 (Spring 1948), 154.

11. Franklin, *From Slavery to Freedom: A History of American Negroes* (New York: Alfred A. Knopf, 1947), 127.

12. Benjamin Quarles, *The Negro in the American Revolution* (Chapel Hill: University of North Carolina Press, 1996), 4–8. This edition offers a new foreword but contains the unrevised text of Quarles's 1961 original.

13. Michael V. Gannon, review of Bennett, *Before the Mayflower*, *Florida Historical Quarterly* 43:2 (October 1964), 197–98; Benjamin Quarles, review of Bennett, *Before the Mayflower*, *American Historical Review*, 68:4 (July 1963), 1078–79.

14. Lerone Bennett Jr., *Before the Mayflower: A History of Black America* (Chicago: Johnson, 1962), 6th ed. (New York: Penguin Books, 1993), 59–61.

15. Benjamin Muse, "Virginia Affairs: PT-As Could Do a Lot for Integration," *Washington Post and Times Herald*, September 26, 1954.

16. Charlotte K. Brookes, "Firm Foundations: A Radio Skit for Negro History Week," *Negro History Bulletin* 17:6 (March 1954), 128–31.

17. Albert Barnett, "Negro History—Taught Only in Jim Crow Schools of the South," *Chicago Defender*, October 13, 1956.

18. Capitol Records did not release the song initially because it was not in line with Cole's usual love ballads and, perhaps, due to its political content. It was released in 2009 as part of a three-song EP honoring the inauguration of President Barack Obama. See "Capitol/EMI Releases Nat King Cole 'Voices of Change, Then & Now' Digital EP Via All Major Digital Service Providers," *International Entertainment News* (online), February 10, 2009, http://internationalentertainmentnews.blogspot.de/2009/02/capitolemi-releases-nat-king-cole.html, accessed February 22, 2017. Cole's lyrics transcribed from "Nat King Cole Night Lights Complete Album Plus 38 Bonus Tracks with New Stereo Sound," *YouTube*, December 27, 2013, at 1:07:35, https://www.youtube.com/watch?v=YAlx2UerHlI, accessed February 20, 2015.

19. Claude Sitton, "Birmingham Gets a Negro Warning," *New York Times*, September 18, 1963.

20. Martin Luther King Jr., *Why We Can't Wait* (New York: Signet Classics 2000), 2–3.

21. A. Philip Randolph, "Three Black Giants," *New York Amsterdam News*, May 15, 1965; Martin Luther King Jr., *Why We Can't Wait* (New York: Signet Classics, 2000), 2–3; "School Decision Freedom Quest's Most Significant Step, Dr. Mays Tells Emancipation Observance, *Atlanta Daily World*, February 13, 1963; Jackie Robinson, "Seeking a Solution," *New York Amsterdam News*, January 5, 1963.

22. Gertrude Wilson, "Misguided Editor," *New York Amsterdam News*, July 14, 1962.

23. Charles Harris Wesley, "Creating and Maintaining an Historical Tradition," *Journal of Negro History*, 49 (January 1964), 30–33.

24. Joseph Moreau, *Schoolbook Nation: Conflicts over American History Textbooks from the Civil War to the Present* (Ann Arbor: University of Michigan Press, 2003), 267–83.

25. "500 Catholic Teachers Get Data on Human Relations Leadership," *Chicago Defender*, March 23, 1963.

26. "Boycott a Thumping Success!" *Chicago Defender*, October 23, 1963; Jeanne Franke, "Racial Pride Stressed in 'Freedom Schools,'" *Chicago Tribune*, October 23, 1963; Gene Roberts, "New Primer Tells History of Negro," *New York Times*, August 15, 1965.

27. Paul Weeks, "Negroes Stage Race March on School Board Hearing," *Los Angeles Times*, June 25, 1963; L. M. Meriwether, "Negro Greats Being Written into Texts," *Los Angeles Sentinel*, July 30, 1964; "D.C. Schools Plan Greater Emphasis on Negro History," *Atlanta Daily World*, January 31, 1963; Moreau, *Schoolbook Nation*, 283–92.

28. "D.C. Schools Plan Greater Emphasis on Negro History," *Atlanta Daily World*, January 31, 1963; Susanna McBee, "Plan to Teach Negro History Here Outlined," *Washington Post*, January 16, 1963; Gerald Grant, "You Can't Just Teach, You Should Mix," *Washington Post*, November 28, 1965.

29. "Scope and contents," *Harris, Middleton A., Collection, 1845–1971*, Amistad Research Center, http://amistadresearchcenter.tulane.edu/archon/index.php?p= accessions/accession&id=406, accessed February 22, 2017; Negro History Associates, *Great Americans Series: The Revolutionary Period, 1770–1790* (filmstrip) (New York: Associates, 1964), 9, 11, 12; *The History of the American Negro* (filmstrip) (New York: McGraw-Hill Text Films, 1965). Text from both filmstrips in the Middleton A. Harris Collection, Manuscripts, Archives, and Rare Books Division, Schomburg Center for Research in Black Culture, New York Public Library; NHA in Box 8, folder 2, McGraw-Hill in Box 8, folder 17.

30. Paul Weeks, "Negroes Stage Race March on School Board Hearing," *Los Angeles Times*, June 25, 1963; "Doctor 'Corrects' Board Member's View of Negroes," *Los Angeles Sentinel*, July 18, 1963; Lerone Bennett, *Before the Mayflower: A History of the Negro in America* (Chicago: Johnson, 1962).

31. L. M. Meriwether, "Negro Greats Being Written into Texts," *Los Angeles Sentinel*, July 30, 1964; "Law Making Negro History Study Mandatory a 'First,'" *Los Angeles Sentinel*, June 17, 1965; Moreau, *Schoolbook Nation*, 291; John Walton Caughey, John Hope Franklin, and Ernest R. May, *Land of the Free: A History of the United States* (New York: Benziger, 1966).

32. "Dr. David S. Muzzey, Historian, Is Dead," *New York Times*, April 15, 1965; Moreau, *Schoolbook Nation*, 287; David Saville Muzzey and Arthur Stanley Link, *Our American Republic* (Boston: Ginn, 1963), 74; Muzzey, *A History of Our Country* (Boston: Ginn, 1941); Muzzey, *Our Country's History* (Boston: Ginn, 1957, 1961); Muzzey and Link, *Our Country's History: Chapter and Semester Tests*, 1st rev. ed. (Boston: Ginn, 1965), 10.

33. Henry F. Graff and John A. Krout, *The Adventure of the American People* (New York: Harcourt, Brace, and World, 1960), 91; Henry F. Graff and John A. Krout, *The Adventure of the American People* (New York: Harcourt, Brace, and World, 1960) 72.

34. Henry F. Graff, *The Free and the Brave*, Annotated Teacher's Edition (Chicago: Rand McNally, 1967), 179.

35. "Black History Focus of New Text," *Chicago Defender*, August 17, 1968; Kathleen Teltsch, "Negroes Say U.S. History Slights Their Heritage," *New York Times*, March 19, 1968.

36. Thomas A. Bailey, "The Mythmakers in American History," *Journal of American History,* 55:1 (June 1968), 6, 17, 14, 7–8; Alan L. Benosky, "Minority Groups and the Teaching of American History," *Social Studies* 62:2 (February 1971), 60–63.

37. Hiller B. Zobel, *The Boston Massacre* (New York: Norton Library, 1970), 303

38. Zobel, *Boston Massacre*, 3–4, 304.

39. Thomas Lask, "Opening Round," *New York Times*, February 28, 1970.

40. Harry Golden, "Only in America: The SCAWDAR," *Chicago Daily Defender*, January 19, 1966; *African American and American Indian Patriots in the Revolutionary War*, ed. Eric G. Grundset (Washington, DC: National Society Daughters of the American Revolution, 2008).

41. "4 Top Business Groups Back Move for Crispus Attucks Day," *Chicago Defender*, March 23, 1963; Ernest R. Rather, "New Holiday" (letter to the editor), *Chicago Defender*, April 4, 1963; "NIA's New Pres. All Out on Rights," *Chicago Defender*, August 26, 1963.

42. "1,000 to Celebrate Crispus Attucks Day," *Chicago Daily Defender*, March 5, 1964; "CIA Committee Plans Crispus Attucks Day," *Chicago Daily Defender*, February 20, 1965; Photo, no title, *Chicago Daily Defender*, March 13, 1965; Photo, no title, *Chicago Daily Defender*, March 16, 1965; "Slate Services in Honor of Martyred Crispus Attucks," *Chicago Daily Defender*, March 4, 1965.

43. "Crispus Attucks and Swahili," *Christian Science Monitor*, February 7, 1968.

44. "Crispus Attucks Will Be Honored by Newark," *New York Amsterdam News*, February 26, 1966; Photo caption, *New York Amsterdam News*, May 27, 1967; Connie Woodruff, "Attucks Parade Hi-lites," *New York Amsterdam News*, March 18, 1967; Connie Woodruff, "Cite Parade Winners at Second Awards Dinner," *New York Amsterdam News*, May 27, 1967.

45. "New Jersey Revised Statutes, 36: 2–1 Crispus Attucks Day," http://law.one-cle.com/new-jersey/title-36/36-2-1.html, accessed February 22, 2017; Doris E. Saunders, "Confetti," *Chicago Daily Defender*, March 12, 1968; Connie Woodruff, "On the Scene . . . in Jersey, *New York Amsterdam News*, February 10, 1968; Connie Woodruff, "Mark 1st Holiday for Afro-Americans," *New York Amsterdam News*, March 9, 1968; "Crispus Attucks Society Plans Second Brotherhood Banquet," *New York Amsterdam News*, October 24, 1970; "Newark School Holiday Set for Negro Patriot," *Los Angeles Times*, March 5, 1968; James R. Dickenson, "In Newark, the Fires of Black Anger Still Smolder," *Los Angeles Sentinel*, May 23, 1968.

46. "Crispus Attucks Day Proposed," *New York Amsterdam News*, April 6, 1968; "Jersey Honors Attucks," *New York Times*, March 5, 1969; "Black Insurance Firms

to Demand Respect for Heroes," *Chicago Daily Defender*, March 17, 1969; "'Black American Day' Is Voted in California," *New York Times*, August 23, 1970; "Bill on Black Holiday Passes," *Los Angeles Times*, August 22, 1970; "200,000 Watch 50,000 March," *New York Amsterdam News*, April 18, 1970;

47. Connie Woodruff, "150,000 Watched as 50,000 Marched in Newark's Parade," *New York Amsterdam News*, April 17, 1071; "Leroi Jones Grand Marshall for Attucks-King Parade," *New York Amsterdam News*, March 27, 1971; Connie Woodruff, "On the Scene . . . in Jersey," *New York Amsterdam News*, April 3, 1971;

48. Kevin Mumford, *Newark: A History of Race, Rights, and Riots in America* (New York: New York University Press, 2007), 161–62;

49. James L. Hicks, "The Story of a Need," *New York Amsterdam News*, October 17, 1964; Loften Mitchell, "Playwright Discusses the Death of Malcolm X," *New York Amsterdam News*, February 27, 1965;

50. "House of Knowledge to Honor Three," *Chicago Defender*, March 2, 1963; "H of K Talks to Center around Jobs for Jobless," *Chicago Defender*, June 13, 1964; Daryl Michael Scott, "The Origins of Black History Month," *Association for the Study of African American Life and History*, https://asalh100.org/origins-of-black-history-month/, accessed February 22, 2017.

51. C. Gerald Fraser, "Powell Says '2d Civil War' Began in Los Angeles," *New York Times*, January 10, 1968.

52. Rev. Jesse Jackson, "The Rev. Jesse Jackson Tells What Blacks of Chicago Want," *Chicago Tribune*, July 19, 1970.

53. Joanne Leedom, "Boston Massacre Echoes in Confrontations 200 Years Later," *Christian Science Monitor*, March 5, 1970. The so-called Chicago Seven had been charged with various conspiracy and rioting charges for their protests at the 1968 Democratic National Convention, but the verdicts in February 1970 acquitted them on most counts. Several were convicted of crossing state lines to incite a riot, but that decision was overturned on appeal in 1972.

54. Stanley G. Robertson, "L.A. Confidential: Faceless Face in the Crowd of History," *Los Angeles Sentinel*, April 25, 1968.

55. Jackie Robinson, "Seeking a Solution," *New York Amsterdam News*, January 5, 1963; "Carmichael May Visit Here Soon," *Chicago Daily Defender*, September 20, 1966.

56. Stokely Carmichael, "Speech Given at Garfield High School, Seattle, Washington, April 19, 1967" (transcript), *University of Washington Instructional Resource Center*, http://courses.washington.edu/spcmu/carmichael/transcript.htm, accessed October 20, 2014.

57. "Editorial: The Boston Massacre and Crispus Attucks," *Negro History Bulletin*, 33:3 (March 1970), 57.

58. Joan Bacchus, Tom Feelings, Ezra Jackson, Francis Taylor, and Bertram Fitzgerald, *Crispus Attucks and the Minutemen* (New York: Fitzgerald, 1967), unpaginated; "Bertram Fitzgerald," *Museum of Uncut Funk* (website), http://museumofuncut-funk.com/2009/05/27/bertram-fitzgerald/, accessed November 15, 2014.

59. "Bertram Fitzgerald"; Tom Feelings, *Black Pilgrimage* (New York: Lothrop, Lee & Shepard, 1972), 12; Alfred E. Cain, *Negro Heritage Reader for Young People* (Yonkers, NY: Educational Heritage, 1965). The same story would appear again in 1991 in Feelings's original format of a young black boy who travels back into time by falling asleep while reading about black history. See Tom Feelings, *Tommy Traveler in the World of Black History* (New York: Black Butterfly Children's Books, 1991).

60. *Crispus Attucks and the Minutemen*, n.p.

61. *Noble Heritage* 1:1 (New York, 1968).

62. Michael William Doyle, "Staging the Revolution: Guerilla Theatre as a Counter-cultural Practice, 1965–68," in *Imagine Nation: The American Counterculture of the 1960s and 1970s* (New York: Routledge, 2002), 71–98; Richard F. Shepherd, "Mr. Interlocutor, Updated, Arrives: 'Minstrel Show' from Coast Slashes at Racial Hypocrisy," *New York Times*, October 21, 1966.

63. Text reprinted in Susan Vaneta Smith, ed., *The San Francisco Mime Troupe Reader* (Ann Arbor: University of Michigan Press, 2005), 35–36. On minstrelsy and its racial stereotypes, see Robert Toll, *Blacking Up: Minstrelsy in Nineteenth Century America* (New York: Oxford University Press, 1974)); Eric Lott, *Love and Theft: Blackface Minstrelsy and the American Working Class* (New York: Oxford University Press, 1993); and W. T. Lhamon Jr., *Jump Jim Crow: Lost Plays, Lyrics, and Street Prose of the First Atlantic Popular Culture* (Cambridge, MA: Harvard University Press, 2003).

64. Eloise Crosby Culver, *Great American Negroes in Verse, 1723–1965* (Washington, DC: Associated Publishers, 1966), 6, 11; "Crispus Attucks," *Black American Heroes of the American Revolution, 1775–1783* (New York: National Association for the Advancement of Colored People, 1969), 7;

65. Edmund F. Curley, *Crispus Attucks: The First to Die* (Philadelphia: Dorrance, 1973), Preface (n.p.), 154–56; "New Books from Dorrance," *Chicago Tribune*, February 24, 1974.

66. "Editorial: The Boston Massacre and Crispus Attucks," *Negro History Bulletin*, 34:3 (March 1971), 52–54; George Washington Williams, *History of the Negro Race in America, 1619–1880*, Vol. 1 (New York: G. P. Putnam and Sons, 1883); 330–33; Esther Forbes, *Paul Revere and the World He Lived In* (New York: Houghton Mifflin, 1942); David Hackett Fischer, *Paul Revere's Ride* (New York: Oxford University Press, 1994), 338–39.

67. Lois Spear, "Negroes in Pre-Civil War History: New Myths in the Making," *Social Studies* 65:7 (December 1974), 310; Bailey, "The Mythmakers in American History."

68. Hazel Garland, "Video Vignettes," *New Pittsburgh Courier*, July 25, 1970; n.t., *Los Angeles Sentinel*, August 16, 1962; Jim Tilmon, "Listen, a Man's Home Is His Castle, Right?" *Chicago Tribune*, May 25, 1969; Vine Deloria Jr., "Grunts to Paternalism: Stereotyping the Indian," *Chicago Tribune*, March 7, 1971; Bill Belton, "The Indian Heritage of Crispus Attucks," *Negro History Bulletin* 35:7

(November 1972), 149–52; Stanley G. Robertson, "L.A. Confidential: Faceless Face in the Crowd of History," *Los Angeles Sentinel*, April 25, 1968.

CHAPTER 8

1. Alice Walker, *Meridian* (New York: Harcourt Brace Jovanovich, 1976), 193–94
2. "The Whispering Bells of Freedom," *Philadelphia Public Art*, http://www.philart. net/art/The_Whispering_Bells_of_Freedom/430.html, accessed August 12, 2015.
3. Karen F. Stein, "*Meridian*: Alice Walker's Critique of Revolution," *African American Review* 20:1/2 (Spring–Summer 1986), 138.
4. Alistair Cooke, "A Warning about the Bicentennial 'Orgy,'" *Los Angeles Times*, April 23, 1975.
5. Barry Schwartz, *Abraham Lincoln in the Post-Heroic Era: History and Memory in the Late Twentieth Century* (Chicago: University of Chicago Press, 2008).
6. *Swing Out, Sweet Land*, November 29, 1970, https://www.youtube.com/ watch?v=3L3XxI6MK8Y, accessed November 26, 2014.
7. *Swing Out, Sweet Land*; "Thursday Highlights," *Washington Post*, April 4, 1971.
8. The ABC statement was presented at a 1972 Senate subcommittee hearing on the current state of planning by the American Revolution Bicentennial Commission (ARBC), which was later reconstituted as the American Revolution Bicentennial Administration (ARBA). Vincent and Robert DeForrest, testimony before the *Hearings before the Subcommittee on Federal Charters, Holidays, and Celebrations* (1972), quoted in Tammy S. Gordon, *The Spirit of 1976: Commerce, Community, and the Politics of Commemoration* (Amherst: University of Massachusetts Press, 2013), 2.
9. People's Bicentennial Commission, *America's Birthday: A Planning and Activity Guide for Citizen's Participation during the Bicentennial Years* (New York: Simon and Schuster, 1974), 9.
10. Gordon, *The Spirit of 1976*, 57.
11. "Should Blacks Celebrate the Bicentennial," *Ebony* 30:10 (August 1975), 35–42; Benjamin Quarles, "Black Americans and the Bicentennial," *Negro History Bulletin* 38:4 (Spring 1975), 387; H. Carl McCall, "Blacks and the Bicentennial," *New York Amsterdam News*, December 3, 1975;
12. "Letters to the Editor," *Ebony* 30:12 (October 1975), 12, 15, 18.
13. "The Bicentennial Blues," *Ebony* 31:8 (June 1976), 152–53. See also Maureen McAleer, "The Legacy of Crispus Attucks in Boston in the Twentieth Century: How Activists, Politicians, and the Public Have Remembered, Commemorated, and Used His Name," master's thesis, Harvard University, 2014, esp. 99–108; and Louis Masur, *The Soiling of Old Glory: The Story of a Photograph that Shocked America* (New York: Bloomsbury US, 2008).
14. McAleer, "The Legacy of Crispus Attucks," 103–4; J. Anthony Lukas, "Who Owns 1776?: The Battle in Boston for Control of the American Past," *New York Times*,

May 18, 1975; Ben F. Carruthers, "Boston Lays Out Black Heritage Walking Trail," *Chicago Tribune*, April 6, 1975.

15. F. R. Bruns Jr., "A Salute to the American Revolution Bicentennial from Grenada," *Washington Post*, March 16, 1975.

16. Leonard W. Stark, "Coin Collector," *Chicago Tribune*, October 5, 1969; Dorothy Budd Bartle, "Black Heroes in History: Medals Honoring Black Americans," *The Museum* (Newark, NJ), 23:4 (1971), 1–20; ARBA "Crispus Attucks, Black American Patriot" button in author's personal collection.

17. Gordon, *The Spirit of 1976*, 4–6.

18. Lerone Bennett Jr., "Remarks at ASALH Sixtieth Anniversary Meeting," *Negro History Bulletin* 39:2 (February 1, 1976), 524.

19. "Historical Calendar Cites Achievements," *Los Angeles Sentinel*, February 12, 1976; Lesley Jones, "School Happenings," *New York Amsterdam News*, November 28, 1970; "The Black Bicentennial Calendar: Two Centuries of Black History in One Year," advertisement, *Jet* 49:11 (December 4, 1976), 28–29; "The Black Bicentennial Calendar: Two Centuries of Black History in One Year," advertisement, *Ebony* 31:2 (December 1975), 111.

20. Advertisements for United (102), American (119), Amtrak (13), and Greyhound (8) in *Ebony* 30:10 (August 1975); Valvoline in *Ebony* 31:6 (April 1976), 81; Jim Beam advertisement in *Ebony* 31:8 (June 1976), 22; Ametco T-shirts in *Ebony* 31:6 (April 1976), 52, as cited in Gordon, *Spirit of 1976*, 58. Identical or similar ads appeared in most issues of *Ebony* and *Jet* in 1975 and 1976.

21. West Virginia's practice and the House of Knowledge events are mentioned by the Association for the Study of African American Life and History in "The Origins of Black History Month," https://asalh100.org/origins-of-black-history-month/, accessed February 22, 2017. See also, "1,700 Launch Freedom Period Here," *Chicago Daily Defender*, July 9, 1964.

22. "Discovering a Black Past," *Atlanta Daily World*, February 19, 1971; "Black History Month," *Wikipedia*, http://en.wikipedia.org/wiki/Black_History_Month, accessed December 17, 2014.

23. "Black History Month Is Supported by Ford," *New York Times*, February 11, 1976; "Excerpted Remarks of President Reagan," *Negro History Bulletin* 47:1 (January/March 1984), 9.

24. "Black History Month Is Supported by Ford," *New York Times*, February 11, 1976.

25. Stevie Wonder, "Black Man," *Songs in the Key of Life* (2xLP), T13-340C2 Tamla 1976; John Doremus, *The Spirit of '76*, SS-24406-01, self-released, 1972; Kenan Heise, "John Doremus, 63, a Top Disc Jockey for Decades" (online obituary), *Chicago Tribune*, July 8, 1995, http://articles.chicagotribune.com/1995-07-08/news/9507080088_1_disc-jockey-radio-united-airlines, accessed February 21, 2015.

26. Stevie Wonder, "Black Man," *Songs in the Key of Life* (2xLP), T13-340C2 Tamla 1976; John Doremus, *The Spirit of '76*, SS-24406-01, self-released, 1972; Kenan

Heise, "John Doremus, 63, a Top Disc Jockey for Decades"; Charlie King and Martha Leader, *Steppin' Out*, FF 492, Flying Fish, 1988.

27. Ricky Ford, "Ode to Crispus Attucks," *Manhattan Blues*, 9036, Candid, 1989; The Bruce Smith Band, "Crispus Attucks," *Get the Picture*, digital release, Bandcamp, 1996, http://thebrucesmithband.bandcamp.com/album/get-the-picture, accessed February 21, 2015; "Crispus Attucks," *Instinct and Music* (blog), March 3, 2011, http://instinctandmusic.blogspot.com/2011/03/crispus-attucks.html, accessed May 3, 2015.

28. "Movie Planned on Life of Hero Crispus Attucks," *Jet*, 44:26 (September 20, 1973), 55; "Guide to the Robert C. Frankenberg Papers," *Northwest Digital Archives (NWDA)*, http://nwda.orbiscascade.org/ark:/80444/xv30113, accessed February 7, 2015; John Cocchi, "Professional Pictures Int'l Charts 12 Properties for Production," *Box Office*, July 1, 1974, 20. Professional Pictures' former president, Elliott Geisinger, confirmed that the film was never made (telephone interview with the author, September 13, 2016).

29. Weston, née Marvin Herskowitz, had been the "Brylcreem man" in television commercials from 1954 to 1962 and also had roles in several daytime soap operas. After a bout with Bell's palsy ended his acting career in the early 1970s, he turned to writing and teaching. See "Interview with Marvin Herskowitz aka Mark Weston," *Whobub*, http://www.whohub.com/marvinherskowitz, accessed February 7, 2015; "Movie Planned on Life of Hero Crispus Attucks," *Jet*, 44:26 (September 20, 1973), 55; "Guide to the Robert C. Frankenberg Papers," *Northwest Digital Archives (NWDA)*, http://nwda.orbiscascade.org/ark:/80444/xv30113, accessed February 7, 2015.

30. Robert Weston, "Crispus" (1987), Playscript Collection, Box 7, Folder MG43, Manuscripts, Archives and Rare Books Division, Schomburg Center for Research in Black Culture, New York Public Library, quoted at 8, 44, 49, 60, 66, 70.

31. "A Lantern for Crispus," Willie Thomas Harris Playscripts, 1951–1984, Box 1, Folder 9, Manuscripts, Archives and Rare Books Division, Schomburg Center for Research in Black Culture, New York Public Library, quoted at 5, 6, 8, 13, 44.

32. Letter, Willie Thomas Harris to Lucy Kroll, agency, October 24, 1985, in Willie Thomas Harris Playscripts, 1951–1984, Box 1, Folder 9, Manuscripts, Archives and Rare Books Division, Schomburg Center for Research in Black Culture, New York Public Library; "Overview—Willie Thomas Harris Playscripts, 1951–1984," New York Public Library Archives and Manuscripts (online), http://archives.nypl.org/scm/20824, accessed February 9, 2015.

33. Sidney Kaplan, *The Black Presence in the Era of the American Revolution, 1770–1800* (Greenwich, CT: New York Graphic Society, 1973), 7–11. Jefferson's quote, from a November 13, 1787, letter to William Smith was, "The tree of liberty must be refreshed from time to time with the blood of patriots and tyrants." See "Thomas Jefferson: Establishing a Federal Republic," *Library of Congress Thomas Jefferson Exhibit* (online), http://www.loc.gov/exhibits/jefferson/jefffed.html, accessed April 7, 2015.

34. Burke Davis, *Black Heroes of the American Revolution* (New York: Harcourt Brace Jovanovich, 1976), 33–40. Other juvenile titles on African American heroes from the post-bicentennial era, with far more limited distribution, include Ann Donegan Johnson, *The Value of Helping: The Story of Harriet Tubman* (La Jolla, CA: Value Communications, 1979); Ida R. Bellegarde, *Phillis Wheatley* (Pine Bluff, AR: Bell Enterprises, 1984); Ida R. Bellegarde, *Mary McLeod Bethune; James Weldon Johnson* (Pine Bluff, AR: Bell Enterprises, 1979); Karlton Stewart, *Black History and Achievement in America: An Overview of the Black Struggle: Its Heroes and Heroines* (Phoenix: Phoenix Books, 1982).

35. Alex Haley, *Roots: The Saga of an American Family* (Garden City, NY: Doubleday, 1976); *Roots* (Burbank, CA: Warner Home Video, 2007, 1977); Matthew Frye Jacobson, *Roots Too: White Ethnic Revival in Post–Civil Rights America* (Cambridge, MA: Harvard University Press, 2006), 42–44.

36. Eugene Cain, *The Black Hero: Teaching Guide* (New York: Scholastic Book Services, 1970), 3, 46–47, 50, 72, 96, 106; Alma Murray and Robert Thomas, eds., *The Black Hero* (New York: Scholastic Book Services, 1970); *A Supplement to Portraits: The Literature of Minorities*, LACO No. 131, June 1972 (Los Angeles: County Superintendent of Schools, 1972), 47–48.

37. Gordon, *Spirit of 1976*, 146.

38. Ella D. Lewis Douglas, "A Bicentennial Review of the Black Contribution to American History," *Social Studies* 67:4 (July/August 1976), 154.

39. James A. Banks, "The Social Studies, Ethnic Diversity, and Social Change," *Elementary School Journal* 87:5 (May 1987), 531–43, quoted at 531, 533, 534, 538.

40. See, for example, Gary B. Nash, Charlotte Crabtree, and Ross E. Dunn, *History on Trial: Culture Wars and the Teaching of the Past* (New York: Alfred A. Knopf, 1997) and Lynne Cheney, "The End of History," *Wall Street Journal*, October 20, 1994.

41. Allen Smith, "Make-up of America—Textbook Style," *Social Studies* 78:5 (September/October 1987), 230–31, 229.

42. Ellen Swartz, "Emancipatory Narratives: Rewriting the Master Script in the School Curriculum," *Journal of Negro Education* 61:3 (Summer 1992), 341.

43. Swartz, "Emancipatory Narratives," 343–44. Swartz identifies the textbook in question as Beverly Jeanne Armento et al., *America Will Be* (Boston: Houghton Mifflin, 1991), with the quoted Attucks passage on 250.

44. Swartz, "Emancipatory Narratives," 354.

45. The textbooks examined are Joseph R. Conlin, *Our Land, Our Time* (San Diego: Coronado, 1985); Donald A. Ritchie, *Heritage of Freedom: History of the United States* (New York: Macmillan, 1985); Ernest R. May, *A Proud Nation* (Evanston, IL: McDougal, Littell, 1985); L. Joanne Buggey et al., *America! America!* (Glenview, IL: Scott, Foresman, 1985); David C. King, *United States History* (Menlo Park, CA: Addison-Wesley, 1986); Pauline Maier, *The American People: A History* (Lexington, MA: D. C. Heath, 1986); Glenn M. Linden, *Legacy of Freedom: A History of the United States*, Vol. 1 (New York: Laidlaw Brothers/

Doubleday, 1986); Diane Hart and David Baker, *Spirit of Liberty: An American History* (Menlo Park, CA: Addison-Wesley, 1987); John Patrick and Carol Berkin, *History of the American Nation* (New York: Macmillan, 1987); Winthrop D. Jordan et al., *Americans: A History of a People and a Nation* (Evanston, IL: McDougal, Little, 1988); Richard C. Brown and Herbert J. Bass, *One Flag, One Land* (Morristown, NJ: Silver, Burdett & Ginn, 1990); Roger LaRaus et al., *Challenge of Freedom* (Mission Hills, CA: Glencoe/McGraw-Hill, 1990); Daniel J. Boorston and Brooks Mather Kelley, *A History of the United States* (Englewood Cliffs, NJ: Prentice-Hall, 1990); Lewis Paul Todd and Merle Curti, *Triumph of the American Nation* (Orlando, FL: Harcourt Brace Jovanovich, 1990); James West Davidson and Mark Lytle, *The United States: A History of the Republic* (Englewood Cliffs, NJ: Prentice-Hall, 1990); Carlton Jackson and Vito Perrone, *Two Centuries of Progress* (Mission Hills, CA: Glencoe/McGraw-Hill, 1991); Henry N. Drewry and Thomas H. O'Connor, *America Is* (New York: Glencoe/McGraw-Hill, 1995); James West Davidson and Michael B. Stoff, *The American Nation* (Englewood Cliffs, NJ: Prentice-Hall, 1995); Thomas V. DiBacco et al., *History of the United States* (Evanston, IL: McDougal Littell/Houghton Mifflin, 1997); Andrew Cayton et al., *America: Pathways to the Present* (Needham, MA: Prentice-Hall, 1998).

46. "major conflict": Linden, *Legacy of Freedom* (1986), 140; "a major role": Davidson and Stoff, *The American Nation* (1995), 148; "drew little reaction": Drewry and O'Connor, *America Is* (1995), 129; "no massive protests": Conlin, *Our Land, Our Time* (1985), 111.

47. Ritchie, *Heritage of Freedom* (1985), 86; Todd and Curti, *Triumph of the American Nation* (1990), 113.

48. "leader . . . first to die": Boorstin and Kelley, *A History of the United States* (1990), 74; "has been called": Brown and Bass, *One Flag, One Land* (1990), 170; "opinion of many": LaRaus et al., *Challenge of Freedom* (1990), 140.

49. "tall man," "West Indies," "well-known," "courage," "terrify any person": Jordan et al., *Americans* (1988), 118; "tall": Maier, *The American People* (1986), 154; "giant stature": Boorstin and Kelley, *History of the United States* (1990), 74; "colonist": LaRaus et al., *Challenge of Freedom* (1990), 140; "active in the Sons of Liberty": Davidson and Lytle, *The United States* (1990), 102.

50. Todd and Curti, *Triumph of the American Nation* (1990), 114.

51. The Attucks doll ornament was created by artist Lawan Angelique, at the invitation of the White House, www.lawanangelique.com/whitehouse.html, accessed August 14, 2007.

52. Wayne Smith, "United States Mint to Sell Commemorative Coins to Honor Black Patriots," *New York Voice* (Harlem, USA), February 25, 1998; "Million Dollar Check to Be Presented to the Black Patriots Foundation; Earnings from Crispus Attucks Commemorative Coin," *Westside Gazette* (Ft. Lauderdale, FL), October 22, 2003.

53. Kristin Haas, *Sacrificing Soldiers on the National Mall* (Berkeley: University of California Press, 2013), 59–95; Smith, "United States Mint to Sell Commemorative Coins to Honor Black Patriots"; "Million Dollar Check to Be Presented to the Black Patriots Foundation; Earnings from Crispus Attucks Commemorative Coin"; James Brooke, "For Black Memorial, It's Build or Bust," *New York Times*, August 4, 1996; "Group Has Less than a Month to Raise $9.5 Million for Black Patriots Memorial, *Jet* 90:21 (October 7, 1996), 18; Reed Abelson, "Backers Struggle to Invigorate Black Patriots Memorial Plan," *New York Times*, February 28, 2000.

54. Haas, *Sacrificing Soldiers on the National Mall*, 59; Dwight, quoted in Haas, 81. Information on the status of the new memorial project can be found at the National Liberty Memorial website, http://libertyfunddc.com/, accessed April 23, 2015.

CHAPTER 9

1. Allison Dorsey, "Black History Is American History: Teaching African-American History in the Twenty-First Century," *Journal of American History* 93:4 (March 2007), 1171–72.

2. The textbooks examined are Sterling Stuckey and Linda Kerrigan Salvucci, *Call to Freedom* (Austn, TX: Holt, Rinehart and Winston, 2003); James West Davidson and Michael B. Stoff, *The American Nation* (Upper Saddle River, NJ: Pearson/Prentice-Hall, 2005); Andrew Cayton et al., *America: Pathways to the Present* (Needham, MA: Pearson/Prentice-Hall, 2005); Daniel J. Boorstin and Brooks Mather Kelley, *A History of the United States* (Boston, MA: Pearson/Prentice-Hall, 2007); William Deverell and Deborah Gray White, *United States History: Beginnings to 1877* (Orlando, FL: Holt, Rinehart and Winston, 2007); Joyce Appleby et al., *The American Journey* (New York: Glencoe/McGraw-Hill, 2009); Joyce Appleby et al., *The American Vision* (New York: Glencoe/McGraw-Hill, 2009).

3. Appleby et al., *American Journey* (2009), 127; Appleby et al., *American Vision* (2010), 61.

4. Mitchell L. Bush Jr., "Crispus Attucks's Heritage," letter to the editor, *Washington Post*, October 2, 1995; "Warriors," *Praying Indians of Natick* website, http://natick-prayingindians.org/warriors.html, accessed January 7, 2015; Michele Morgan Bolton, "Two Towns Claim Crispus Attucks," *Boston Globe*, February 24, 2008, on *HighBeam Research*, https://www.highbeam.com/doc/1P2-15408955.html, accessed February 22, 2017.

5. Deverell and White, *United States History* (2007), 101.

6. Patricia Bradley, *Slavery, Propaganda, and the American Revolution* (Oxford: University Press of Mississippi, 1998), 55–56; Patricia Bradley, *Slavery, Propaganda, and the American Revolution*, 59–61.

7. James Oliver Horton and Lois E. Horton, *In Hope of Liberty: Culture, Community, and Protest among Northern Free Blacks, 1700–1860* (New York: Oxford University Press, 1997), 52–54. The main problem with the description of the massacre is the

authors' reliance on problematic nineteenth-century sources like William Nell and Hewes's *Traits of the Tea Party*. The source cited for the "letter" to Hutchinson is a 1968 reprint of George Washington Williams's 1883 *History of the Negro Race*. As discussed in Chapter 4, Williams made the same error in ascribing Adams's words to Attucks. For another example of historians too readily accepting their sources' accounts at face value, see Mitch Kachun, "Antebellum African Americans, Public Commemoration, and the Haitian Revolution: A Problem of Historical Mythmaking," *Journal of the Early Republic* 26:2 (Summer 2006), 249–74.

8. Peter Linebaugh and Marcus Rediker, *The Many-Headed Hydra: Sailors, Slaves, Commoners, and the Hidden History of the Revolutionary Atlantic* (Boston: Beacon Press, 2000). All quotations are taken from Marcus Rediker, "The Revenge of Crispus Attucks; or, the Atlantic Challenge to American Labor History," *Labor Studies in Working Class History of the Americas* 1:4 (2004), 35–45, quoted at 38.

9. James A. Banks and Cherry A. Banks, *March toward Freedom* (Belmont, CA: Fearon-Pitman, 1978), 21.

10. *African Americans in U.S. History, through 1877*, Vol. 1 (Englewood Cliffs, NJ: Globe Books, 1989), 18. The authors seem to have conflated Saint-Gaudens's Boston Common monument to Robert Gould Shaw and the Massachusetts 54th USCT and Robert Kraus's Attucks or Boston Massacre monument. The latter is not a "statue" of Attucks, though it lists his name and one might try to find his likeness in the bas-relief, based on Revere's engraving, which graces one side of the plinth.

11. *The African American Experience: A History* (Englewood Cliffs, NJ: Globe Book, 1992), 18.

12. John Hope Franklin and Alfred A. Moss Jr., *From Slavery to Freedom: A History of African Americans* (Boston: McGraw-Hill, 2000), 79, 81–82. Salem and Poor indeed did participate in the Battle of Bunker Hill in 1775. An odd quirk of the 2000 edition is the small image of the Revere engraving on the chapter title page, whose caption indicates that it depicts not the Boston Massacre but "the Battle of Bunker Hill, where Crispus Attucks lost his life and where such well known blacks as Peter Salem and Salem Poor fought."

13. Unlike earlier editions of *From Slavery to Freedom* or Lerone Bennett's *Before the Mayflower*, many of these new texts contained extensive illustrations, maps, graphs, and tables; chapter reviews; test banks; study guides; multimedia supplements; and other typical accoutrements of the textbook genre. Over the years, Franklin's *From Slavery to Freedom* did begin to be marketed explicitly as a textbook, with the accompanying study guides, test banks, and other supplementary materials. The book's transition from monograph to textbook was complete by 1994, when textbook publisher McGraw-Hill replaced trade publisher Knopf, whose last edition of the book had appeared in 1988.

14. James Oliver Horton and Lois E. Horton, *Hard Road to Freedom: The Story of African America* (New Brunswick, NJ: Rutgers University Press, 2000), 59–62.

15. Darlene Clark Hine et al., *The African-American Odyssey* (Upper Saddle River, NJ: Prentice-Hall, 2000), 74.

16. Joe William Trotter, *The African American Experience* (Boston: Houghton Mifflin, 2001), 106.

17. Clayborne Carson et al., *The Struggle for Freedom: A History of African Americans* (New York: Pearson-Longman, 2007), 104.

18. Nell Irvin Painter, *Creating African Americans: African American History and Its Meanings, 1619 to the Present* (New York: Oxford University Press, 2006), 55, 64–65, 437.

19. Thomas C. Holt, *Children of Fire: A History of African Americans* (New York: Hill and Wang, 2010).

20. Holt, *Children of Fire*, xvi.

21. For example, Michael Lee Lanning, *The African American Soldier: From Crispus Attucks to Colin Powell* (Secaucus, NJ: Citadel, 1997); Robert Edgerton, *Hidden Heroism: Black Soldiers and America's Wars* (Boulder, CO: Westview Press, 2002), cited at 16; Catherine Clinton, *The Black Soldier: 1492 to the Present* (New York: Houghton Mifflin, 2000); Clinton Cox, *Come All You Brave Soldiers: Blacks in the Revolutionary War* (New York: Scholastic Books, 1999); Douglas R. Egerton, *Death or Liberty: African Americans and Revolutionary America* (New York: Oxford University Press, 2009), cited at 55–56.

22. Kareem Abdul-Jabbar, *Black Profiles in Courage: A Legacy of African-American Achievement* (New York: Perennial, 2000), xx–xxii.

23. Abdul-Jabbar, *Black Profiles in Courage*, 38.

24. Abdul-Jabbar, *Black Profiles in Courage*, 38–47. Bennett is the only other account that has Attucks leading the attack on Murray's Barracks. No witnesses at the soldiers' trial placed Attucks in that mob, though John Adams did intimate it in his closing arguments. See "Rex v. Preston; Rex v. Wemms," in *The Adams Papers Digital Edition*, ed. C. James Taylor (Charlottesville: University of Virginia Press, Rotunda, 2008), http://www.upress.virginia.edu/content/adams-papers-digital-edition, accessed February 22, 2017.

25. Abdul-Jabbar, *Black Profiles in Courage*, 44–47.

26. George Washington quote: Columbus Salley, *The Black 100: A Ranking of the Most Influential African-Americans, Past and Present* (New York: Citadel Press, 1998), 67; Catherine Reef, *Black Fighting Men: A Proud History* (New York: Twenty-First Century Books, 1994). Christopher Snyder quote: Claud Anderson and Brant Anderson, *More Dirty Little Secrets about Black History, Its Heroes and Other Troublemakers*, Vol. II (Bethesda, MD: PowerNomics, 2006). Other texts reviewed include Jim Haskins, *One More River to Cross: The Stories of Twelve Black Americans* (New York: Scholastic, 1992); Kathryn I Bel Monte, *African-American Heroes and Heroines: 150 True Stories of African-American Heroism* (Hollywood, FL: Lifetime Books, 1998); Anne Beier, *Crispus Attucks: Hero of the Boston Massacre* (New York: Rosen, 2003); Monica Rausch, *Crispus Attucks* (Milwaukee,

WI: Weekly Reader Early Learning Library, 2007); Joanne Mattern, *The Cost of Freedom: Crispus Attucks and the Boston Massacre* (New York: Rosen, 2007).

27. Introductory comments by Geoffrey Scheurman, preceding Joy Hakim, "Choosing Five Americans Who Got It Right, or History for Young Minds," *OAH Magazine of History* 20:4 (July 2006), 12; Joy Hakim, *A History of US: From Colonies to Country, 1735-1791*, 3rd ed. (New York: Oxford University Press, 2003), 63–64.

28. *Kirkus Reviews* 61 (December 1, 1993), 1528; *Booklist* 90 (January 15, 1994, 925; Ann Rinaldi, *The Fifth of March: A Story of the Boston Massacre* (San Diego: Gulliver/ Harcourt Brace, 1993), ix.

29. Rinaldi, *The Fifth of March*, 91–94.

30. Rinaldi, *The Fifth of March*, 200, 205–7, 212.

31. Rinaldi, *The Fifth of March*, 323–28.

32. Rinaldi, *The Fifth of March*, 323–28. Some reviewers have found fault with Rinaldi's presentation of minorities. Critics of a 1999 novel about the Carlisle Indian School in the late nineteenth century claim she "relied on stereotyped images of Native Americans." A review of a 2007 novel about slavery and the underground railroad found "distressing" Rinaldi's "perfunctory treatment of the black characters, who are poorly developed and at times marked by stereotypical traits." The treatment of one black character in particular "casts the novel in an irritatingly paternalistic light." See Rinaldi's *My Heart Is on the Ground: The Diary of Nannie Rose, a Sioux Girl* (New York: Scholastic, 1999) discussed in Jeanne Blain McGlinn, *Ann Rinaldi: Historian and Storyteller* (Lanham, MD: Scarecrow Press, 2000), 17, and Rinaldi's *The Ever-After Bird* (Orlando, FL: Harcourt, 2007) discussed in Bruno Navasky, "Freedom Train," review essay, *New York Times Book Review* November 11, 2007), 42.

33. Rush Limbaugh, *Rush Revere and the First Patriots: Time Travel Adventures with Great Americans* (New York: Threshold Editions, 2014), 159–61.

34. Nas, "You Can't Stop Us Now," *Untitled* (2xLP), B0011505-01, Def Jam Columbia, 2008; Gezus Zaire, "Hip-Hop 2008: A Salute to the Veterans," *Cleveland Call & Post*, December 31, 2008, C8; Shaheem Reid, "Nas Previews Controversial Album for MTV News: 'I'm here to rap about what I feel,'" *MTV News*, May 13, 2008, http://www.mtv.com/news/1587428/nas-previews-controversial-album-for-mtv-news-im-here-to-rap-about-what-i-feel/, accessed February 20, 2015; Prophetix, "Crispus Attucks," *High Risk*, Asylum Entertainment, 2002.

35. David Nicholson, "Hailstork Concerto Debuts," *Daily Press* (Norfolk), November 12, 2005; "P," *The Virginia-Pilot* (Norfolk), December 8, 2011; Malcolm Venable, "In Memory of Slain American Patriot Crispus Attucks a New Cantata Is to Be Performed Saturday at the Glorious Attucks Theatre, Named for Him, Written for the Occasion by Man of the Arts Dr. Adolphus Hailstork," *Virginia-Pilot*, October 20, 2005.

36. Common, *The Dreamer, The Believer* (Warner Brothers 2011); Andy Gill, "Album: Common, The Dreamer/The Believer," *Independent*, December 16,

2011, http://www.independent.co.uk/arts-entertainment/music/reviews/album-common-the-dreamerthe-believer-warner-bros-6277921.html, accessed May 7, 2016.

37. "Crispus Attucks lyrics," *Genius*, http://genius.com/Merc-versus-crispus-attucks-lyrics, accessed February 20, 2015; Merc Versus Facebook page, https://www.facebook.com/mercversus7, accessed February 20, 2015.

38. Ice Cube, "It Was a Good Day," Music Video, *YouTube*, https://www.youtube.com/watch?v=h4UqMyldS7Q, accessed February 22, 2017; "Crispus Attucks 'Today Was a Good Day,' with Wayne Brady, JB Smoove & Michael Kenneth Williams," *Funny or Die*, http://www.funnyordie.com/videos/bc018e0780/crispus-attucks-today-was-a-good-day-with-wayne-brady-jb-smoove-michael-kenneth-williams, accessed February 21, 2015.

39. Website for *Liberty!*, http://www.pbs.org/ktca/liberty/, accessed February 23, 2015; *Liberty! The American Revolution*, episode 1: "The Reluctant Revolutionaries, 1763–1774" (Alexandria, VA: PBS DVD Video, 1997); *The Revolution*, episode 1: "Boston Bloody Boston," Steven Strept, producer (New York: A&E Television Network, 2006).

40. *John Adams*, DVD, produced by David Coatesworth and Steven Shareshian (New York: HBO Films, 2008); "Why the Dramatic License in 'Sons of Liberty' is a Problem," *Past in the Present*, January 29, 2015, https://pastinthepresent.wordpress.com/2015/01/29/why-the-dramatic-license-in-sons-of-liberty-is-a-problem/, accessed February 22, 2017; *Lizzy McGuire*, Disney Channel, season 2, episode 26, "A Gordo Story," aired February 28, 2003, https://www.youtube.com/watch?v=3g-mh9py6rLw, accessed February 22, 2017; *30 Rock*, National Broadcasting Company, "Winter Madness," season 4, episode 11, http://en.wikipedia.org/wiki/Winter_Madness#Cultural_references, accessed February 24, 2015.

41. "United We Stand," *Liberty's Kids*, first aired on PBS stations September 4, 2002; *Liberty's Kids: The Complete Series* (Los Angeles, CA: Shout Factory, 2002).

42. *Marvel's Luke Cage*, Season 1, Episode 2, "Code of the Streets," *Netflix*, Aired September 30, 2016.

43. Jeremy Fuster, "'Luke Cage': The True Story behind Luke's Hero, Crispus Attucks," *The Wrap*, October 1, 2016, http://www.thewrap.com/luke-cage-the-true-story-behind-lukes-hero-crispus-attucks/, accessed December 14, 2016.

44. "A Man Named Crispus (2013) movie," *MoviesPictures*, http://moviespictures.org/movie/A_Man_Named_Crispus_2013, accessed February 9, 2013; "Gabriel Bologna, biography," *Internet Movie Database (IMDB)*, http://www.imdb.com/name/nm0093232/bio?ref_=nm_ov_bio_sm, accessed February 15, 2015.

45. It should be kept in mind that Google and other Internet search engines tend to tailor search results to the usage patterns of the IP address from which the search originated. My search was made from my home network using the laptop computer on which this book was written. The same search from other IP addresses might bring differently arranged results, though the broader patterns of Attucks's presence on the Internet would be very similar.

46. Melita D. Myles, "Crispus Attucks Gave His Life for the Battle," *Philadelphia Tribune*, 118:25, February 12, 2002.

47. "Crispus Attucks: First American Patriot," *New York Beacon*, 9:6, February 13, 2002.

48. Leroy Vaughn, "Our Heritage: Blacks and the Revolutionary War," *Los Angeles Sentinel*, 64:37, December 16, 1998.

49. Kendall Wilson, "Experts Recall Blacks' Role in Revolutionary War," *Philadelphia Tribune*, 115:66, July 2, 1999.

50. "He Was the First to Die for American Freedom," *The Bay State Banner* 30:21, February 9, 1995; Kay Bourne, "Activists Celebrate Legacy of Slain Black Revolutionary," *Bay State Banner*, March 11, 2004.

51. Yussuf J. Simmonds, "The Black Soldier," *Los Angeles Sentinel*, January 11–17, 2007.

52. Kwame Ansah, "Telling the Real Truth About American Race Relations," *The Jacksonville Free Press*, March 25, 1998. Historians writing about blacks' support for the British prior to Ansah's article include James Oliver Horton and Lois E. Horton, *In Hope of Liberty: Culture, Community, and Protest among Northern Free Blacks, 1700–1860* (New York: Oxford University Press, 1997), and Sylvia R. Frey, *Water from the Rock: Black Resistance in a Revolutionary Age* (Princeton: Princeton University Press, 1993).

53. H. D. S. Greenway, "Whitewashing the Founding Fathers," *Boston Globe*, April 25, 2006; Simon Schama, *Rough Crossings: Britain, the Slaves and the American Revolution* (New York: Ecco, 2006).

54. Michael P. Quinlan, "A Lesson for Today from the Boston Massacre," *Boston Globe*, March 5, 2001.

55. Treesa Wiltz, "Cyber Street Beat: At the Web Site Cheerfully Devoted to Skewering 'Urban' New Media, an Anonymous Self-Styled Revolutionary Is Getting' 'Wiggy' Wit' It," *Washington Post*, January 23, 2001; Aliya S. King, "A Conversation with . . . John Lee," March 5, 2009, http://aliyasking.com/2009/03/05/a-conversation-withjohn-lee/, accessed April 14, 2015.

56. Cory Booker, *The Colbert Report*, November 20, 2008, http://thecolbertreport. cc.com/videos/ag7dg1/racism-is-over---cory-booker, accessed April 14, 2015; quotation from DVD cover, Spike Lee et al., *We the People: From Crispus Attucks to Barack Obama*, More Perfect Union LLC, Terrelle Taylor, director, 2014 [2009]; Ta-nehisi Coates, "Fear of a Black President," *Atlantic* (online), August 22, 2012, http://www.theatlantic.com/magazine/archive/2012/09/fear-of-a-black-president/309064/?single_page=true, accessed April 14, 2015.

57. Crispus Attucks Brigade website, http://tedhayes.us/uscab/, accessed April 14, 2015; Francis Taylor, "Crispus Attucks Brigade Clashes with Blacks Supporting Guest Worker Program," *Los Angeles Sentinel*, 71:58, April 27–May 3, 2006.

58. Crispus Attucks Tea Party press release, reprinted in Kathleen McKinley, "Conservative Blacks in Houston Form Crispus Attucks Tea Party," *Texas Sparkle: A Blog about Politics and Issues with Kathleen McKinley*, January 11, 2011,

http://blog.chron.com/texassparkle/2011/01/conservative-blacks-in-houston-form-the-crispus-attucks-tea-party/, accessed April 14, 2015.

59. Greg Freeman, "Reader Goes to Bat for Idea of Erecting Crispus Attucks Statue," *St. Louis Post-Dispatch*, October 17, 2002; Yvonne Samuel, "Crispus Attucks; Early Black Patriots Draw New Interest," *St. Louis Post-Dispatch*, February 5, 2003; Ben Westhoff, "Burnt to a Crispus; A Monument to an African American Symbol of U.S. Independence? Don J. Smith Asks (but not very politely): Why Not?" *Riverfront Times* (St. Louis), September 10, 2003.

CONCLUSION

1. Anita Danker, "A Bridge for Crispus Attucks," *Historical Journal of Massachusetts* 36:1 (Winter 2008), 57–70; Benjamin Wallace-Wells, "Revolt Revisited: Framingham Bridge Flap Revives Issue: Was Attucks a Colonial Hero or Thug?" *Boston Globe*, February 9, 2000; editorial, "A Bridge for Attucks," *Boston Globe*, February 17, 2000.

2. Danker, "A Bridge for Crispus Attucks"; Wallace-Wells, "Revolt Revisited"; editorial, "A Bridge for Attucks."

3. Maier quoted in Wallace-Wells, "Revolt Revisited"; Alfred F. Young, "The Trouble with the Freedom Trail," *Boston Globe*, March 21, 2004.

4. Danker, "A Bridge for Crispus Attucks," 69.

5. Danker, "A Bridge for Crispus Attucks," 65–70; Dennis Wepman, "Peter Salem," *American National Biography* (online), February 2000, http://www.anb.org/, subscription database, accessed April 16, 2015. These two sources differ on some details of Salem's life, most notably whether he died in the Framingham poorhouse, as Wepman indicates, or avoided that fate through the beneficence of his former owner, as Danker contends. See also Margot Minardi, *Making Slavery History: Abolitionism and the Politics of Memory in Massachusetts* (New York: Oxford University Press, 2010), 49–56.

6. Some scholars question whether the black man behind Grosvenor in Trumbull's painting depicts Salem or another black servant; there is also another black figure in the painting who may or may not have been intended to represent Salem. Danker, "A Bridge for Crispus Attucks," 65–70; Wepman, "Peter Salem," accessed April 16, 2015.

7. Danker, "A Bridge for Crispus Attucks," 68–70.

8. Scot French, *The Rebellious Slave: Nat Turner in American Memory* (Boston: Houghton Mifflin, 2004); Douglas Greenberg, ed., *Nat Turner: A Slave Rebellion in History and Memory* (New York: Oxford University Press, 2004); William Styron, *The Confessions of Nat Turner* (New York: Random House, 1967); John Henrik Clarke and William Styron, *William Styron's Nat Turner: Ten Black Writers Respond* (Boston: Beacon Press, 1969); Frank Christopher et al.,

Nat Turner: A Troublesome Property, DVD (San Francisco: California Newsreel, 2002); Nate Parker, et al., *The Birth of a Nation* (Fox Searchlight Pictures/20th Century Fox Films, 2016).

9. On the role of violence and death shaping masculine and patriotic ideals, see Mark S. Schantz, *Awaiting the Heavenly Country: The Civil War and America's Culture of Death* (Ithaca, NY: Cornell University Press, 2008), and Cecilia O'Leary, *To Die For: The Paradox of American Patriotism* (Princeton: Princeton University Press, 2000).

10. The literature on white conceptions of black violence and on the use of violence to control black behavior is vast and includes sweeping surveys, microhistories, and sociological analyses. A few representative titles include Winthrop D. Jordan, *White over Black: American Attitudes toward the Negro, 1550–1812* (Chapel Hill: University of North Carolina Press, 1968); George M. Frederickson, *The Black Image in the White Mind: The Debate on Afro-American Character and Destiny, 1817–1914* (New York: Harper & Row, 1971); Joel Williamson, *The Crucible of Race: Black/White Relations in the American South since Emancipation* (New York: Oxford University Press, 1984); William F. Messner, "Black Violence and White Response: Louisiana 1862," *Journal of Southern History* 41:1 (February 1975), 19–38; Katheryn Russell-Brown, *The Color of Crime*, 2nd ed. (New York: New York University Press, 2009); Sarah N. Roth, "The Politics of the Page: Black Disfranchisement and the Image of the Savage Slave," *Pennsylvania Magazine of History and Biography* 134:3 (July 2010), 209–33; Grace Hale, *Making Whiteness: The Culture of Segregation in the South, 1890–1940* (New York: Vintage, 1999); Glenda Elizabeth Gilmore, *Gender and Jim Crow: Women and the Politics of White Supremacy in North Carolina, 1896–1920* (Chapel Hill: University of North Carolina Press, 1996).

11. On the spate of killings of black men and women since 2012, the emergence of Black Lives Matter, and related topics, see, for example, Collier Meyerson, "How Michael Brown Changed Our Perceptions of America," *Fusion*, August 6, 2015, http://fusion.net/story/178654/how-michael-brown-changed-our-perceptions-of-america/, accessed March 29, 2016; Shannon Luibrand, "Black Lives Matter: How a Death in Ferguson Sparked a Movement in America," *CBS News*, August 7, 2015, http://www.cbsnews.com/news/how-the-black-lives-matter-movement-changed-america-one-year-later/, accessed March 29, 2016; Ta-Nehisi Coates, "Letter to My Son," *Atlantic*, July 4, 2015, http://www.theatlantic.com/politics/archive/2015/07/tanehisi-coates-between-the-world-and-me/397619/, accessed March 29, 2016.

12. Recent academic works discussing African Americans in the Revolutionary era include Edward Countryman, *Enjoy the Same Liberty: Black Americans and the Revolutionary Era* (Lanham, MD: Rowman & Littlefield, 2012); Alan Gilbert, *Black Patriots and Loyalists: Fighting for Emancipation in the War for Independence* (Chicago: University of Chicago Press, 2012); Julie Winch, *Beyond*

Slavery and Freedom: Free People of Color in America from Settlement to the Civil War (Lanham, MD: Rowman & Littlefield, 2014). Other scholarly works offer responsible treatments of the "actual" Attucks while also addressing the ways in which a "mythic" Attucks has been constructed to suit various purposes. See, for example, Stephen Kantrowitz, *More than Freedom: Fighting for Black Citizenship in a White Republic, 1829–1889* (New York: Penguin, 2012); Margot Minardi, *Making Slavery History: Abolitionism and the Politics of Memory in Massachusetts* (New York: Oxford University Press, 2010); Tavia Nyong'o, "'The Black First': Crispus Attucks and William Cooper Nell," in *Slavery/Antislavery in New England*, ed. Peter Benes, *Annual Proceedings of the Dublin Seminar for New England Folklife*, Vol. 28 (Boston: Boston University Press, 2005), 141–52; Elizabeth Rauh Bethel, *The Roots of African-American Identity: Memory and History in Free Antebellum Communities* (New York: St. Martin's Press, 1997); Maureen McAleer, "The Legacy of Crispus Attucks in Boston in the Twentieth Century: How Activists, Politicians, and the Public Have Remembered, Commemorated, and Used His Name," master's thesis, Harvard University, 2014; Robert J. Allison, *The Boston Massacre* (Beverly, MA: Commonwealth Editions, 2006); Neil L. York, *The Boston Massacre: A History with Documents* (New York: Routledge, 2010). The inaccurate assertion that Attucks wrote to Hutchinson is repeated in Manisha Sinha, *The Slave's Cause: A History of Abolition* (New Haven: Yale University Press, 2016).

13. Compiled Facebook responses are in the possession of the author.
14. For discussion and critiques of White's impact, see, for example, *Metahistory: Six Critiques*, Wesleyan University Center for the Humanities (Middleton, CT: Wesleyan University Press, 1980); Frank Ankersmit, Ewa Domanska, and Hans Kellner, eds., *Refiguring Hayden White* (Stanford, CA: Stanford University Press, 2009); and Herman Paul, *Hayden White: The Historical Imagination* (London: Polity Press, 2011).
15. Hayden V. White, "The Burden of History," *History and Theory* 5:2 (1966), 111–34, quoted at 127, 130. See also White, "The Culture of Criticism," in *Liberations: New Essays on the Humanities in Revolution*, ed. Ihab Hassan (Middletown, CT: Wesleyan University Press, 1971), 55–69; White, *Metahistory: The Historical Imagination in Nineteenth Century Europe* (Baltimore: Johns Hopkins University Press, 1973); White, "The Tropics of History: The Deep Structure of the *New Science*," in *Giambattista Vico's Science of Humanity*, ed. Giorgio Tagliacozzo and Donald Phillip Verene (Baltimore: Johns Hopkins University Press, 1976), 65–85; A. Dirk Moses, "Hayden White, Traumatic Nationalism, and the Public Role of History," *History and Theory* 44:3 (October 2005), 311–32; Ewa Domanska, "Hayden White: Beyond Irony," *History and Theory* 37:2 (May 1998), 173–81.
16. White, *Metahistory*, 130, 8; Moses, "Hayden White," 311–12.
17. Said quoted in Aleida Assmann, "Transformations between History and Memory," *Social Research* 75:1 (Spring 2008), 66.

18. Wulf Kansteiner, "Finding Meaning in Memory: A Methodological Critique of Collective Memory Studies," *History and Theory* 41:2 (May 2002), 180. Kansteiner and I both use the term "collective memory" to refer to the concept of a social group's generally shared understanding of the past; other scholars working in the field of history and memory prefer other terms—social memory, cultural memory, public memory, and others—to refer to the same concept. As Kansteiner's definition suggests, the term should not be taken to imply that all members of the group have the same understanding. Negotiations of meaning are continuously in flux, even as members of the group tend to embrace some broadly shared understandings. The literature in this field is vast and growing. Some of the works that have been most influential in shaping my own approach to history and memory, and that are most relevant to this study, include Michael Kammen, *Mystic Chords of Memory: The Transformation of Tradition in American Culture* (New York: Knopf, 1991); Michel-Rolph Trouillot, *Silencing the Past: Power and the Production of History* (Boston: Beacon Press, 1995); David Blight, *Beyond the Battlefield: Race, Memory, and the American Civil War* (Amherst: University of Massachusetts Press, 2002); Eric Hobsbawm and Terence Ranger, eds., *The Invention of Tradition* (New York: Cambridge University Press, 1983); John R. Gillis, ed., *Commemorations: The Politics of National Identity* (Princeton: Princeton University Press, 1994); Alfred F. Young, *The Shoemaker and the Tea Party: Memory and the American Revolution* (Boston: Beacon Press, 1999); Geoffrey Cubitt, *History and Memory* (Manchester, UK: Manchester University Press, 2007); David Gross, *Lost Time: On Remembering and Forgetting in Late Modern Culture* (Amherst: University of Massachusetts Press, 2000); David Lowenthal, *Possessed by the Past: The Heritage Crusade and the Spoils of History* (New York: Free Press, 1996); Jay Winter, *Remembering War: The Great War between Memory and History in the 20th Century* (New Haven: Yale University Press, 2006); Jeffrey Olick, "'Collective Memory': A Memoir and Prospect," *Memory Studies* 1:1 (2007), 19–25; Patrick Hutton, "Recent Scholarship on Memory and History," *History Teacher* 33:4 (2000), 533–48; Kerwin Lee Klein, "On the Emergence of Memory in Historical Discourse," *Representations* 69 (2000), 127–50; Aleida Assmann, "Transformations between History and Memory," *Social Research* 75:1 (Spring 2008), 49–72.

Index